Dream Machine

SAMIR DAYAL

DREAM MACHINE

Realism and Fantasy in Hindi Cinema

TEMPLE UNIVERSITY PRESS
Philadelphia • Rome • Tokyo

TEMPLE UNIVERSITY PRESS
Philadelphia, Pennsylvania 19122
www.temple.edu/tempress

Published 2015

Library of Congress Cataloging-in-Publication Data

Dayal, Samir.
Dream machine : realism and fantasy in Hindi cinema / Samir Dayal.
pages cm
Includes bibliographical references and index.
ISBN 978-1-4399-1063-4 (hardback : alk. paper) — ISBN 978-1-4399-1064-1 (paper : alk. paper) — ISBN 978-1-4399-1065-8 (e-book) 1. Motion pictures—India—History. 2. Motion pictures, Hindi—History. 3. Realism in motion pictures. 4. Fantasy in motion pictures. I. Title.
PN1993.5.I8D395 2015
791.430954—dc23

2015003431

♾ The paper used in this publication meets the requirements of the American National Standard for Information Sciences—Permanence of Paper for Printed Library Materials, ANSI Z39.48-1992

Printed in the United States of America

9 8 7 6 5 4 3 2 1

For Laura

Contents

Acknowledgments

Writing this book has been, in the main, a solitary exercise. Still, along the way, I incurred many debts that deserve acknowledgment, and indeed it is a pleasure to name some of the many influences, friends, colleagues, and fellow travelers who have, in both particular and general ways, left an imprint on my thinking. Even those I mention here who did not see drafts of the material that found its way into this book have been helpful in various other ways. The people I am able to acknowledge here are named more according to a sense of their personal significance than anything else. Some of these acknowledgments will surprise the named parties. Needless to say, responsibility for any shortcomings rests with me alone.

A first important debt is to students with whom I have been able to test some of the ideas presented in this book, and I am deeply grateful for their helpful comments and enthusiastic engagement. Teaching them was itself an education. More generally, I have learned much from scholars in the fields of postcolonial studies and literary and cultural theory, including Cyrena Pondrom, Martin Schwab, Dilip Gaonkar, Hortense Spillers, W.J.T. Mitchell, and R. Radhakrishnan. Through his personal example, Hans Robert Jauss taught me something about the practice of scholarship, even though our acquaintance was brief.

I had the good fortune to attend a seminar on literary theory at Georgetown University, where Gayatri Chakravorty Spivak, whose work has been important to my own, was a presence. Another seminar on theory was also a source of inspiration: although, considering the evolution of this project since that time, Homi Bhabha and members of a seminar he led at the Dartmouth School of Theory and Criticism may not recognize a direct link, they helped me formulate some of my initial questions and theoretical framings for this book.

Another valuable collaboration was with Ann Kibbey, editor in chief of *Genders*; I enjoyed working with her as a member of the journal's editorial board, and I vividly remember our productive discussions of various ideas that, though transformed, found their way into this book. I feel fortunate to have been able to collaborate on other scholarly projects—sometimes directly related to the arguments presented in this book—with colleagues such as John Hawley, Deepika Bahri, Lavina Shankar, and particularly Margueritte Murphy. Colleagues in more distant places also provided productive collaboration, including Jopi Nyman in Finland; Mina Karavanta in Greece; Bent Sorensen and Camelia Elias in Denmark; and Monika Mueller, Dorothea Fischer-Hornung, Monika Fludernik, and Heike Raphael-Hernandez in Germany. Older debts also deserve acknowledgment: to Vikram Poddar and particularly to Akumal Ramachander, both of whom were early interlocutors in the best tradition of the passionately argumentative Indian.

Colleagues and friends in Boston who have lent support and been generous in providing intellectual companionship include Arindam Dutta (to whom I gratefully acknowledge an early debt that dates from even before he came to MIT and that, in his generosity, he has probably forgotten). This collaboration resulted in the creation of the South Asian Studies Consortium, which I cofounded along with Arindam, Jyoti Puri, Jalal Alamgir, and others and which has been a source of intellectual stimulation, though it also invariably evokes great sorrow at the memory of Jalal's devastating and untimely death in 2011. I express my enormous gratitude to another Boston-area colleague and co-conspirator, Rajini Srikanth, who has been an indefatigable and unfailing comrade on many projects over the years. I cherish her realistic idealism and, most of all, her friendship.

Other friends and colleagues who have, in large and small ways, been supportive include Tuli Banerjee, Miriam Chirico, Ayesha Jalal, Amitava Kumar, Geeta Patel, and Lakshmi Srinivas. I am particularly grateful to Harleen Singh for her warm friendship over many years and for inviting me to teach a class at Brandeis University. A special thank-you goes to Judith Feher Gurevich for her hospitality and for her encouragement, both personal and professional, and especially to Frances Restuccia, whose passion for rigor and commitment to clarity I admire and whose exhortations I deeply appreciate. Frances's intellectual alacrity and friendly goading helped move this book along; she reminded me frequently that while getting it right was important, the perfect is the enemy of the good. Judith, Frances, and Kalpana Seshadri were important presences at the Psychoanalysis Seminar at Harvard University's Humanities Center, which has been crucial in helping me refine some of the arguments I put forward in this book.

Early versions of some chapters, or related material, were presented as conference papers and invited lectures. Many audiences at a variety of institutions offered valuable comments and questions that served to improve this book. These early versions of chapters and associated material were delivered at a variety of institutions both within the United States, ranging from the University of Illinois at Chicago (at the invitation of Rocio Davis) to the Harvard Film Archive (where at the kind invitation of Meena Hewitt, of Harvard's South Asia Initiative, I introduced a retrospective on the films of Raj Kapoor), and at a variety of non-U.S. locations, including the University of Porto in Portugal, the University of Hong Kong, the University of Padua in Italy, the University of Riga in Latvia, the University of Belgrade in Serbia, the University of Madrid-Complutense in Spain, and the University of Warsaw in Poland. I express my special gratitude to Ewa Łuczak for inviting me to deliver a keynote speech at the University of Warsaw in May 2010 and a lecture to a different audience in May 2011. On both occasions I received warm hospitality and productive feedback from the responsive audiences; Ewa's energy and spirit were as impressive as they were infectious.

I gratefully acknowledge travel and research grants and support from Bentley University: this support was invaluable in enabling me to complete the research for the book and travel to conferences and archives. I thank the library staff at the Film and Television Institute of India (FTII) in Pune and at the National Film Archive of India in Bangalore. Travel to both was made possible by grants from my home institution. I also express my deep gratitude to Amy Galante at the Baker Library for her resourcefulness in finding obscure interlibrary loan materials and to other librarians for acquiring materials on very short notice.

I thank Caitrin Lynch for her insightful and constructive comments on an early draft of a chapter that I presented as a fellow of the Valente Center at Bentley University. I gratefully acknowledge the Valente Center's generous underwriting of a leave to complete the chapter and thank members of the Valente Seminar for stimulating conversation. I am fortunate to have supportive colleagues within my own institution, and especially within my department; on several occasions they offered commentary on ongoing work. It is a great joy to be a member of a department of scholars with such wide-ranging interests and strengths.

I am particularly grateful to the anonymous readers for Temple University Press, whose detailed reports pushed me to compress, refine, and recast my arguments. Some readers saw the manuscript more than once, and their suggestions helped make this a better book. Kim Vivier and, at Temple University Press, Sara Cohen, Joan Vidal, Gary Kramer, and most particularly Janet Francendese were a pleasure to work with. I feel blessed to have had Janet's assistance; she was especially helpful and responsive at every phase of the process, shepherding the book through to publication.

My deepest thanks go to my family. Vineeta and Purshotam Dayal, my parents, and my siblings, Ronnie and Vandana, have been extremely supportive. I thank Deven and Mira for putting up with me as I wrote this book and for their love and unquestioning faith. It was Mira who, at my special request, created the design concept for the cover of this book. And finally to Laura, who has never wavered, I dedicate this book.

Dream Machine

Introduction

Mirror and Lamp

In 2013 India celebrated a hundred years of cinema. During its century this cinema, and in particular Hindi-language popular cinema, arguably the most important of several cinema industries in the Subcontinent, has been both mirror and lamp—reflecting "Indianness" back to Indians at home and abroad, but also shaping Indianness. Movie-going in India is a special sort of pleasure—for many affording rare access to privacy, a sometimes three-hour-long respite from noise and heat in an air-conditioned, carpeted interior, where one can be alone with oneself among others, in the dark. This pleasure necessarily induces a different relation to interior, psychic space, without having to submit to sleep, even absenting the enjoying ego from the enjoyment: this is as close to accessing (unconscious) desire as most ever come, and could even be considered a kind of wild psychoanalysis. For many Indians without the means, it affords opportunities to travel ("transport"?), if only on the wings of fantasy: to alternative realities, foreign locales, alien cultures, unfamiliar aesthetics of self and unaccustomed social arrangements, pleasurable disorientations of everyday life. The "dream machine" is also a space-time travel machine—"motion" pictures *move us* to different zones, to unaccustomed emotions.

Sitting in darkened cinema theaters in India, the spectator might also be struck by how often Indianness itself is what is being screened—in both senses. Hindi cinema has been, to change metaphors, a "dream machine," producing images of collective or national identity that, with every iteration, prove more transitional, contradictory, and elusive or enable us to screen truths about ourselves from ourselves. There is a double valence to the "moving pictures" of Hindi cinema: what *moves* audiences of this extremely popular cultural form is on the one hand the reflection of what is constructed as everyday Indian life and on the other hand the production of fantasies—and fantasmatic displacements—of an essential, primordial, idealized Indianness that is yet unachieved. This doubleness hints at an anxiety about the reliability and integrity of presumed anchors of national identity. Realist representations "screen" that anxiety behind images that blur or fissure and finally undo the very categories of Indianness assumed to be givens. This book reframes Hindi cinema as a domain where fantasy is as important as realism, a site for the simultaneous construction *and* deconstruction of Indianness.

The genre "Bollywood," associated with Bombay (Mumbai) and Pune, emerged around 1931. Madhava Prasad reminds us that the coinage can be traced back to a description of films produced in Tollygunge studios in Kolkata as "Tollywood"; this description was subsequently extended to films produced in the Bombay (Mumbai) film industry as "Bollywood."[1] Initially a deprecatory journalistic label, "Bollywood" has since the 1980s become a transnationally recognized metonymic signifier, sometimes overshadowing the broader category of Hindi cinema. Some, admittedly, embrace it as enhancing Hindi films' visibility on the global cinema circuit. Here I use the term "Hindi cinema" because it is the accurate term for the majority of films I discuss, along with some strategically chosen exceptions such as *Slumdog Millionaire* (Danny Boyle, 2008).

No other recently published book, to my knowledge, offers as sustained a discussion as this one does of the role of fantasy in Hindi cinema. Of course, I do not claim to be the first or sole observer of fantasy in this cinema, and here I take the opportunity to indicate how my approach is significantly different from that of comparable studies. Indeed, I have learned much from these studies, including those that discuss either realism or fantasy, or both.

Among comparable books is Prasad's *Ideology of the Hindi Film: A Historical Construction* (1998). Its chief concern is with (especially Marxist) theory and its import for film studies. Though my own analysis also identifies the ideological underpinnings of dominant narratives in Hindi films, my approach is different in its conceptualization of their narratological strategies, philosophical premises, and particularly the structuring dialectic of realism and fantasy. Another comparable book concerned with ideological analysis is Ravi Vasudevan's edited anthology, *Making Meaning in Indian Cinema* (2000): the various essays discuss an assortment of topics, including fashion, gender, and the ideology of the family and domestic arrangements in 1950s-era Hindi cinema. The collection's declared focus is on how popular Indian cinema makes *political* meaning, but it is an edited anthology, whereas my own book is a much more sustained argument about how such meaning-making is best understood within the frame of the dialectic of reality and fantasy.

Vijay Mishra's *Bollywood Cinema: Temples of Desire* (2002) is another comparable book. This is a compendious and erudite discussion of Bollywood cinema as a storehouse of images of a pan-Indian culture rich in traditions as well as cinematic genres ranging from the epic to the Indian gothic; it elaborates on the role of religion and gender dynamics within the film industry. Mishra's book, like mine, considers the influence of contemporary popular culture on Hindi cinema, and like mine it is sensitive to the significance of the diaspora in shaping some of the concerns of Hindi films. An important point of contrast is that whereas Mishra suggests that Bollywood films are "temples" of the desire for community and a pan-Indian national culture, my own book extends this important point by exploring the rich veins of complication and contradiction introduced by the irruption of fantasy within sanctioned narratives of Indianness. Fantasy, I demonstrate, often encodes suppressed or repressed desires that fissure the surface, or skin, of the popular Hindi film, revealing important fault lines of identity and society.

A competing book that, like mine, attends to the constitutive contradictions of Indian films is Jyotika Virdi's *The Cinematic ImagiNation: Indian Popular Films as Social History* (2003). My book shares with Virdi's an interest in approaching Indian cinema as a national-popular matrix in which one can trace narratives of the emergent nation. Yet Virdi seeks to show how the notion of the nation manages to cohere despite contradictions and internal conflicts; she draws attention to the conflicted relationship between the national and the transnational. Virdi's argument, like mine, is informed by film theory, cultural studies, and postcolonial theory, as well as psychoanalysis—especially in her discussion of masculinity, which accords with much in my own discussion of the "Angry Young Man" films of the mid-1970s, and in her treatment of the "Avenging Woman." Yet ultimately her focus on the figure of the family distinguishes it from my argument, which is more concerned with the way the dialectic of realism and fantasy allow a much broader and richer range of themes to be highlighted, well beyond the family dynamic.

Lalitha Gopalan's *Cinema of Interruptions: Action Genres in Contemporary Indian Cinema* (2002) is another competing book, employing analytic strategies and theoretical idioms more familiar in Western film studies. It proposes to refract Western film theory "through a reading of interruptions in Indian films."[2] My book shares Gopalan's interest in the significance of these "interruptions," as well as a methodological commitment to resisting a provincial theoretical framing of Hindi cinema. Yet Gopalan's book, pivoting on the erotic conceit that cinema "proposes" to us, is avowedly a treatment of *action genres.* My book differs markedly in its broader generic reach and its emphasis on a more transnational analytic, without discounting or discrediting popular reception—domestic discourses of pleasure, Subcontinental articulations of social norms, rooted mores, culture, or everyday praxis. Informed by postcolonial discursive strategies, my approach makes explicit the function and significance of contradictory desires or "nonrealistic" elements that arise within the main narratives of Hindi cinema. It more consistently traces the subtle and complex ways in which fantasy, as conceived in film theory, works in a dialectical relationship with the social text of this cinema to produce meaning—or to raise difficult issues. These distinctive features are most evident in the close readings I present of particular films.

Other books invite more attenuated comparison with mine, and I note a few in passing, including the many general surveys of the film industry such as Nasreen Munni Kabir's *Bollywood: The Indian Cinema Story* (2001), a somewhat enthusiastic and uncritical overview. Other works, such as the more recent *Global Bollywood: Travels of Hindi Song and Dance* (2008), edited by Sangita Gopal and Sujata Moorti, may appear to present a competing approach, but they are only glancingly comparable. Essays contained in *Global Bollywood*, for instance, deal with "fantasy sequences." Yet they largely discuss only "song and dance" routines and *filmigit* (film music), the most elementary level of "fantasy." My book is very different from these and several others quoted or cited in its pages, in its consistent, sustained, and multilayered appreciation of the relationship between realism and diverse forms of fantasy. There are certainly many other books that touch on themes discussed in my book, or discuss realism and fantasy, but they do so without developing that relation in depth, across different genres and subgenres, across the nation's boundaries, or over the period covered by my analysis, from Independence through the post-1990s liberalization era and into the present. I cannot here survey the vast range of commentary and scholarship on Hindi cinema (let alone "Indian cinema"). While there is a vibrant industry of commentary on Indian cinema, many published works do not meaningfully compete with my own particular approach, although I gratefully acknowledge that I have learned much of what I know from this rich body of work.

Here it might suffice therefore to observe that my book is framed by two kinds of analyses of Hindi cinema, and some of these along with the works discussed above are presented summarily in the next two endnotes. One kind of analytic approach, reflected in works dating from the 1990s through the early 2000s, highlights social and aesthetic realism; social issues including poverty, work, and development; class and neofeudal social conditions; crime, violence, and the law; and gender, sexuality, and the family.[3] A second, produced roughly between 2000 and the present, focuses more on industry changes, audience or reception studies, historicist (re)framing, and globalization's influence.[4]

What then is the singular contribution of my book? While several of the other works on Hindi cinema have suggested that cinema reflects the image of the imagined nation as it has developed since Independence, they have tended to emphasize primarily the major social or cultural themes and the realist narratives. It is a diacritic of my approach that "Indianness" remains an important conceptual category, but I draw attention to the subtle yet powerful centrifugal forces that are increasingly represented in cultural forms, principally the cinema: Indian identity is growing more "flexible" or fungible today as compared with the early and emergent national identity of the immediately post-Independence era of the 1940s and 1950s. Nationalism must be historicized and understood as dynamically changing with the increasingly globalized flows of culture, people, goods, and capital; indeed, nationalism is taking new and occasionally virulent, but always politically significant, forms—as with the recent election of the new prime minister, Narendra Modi. It is especially important to recognize how globalization as an external force and post-1990s liberalization have wrought changes in Indians' self-image. No mirror is more revealing than Hindi cinema.

My project focuses attention on recognizing the contradictions of Hindi cinema, and the contradictory play of realism and fantasy (including the often overlooked or repressed dimensions of psychic life and marginalized desire), as *productive,* and on tracing the increasing disaggregation of "Indianness" in response to the forces of globalization and economic liberalization. In highlighting, unlike most other comparable studies, the subtle but significant—and often misunderstood or neglected—role of fantasy, my book does not in any sense neglect the fascinating subtleties or complexities of Hindi cinema's commitment to represent the social in a realist mode. Neither do I suggest that fantasy is more important than realism in Hindi cinema. Far from it. Rather, it is in the interplay of the realistic and the nonrealistic elements that we can fully appreciate the richness of this cinema, and it is in close textual analysis that this richness can emerge. As always, God and the Devil are in the details.

The customary attitude to fantasy in Hindi films can be characterized as a tendency to deprecate it as mere attraction or distraction—even mere silliness. Nor does most commentary, including scholarship, seriously and consistently analyze the dialectical relationship between fantasy and realism, even when that relationship is noted. While there are books that discuss fantasy in Indian cinema, few attempt to track it diachronically, as I do, from the time India gained independence from the British in 1947 to the contemporary conjuncture—in order to trace the sometimes vexed and contradictory fashionings of Indian identity. In that contemporary conjuncture, I suggest in my Conclusion, globalized mediascapes require an interrogation of the integrity or sustainability of the category "Indianness" in Indian cinema generally. Hindi cinema, I argue, is increasingly the locus classicus for the construction of the public image of Indian identity, as contrasted with other major cultural forms such as classical music, dance, or even the news outlets—access to which after all remains limited for many, even for the vast majority. Throughout, my book intentionally and consistently focuses on familiar mainstream examples while also considering less iconic films, in order to track what I call "condensations" of the dominant Indian sensibility or temper at a given historical and cultural moment.

Perhaps what remains most distinctive about the analysis offered in my book, then, is that it draws out the diversity of forms of fantasy, from the most commonplace sense of the "fantasy sequence," familiarly known as the "song-and-dance routine," to expressions of psychic life inadmissible otherwise, at the level of the diegesis, and highlights their subtle and sometimes disruptive or destabilizing momentum. For all these various forms are in fact operative, sometimes simultaneously, in Hindi cinema, and far from providing mere escapism of the kind too often pejoratively associated with "Bollywood," the seams of fantasy threaded through these films offer rich and often unorthodox possibilities for meaning-making and self-fashioning.

Contradictions and Condensations

Popular Hindi films reproduce a constitutive contradiction of cinematic representation. In even the most formulaic realist narratives, for example, the hero proclaims his patriotism, and his actions serve as object lessons in good Indian citizenship. Yet antirealist elements fissure the surface narrative, offering pleasurable ruptures of or anxious *supplements* to the sanctioned mimetic narration; they often interrupt realist diegesis, interposing defamiliarizing and destabilizing fantasies. The formula narrative surface may be disfigured by a "stain" that nonetheless has a pressing claim to psychic truth otherwise inexpressible.

Perhaps the dialectic between realism and fantasy is endemic to the cinematic apparatus. The film screen or photograph, Stanley Cavell remarks, is unlike a painting because it implies a reality "behind" itself, extending outside its edges, constituted by the inadequacy of representation. The screen always screens its existence from the spectator, and screens the spectator from the projected world, making the viewer unviewable—and therefore absolving him or her from having to make ethical decisions the characters face in the diegesis, while indulging pleasurable fantasies. The "world viewed" onscreen cannot claim existence as a predicate. It does not exist *now:* there is always a time lag. Yet spectators may suspend disbelief, fully captivated by/in the fantasy screened now *as* "the [real] world."[5]

André Bazin's influential account of realism suggests that cinema, like the photograph, "actually contributes something to the order of natural creation instead of providing a substitute for it"; this argument somewhat paradoxically entails the notion that the camera itself should not be *seen* as *distorting* "the natural" order, for naturalness implies immediateness, or more precisely nonmediation. The camera, David Bordwell clarifies, "should not stray" over this representational axis of meaning-making but should obey the 180-degree rule.[6] In practice, and famously in the work of the great Yasujirō Ozu, the camera occasionally does stray over the axis, without shattering the realist illusion. A commitment to realism *as stylistic convention* is more important than rigid adherence to a body of realist *techné* or formalist dogma.

It is instructive to contrast formalism and realism. Formalists focus on filmic techniques: editing, montage, fast and slow motion, low and high camera angles, the manipulation of two-dimensional mimesis of reality. Rudolf Arnheim, Sergei Eisenstein, and other formalists skeptical about film's capacity to capture the full visual experience of reality championed film's compensatory or supplementary virtue—its expressive and artistic potency. Votaries of realism such as André Bazin, Siegfried Kracauer, and Stanley Cavell, by contrast, emphasize that the "world viewed" by the camera *is* indeed capable, through such techniques as the long take, deep focus, minimal and continuous editing, of capturing and rendering reality, without need for specious supplements such as montage or expressive manipulation of the two-dimensional representation. Film's art consists in its perfect re-presentation of the world.[7] This is not naive verisimilitude. Cavell cites the insistence of realists such as Irwin Panofsky and Bazin that "the medium of movies" was "reality as such"; both "wish, correctly, to emphasize that on film reality is not merely described or represented. But obviously it is not actually present to us either. . . . [W]hat makes the physical medium of film unlike anything else on earth lies in the absence of what it causes to appear to us; that is to say, in the nature of our absence from it; in its fate to reveal reality and fantasy . . . by projections of reality . . . in which . . . reality is freed to exhibit itself."[8]

Hindi cinema cannot be reduced to either naive realism or escapist fantasy: it makes a more complex, if implicit, claim to indexicality. Mary Ann Doane theorized the "medium specificity" of film, identifying its most striking characteristic as "indexicality," the "ability to capture time and movement" or "life itself." The "experience of a medium is necessarily determined by a dialectical relation between materiality and immateriality," and therefore between realism and fantasy.[9]

As *method* or technique, cinematic realism can be self-effacing (hiding the machinery of representation) or self-reflexive. It renders the real in a presumptively transparent manner or admits that reality is captured (honestly) if artfully—but not distorted.[10] Filmic narratives are interesting because of complications and interruptions; fantasy infiltrates even the most innocent representations and self-representations, complicating naive realist notions of mimesis. While at one level Hindi cinema cleaves to the Bazinian ideal of realism, relying on mise-en-scène more than montage, claiming to reconstitute the world without manipulating space and time, at another it accommodates the distortion of everyday reality, disrupting logical sequence or disordering "commonsense" perception through nonrealistic or fantasy elements. Realism and fantasy are bound in an epistemological parallax, or dialectic in Walter Benjamin's sense, as condensing "history at a standstill" in the cinematic image, but also as the commonplace and commonsense notion of a dynamic contradiction where the real and the imaginary, the fantasmatic or even the Real, are palimpsested or antithetically configured. This antithesis evokes Sigmund Freud's opposition of the reality and pleasure principles, and Jacques Lacan's elaboration of the orders of the Symbolic, Imaginary, and Real. In the cinematic dialectic, fantasy elements destabilize the realist diegetic world of even mainstream Hindi films *and* unleash desire (or even "drive") expressed as alternative "imaginary" possibilities.

I begin by framing the general argument of this book, introducing the dialectical opposition of realism and fantasy as a key modality. Next I present a brief overview of the history of Hindi cinema, followed by a consideration of Hindi cinema's claim to be the national cinema. After defining some key terms, including the "dream machine" of the title, I consider the implications of the dialectic of realism and fantasy and foreground the problematic of Indianness. Finally, I outline the individual chapters, highlighting their arrangement in a sequence spanning the period of postcolonial Hindi cinema roughly from Independence in 1947 to today. Tracing this arc over the decades, I suggest that Hindi cinema functions as both mirror and lamp of Indianness, representing and simultaneously defining historically specific "condensations"—desublimations, refractions, or crystallizations of shared consciousness.

These condensations index the reigning cultural climate or constellations of sociopolitical/cultural identity at different historical conjunctures: the "social realism" that defined Hindi cinema's Golden Age from about 1940 through the 1960s, the emergence of a righteous "anger" that informed the Angry Young Man and the Avenging Woman cinema in the 1970s through the 1980s, the emergence of a new cosmopolitanism emerging in the neoliberal 1990s, and the current constellation under globalization. This current constellation is widely represented as a culture-flattening diffusion of a McDonaldized (U.S.-oriented) monoculture, "centrally conceived, controlled, and comparatively devoid of distinctive substantive content," producing nothing. Yet there have been reactive condensations that may be interpreted as "glocalizing," "indigenously conceived, controlled, and comparatively rich in distinctive substantive content"; these have, as George Ritzer puts it, led to the "expansion of something," even if it was the expansion of the imagination.[11] Critical studies have registered these condensations but have not always understood or considered seriously the dialectic of realism and fantasy through which they are cinematically rendered.

There is a vernacular utopianism inherent in all fantasy. Ernst Bloch derided the utopianism of daydreams and storytelling produced as salve against perceived deficits of experience as "simple, false, disengaged and abstract." From his Marxist perspective, a "concrete" utopianism, requiring "tarrying with the negative," reliant on action oriented toward social change, was preferable to compensatory fantasies of the "cowardly 'as if,'" even if it imagined a better world.[12] Yet compensatory fantasies tendered in works of fiction, art, and film provide emotional and psychical sustenance, aesthetic pleasure, and intellectual resources, challenging and redressing the status quo. For Freud, psychical reality, as Cornelius Castoriadis explains, is not subordinate to our perception of "reality" but its foundation, albeit guided by the pleasure principle. Fantasy is not mere escapism.[13]

Post-Independence Hindi cinema is a rich site for mapping a *collective consciousness* in specific phases of the nation's cultural history. My approach foregrounds the circulation and convergences of fantasies that reveal what is conventionally inexpressible—but psychically true. Paradoxically, Hindi films presume to condense an immutable Indianness ("traditional values") *and* simultaneously narrate a becoming-national, negating that immutability. The project of figuring and configuring national culture is continually interrupted and disaggregated by processes of political transformation and cultural fragmentation, increasingly global flows, and unruly identifications, rendering Indianness not molar but molecular. This is consistent with centrifugal national/cultural trends in China and other countries, Slavoj Žižek suggests; we don't really understand the processes involved—and need new theories to explain them.[14] As Ashish

Rajadhyaksha writes about Indian cinema, "There appears to be something out there that still needs 'an account.'"[15]

The Idea of Indianness

Hindi cinema may be entertainment, even a "spectacular" apparatus in both senses of the word. But since Independence it has also inscribed, in Gyan Pandey's words, the "biography of the nation-state," charting its avowedly "secular, democratic, non-violent course," and its linchpin, the idea of Indianness.[16] Yet that worlding is fissured and shifting: "Indianness . . . finds itself in a constant state of transition, dually combating and incorporating outside sources."[17] Pandey's "biography" must countenance the idea that the object of that biography is invented as much as represented.[18]

Eric Hobsbawm writes that the affirmation of national identity requires the *invention* of "tradition."[19] He is responding, Joan W. Scott reminds us, to a call to reassess Stalinist historiography, "with its ahistoric notions of workers and class struggle," to complicate any primordialist or ahistorical project of defining national identity, for "although we take identities for granted as rooted in our physical bodies (gender and race) or our cultural (ethnic, religious) heritages . . . they don't follow predictably or naturally from them."[20] Like other identities, Indianness is not a primordial and immutable essence but a dynamic construction that encodes its own deconstruction.

My argument extends Benedict Anderson's thesis in *Imagined Communities* that print capitalism was instrumental in defining national identity as a political community "imagined as both inherently limited and sovereign."[21] The meaning of Indianness is not exhausted by reference to a territorially bounded, sovereign national essence. Anderson himself acknowledges that even large nations have finite but *elastic* boundaries. Indianness denotes an elastic, *imaginary*, and not only political identity; as such, it "supplements" and exceeds actual instantiations.

This is where fantasy enters the dialectic. In *Hindu religion and mythology* heaven is the zone where fantasies are fulfilled, the priceless *chintamani* (jewel of one's deepest fantasy) found. In *Hindi cinema* fantasy is laminated to this Ur-meme of one's deepest desires, illustrating the "complicated dynamic of recognition and misrecognition that brings a sense of identity into being and *calls that identity into question*."[22] Popular Hindi films reveal a "logic" of disavowal—disavowal of what one is driven to believe or of whom one is driven to identify with. Judith Butler describes such identification as "an identification that one fears to make only because one has already made it."[23] Similarly Julia Kristeva, echoing Nietzsche, highlights "this incredible need to believe," the "narcotic that makes living easier, for—happy infantile and amorous trauma—it is the foundation of our capacity to be . . . *speaking beings*."[24] Fantasy unleashes possible identifications supplementing mimetic representations of essentialized identities, including religious and national identities—a negation of what Fredric Jameson, in theorizing realism, refers to as "the time of the preterite."[25]

I foreground contradictions embedded in narratives of national "Hindu" identity in social realist films *and* relatively innocuous popular melodramas. Such contradictions are endemic to the tentative self-fashionings of post-Independence secular socialism and representations of Indianness in the contemporary globalized conjuncture. India's information technology boom and new cultural prominence are celebrated in campaigns of "India Shining" and "poised" but are also accompanied by anxieties about Indianness becoming deterritorialized and disaggregated. The film star Amitabh Bachchan was recruited to present this new narrative of India: his significance as an iconic, "nonrepresentative representation" of Indianness is discussed in Chapter 3.[26] Bachchan exemplifies a Bazinian realism, illustrating how it is "at the ontological level that the effectiveness of the cinema has its source," how the screen "put[s] us 'in the presence of' the actor" himself.[27]

Uniquely among major film industries, Indian cinema functioned, Roy Armes reminds us, even when national sovereignty was denied to citizens.[28] The Indian cinema industry was active forty years before the end of the British Empire but flourished after Independence, superseding other forms of cultural production in *mediating* the representation of national, sovereign identity, enabling the construction of fantasy identifications.[29] It also furnishes an object lesson in a performative paradox: that the very performance of national or personal identity in cinema and life frustrates attempts to fix an immutable essence. This double potentiality of cinema as representation and performance gains from a brief historical perspective, which I offer below.

Historical Retrospective

In Paris on March 19, 1895, the Lumière brothers presented the world's first film on their newly patented cinematograph. Only a year later, films were being made in India, well before the country became a sovereign democratic republic in 1947. Even in the earliest domestically produced feature-length "mythological" film, *Raja Harishchandra* (1913), melodrama operates as a *hinge* in the dialectic between realism and fantasy. The genre of the "mythologicals"—what Salman Rushdie dubbed the "theologicals"—was eclipsed in the 1950s by the rise of the Hindi Socials.[30] This "Golden Age" cinema of the 1940s through the 1960s was committed to a social realism, displacing the melodramatic tendencies of silent films. Only a handful of the thirteen hundred silents survive.

Yet fantasy was always a key element of Hindi cinema. Fantasy sequences are conventionally associated with song-and-dance interludes; even the first talkies featured them prominently, beginning with *Alam Ara* (Light of the World, Ardeshir Irani, 1931), featuring seven songs.[31] Other films had more (forty and even sixty) until a consensus emerged that too many were deleterious though a few were de rigueur.[32] Unlike Hollywood narrative (linear and "psychologized"), mainstream Indian cinema "offers us a different order of diegesis," more like that of the *Ramayan* and *Mahabharat*.[33] These ancient epics render real and imaginary ("fantasy") time in parallax view, mundane temporality nested within cosmic and mythic time.

Although the *natya* (traditional dance) of classical Sanskrit theater declined with the language (between the tenth and twelfth centuries), Sanskrit dramatic traditions bequeathed to Indian cinema lineaments of form.[34] Classical *rasa* theory (in which connoisseurship of art, and particularly of drama, is associated with the cultivated appreciation of the aesthetic essence of the work of art as a whole, as well as of each formal element) was always fundamental. Folk traditions and other dramatic forms came to the fore. From Bengal came *Yatra* or *Jatra,* from Uttar Pradesh Ram-and-Krishna *Lila* ("play" in both senses), from Gujarat *Bhavai,* from Tanjore *Bhagavata Mela,* from Tamilnadu *Terukuttu,* from Andhra Pradesh *Vithinatakam,* and from Karnataka *Yakshagana.* Also influential were performances of *bahurupis* (itinerant performers), as well as *tamasha* and other street performances.[35]

Silent films relied on visual representation of the body to carry meaning. Sound facilitated the studio system's emergence and flourishing from the 1920s through the early 1950s. Film was culturally unifying, speaking to and for people across mutually unintelligible languages—witness the massive box-office success of India's first "talkie," *Alam Ara,* made sixteen years before Independence. Sound capitalized on Parsi theater's influential Hindi-Urdu performance tradition (dating from the nineteenth century). Parsi theater "displayed an odd mixture of realism and fantasy, narrative and spectacle, music and dance, lively dialogues and ingenious stagecraft, all amalgamated within the accepted narrative discursivities of melodrama."[36] Theatrical houses that clearly bore the imprint of Parsi theater, especially in the realms of song and dance alongside dialogue, included the Elphinstone Dramatic Company and the Victoria Theater Company, in name and melodramatic form also influenced by Victorian theater.

In the work of producers of the post–World War I era, including Chandulal Shah, Ardeshir Irani, and J.B.H Wadia, one can already discern a self-reflexivity about "Indianness"—witness Dhiren Ganguly's *Bilet Pherat* (Foreign Returned, 1921). This self-reflexivity grew in the late 1920s through the 1930s with the rise of the Studio Era. V. Shantaram's Prabhat Film Company was inaugurated in 1929, Birendranath Sircar's New Theatres of Calcutta in 1930, and Himansu Rai and Devika Rani's Bombay Talkies in 1935. Scores of less important companies—nearly ninety in all, emerged in western India alone: Imperial Film Company, Wadia Movietone, Ranjit Movietone, Sagar Film Company, Paramount Film Company, and many others, each generically specialized. Wadia Movietone, for instance, became identified with *Hunterwali* (The Huntress, Homi Wadia, 1935), featuring Nadia the eponymous Huntress.

Postcolonial Hindi cinema was framed—and influenced—by two events: World War II and Independence. As the studio system crumbled, compensatory developments buoyed the film industry: the boom in "black money financing," the rise of independent producers, and the emergence of the Indian People's Theatre Association (IPTA), an antifascist initiative for artistic innovation, in

1942. Eminent members included Ritwik Ghatak, Mrinal Sen, K. A. Abbas, and Raj Kapoor.[37] The pre-Independence state deprecated and dismissed the cinema industries as an alien cultural form.[38] Yet from the 1960s the government began to intervene more directly in film financing and regulation through official censorship codes. Remarkably, India only liberalized the film industry in 1998, granting it official industry status in 2001.[39]

A National Cinema?

Indian films in general have been produced under an informally capitalist regime despite the absence of a state capitalist system, Prasad suggests, in ideological contravention of state-sponsored secular socialism.[40] Each decade of Indian cinema produced an iconic film or films definitive of the Zeitgeist. This serves as rough organizing principle for my chapters, each focusing on key films from each decade as representative *condensations.* Jawaharlal Nehru, India's first prime minister, appointed the S. K. Patil Film Inquiry Committee. Its report linked the commercial and cultural spheres, noting increasing private investment and endorsing the Films Division's support for social realist cinema. It underwrote Hindi cinema's claim to be the national cinema. The commission's ideological leanings were evident in its support of "realist rootedness versus indigenous mass culture, nationalist utopia versus the regionalist components of nationalism."[41] The creation of the national film archive and a national film institute further consolidated the Hindi cinema industry. However, dissenting opinions began to emerge about the legitimacy of Hindi cinema's self-proclaimed priority, particularly because it entailed the marginalization of other cinemas. Recently, Hindi cinema—including Bollywood, Hindustani (a blend of Hindi and Urdu), "Hinglish" (a blend of Hindi and English), and diasporic cinema—has enjoyed success nationally and internationally.[42] So have hybrid musicals such as Andrew Lloyd Webber's *Bombay Dreams,* stage shows, and films such as *Moulin Rouge* (Baz Luhrmann, 2001). But is it meaningful to speak of *Hindi* cinema as a national cinema?

"The emergence of Bollywood as a space of cultural production and expression that is now decidedly global," Anandam Kavoori and Aswin Punathambekar observe, "spells trouble for categories such as 'Indian cinema,' 'nation,' 'public,' 'culture,' 'modernity,' 'identity,' and 'politics.'" They note that Padma Lakshmi and Freida Pinto may be nominally "Indian," but they are really transnational "brands." Aishwarya Rai "made it to the cover of *Time* magazine, and even taught Oprah Winfrey and her viewers to wear a sari," but her Indianness was hardly the point of interest. Other signs of Bollywood's globalization include an episode of *The Simpsons* in 2006 in which the Simpsons' trip to India concludes with a *filmi* song-and-dance routine. Shekhar Kapur, acclaimed director of *Elizabeth* and *Bandit Queen,* predicted that Bollywood will "define and dominate global entertainment in the twenty-first century."[43] As modernity itself grows more "liquid," in Zygmunt Bauman's phrase, modern Indianness is correspondingly becoming more disaggregated;[44] this is an important argument in my Conclusion. Indianness resists fixing, and is becoming increasingly deterritorialized, "a heterogeneous imaginary that draws energy from historical formations of colonialism and postcolonialism, discourses of diversity, and exercises of bureaucratic power."[45] My book tracks this imaginary in Hindi cinema over the decades since Independence.

Popular Hindi cinema does not compare favorably with the best international cinema. It often fails to meet minimal standards of "realism," being predisposed to "fantasy sequences" featuring song-and-dance episodes at odds with the diegetic continuum, sentimental dialogue, melodramatic plotting, ridiculous comedy, risible heroes and heroines, repressed sexuality, outworn social mores or reactionary moralism, cliché "philosophy," shopworn traditionalism and spirituality, unconvincing mise-en-scène, and generally low production values. Excepting parallel or art cinema (Satyajit Ray, Shyam Benegal, and other luminaries), the cinema rarely seems invested in high art: image texture, the crystallization of time, or the fluid framing and shifting focus within an uncut shot that enrich, for instance, Chris Marker's *La Jetée* (1962) or *Sans Soleil* (1983). But neither is Hollywood. Realism is not a standard but a convention.

A better appreciation of Hindi cinema requires "thick" description, as Clifford Geertz might put it, engaging the dialectic or parallax between realism and fantasy. This poses a challenge for audience reception: commentators frequently undertheorize the role of fantasy, underestimating how "popular cinema remains unencumbered by any obligation to reflect reality"; besides, "Bollywood is selective" in "maintaining, affirming and/or 'resituating'" Indianness as "systems of values."[46] Hindi cinema cannot "fix" an echt Indianness because representation is always imperfectly achieved. Yet inadequation is a source of creativity.

Besides, identity itself is a deficient category.[47] Hindi cinema is "implicated in strategies of containment, subjugation and resistance rather than emanations of fixed homogeneous categories such as class, gender or race."[48] Rather than sedimented identities, it is better to speak of *actants* in global networks—circulations of culture, information, goods, and capital, as Bruno Latour reminds us: "By following circulations we can get more than by defining entities, essence or provinces."[49] And these circulations encompass more than what Kuan-Hsing Chen defines as the ambit of "Asian" studies, a project of "deimperialization": elaborating "authentic" subject-constructions to counter imperialism's stereotypes.[50] The signifiers of "Asia," like those of "India," need to be assessed against the backdrop of neoimperialism; Indianness is also implicated in official discourses of modernity. Thus *Mother India* (1957), discussed in Chapter 2, ought to be contextualized with reference to Nehru's programs of development, industrialization, and agricultural modernization. These programs informed communications policy in India's first Five-Year Plan (1951), drafted four years after Independence. It postulated that "an understanding of the priorities which govern the Plan will enable each person to relate his or her role to the larger purposes of the nation. . . . All available methods of communication have to be developed and the people approached through the written and the spoken word no less than through radio, film, song and drama."[51]

If Indianness is simultaneously a material reality and a discursive and even fantasmatic construction, the drive to mimeticism finds its natural matrix in the Golden Age of social realism—particularly in the films of Raj Kapoor and Mehboob Khan. Social realism was a discursive frame in which religion and community, sexuality and gender, class, national character and regional difference, caste and ethnicity, even skin color, were parsed to conform to regularities and patterns—ideological *condensations*—such as secular socialism. But the parallax of realism and fantasy gestures toward an *excess, a remainder,* though their parallax requires spectators to view the film in stereopsis, combining both. Besides, social realist discourse about Indianness runs up against fantasy *identifications* not contained within regularized and reified *identities,* as I show in Chapter 1, discussing the film *Awaara,* whose protagonist perversely embraces the disparaging label ascribed to him: *awaara* (savage/vagabond).

Another condensation of Indianness has been around confessional, religious, or ideological *belonging,* particularly *Hindutva* ("Hinduness"). This was an invention of the nineteenth century, and as Chapter 4, on "terrorism cinema," shows, conflates Indianness and Hinduness on the mythological warrant of primordial Hindu cultural community.[52] Yet Hindi cinema also propagates a centrifugal drive, propelled from reified identity by fantasmatic or imaginary identification, fueled by global cultural flows. These flows pose a challenge to cultural insularisms; popular Hindi cinema accelerates "disaggregation" of Indianness even when national narratives attempt to contain it.

A commonplace of Western cinematic traditions is that "all that remains of the national specificity question is a vague memory of a certain unease about the national film enterprise itself."[53] Yet Hindi cinema remains obsessed with Indianness, coded in the claim of being the national cinema, which might be an unsustainable notion.[54] Ray's famous *Pather Panchali* (Song of the Road, 1955) is very different from *Mother India,* discussed in Chapter 2, though both are icons of the Golden Age. *Pather Panchali* appeared only two years earlier, yet it projects a radically different sensibility. It was shot in black-and-white while *Mother India* was shot on Gevacolor negatives and then transposed to Technicolor stock. Furthermore, Ray's neorealism contrasts with the complicated—inconsistent—social realism of Khan's film. Benegal, the famous Bengali filmmaker, was critical of the presumption that while Hindi filmmakers (such as the secular nationalist Raj Kapoor) "were somehow more representative of India," Bengali filmmakers like Ray "only represented Bengal."[55] Clearly, Telugu or Tamil cinema has different aesthetics—and habitus—from Hindi or Punjabi cinema, let alone diasporic cinema. The local, furthermore, is not to be subordinated to the regional, national, or global. Tamil or Telugu cinemas often present dissident constructions of national culture. Such distinctions, though beyond the scope of this book, are crucial: they demand due modesty in pronouncements about "Indianness."

If national identity is understood as the *demos,* Seyla Benhabib emphasizes, there is "no way to cut" the "Gordian knot linking territoriality, representation, and democratic voice."[56] But, however fugitive, the imaginary of Indianness "masks the hierarchy of subject positions and belonging divided along the lines of gender, class, ethnicity, and caste."[57] It is impossible to designate a national cinema in a country with twelve major languages, a thousand dialects, many ethnic groups, over a billion inhabitants, and a diaspora spread across the "Brown Atlantic" and Asia, the Americas, Europe, and Africa. There is a huge diversity of religion and region, rural versus urban, educated versus unlettered. Can Hindi cinema meaningfully claim to represent Indianness—even as what Fredric Jameson termed "national allegory," a formulation for which Jameson was roundly criticized, notably by Aijaz Ahmad?[58]

Hindi cinema *is* arguably a "legitimate metaphor" for Indian society and politics, which "appear to have merged."[59] Its claim to be a national cinema rests on the ability to reflect *and* fashion shared constellations of identity—as mirror and lamp. Ravi Vasudevan underscores its power to circulate a "reproducible image" of Indianness.[60] Similarly, Ernest Gellner suggests nationalism is the nation's mother, and not vice versa.[61] Yet Perry Anderson criticizes Gellner for underestimating cinema's role in the mimesis of national identities.[62] A national cinema condenses a singularity fantasmatically projected (a posteriori) as defining essence of "the people." Often this projection is an anxious reaction to real or imagined threats. Therein lies a paradox. As Žižek notes, the national "Thing" is "conceived as something inaccessible to the other and at the same time threatened by" that other.[63] Instead of the anxious fetish of "authentic" identity, Indianness might be conceptualized as relative and "differentiative," politically *equivalent* to other sovereign national identities and *differentiated* from them not as commodified reification but as motivated identification.

By century's end India will be among the four largest economies. The film industry consistently outperforms other contributors to the annual GDP and is expected to grow, in this era of increasing media convergence. Localization—or "glocalization"—is nevertheless crucial. Hindi cinema, in Vasudevan's words, is not only a "matter-of-fact everyday space"; it is also adjunct to "a broader space, in the market, near factories, schools, office blocks, in a mall, in residential areas."[64] However, cinematic space is to be conceptualized not as territorially circumscribed within a cinema complex but as extending seamlessly into virtual (online, global) spaces opened up by new media.[65]

It would be hard to exaggerate the importance of the *virtual* production of hyperinvested "identity" constructs on television and the silver screen. These constructs can be ideologically regressive, antiminoritarian: is this not the case with the massively promoted and widely promulgated serialized Hindu epic *Ramayan?* The first episode was telecast on Doordarshan's National Television Programme, charged with the dissemination of a patriotic Indian (Hindu majoritarian) sensibility. Produced and directed by Ramanand Sagar, that first broadcast was followed by seventy-seven weekly episodes. Though panned by critics and secular intellectuals as a "communalist," Hindu nationalist narrative, its success was unprecedented. Subsequent events seemed to suggest the antisecularist consequences of this mass-mediatic phenomenon: three years after the telecast, tensions between Hindu and Muslim communities erupted in a series of riots across northern India, culminating in December 1992's destruction of the Babri Mosque by Hindu extremists.[66] Just as scandalously, the 2002 communal riots in Gujarat resulted in the deaths of more than one thousand people under the watch of BJP's Hindu fundamentalist leader Narendra Modi, who in 2014 became India's newly elected prime minister. There are many parallels in Hindi cinema for Hindu nationalism relayed through the *virtual* hyperinvestment of Indianness.

Comparisons with radio and TV provide illuminating parallels for resistance to Hindi cinema's claims to being a national cinema. The television industry has been criticized for nationalist bias; while experimental broadcasts date from 1959, general Hindi-language services were inaugurated on August 15, 1965 (Independence Day), and in 1966 the Chanda Committee Report called for the autonomous incorporation of television. Radio is much older. In 1957 the Director General of Information and Broadcasting announced the state's intention to change the name of All India Radio to "Akashvani" (Voice from the Skies), which was interpreted as evidence of a long-standing bias toward Hindi. In the 1970s the Verghese Committee recommended the creation of an autonomous national broadcasting corporation, a single comprehensive entity. In the 1980s the Joshi Committee advocated a more autochthonous rather than "derivative" idea of modern Indianness.[67] Both media industries privileged Hindi.

The attendant controversies were heightened by the separation of government-sponsored radio and television services on April 1, 1976, through the establishment of the national network Doordarshan.[68] The Constitution of India provided in Articles 343–351 for Hindi (Devanagiri script) to be "the official language of the Union," with English remaining the "subsidiary national language" to facilitate governmental communication among the national and interstate agencies.[69] Arvind Rajagopal underscores how for Doordarshan *national programming* denotes "an emergent category of software in Indian television drawing upon mythological and historical sources, and portraying an idealized past" that is "projected as the crucible for shaping Indian identity."[70] The dispute demonstrates how the ideologically motivated production of national identity solicits an equal and opposite reaction, or deconstruction.

Resentment against the de facto hegemony of Hindi in radio and television extends to the domain of cinema. Although there are other cinemas (Tamil, Bengali, Malayali, and others), Hindi cinema is primus inter pares and influential as a dominant *cultural* model. There is the unarguable demographic preponderance of Hindi speakers in the country. Neither can we dispute the unsurpassed *volume* of the Hindi film output. Taken together, the Indian film industries produce between eight hundred and nine hundred films annually, in various languages. Hindi films outnumber all others. A third factor is that

Hindi speakers—often religiously identified as Hindu—wield *political as well as economic power.* Many Hindi-language films are funded, directed, "performed," and distributed by members of the Hindi-speaking community, representing shared ideological, religious, political, and economic interests. For these reasons and its long history, Hindi cinema *is* the undisputable major presence in the Subcontinental mediascape: it is practically the national cinema.

Admittedly, there is a measure of contingency in my focus on a few examples of Hindi cinema. I do not discuss the significant production from regional film industries, whether in Bengali or Tamil, Telugu, Malayalam, or Kannada, although these "regional" cinemas "articulate vastly different concerns and address local identities within India."[71] I leave untouched hundreds of other important or interesting films, including minor or small, low-budget films. While I select representative films, these selections may seem arbitrary. For instance, I do not discuss the very important film *Ankur* (Seedling, Shyam Benegal, 1974) but I discuss two films from the following year (1975), *Deewaar* and *Sholay,* and knowledgeable readers might find such selection arbitrary, given that Benegal's film is artistically superior to the two popular hits. My selections may seem to other readers, especially experts, all too predictable. Yet this is not a book exclusively for experts. I acknowledge and accept my limitations. I also affirm the value of considering landmark or otherwise important Hindi films that define Hindi cinema, precisely because my premise is that that *popular* cinema helps define Indianness.

Inside the Dream Machine

My title, *Dream Machine,* apostrophizes an actual machine (a dream machine or "dreamachine") that uses stroboscopic flickering light to induce hypnagogic effects on a subject. The machine is simple: a cylinder with side perforations. It is contemporaneous with the traditional record player, the gramophone—also rotating on a turntable at the rate of 78 or 45 revolutions per minute. Grand claims have been made about its profound effect on the brain. I adapt the image to exploit the broader implications of the dream machine's hypnagogic power, highlighting the immersive experience of cinema and its *double séance*: in the hypnagogic state one is simultaneously in the real world and transported elsewhere. The dream machine is most effective if the subject's eyes are closed. To dispel the effect, the subject need only reopen them. This suspension between the actual and the hypnagogic is a suggestive image for Hindi cinema's "suspension" between realism and fantasy.

Hindi cinema certainly evokes the dream machine: purveying dreams, reflecting Indianness back to subjects who identify with aspects of the national imaginary through "projection," in Mary Ann Doane's phrase.[72] The cinematic dream machine projects and (re)produces condensed images of Indianness at specific historical conjunctures—but *also* tests conventional limits of *realism* and what is taken to be *reality* by interposing competing fantasy identifications and truths. Entering the dream machine of cinema offers both scopic and visual pleasure, licensing temporary indulgence of otherwise impermissible desires, hopes, aspirations, and fears. Exiting the machine's hypnagogic state (or just the theater) and reentering "reality" can itself be revealing. An even broader interpretation might assimilate Hindi cinema to Michael Hardt and Antonio Negri's category of "social machines that create and recreate the identities and differences . . . understood as the local."[73] As an apparatus (re)producing the local (Indianness), the cinema machine (the camera-projector mechanism) "become[s] a 'larger social and/or cultural and/or institutional 'machine' for which the former is only a point of convergence of several lines of force in the latter."[74] There are other important referents of the dream machine metaphor, including the technology, or industry, of image production. Bernard Stiegler suggests that "*industrial temporal objects* are the new century's determining elements."[75] This book approaches Hindi cinema as a technology for producing condensations of national culture—including national *fantasy*. It is in this sense too a "dream machine."

My book's title also invokes a machinic mirroring: the dream machine suggests cinema's ability to function like the *dispositif*: the spectator is captured by the cinematic apparatus, suspended between reality and fantasy *and* interpellated within the public sphere of democracy, which Žižek conceptualizes as a "formal link of abstract individuals."[76] Jürgen Habermas theorizes this functioning of the public sphere, and Oskar Negt and Alexander Kluge elaborate the notion of the *cinematic* public sphere mediating between state and civil society, facilitating the *representation* (here, of Indianness to Indians) but also *producing* cultural identity.[77]

Certainly the category "public sphere" ought to be invoked with caution. The Habermasian desiderata are not met in every case: Hindi cinema is not necessarily in counterpoint to the discourses of the state; neither is it always genuinely transparent, open to participation from all parties of implied publics. It is not consistently oppositional or linked to the public exercise of reason (following Kant's important distinction between public and private). Further distinctions, having to do with class, ought to be noted too. Yet with Kavita Daiya I argue for construing Indian cinema as a public sphere text.[78]

At least *social realist* Hindi cinema is able to produce a kind of counterpublic and a countermemory, unlike Bollywood extravaganzas, facilitating reflections in a way analogous to Kant's public reason, which "must always be free," while the private use of reason "may often be very narrowly restricted" without hindering the project of enlightenment.[79] Counterpublics may aspire to this kind of "freedom": it would be hard to imagine, given rates of public literacy and the economic conditions of most Indians, a more effective public sphere than cinema.

Yet public reason is hardly cinema's primary concern. In a globalized era we are increasingly caught up in what Guy Debord has described as the "society of the spectacle."[80] Hindi cinema too is driven by imperatives of entertainment. But it is also impelled by the forces of desire for what is publicly disallowed/disavowed and by desire for a "deconstructive reinvestment" of traditional values threatened by modernity and globalization. Vasudevan highlights the melodramatic mode of realism as a supplementary relation between the ideologically sanctioned status quo and the transgressive force of fantasy; melodrama can potentially "undertake a narrative and performative operation which allows for forbidden, transgressive spaces to be opened," if only to be folded back into "a moral order."[81] Accordingly, "realist" and "fantasy" representations may be differentiated *modalities,* with fantasy augmenting, refracting, or supplementing realism. This supplementarity, furthermore, is heterogeneous and segmented, ranging from song-and-dance routines to fantasy in the psychoanalytic sense, tapping into unconscious reservoirs of psychic life including fantasy scenes of seduction crucial to the Oedipus complex and therefore to subjectivation, exceeding conscious reality and the "symbolic."[82]

Freud had already in 1897 come to recognize that theories of seduction may be produced by fantasies, not necessarily actual sexual seduction or abuse. Still, invoking a psychoanalytic interpretation of fantasy in this context will provoke familiar objections that Western psychoanalytic constructs—especially the crucial structure of the Oedipus, the model of the drives, the operation of desire within the Symbolic, and the notions of collective or individual fantasy—are alien to the Indian context. The eminent Indian psychoanalyst Sudhir Kakar suggests that psychoanalysis has had only a slight influence on Indian culture, yet even he has explicitly employed a psychoanalytic lexicon to describe the "everyday fantasy" and intimate relations among Indians.[83] In any case, fantasy is Hindi cinema's stock-in-trade: the power of fantasy "comes to our rescue by extending or withdrawing the desires beyond what is possible or reasonable" in a given social milieu; fantasy opens onto an alternative "world of imagination . . . fuelled by desire . . . [w]here we can continue with our longstanding quarrel with reality."[84] Psychoanalysis, even if a "derivative" discourse within Hindi cinema studies, provides a critical vocabulary for understanding psychic life.[85]

Arguing that the translation of fantasy must inevitably assume a catachrestic quality, I have dealt elsewhere with whether psychoanalytic and other Western theoretical categories can travel.[86] Prominent postcolonialists such as Gayatri Spivak and Homi Bhabha have regularly employed Freudian and Lacanian categories in discussing non-Western texts.[87] And students of Hindi cinema, including Madhava Prasad, Jyotika Virdi, and Lalitha Gopalan, have applied presumptively "Western" theoretical categories extensively. Still, the psychoanalytic category of fantasy is admittedly a recalcitrantly local projection, and must be acknowledged as prohibitive of translation both figuratively and geographically—or championed as a primary mode for the obdurate reaffirmation ("return") of the local even or especially *from within* the spaces of the hegemonic universal, a process Spivak, along with Peter Geschiere and others, has theorized.[88] Admittedly, there are misuses of psychoanalytic categories such as "extimacy," but that is a different problem.[89] Untranslatability here is precisely resistance to what Spivak terms "the law of the strongest."[90]

Hindi cinema's "untranslatability" is an effect of the dialectic between realism and fantasy—manifested as culturally specific, rather than medium specific, idiom: overstylization. And much of this emotionally as well as technically overstylized/oversaturated treatment is most visible in antinaturalist modes, particularly "fantasy" sequences.[91]

Realism *with* Fantasy: A Representational Parallax

Realism and fantasy in the cinematic construction of Indianness are interpenetrative discourses. Especially in "postparallel" cinema from the late 1990s, Bollywood-style "fantasy" sequences function dialectically or in parallax with realist diegesis, modulated by the use of "narrative-governed montage logic, realist camera eye, and big-name Bollywood stars."[92] Yet fantasy elements have a very materialist substrate: "filmi" songs are produced separately in studios designed to record "playback" singers. Shot separately, subsequently incorporated into films, they can be distributed independently and sold before the film's release. They may provide fora for covert or sub-rosa product placement, subliminal advertising, visceral enticements to consumerism, promotion of tourism, and marketing of the soundtrack as "playback" songs or packaged as music video. This selling of "fantasy" supports a vertically parallel economy in the music, tourism, and advertising industries. Elements of "fantasy sequences" thus have a *commercial* dimension and a *modular* quality, an afterlife as well as an anterior existence beyond the story.

Sophisticated cinephiles might deprecate playback singing, in which a professional singer's voice is "picturized" or synchronized by playing back the recording on set while the action unfolds, actors lip-syncing the words. But "Indians are used to the concept of playback singing and they would rather have a beautiful song on screen from a beautiful woman than have a beautiful woman singing in a very bad voice."[93] Partha Chatterjee goes so far as to assert that traditionally song sequences were "the most important component of the Bombay film."[94] While elite cultural forms (classical dance and theater) and "commercialized popular cultural forms" are "perceived as Western influenced and overtly erotic," song-and-dance fantasies "offer a powerful alternative to the Brahminic renditions of Indian culture" and could politically or ideologically interrupt the status quo.[95]

Fantasy can be formally intensive or extensive: intensive in the sense that "music and song [and dance] in popular cinema define and propel plot development,"[96] and extensive in that they also extend the realistic narrative in parallax with nondiegetic dimensions.[97] *Filmi* fantasy also presents aspirational and emotionally involving narratives.[98] These, however, complicate received interpretations of Indianness, sometimes making available transgressive narratives and counterhegemonic identifications.[99] They also enable as yet unscripted identifications or identities to come.[100]

Fantasy operates on two registers: the *formal* (or profilmic) and the *psycho-*

political. As *filmi* convention, it takes the form of "interludes" or song-and-dance routines that *seem* mere diversions or interruptions: flashbacks, flash-forwards, alternative realities, imaginary sideline trips, visitation by spirits, gods, or ghosts. Yet fantasy may also reconfigure psychic/erotic, political, nationalist, ideological, religious, social, economic, or philosophical imaginings that could otherwise (as part of the "realist" narrative) risk offending paying audiences or ruffling feathers among the powerful. Fantasy may address or *redress* reality, reimagining "real" social arrangements and unrealized agential possibilities. It may also lend itself to consumerist blandishments, religious/ideological manipulation, and illiberal pedagogies.[101]

Increasingly experimenting with "fantasy" elements, contemporary Hindi cinema has tried to accommodate unruly identifications not constrained within normative boundaries, including expressions of narcissistic fandom. Fantasy may be simultaneously integral to the diegesis (in flashback, for instance) and project an embellished alternative to, or escape from, unsatisfying actuality, to imagine a better future. Fantasy may function as a symptomatic, minoritarian countertext, interrogating dominant discourses to re-cognize and "distantiate" ideology—even though ideology is in the Althusserian interpretation both irreducible and invisible to our self-constructions; this is often only a potentiality in most popular films, but it would be cynical to discount it. Even lowbrow fantasy sequences offer self-reflexive commentary on popular and elite culture: witness the self-consciously kitschy sequences in *Dabangg* (Audacious, Abhinav Kashyap, 2010) and its sequel, *Dabangg 2* (Arbaaz Khan, 2012).

Gopalan argues that fantasies "both block and propel the narrative in crucial ways. . . . [W]e find pleasures in [the] interruptions and not despite them"; *interrupted pleasures,* she suggests, are akin to coitus interruptus, presumably also linked to frustration.[102] She references Laura Mulvey's argument that Hollywood cinema exhibits a scopophilic tendency to fetishize parts of a woman's body "*in excess* of narrative needs": fetishization as spectacle.[103] Yet invoking the register of "desire" raises a host of issues, including the neglected register of pleasure—the locus classicus of fantasy is the terrain of sexuality and sexual difference, after all.[104] Gayatri Gopinath, Jigna Desai, and others trace the "impossible desires" circulating in films of the South Asian diaspora, representing non-heteronormative sexualities; I discuss such films in Chapter 6.[105] My specific interest is in exploring the psychic possibilities subtended by these impossible desires, and not just "territorial fantasy," via readings of key popular films.[106]

The salience of fantasy in Hindi cinema indexes an emphasis on subjectivity, something the Marxist realist György Lukács would undoubtedly have considered a regressive and "unhistorical" characteristic, as evidenced by his suggestion that the "greatest obstacle to an understanding of history lay in the Enlightenment's conception of man's unalterable nature"; Hegelian philosophy, Lukács observed, "sees man as a product of himself and of his own activity in history."[107] To take subjectivity and identity seriously is impossible without an understanding of psychic life. Yet psychoanalytic readings of Hindi cinema are rare, and the relationship between the body and psychic life undertheorized. As laminar surface, the body, Michel Foucault writes, "is the inscribed surface of events (traced by language and dissolved by ideas), the locus of a dissociated self (adopting the illusion of a substantial unity), and a volume in perpetual disintegration. Genealogy, as an analysis of descent, is thus situated within the articulation of the body and history."[108] Such a genealogy might offer a map of evolving cinematic images of "Indianness." But a psychoanalytically rigorous interpretation would insist that fantasy speaks the subject's *unconscious* desire, exceeding the grasp of rational control and escaping the orbit of orthodox discourse.

Cinema as a machine for unleashing desire opens up a space set against both the private sphere and the inevitably agonistic public sphere. If realism and fantasy are dialectically related, my project is to explore the dialectical contradictions as *productive*. Fantasy has a *political* as well as *psychic* effectivity, and I track it in an intersectional matrix that imbricates nation, class, race, gender, and sexuality.

A psychoanalytic (especially Lacanian) account of fantasy enriches our apprehension of the (partial) objects of desire that constitute experience and subjectivity—as in the classic formula for fantasy, $\$\lozenge a$, linking the barred subject to *l'objet a*. It also provides an opportunity for a haptics of desire, an oblique representation of propriocepsis: another route to accessing the body as gendered social construction, and even as animal.

Fantasy is more than escapist lure, more than caricature *filmi* "attraction"—or worse, "distraction," or even "interruption," in Gopalan's negative sense.[109] Articulated as link between individual desires and national or cultural identitarian doxa, fantasy functions as excess, or excrescence. Žižek explains that "the standard notion is that one can only arrive at the final truth at the end of a series of errors, so that these errors are not simply disregarded, but are 'sublated' in the final truth, preserved therein as moments within it. What this standard notion misses, however, is how the previous moments are preserved precisely as superfluous."[110] Fantasy is preserved *as superfluous*, even occasionally fanciful and escapist, within the realist trappings of mainstream Hindi melodrama. It is not *therefore* insignificant.

To return to Rajadhyaksha's speculation, perhaps it is this dialectic between realism and fantasy that "still needs an account." In the first instance, to adapt Žižek's framing to my purposes, what is remarkable is not only the persistence of the cinema, "notwithstanding the obsolescence of its most distinctive technological vehicle, celluloid," but also the very idea—confection of realism and fantasy—of India: "an equally stubborn presence, despite the foundational transformations . . . since the onset of globalization."[111] That stubbornness constitutes a reaffirmation of autochthony, what Geschiere terms the "global return to the local," or simply the persistence of the local.[112] Though cautioning against uncritical reliance on Western theory, Wimal Dissanayake acknowledges that because of the interanimation of the global and the local, it is "almost as if Foucauldian heterotopias are in operation."[113] Global socio-politico-cultural processes have penetrated the experience of everyday existence. How then do we understand modern Indianness, that fugitive, ambivalent yet stubborn presence, if modernity is itself a complex and elusive category?[114]

Exploring changing cinematic constructions of postcolonial cultural identity, this book suggests that the more the ("realist") national narratives seek to fix a cultural identity, the more they are confronted by the plasticity and fungibility of Indianness. Yet if Hindi cinema is a mirror, it is also a site for the construction of screened fantasies about imagined selves and "imaginary homelands," and the enunciation of pleasurable identifications.

The Chapters

The chapters trace the trajectory of Hindi cinema from early postcolonial cinema through the 1990s into the contemporary moment. Framed by the Introduction and the Conclusion, the book is divided into three sections. The first, titled "Postcolonial Hindi Cinema: Bad Subjects and Good Citizens," contains three chapters, focused on films reflecting or constructing images of the postcolonial Indian citizen, particularly along the axes of class, gender, the family, and social or legal institutions. Section II, "Reimagining the Secular State," contains two chapters concerned with films that revisit the articulation of secular state and society. Section III, "Diasporic Cinema and Fantasy Space: Nonresident Indian Aliens and Alienated Signifiers of Indianness," contains three chapters concentrating on films from the post-1991 liberalization era, and especially Middle Cinema, featuring middle-class Indians, particularly diasporics or nonresident Indians (NRIs). Several of the later films betray growing anxiety about the transnational disaggregation and dispersal of "floating" signifiers of Indianness; others engage with a new cosmopolitanism. The Conclusion draws the three sections together, suggesting that this cinema's often anxious attempts to shore up Indianness reveal ironically how Indianness is itself becoming more disaggregated.

I consider landmark, even epoch-defining, films that condense key elements of their social moment and milieu through the decades since Independence in 1947. The book strategically alternates between close reading and broader analysis of films to anchor discussion, singly or in signifying clusters, illustrating "condensations" of the national imaginary. Chapter 1 analyzes *Awaara* (Raj Kapoor, 1951) as emblematic of an immediately postcolonial crisis of national (social realist) self-construction. This "Hindi Social" traffics in the idioms of social realism, depicting the harsh postcolonial reality faced by young men like the protagonist Raj, while the rich live extremely lavish lives—and lavish lies. The film subtly presents a crisis of masculinity and attendant disillusionment with official mythologies of a modern, recently decolonized India.

Chapter 2 takes up the critique of the mythopoetics of the nation, focalizing the synecdochic female protagonist of *Mother India* (Mehboob Khan, 1957). Another classic of Golden Age cinema, the film crystallizes and ironizes the overdetermined meme of motherhood, highlighting contradictions between the fantasy subtended by the idealized "Mother India" and the postcolonial reality of non-urban women—and rural India.

Chapter 3 discusses two subgenres of Hindi popular cinema from the 1970s and 1980s, rather than focusing on a single film; a crisis of gendered social politics converges in the complementary figures of the Angry Man and the Avenging Woman in these subgenres. The first subgenre is represented by two films, *Deewaar* (The Wall, Yash Chopra, 1975), and *Sholay* (Embers, Ramesh Sippy, 1975), registering popular resentment—righteous and particularly masculine "anger"—against the status quo. Films in the second subgenre depict the corollary anger condensed in the figure of the Avenging Woman: *Insaaf Ka Tarazu* (Scales of Justice, B. R. Chopra, 1980) and *Zakhmi Aurat* (Wounded Woman, Avtar Bhogal, 1988). The question is whether that "anger" presents genuine—and viable—responses to oppressive social conditions or whether they are compensatory "fantasies" of resistance and revenge.

Chapter 4 likewise considers a cluster of films rather than a single example, identifying a historically specific condensation of anxiety cathected onto the figure of the terrorist during the 1990s and early 2000s. "Terrorism cinema" condenses and desublimates the diffuse concern about cultural/social sovereignty and military insecurity as a crisis of the official doctrine of state secularism. This chapter offers readings of particular films within the cluster, such as *Roja* (Mani Ratnam, 1992), *Dil Se* (From the Heart, Ratnam, 1998), *Mission Kashmir* (Vidhu Vinod Chopra, 2000), *A Wednesday* (Neeraj Pandey, 2008) and *My Name Is Khan* (Karan Johar, 2010). The chapter parses political rhetorics and visual grammars used to represent and imagine responses to the threat of the terrorist, and simultaneously to register challenges to secularism *and* fantasies romanticizing and eroticizing the terrorist.

Chapter 5 focuses on *Lagaan: Once upon a Time in India* (Ashutosh Gowariker, 2010), which imaginatively returns to the colonial era of the late nineteenth century, retrospectively reconstructing a fantasy India. This recuperative narrative is organized around the conceit of a cricket match between the British colonials and unlettered peasants. The match propagates the fantasy of a counterfactually secular India—an object lesson to contemporary Indians. But it is a richly layered and conflicted fantasy, palimpsesting real and psychic terrains of interracial contact and contest—and the emotionally fraught confoundings of interracial romance.

Chapter 6 explores cinematic geographies of desire—"fantasies" of alternative sexual arrangements, non-heteronormative spaces presumptively *queering* Indian culture because accommodative of nontraditional, even transnational, models of sexuality—in two key examples: *My Beautiful Laundrette* (Stephen Frears, 1985) and Deepa Mehta's *Fire* (1996). It also discusses other, less well known LGBTIQ-themed films featuring South Asians—films responsive to global LGBTIQ discourses of rights and social realignment.

Chapter 7 foregrounds a newly condensing cosmopolitan sensibility in diasporic South Asian cinema, against the backdrop of broader sociopolitical developments, particularly post-1991 neoliberalism. The chapter examines a cluster of illustrative films, many challenging a narrow definition of Hindi cinema: not only *My Beautiful Laundrette,* discussed in the previous chapter, but also *Mississippi Masala* (Mira Nair, 1991), *Bhaji on the Beach* (Gurinder Chadha, 1993), *Dilwale Dulhania Le Jayenge* (The Brave Heart Wins the Bride, Aditya Chopra, 1995), *My Son the Fanatic* (Udayan Prasad, 1997), *Aa Ab Laut Chalen* (Let's Return Home, Rishi Kapoor, 1999), *ABCD* (Krutin Patel, 1999), *American Desi* (Piyush Dinkar Pandya, 2001), *East Is East* (Damien O'Donnell, 1999), *Bend It Like Beckham* (Gurinder Chadha, 2001), *Monsoon Wedding* (Mira Nair, 2001), and others.

Chapter 8 tracks the condensation of a new ethical and aesthetic sensibility in the cinematic representation of Indianness, focusing on a singular if paradoxical example—Danny Boyle's *Slumdog Millionaire* (2008). The film marks a watershed for the "Hindi cinema" industry. Though not strictly speaking a Hindi film, it puts the category in question precisely by *displacing* "Bollywood" as well as "Indianness" itself in several registers. Topics discussed include controversies attending the reception of the film, particularly Boyle's alleged proclivity for luxuriating in the most unpleasant realities of slum life in India—"poverty porn."

The Conclusion draws together the book's arguments. I revisit the vast range of films surveyed in this book but also consider other cultural forms, including novels, television, musicals, music, and even animation, highlighting issues of cultural "property," appropriation, misappropriation, and expropriation raised by the cross-cultural borrowings and hybrid instantiations of markers of Indianness. Increasingly fissured, Indianness is subject to centrifugal forces and tends to greater disaggregation rather than toward singularity or reification. *Neither* Indianness nor the modular Indian citizen-subject nor Indian cinema should be conceptualized as embodying a primordial and reified essence, but rather should be seen as constructed within and by an ultimately global circulation of actants—and by fragmentary, floating signifiers.

I

POSTCOLONIAL HINDI CINEMA

Bad Subjects and Good Citizens

1

The Wish to Belong, the Desire to Desire

The Emergent Citizen and the Hindi "Social" in Raj Kapoor's Awaara

The year 2014 marked the twenty-fifth anniversary of Raj Kapoor's death in 1988, which seemed to have been scripted so melodramatically that it might have made even a Bollywood director blush: soon after the film industry's most prestigious award, the Dadasaheb Phalke award for contributions to Indian cinema, was conferred on him by the country's president, Kapoor collapsed and died. Kapoor won many accolades besides the prestigious Padma Bhushan, including nine Filmfare awards and two nominations for the Palme d'Or at the Cannes Film Festival. He was one of the most admired directors of Hindi cinema's Golden Age, from about 1940 through about 1961, and it would be hard to find many who are more representative of popular Hindi cinema from that important phase of Indian cultural history. His film *Awaara* (Vagabond, 1951) is possibly his grandest achievement, although he himself was most fond of a film he directed nearly twenty years later, *Mera Naam Joker* (Call Me the Joker, 1970). It is for these reasons that my first chapter focuses on *Awaara*.

If Kapoor's death was dramatic, his career was also larger than life. He was born in what became Pakistan after Indian Independence and Partition in 1947 into the first family of Indian cinema, five generations of which have been prominent on the silver screen. The first generation was that of B. N. Kapoor. Raj's father was the eminent actor Prithviraj Kapoor. Raj was the eldest of six; his siblings Shashi and Shammi were major film stars. His children, Rishi and Randhir, and grandchildren Karishma and Kareena Kapoor, have been significant presences in the industry. Certainly Raj Kapoor became an icon in his own right and was not just a member of a dynasty.

Neither did Kapoor emerge in a historical and political vacuum. It helps to remember the context in which he was steeped. In 1947 India had undergone perhaps the signal moment of its modern history: independence from two hundred years of British colonial rule. Jawaharlal Nehru became the first Indian prime minister, and his vision, a marked contrast with that of Mahatma Gandhi, was an important influence on the course of the country's subsequent development, which is sometimes for convenience divided into the Nehruvian chapter and the post-Nehruvian chapter. The Nehruvian chapter of India's modern political formation was characterized by a commitment to secular socialism; centralized government; protectionist economic policies; state intervention in policies on censorship, morality, and education; state control of transportation, heavy industry, banking, and communications, especially under the Five-Year Plans; and strategic nonalignment, which became official after the 1955 Bandung conference. The Nehruvian chapter could be said to have ended with the assassination in 1984 of Nehru's daughter Indira Gandhi, who was also prime minister of India at the time. The post-Nehruvian chapter of India's modern political history was marked not only by this epochal assassination but also by an era of successive "transitional" governments, including those headed by Rajiv Gandhi, Indira's son, who would himself be assassinated, and another government headed by Narasimha Rao, but most signally a government under the right-wing Bharatiya Janata Party (BJP). There was a radical break with the Nehruvian era during this period, also attended by the breakup of the Soviet Union in the 1980s, and India did a volte face from its former orientation to the Soviet Union toward the West. More recently in this post-Nehruvian phase, and especially after the software boom and the liberalization of the economy starting in 1991, India has come to think of itself as a player on the global stage. Kapoor died at the cusp of the era of economic liberalization, as India turned increasingly toward globalized capitalist economy and culture. So he was witness to an enormous cultural transformation and represented aspects of it in the films he directed through the decades.

The Golden Age and the Social Realist Text

Kapoor, like Mehboob Khan, another famous auteur of the Golden Age of Indian cinema whose own iconic film, *Mother India* (1957), is the focus of Chapter 2, was influenced by the neorealists (particularly Vittorio de Sica) and the German expressionists (including Fritz Lang, Friedrich Murnau, and Robert Wiene) as well as Federico Fellini and Hollywood filmmakers such as Frank Capra, Orson Welles, and Alfred Hitchcock. As a major director and head of his own studios (RK Films), which he established in 1948 at the age of twenty-four, Kapoor was the youngest film studio owner of his time, and consequently enjoyed unprecedented artistic freedom as a director—to the point of showing a kiss in one of his "fantasy sequences" (in *Satyam Shivam Sundaram* [1978] before the ban on kissing was officially lifted) and even showing some nudity in one of his films (the aforementioned *Mera Naam Joker*). More important, he exercised control over and demonstrated mastery of all the major aspects of filmmaking.

Dissanayake organizes Indian cinema into the categories of "the popular, the artistic, and the experimental"; only the last two are presumed capable of interrupting and interrogating "the hegemonic project of the nation-state." *Pace* Dissanayake I suggest that popular Hindi cinema is often deceptive in its interrogation and implied critique of the status quo—and perhaps the more effective precisely because it reaches a broader audience.[1] And certainly Kapoor's films blurred the boundaries of these categories, as I argue below.

Kapoor's filmmaking, including camera work and stage design, evidenced his eagerness to experiment with the visual surface. Some of this experimentation, such as the green screen and the kaleidoscope effects on display in *Aag* (Fire, 1948) and his other early black-and-white films, may seem amateurish today. It is important to remember that they were made long before computer-generated imaging became available.

Before he became known for his directorial genius, however, Kapoor was a member of the activist and antifascist Indian People's Theatre Association (IPTA), formed in 1942, five years before Independence and during World War II, and the experience was formative. At this time the "star system" arose, and Kapoor was influenced by it, becoming a star actor himself. As director he had both a commitment to social issues and a deep instinct for the theatrical, for blocking, and for artistic choreography. Theatrical instincts and strong ideological convictions that developed in his collaboration with the IPTA would combine in his cinema direction with an instinct for dramatic storytelling, starting from his earliest directorial work in a film like *Aag*, the setting of which is the theater.

Tracing some of the connective threads of Kapoor's oeuvre also helps us to see the critical and sustained supplementary role of fantasy in his films. In *Aag*, made in 1948, Kapoor's first year as the owner of his own studio (RK Films), the protagonist, Kewal, sets fire to his own theater and in the process burns his face, scarring it grotesquely. Although he survives, his beloved Nimmi is repulsed by the disfigurement. As he emerges from the ruins of his theater and the ruin of what Nimmi had seemed to value, Kewal taunts her bitterly—telling her that physical beauty, what she had loved in him before he was burned, is fleeting. This theme of superficial beauty, of appearance versus reality, was a main thread linking his films. In a film made three decades later, *Satyam Shivam Sundaram* (Truth, Goodness, Beauty, 1978), the handsome engineer who has come to inaugurate a new dam in a village (a metonym for the social realist dimension of the progress of postcolonial modernity) hears Rupa's religious singing and falls in love with her voice and her attractive figure, and even asks for her hand in marriage. Rupa's voice has become a partial object of desire because despite his efforts he is unable to see the disfiguring scar she carries on her otherwise beautiful face and he constructs a compensatory fantasy—the Hindi word *kalpana* is explicitly used by him to signify fantasy—of what she really looks like on the premise that a beautiful voice could come only from a beautiful body, a beautiful face. This Socratic fantasy is also entertained by Rupa herself: receiving such adulation from her lover, who composes over-the-top poems to her beauty, she is carried away and, as she gazes at her disfigured face in the mirror during one fantasy sequence, begins to see images of herself restored to perfection. This fantasy sequence segues into a more conventional fantasy where the images of her as perfect are then actualized (not realized): Rupa is seen dancing, beautiful, unscarred, and engaged in a duet with her lover. There is no "realism" here: the scenery is utterly and breathtakingly defiant of any earthly landscape, and in fact within the fantasy sequence the notion of fantasy becomes, with unusual self-reflexivity, a running joke, as Rajeev is shown trying to embrace a woman who disappears right before his eyes. Rupa too speaks in fantasy to her reflection in the mirror, but the mirror does not reflect the real Rupa—whose name significantly means (beautiful) "form." This is not just a reference to her body. It is also a reference to the problematic of realism versus fantasy. Rajeev marries Rupa without seeing her face entirely, and on their wedding night he is aghast when he discovers that she is disfigured, de-"formed" in mockery of her name. He disowns her and runs away from the wedding, literally chasing the beautiful fantasy. And, obligingly, Rupa appears to him at their favorite meeting point. The real Rupa also appears to him and allows him to embrace her as long as he agrees not to lift up her perpetual veil (it is tempting to contrast her with the Real—with a capital *R*—Rupa, especially given the truly repulsive special effects superimposed on the real—living—Rupa's face by the director).

When that flesh-and-blood Rupa becomes pregnant, Rajeev cannot comprehend how it is possible and heaps insults on her, saying that he was seeing a different woman. In a departure from the conventional sexist melodrama that popular films often purvey, Rupa confronts Rajeev with the issue of gendered hypocrisy: if she is a whore, as he suggests, then what does that make him? This marks a turning point in the film, for it releases Rupa from her role of demure Indian woman, unable to stand up to the sexism and patriarchal mores of her society. When her beloved father dies of shock on her revelation of the pregnancy and Rajeev's obstinate rejection, Rupa is reborn as a fearless woman, no longer bound by propriety, and she leaves Rajeev. Surely this moment is no less resounding than Nora's departure from her house in Henrik Ibsen's *A Doll's House,* when she slams the door behind her as she leaves her husband, Torvald. Rupa's departure from her home is a pivotal moment of social critique, the obligatory "happy ending" notwithstanding.

Seeing continuities among his directed films highlights the inventiveness with which Kapoor blended realism and fantasy. What is crucial is that much of the drama of the fantasy sequences in *Satyam Shivam Sundaram* depends on everyone's awareness of the contrast between the fantasy being indulged and the unpleasant reality of Rupa's disfigurement—everyone, that is, except Rajeev himself! Interestingly, Rupa counsels him to trust not the eyes but the heart—this is tantamount to elevating fantasy as more reliable than appearance (what appears to be reality). In context, this makes sense. And Rajeev playfully agrees to keep his eyes closed, saying it is apparently only in this way that he can have Rupa.

As I argue however, it is the fantasy sequences of *Awaara* that remain unsurpassed in their psychological complexity by those films that followed it in Kapoor's oeuvre, and in *Awaara* we can find lineaments of the technical and thematic complexity of Kapoor's fantasy sequences in later films. Kapoor's auteurist genius also manifested itself in the domain of music, for which he had a natural ability and talent. This talent remains unusual even among directors of Indian films, with a few exceptions such as the great Satyajit Ray. It is often underappreciated that Kapoor wanted to be a music director before he became a film director. It was he who introduced to the film industry the famous music director duo Shankar-Jaikishan and lyricists Hasrat Jaipuri and Shailendra. Kapoor was the first Indian director to use color, in *Sangam* (Meeting, 1964), and with this film he also inaugurated the trend toward foreign location shooting, which soon became a sine qua non for popular Hindi cinema: audiences began to feel entitled to some armchair tourism.

Kapoor also became known for extravagant staging or mise-en-scène, especially in *Awaara*. Yet, I argue below, *Awaara*'s often comedic and spectacular mise-en-scène should not distract us from the film's seriousness, from its forceful cultural critique. The protagonist may be a clowning *awaara*, or vagabond, but he is modeled on Charlie Chaplin's tramp, like the eponymous tramp in *Shree 420* (1955), a film Kapoor directed, produced, and starred in, again playing a vagabond named Raj. *Shree 420* is continuous with *Awaara* in other important ways: Nargis is once more the love interest Vidya, and there are other subtle analeptic links to *Awaara,* including the repetition of a musical motif played by street musicians. *Shree 420* likewise has a fundamentally (but not exclusively) comedic structure. It mocks gentlemanly virtues and respected pillars of society who are in truth frauds, just as *Awaara*'s vagabond protagonist had fingered the rich and powerful as frauds and profiteers. (In common parlance a "*shree* 420" is a carnivalesque trickster figure, poking fun at society, especially, in this case, the bourgeois aspirations and pretensions of the upper classes in post-Independence India; the term derives from the Indian Penal Code's Section 420, which makes crimes of theft punishable by law.) Notably, the later film is set in the city—Mumbai—iconic of Indian modernity, and it opens with a song sequence that contains possibly the most famous lines of early cinema: "My shoes are Japanese / My trousers English. / On my head is a Russian hat / But my heart's Indian for all that."

It is worth noting that there are moments in *Shree 420* in which astonishing special effects are used to project fantasmatic projections: in one scene a snake, representing evil, appears as a hallucinatory fantasy in a sari that has just been discarded by Vidya, and in another scene a ghostly alter ego of Vidya appears in a double exposure, as a fantasized image, and this vision is incorporated into a complex and extended song-and-dance "fantasy" sequence. A third double exposure features Raj himself, dressed in a dark suit and gazing into a mirror that reflects back the apparition of the vagabond Raj. Each of these hallucinations comments on the narrative in powerful if "magical" ways, but all flout realist conventions while being central to the film's meaning-making. The end of the film projects another fantasy, this time utopian, of an alternative reality representing a vision of a more humane postcolonial state and (an impossible) future in which the poor will be able to build their own homes. There can be no doubt, in other words, that as an auteur Kapoor was very conscious that he was presenting a systematic and systemic interrogation of the meaning of modern Indianness, and the genealogical trajectory suggests semantic richness and cultural depth as well as the director's sustained obsessions.

The dominant cultural framing of India's Golden Age cinema, Ravi Vasudevan observes, was that "it was related to the formation of an art cinema, that it addressed a (potential) art cinema audience and, in turn was premised on a notion of social difference," as contrasted with commercial cinema's "infantile," florid, sentimental, melodramatic popular mode.[2] Vasudevan acknowledges that critics such as Kobita Sarkar saw some potential in popular film to achieve social realism, inspired in part by Italian neorealism, though "limited by melodramatic characterization and narrative."[3] And while Golden Age films including *Awaara* hold a mirror to postcolonial Indianness, they also complicate the image of the nation and postulate alternative imaginings of Indianness for *mass audiences* as well. Golden Age films problematize—preeminently through disruptive "fantasy" and fantasmatic subtexts—received narratives of nation, and this is a source of insight and richness.

The Contradictions of "Indianness"

The contradictions of "Indianness" are figured in *Awaara* in the opposition of two pivotal categories: *gentleman* and *vagabond* (*awaara*). Their opposition is brought to crisis primarily in often underestimated "fantasy sequences," including flashbacks, "song-and-dance" routines, and phantasmagoric nightmares elaborately staged in the interstices of the main narrative. Fantasy cannot be overlooked in any analysis of Hindi cinema's role in reflecting *and constructing* the image of postcolonial Indianness as both mirror and lamp. But here the opposition is structurally crucial.

Not only is "family" a governing paradigm, but the film is also an archetypically family affair. The protagonist, like the director himself, is named Raj, and is arguably his mouthpiece and alter ego. Raj Kapoor's real-life father, Prithviraj Kapoor, plays Raj's on-screen father, Judge Raghunath; his youngest real-life brother, Shashi Kapoor, plays Raj's younger self. And Prithiviraj's father, Dewan Bashwanath Kapoor, has a cameo role, the only time he ever appeared in a commercial film. Thus four generations of Kapoors appear in the film, though never in the same frame. Set alongside his other personae in films such as *Shree 420*, Kapoor's protagonist is a landmark of his cinematic autobiography, an inscription of the auteur's autoaffective relation to himself and his idea of Indianness.

Family as paradigmatic *theme* or motif is pivotal in several registers. Judge Raghunath is the scion of a prominent feudal family. His father was a "feudal lord," a neocolonialist successor to the British, a member of the powerful landed ruling elite.[4] A flashback takes us back to where the story, though not the film, begins: family trouble in the Judge's own household. Raghunath had sent Jagga, son of a criminal, to jail for rape—a charge that had not been proved in court beyond reasonable doubt. Jagga escapes from prison and kidnaps Leela, Raghunath's wife, seeking what might be termed "criminal" or indeed (mytho)poetic justice. When he discovers she is (already) pregnant, Jagga changes his strategy, patterning his revenge according to well-known mythological memes. After four days, enough to suggest that she has been dishonored, he releases her back to the Judge. Initially, like Rama in the *Mahabharat*, who retrieves Sita from her demonic abductor Ravana, the Judge is happy to have her home. Soon, however, his mind is poisoned by others and he rejects Leela as defiled in the eyes of an unforgiving orthopraxy, just like Rama even after Sita had proved her chasteness in her trial by fire (*agnipariksha*). The Judge is also being considered for promotion to an important office, and a blemished reputation could dash his hopes.

Leela gives birth to Raj in poverty. This is a monumental event, for family practically defines Indianness in the popular mind. Leela's disgrace has major repercussions for Raj: deprivation of his due place in "good" society, a life of alienated poverty, disgrace, and crime. Raj becomes a bad citizen and finds a surrogate father in none other than Jagga. But he also finds love when he is reunited with his childhood friend Rita, the Judge's ward and a lawyer. Rita (played as an adult by the iconic Nargis) teasingly calls him uncivilized (*junglee*, savage), though he has the dress and comportment of a gentleman. Raj fails to become a true gentleman, perversely embracing his déclassé status as an *awaara*. While he desires to desire happiness, he cannot accept Rita's love without suspicion, and he scuttles his chance of happiness with her at the precise moment when it seems within his grasp. Raj's story tracks his exclusion and alienation, raising questions about his constitution as citizen subject and imbricating discourses of class, gender, biological inheritance, criminality, and law (*kanoon*)—themes permeating Kapoor's oeuvre, from the early film *Barsaat* (Monsoon, 1949) to the relatively late *Bobby* (1973).

Raj, discovering that Jagga had ruined his mother's life, kills him in an act of surrogate parricide. Later Raj learns that Raghunath is his real father, and confronts him, nearly committing actual parricide. For this criminal threat, he is produced before Judge Raghunath in court—defended, as melodramatic formula dictates, by Rita, the lawyer. Yet there is something subversive about Rita's "maiden voyage" into the realms of the law as a woman defending the hero.[5] Albeit with ritual respect, Rita sharply interrogates Raghunath, her guardian and mentor, in his own courtroom, successfully discrediting this pillar of Indian society and his shabby personal conduct vis-à-vis his family. Raj gets a light sentence (three years in prison); Rita promises to wait for him, in the vaguely inconclusive conclusion.

Raj remains an outsider throughout the film, and the inconclusiveness of the ending is significant—underscoring the fact that no fantasy produced in this courtroom drama could promise resolution, given the overwhelming reality of social injustice. Raj's story is superficially that of a man's unjust subalternization, but it ironically also questions the privilege denied Raj, drawing attention to the flawed social contract. It is crucial that Raj retains something excessive and unruly, that he stays the *awaara*, the *junglee*, the animal, the vagabond. This identity is postulated as embodying a critique of the trajectory of postcolonial Indian modernity—literally, in Raj's body, rendered "*junglee.*"

Iqbal Masud writes that the film "introduced a self-conscious element of 'modernity' into Indian cinema. The title itself with its echoes of rootlessness, 'lost generation' and a free-floating, amoral consciousness, recalls Walter Benjamin's analysis of the Baudelairean city with its twin archetypes of the Dandy and the Apache." It is an exemplarily urban film, one of the first postcolonial films that *imagine* a possible urban Indian identity in the cinematic public sphere.[6] In brief, Raj here tests/puts to the proof a modern male identity *dandified, and situated pointedly in the modern Indian city,* and the test is of vital interest to anybody concerned with the question of what the new Indian can be. The importance of this metropolitan identity is missed even by otherwise astute observers such as Gayatri Chatterjee, who puzzlingly begins her reading of *Awaara* by remarking that we get information that is, according to her, simultaneously revealing and irrelevant, such as that Raghunath's father "was a big landlord, a Talukdar, somewhere in U.P., '*but he liked to spend most of his time in Bombay.*' The italicized part of the information is however unconnected with the narrative."[7]

Thus in the film a contradiction emerges between the family as a real human relation and the family as simultaneously a microcosm of the state and its occultation. Hegel writes that the family "stands opposed to its own actuality when explicitly conscious; as the basis for the actuality of the nation, it stands in direct contrast to the nation itself; as the *immediate* ethical existence, it stands over against the ethical order which shapes and preserves itself by work for universal ends": the Indian equivalent of the Roman *Penates* of the family, who "stand in contrast to the universal spirit."[8] In other words, there is a contradiction between the official construction of the national family and the family functioning as cellular reproduction, in every sense of the word. This is a kind of ecology and politics of biopower.

There is, furthermore, a simultaneous contradiction and a relation of *mutual* reproduction between state and family. On the one hand, the state is constantly being apostrophized in Hindi cinema by representations of the exemplary family, especially in times of crisis. On the other hand, the nation is regularly presented not in the bloodless form of institutions of biopower and bureaucracy but as the nuclear or extended family. Yet rarely has the contradiction between the state mythology and the image of the family in Hindi cinema been so stark.

Being framed by the Judge and failed by the legal system not only fills Jagga with a ressentiment that drives him to the very social pathology for which he was initially wrongly convicted. In the context of the film, it also propels him to what can only be termed the righteous and *philosophic* rage of the wronged.

His primary motivation for being a bandit is not venal but theoretical. In establishing that social pathology is a product not so much of nature as of nurture, or cultural deformation, he avowedly wants to prove the Judge wrong precisely for nurturing an extrajudicial prejudice based on a genetic fallacy: that "good people are born to good people, and criminals are born to criminals." He is also a living indictment of the Law and the state. It is remarkable that while Jagga himself is not exactly a charmer, an impartial viewer can see the justice of his complaint against the Judge: the Judge's premise is repeatedly undermined in the diegesis. The "outlaw" Jagga is thus surrogate not only for the lawmaker (the Judge) but for Raj, the dissenting non-gentlemanly "junglee."

The title *Awaara* suggests the protagonist's exceptional status, his vagabondage indexing his exclusion from *any* proper family, whether the national family to which as a citizen-subject he notionally belongs or the bourgeois family to which he desires to belong. The film engages with the place of unruly desire in the modern Indian bourgeois family and with the sanctioned canalization and regulation of personal desire in the context of the national family and interrogates the norms of inclusion and exclusion from the folds of those two versions of family. Its themes are the unruly desire to desire and the frustration of the wish to belong.

An important consequence of Raj's being denied his patrimony and birthright to a proper family by his own father, a pillar of the legal establishment, is that his desire as subject is thwarted. In the strict psychoanalytic sense, this imperils his status as subject, let alone as *zoon politikon*, or political being. As an "*awaara*," or vagabond, Raj is designated as "extimate" in the sense elaborated by Jacques Lacan: simultaneously representative of the new postcolonial Indian citizen-subject and irreconcilably exiled, abjected, from that status: through him, Kapoor radically deconstructs some of the foundations of that postcolonial subjectivity. This self-contradictory play of Raj's desire and the self-divided tropology of family make this film a rich and early complication of the cultural project of defining Indianness in postcolonial India.

The Judge, the Gentleman, and the *Junglee*

Eventually, Raj is established as a sympathetic figure despite having grown up under the tutelage of a criminal and an impoverished mother—hardly, in the Judge's judgment, conditions that he would expect to produce a "gentleman," which in the lexicon of the film (or more accurately, in the semantic and philosophical grammar that links and divides the Judge and Jagga) constitutes social excellence and virtue. Like Jagga himself, Raj is positioned with respect to the law structurally as a pervert (in the sense given the term by Jacques Lacan, as he draws together Immanuel Kant and the Marquis de Sade). He shows up the injustice of this justice, its inhumanity. The law is not just an abstract code. It is also embodied in the citizen-subject, and this is why the individual story of Raj is a microcosmic representation of larger questions the film poses regarding the state. Hegel conceptualizes this instantiation of the Law as a commutative relation between individual and state: the Human Law, he writes, "has its being essentially in the form of self-conscious actuality. In the form of universality, that spirit is the law known to everybody, familiar and recognized, and is the everyday Customary Convention (*Sitte*); in the form of particularity it is the concrete certainty of itself in any and every individual; and the certainty of itself as a single individuality is that spirit in the form of Government."[9]

It could plausibly be argued that Raj, having in the final sequence of the film accepted his just sentence but also having delivered his chastisement of the unjust system, is not merely folded back into conventional moral virtues. What we have is not merely social realist comedy with a moral lesson. Rather, he retains something beyond the social pieties, something perhaps a little more aligned (while not being identical) with what Machiavelli would have understood as *virtù*. Machiavelli was, of course, referring to qualities desirable in a prince, but the concept refers to personal qualities that a good if ordinary man might also wish to cultivate; it is perhaps an interesting coincidence that while he is intended to represent an Everyman, Raj's very name is related to the Hindi word for "king." As an ordinary but good man, then, Raj exhibits a certain excessive, outlaw bravery, resourcefulness, daring, and ruthlessness—desirable qualities of (gentle)manliness. Under the British "raj," the undermining of Indian masculinity and a consequent shoring up of British manhood was precisely the most debilitating of all threats to colonial Indian identity, and one of the preeminent modes for the assertion of British colonial male superiority. In its immediately postcolonial moment, it is hardly surprising that the film is focused on (gentle)manliness as a key attribute of the masculine Indian subject; my argument throughout this book is that Hindi cinema is above all the mirror and the lamp of Indian identity construction, of Indianness.

The film thoroughly undermines the position of the Judge not only via Rita's lawyerly interrogation but also in Raj's stinging castigation of the Judge and the social norms his court professes and enforces. This indictment is equally a powerful commentary on the newly postcolonial nation of India, which had gained its independence from British colonial rule a scant four years before the release of this film. As Gayatri Chatterjee writes, the courtroom "is the arena where the grievances are voiced, where there is an appeal to the establishment, not through law-books but through the heart. That is why [forms of protest like Raj Kapoor's film] are never 'realistic,' but are always popular."[10] Only in the end is Raghunath able to tearfully acknowledge not only the mistake on which his entire personal and professional life has been built but also Raj as his son and, implicitly, as a good man and a gentleman. It is only by appeal to the heart and to the social link that a just social order can be achieved. This is the contradiction between the individual *citoyen* and the abstract individual postulated by the universalist language of the state law expressed—and only expressible via—"fantasy."

As Slavoj Žižek theorizes it, this is the "formal link of abstract individuals. . . . [D]emocracy implies a split between the abstract *citoyen* and the *bourgeois* bearer of particular, 'pathological' interests, and any reconciliation between the two is structurally impossible."[11] The visual representation of fantasy disrupts the main narrative, which does its ideological work. Fantasy must be read symptomatically, as Marx and Freud would have it. And as Žižek elaborates this symptomatic reading, it is the fantasy that structures social reality and gives it a specific meaning.

But fantasy also circulates in a more complex psychic economy than mythological romance. Fantasy renders fungible subject positions and object choices: as psychoanalytic theory tells us, the formula for fantasy is $\$\Diamond a$; the subject is an effect of its relation to the *objet a* of desire. As J. B. Pontalis and Jean Laplanche put it in "Fantasy and the Origins of Sexuality," the origin of fantasy for Freud lies in the "hallucinatory satisfaction of desire, in the absence of a real object," in which the subject forms "no representation of the desired object" but "is himself represented as participating in the scene," and this staging of desire simultaneously produces the partial object of desire the subject believes he or she has lost—and constitutes that subject.[12] There is no fixed position for either subject or partial object. The partial object falls as soon as it is grasped, giving way to another in an endless chain. Similarly, the subject slips from subject position to subject position depending on the play of desire being staged. I read the films selected for discussion here as staging the play of desire and subject in the social field, represented cinematically as mise-en-scène: irradiated by a range of political, historical, economic, gendered, class, racial or ethnic, and national discourses, and infiltrated by ideologies that are in tension. Fantasy appears in textured social interaction, even failed interaction.

The recent turn to fantasy as a focus of study in film studies articulates the psychic and the social "without seeing either side of the equation as wholly contingent on, or reducible to, the other."[13] For there is, as Freud showed, a "psychical reality"—the unconscious *Wunsch*—that is more than the negative or antithesis of actuality or social reality and more than a psychological account of behaviors not fully obvious to a casual observer. Psychic reality is not an inferior reality. Hindi cinema, as a "dream machine," turns on this premise, trafficking in fantasy in various registers.

The most resonant fantasy of the film occurs at what seems to mark a turning point in Raj's life. The "cause" of Raj's desire is presented within a fantasy sequence that, although a directorial afterthought tacked on at a late stage in shooting, is remarkable for brilliant cinematography and staging, for the "eclecticism of its musical borrowings from Western classical music, Goan and Russian folk songs and the choral songs of the Indian People's Theatre Association (IPTA)."[14] In this fantasy Raj appears to be chastened by his "missed encounter" with evil—evil from which he seeks to escape into the world of love through union with Rita. The "fantasy" puts Raj in closer touch with his "real" feelings, an interoceptive sensing of his psychic pain. The fantasy is thus not a distraction or an extravagance on the part of the director; even though it is extravagantly "mise-en-scène," in purely cinematic terms it is narratologically purposive.

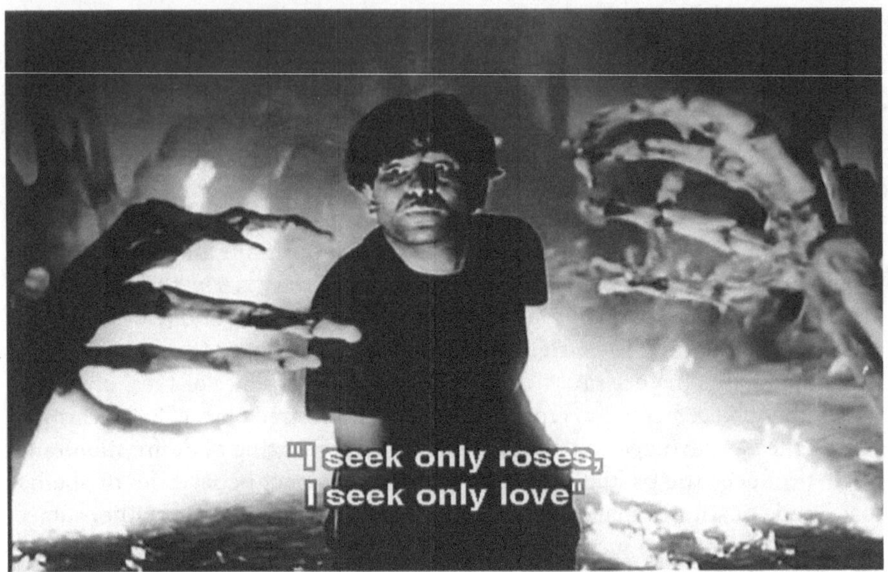

Figure 1.1. Raj (Raj Kapoor) tormented by his fantasies in *Awaara* (dir. Raj Kapoor, 1951).

In this fantasy that alternates between a heavenly realm where Rita offers love and a hell (*narak*) of fire, skeletons, and ghouls, Raj sings plaintively, "I seek only flowers (*phool*) / I seek only love (*pyaar*) / I seek only spring (*bahar*)" (see Figure 1.1).

The stunning set for this dream sequence in *Awaara* was designed by M. R. Achrekar and, together with the equally impressive choreography by the Frenchwoman Madame Simkie, it offers an extraordinary example of the visual opposition of realistic and fantasy elements. The sequence features what would have been for the time impressively distortive "special" effects, with dizzying visual puzzles of scale and dimension and with low-key (with fill) or high-contrast lighting and nightmare chiaroscuro reflecting the state of Raj's unconscious mind. The choreography is brilliant; its improbable juxtapositions of meditative statues in one segment are contrasted with an overwrought mise-en-scène in which grotesque figures seem to threaten Raj in another segment, and it has clever and often subtle visual bridges between Rita as the emblematic angel of the first part of the dream and the representation of then state-of-the-art special effect of superimposition (using a matte shot) to project Jagga as the improbably large éminence grise brooding over the second part. This is an example of iconic framing of space, perspective, and bodily movement—an organization of the image, "relocated in the individual" though it may be, in which a stabilized critique of the existing social order is conveyed.[15] But it is also augmented by intertextual richness. The lovelorn male protagonist, repelled by a reality that militates against an authentic happiness, seeks refuge in imagination, poetry, and other forms of withdrawal from imperfect social reality. Raj's dissension is most powerfully expressed in his autoaffective identification as "animal" rather than "gentleman": as *junglee, awaara.* The sequence was a technical watershed in the practice of filming "fantasy sequences." It inaugurated a practice of setting songs within a dream, songs that reveal or express something important to the characters that could not be presented so powerfully in the main, realistic narrative—particularly psychic truth.

Formal antecedents for the film include generic linkages to Italian neorealism, but the fantasy elements in *Awaara* are a countercurrent to the main diegesis—even superseding the realist diegesis. This is a formally significant internal contradiction in a film that is presumptively in the realist tradition, even an hommage to Italian neorealism. As Gilles Deleuze insightfully points out in *Cinema I: Image-Movement,* however, Italian neorealism itself does not hew to realism or naturalism. Rather, it participates in what Dana Polan in a review of Deleuze identifies as "a kind of modernist anti-realism in which space has no real existence."[16] This evacuation of space is the most striking visual achievement of the stagy fantasy presented in *Awaara,* and doubles as a metaphor for the kenosis of the protagonist himself, as he sings his song wishing not to be in the real world of suffering but to be removed from it into the timeless and spaceless realm of love and happiness. But this is, of course, a fantasy.

A figural model for the lovelorn protagonist is the figure of Devdas, originally created in Saratchandra Chatterjee's 1917 novel of that name. This poet grows up with his childhood friend Parvati; as they approach adulthood, they fall in love. But they cannot marry because their families will not permit it on account of differences in caste. Devdas spurns the world because he "wants only love"—to use the words from Raj's fantasy—but cannot have love. The film version by P. C. Barua in 1935, in which the disaffected poet was played by K. L. Saigal, struck a chord, and another version was made in 1955 by Bimal Roy with Dilip Kumar in the lead. A much more opulent version was made in 2002 by Sanjay Leela Bhansali, the "sensitive" poet Devdas being played by the sentimentalist actor of overblown gestures Shah Rukh Khan, and the part of the lower-caste Parvati by the equally renowned beauty Aishwarya Rai. A similar renunciant is at the center of another important film, *Pyaasa* (The Thirsty One, 1957), from the Golden Age director Guru Dutt and made in the same year as *Mother India* (Mehboob Khan, 1957), discussed in Chapter 2. Vijay, the protagonist, is a tortured poet in postcolonial India, but his sensibility seems modeled on the image of an inward-looking Indianness, soulful and melodramatic. While the heart-of-gold courtesan brings his works into the public eye, he himself does not wish to be in it. He wants not fame or money but poetry and love—the inner life of psychic authenticity. The Devdas and Vijay figures are analogues for Raj, and comparison with these and similar characters in Hindi cinema contributes to the understanding of the circulation of the social meme of the sensitive male who declines the blandishments of social success.

Vectors of Realism and Fantasy

I read *Awaara* in terms of the bifurcated vectors of Raj's development, one arguably a conventional *realist* narrative in which Raj is redeemed by Rita's love and transformed from a criminal into a virtuous Indian citizen, and another much more contradictory narrative, vectored through a fantasmatic and unruly expression of a socially excessive desire in which he embraces his "*virtù*" as a "*junglee*," delivering a powerful critique of the state. We cannot underestimate the import and the importance of the film's ambition to intervene in a discourse of cultural citizenship. The *fantasmatic* vector is exemplarily represented by the dream sequence. Perhaps because this film is a prime exemplar of the "Hindi Social" and its dominant ideology of social realism, critical discussions of the film have tended to focus on its social commentary and have neglected its fantasy elements, and particularly this key dream sequence.[17] My own discussion emphasizes the fantasmatic subtext—its extraordinary oneiropoetic suggestiveness and aesthetic brilliance, but also its critical role as "dangerous supplement."

The upshot of Raj's nightmarish fantasy (Figure 1.1) is the resurgence of a desire *to desire* that had lain dormant or occluded in his everyday life: he desires beauty, freedom, love, and happiness, not necessarily the kind of social success implied by becoming a gentleman like the Judge. His actual love life in the realist narrative seems to be caught in the dilemma or contradictions highlighted by the fantasy. In the realist mode, that is to say in the diegesis, the conflicts between his actual existence and his fantasized life are brought home repeatedly. The sharpest point of this conflict between reality and his fantasy or desire irrupts in a lovers' quarrel he has with Rita. In a two-shot that starts off as a romantic, even rather sexy, clinch, when she is changing out of wet clothes behind a modest towel, Raj comes up on her and Rita (playfully) chides him, calling him an animal or savage—a "*junglee*" (see Figure 1.2).

Rita employs the playful term as mere sexual banter, but it sticks like a thorn in Raj's side. Perversely, Raj insists on misrecognizing the term as deprecation. But perhaps he is not entirely mistaken in his misprision: for arguably the exchange reveals a psychic truth—a reality—to himself; it becomes autoaffective. Indeed, as the diacritic of their relationship and of the film's major themes, the term takes on the parabolic aura of a semantic marker of class difference.

Evoking Raj's Everyman anxieties about his inadequacy as a "gentleman" and his inadequation to the modular form of modern citizen-subject, or his insinuated failure, in Rita's eyes, as a proper object of love, the term "*junglee*" functions as a motif around which the film's narrative contracts—and Raj finds that it is a glove that fits him. It is an ideologeme indexing the question of nature versus nurture that divides the class/world of Judge Raghunath from that of the bandit rival and "antihero" Jagga.

But I would stress that the fantasy more importantly constitutes an encounter with the Real: with the coercive reality beyond the web of what sustains society's pleasant fictions, such as the fiction that a woman of Rita's background

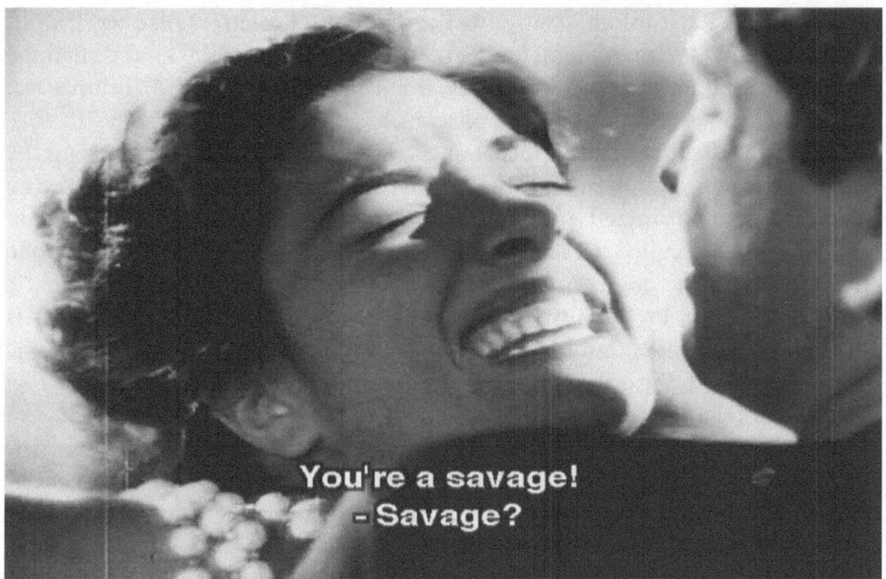

Figure 1.2. Rita (Nargis) calling Raj (Raj Kapoor) a "savage" in *Awaara* (dir. Raj Kapoor, 1951).

can simply fall in love with someone like Raj without social complications. She calls him an animal in an erotically charged joke, but he (unconsciously, fantasmatically) "re-cognizes" this as the truth about what he is underneath the facade of being a gentleman that he presents to the world (dressing in Western suits, pretending to play the piano, affecting a cosmopolitan dandyesque style, lying to his mother about traveling to the West rather than telling her the ugly truth that he had been away in jail). My psychoanalytic interpretation would find confirmation in Vasudevan's description of the Hindi Social's project of formulating "an alternative order of cinema conceptualizing a different, more sensitive, *psychological,* humanist and 'adult' order of personality."[18]

The irony of Raj's self-recognition in the animalistic category "*junglee*" takes on a piquant resonance in the film's staging of his encounter with a dog. This mise-en-scène exemplifies the "tableau" postulated by Vasudevan, summarizing a poignant psychic truth about Raj's emotional life.[19] Jobless, Rita-less, and Jagga-less, unable to be saved by his poor mother, Raj addresses a stray dog, saying that the only difference between them is that the dog is an animal and he is a human being. He seems to be posing the question, what good is it being human if one is to live like a stray dog? Both are tramps ("*awaaras*"), nameless, homeless, and loveless. Indeed, Raj repeats the word "human" (*insaan*) sardonically, underscoring the irony.

As Raj commiserates with the dog, a man walks carelessly past, roughly brushing the dog. Raj protests aloud, and the man, clean-cut and wearing a good suit, retorts, "Mind your tongue! Bloody savage," using the same word Rita had used playfully. Raj leaps up, strangling the man until the latter falls away limply. It is implied that the man might have suffered a worse fate at Raj's hands had the portrait of Rita not risen up uncannily, fantasmatically, before his mind's eye, an image of the better angel of his conscience.

Significantly, this image appears at the level of fantasy, superimposing the image of the photograph of a young Rita over Raj's face, as if reality were being subsumed by a feminized and spectral version of his conscience, or of what Freud might have called his *Ideal Ich.* His "becoming animal" in this parabolic encounter with the dog is redeemed but also highlighted by this fantasmatic image of a higher, loving humanity as embodied in the good woman. This is a fantasy of humanism, no longer at war with the animal. Indeed, his psychic identification with the dog approaches the condition of autopoiesis, self-making, in the act of relation to the dominant social text.

Raj's "becoming animal," then, is reinscribed in the grammar of extrasociality—he is the outlaw, the undomesticated anti-gentleman (or ante-gentleman?), the criminal. What looks like a throwaway or minor sequence actually subtends larger concerns: the assimilation of Raj's status to the level of a stray dog, this "becoming animal," is thematically significant, and is not to be read only as a reduction in stature for the human. Rather, there are two important implications of his Imaginary (in the psychoanalytic sense) identification with the stray dog.

First, the conscious and sardonic identification with the dog has a particular depth and is a significant autoaffection. In thinking the other's (here, the dog's) intimate relation to the self, there is a thinking of the self: the encounter with the other is an encounter with the self at the same time; heteroaffection is intimately bound to autoaffection, or the effect on the self. This is what Derrida theorizes in *The Animal That Therefore I Am.*[20] In relation to the other (*l'autre*), there is a self-relation, a relation to the I (*le moi*). This is the sense in which the epithet "*junglee*" is irreducibly embraced by Raj, not just at the superficial analogical level of being *like* an animal but in a much more profound, unconscious level as well, in a process of introversion of the other. This is the irreducible trace that, even when he seems to be "reformed" at the end of the film, Raj declines, as it were, *unconsciously* to give up: an excessive, unruly dissent.

For if the film encodes the power of Raj's emergent extrasociality—"*jungleeness*" or *awaarapan,* it appears to retreat behind the screen of social propriety, humanism, love, gentlemanly virtue, bourgeois domesticity, and other social bromides. Yet the trace remains as an intransigent remainder, an essential dissension, and Raj remains an *awaara* at some core place in his relation to himself and his relation as citizen-subject to the state.

This is why the contradictions of the film are insightful, provocative: without this contradiction the film would be betraying its title, its driving conceit, its tropological brilliance. Not only the provocatively ambiguous ending but also Raj's unruly parody of the code of the gentleman and the antisocial parable of *awaarapan* embodied in his often comedic performative would be rendered nugatory and, what's worse, would renounce or put under erasure its critique of the social order. We cannot forget here Raj Kapoor's progressive/left ideology, an ideology whose account of society turned on the crucial operation of class struggle. This ideology was central to his reputation and was what endeared him to the Soviet Union, as noted earlier in this chapter. On his travels to that country in the mid- to late 1950s Kapoor was hailed as a people's champion and lionized as "Tavarish Brodyaga" or "Comrade Vagabond"; indeed, he cultivated the corresponding attitudes at home deliberately. Yet it was not only in the Soviet Union that Kapoor's film was popular. Winning a wide viewership in other parts of Asia and the Middle East, it was a hit in China, and there too his political critique was not lost on viewers.

Second, in enacting a fall from his status as the high-born son of the Judge to a status no higher than that of a stray dog, Raj's pastiche performative burlesques the very notion of gentleman. In that specific sense he delivers a powerful social critique, as eponymous *awaara.* He is the protagonist of this exemplary Hindi Social, but also a namesake, mouthpiece, and alter ego of the director. The more or less happy ending does not negate Raj's (irreducible if unconscious) disavowal of the status of gentleman to which he was born, a class that inherited the mantle of power from the British colonials. They know how to game the system, earning the rewards of being "gentlemen" while those like Raj earn only bitter calumny for being "dacoits," thieves, and "*awaaras*." It is implied that Raj's rough *virtù,* then, is more admirable than the virtue performed by these "gentlemen" whom postcolonial Indian society, eager to establish its credibility as a modern civilization, honors—indeed fetishizes.

Raj's caustic inversion—even carnivalization—of the implied hierarchy of the gentleman over the *awaara* is dramatized in the scene in which—having eluded the police in a stolen car—he encounters Rita at the grand home of the Judge (now her guardian). During this visit Raj cleverly reveals and hides what he really is: he proclaims he is a thief, though he appears to be a gentleman; he is hiding the truth in plain sight by proclaiming it. He simultaneously produces a brilliant send-up of and witty polemic against the code of the gentleman and against bourgeois ideology and capitalism. He lambastes the Judge and his ilk as shams and crooks who dress as he himself is dressed—like a gentleman, or *shareef*—and fleece the system. His radical disassociation of class from true virtue is wild class analysis.

Raj's elaborate self-presentation as a gentleman is achieved under false pretenses—and obviously in the surface narrative, the humor of the film, its "entertainment" value, inheres in the fact that the audience is in on the joke. However, it is through the contradictions of his performative that Kapoor's social critique can be "archaeologically" extracted. For Raj does not merely fail to be a gentleman. The real point of the film is that he undercuts the very premises of the aspiration to gentleman status—the aspiration to social success—in the film, throwing away his every chance, it would seem, at conventionally recognizable success in that endeavor. He reveals, through the contradictions and cracks in his performance, his unconscious desire: he prefers at some level his uncivilized vagabond self. He does not cede on his desire, thereby enacting the cardinal rule of being true to himself in the psychoanalytic register. As Lacan put it, the cardinal rule for the subject inheres in "*ne pas ceder sur son désir.*"[21]

The *Awaara* and the Auteur

It is impossible to render a full account of *Awaara*'s intervention as Hindi Social without reading it as a part of the director's political autobiography. And it is impossible not to recognize in the figure of the *awaara* a mouthpiece for the auteur's implied critique of Indianness: the film is not the kind of comedy in which the ending resolves all key contradictions—gentleman versus vagabond, nation as expressed in representative institutions such as the court versus the family and blood. It is in this—critical—sense that *Awaara* should be construed as a paradigmatic representative of the Golden Age of Hindi cinema. It is anything but a propagandistic or chauvinistic celebration of Indianness. Having been made just over three years on from Independence, it is perhaps a little surprising that the film seems so disenchanted with modern Indianness. A renovation of cultural pride updated and made suitable for the immediately postcolonial moment must have been a felt need for the citizenry, even as Indians flocked to see this cultural product of a newly reorganized Indian cinema industry.

Commentators on the film have not always shown how explicitly *Awaara* articulates its critique of Indianness from within the framework of state and civil society's institutions such as the court system and the family. It is the family that ultimately legitimates individual thought and action in—and between—the private and the public spheres. But above all the family is the nation in microcosm. An exploration of postcolonial male subjectivity, and perhaps even more female subjectivity (given the propensity of nationalist discourse to entrust the national Thing in the matrix of the real and fantasmatic domestic spaces of "home"), must be considered within a familial conceptual structure. Writ small, the precise contours of this private-sphere identity were still an unsettled matter in the early years after Independence, and the agon of Raj's questioning of the state's and social institutions' relation to the marginalized citizen could be read as a test case for the status of postcolonial Indianness. By the same token, the film can be read as elaborating a progressive agenda for the emergent republic, a proposal for the reconstruction or makeover of the normative if emergent male citizen-subject—as well as an element of the political autobiography of the director. This chapter undertakes a kind of archaeology of this progressive project in *Awaara*, particularly though not exclusively through the nonfrontal approach of reading nondiegetic and especially fantasy elements alongside the realist narrative.

In Kapoor's film Raj stands at the crossroads of reality and potentiality, or reality and fantasy. As a figure of a collective fantasy too, he embodies the aspirations of the new Indian male; the fantasy of potential plenitude is the more poignant here because it threatens constantly to reveal itself as impotence. Though adrift as an outcast—*awaara*—he looks like a caricature of the presumptively successful modern citizen. He looks like a leading man dressed in a suit, able to fake his way into the image of a cosmopolitan traveler; he is also able to insinuate himself into the home of an extremely wealthy and important judge who happens to be the father of a beautiful and nubile socialite daughter into whose affections he is also able to insinuate himself.

An underlying argument of this chapter is that the central theme of Raj's exclusion from civil society is really metonymic of a larger meditation on the nature of Indian democracy, and indeed on democracy as such. The director seems to be saying that if India aspires to secular democracy after suffering long under colonial rule, it needs to confront a fundamental and constitutive problem with democracy. As Žižek reminds us, democracy can only be a "formal link of abstract individuals," which is to say that there persists a constitutive split within democracy between the abstract citizen-subject (*citoyen*) and "the *bourgeois* bearer of particular, 'pathological' interests," and furthermore that any "reconciliation between the two is structurally impossible."[22]

The split manifests as the definitive parallax of realism and fantasy in Hindi cinema. From one perspective (the official narrative) the abstract individual is interpellated by discourses of democracy as anchoring the Symbolic order: the citizen-subject is the designated bearer of democratic rights and responsibilities. From another perspective this nominal construction of the abstract individual is complicated and interrupted by individual or group *fantasies* of alternative, dissident, or utopian self-understandings. No democracy can balance all these particular claims of individuals or groups. Just as "planetary" democracy is dissolved as soon as it encounters the "pathological" national "Thing" (*das Ding*), so also a national democracy is undone as soon as it encounters particular and competing particular fantasy *supplements*—what Žižek might call competing materialized *enjoyments*—in which it is necessarily instantiated. As he writes, "It is in the very nature of fantasy to resist universalization: fantasy is the absolutely particular way every one of us structures his/her 'impossible' relation to the traumatic Thing."[23]

My reading of Kapoor's film also corroborates Žižek's observation that the "field of the law, of 'rights' and 'duties' . . . pertains by its very nature to the dimension of universality[;] it is a field of universalization brought about by equivalent exchange, which is why the formula of fantasy as irreducible to the dimension of universality is $\$\Diamond a$, i.e., the subject confronted with this 'impossible' surplus."[24] The individual subject's enjoyment can never be totally contained within the universal. Žižek wants here to limn the incommensurability of ideas of democracy as a universal principle on the one hand, and, on the other, ideas about communal and individual fantasies. The community or the individual is as noted only the abstract category: and in one sense *Awaara* is a good illustration of the contradiction to which Žižek points. For, at one level, the film asks: what kind of modern democracy is India if someone like Raj can find himself excluded within/from it? What is the status of Indian citizenship, of the bourgeois Indian family, of marriage, of law, of the criminal justice system? What guarantee does biological inheritance/patrimony provide? What is the role of culture in excluding someone like Raj, of class, if someone like Raj can test its limits by falling on the wrong side of it through no fault of his own, even if he was born into society's upper echelons? In Hindi cinema the question of the individual is not, or not just, the formal question Žižek explores, having to do with the abstract category of the individual at odds with the universalism of democracy. Rather, it is keenly engaged in exploring the idiom of the hero's or heroine's particular fantasy, the very content of specific individual life experiences that is highlighted in the dialectic of realism and fantasy, or the fantasies that drive a particular group or class. This is so even if the individual, Raj in this case, is meant to be generic, a representative representation of Indians, to raise general questions about Indian society at a particular moment in the nation's history. This is why the dialectical relationship between fantasy and the context or social milieu ("reality") is a main focus of my discussion in this book.

Raj is excluded from the democratic public sphere by the accidents of his circumstance. He is reduced to a subject position in which he feels he is denied the right even to desire happiness as either an *awaara* or an aspiring gentleman. So he must fall between, neither fish nor fowl. That is why he is hypersensitive in his confrontation of Rita when she playfully calls him a "*junglee*," a savage. Insisting on owning this dehumanizing—self-flagellating—label in an act of mimetic citation, Raj acknowledges the truth of the characterization, beyond what Rita meant. This "*junglee*" status is the only intermediate position open to him, between belonging as participant in the public sphere and enjoying domestic bliss in bourgeois companionship.

That perhaps is also why he scuttles his own chance of happiness and acceptance in his senselessly self-destructive behavior in a bizarre scene at Rita's twenty-first birthday party. Raj seeks a loan of a thousand rupees from Jagga, to buy clothes to look right and a gift for Rita. Jagga mocks him, observing that it seems that "gentlemanliness" (*sharifat)* is going cheap (*bazaar me bik rahi hai*) and Raj wants to buy some. But Jagga points out sarcastically that he is not the sort of gentleman who loans money for such squandering. Raj will have to earn the money the old-fashioned way: stealing, robbing, perhaps even killing. Raj refuses, having resolved to be good.

Raj's bitter avowal of the label of *awaara* is what perhaps explains his strange levity and incomprehensible insensitivity as he hands Rita a necklace he has stolen (from the Judge himself) without a box, and his strange inability to be embarrassed when faced with the clear evidence that the empty box that Judge Raghunath hands Rita at the same time is the box from which it is evident he stole the necklace. All the time, as he does every time he is in this grand house of the Judge, he tells the truth (speaks "the Real") as if it were an offhand, witty lie. When Rita asks him why such an expensive gift, he says, "For you, nothing is too expensive. Besides, I stole it." This is an ironic confession that, as is customary in Raj's banter with Rita, hides the truth with, or behind, the truth.

As Rita takes him to meet the Judge, presuming that it will be their first meeting, Raj spots the man from whom he has stolen the necklace. As the recognition dawns on everyone, Raj slips away through the front door this time, the tuxedoed gentlemen and ladies, including Rita, watching his retreating back. Raj is ironically wearing a white jacket, contrasting with the black tuxedoes of most of the men. The black-versus-white theme plays with the customary associations of good and evil, and is repeated frequently in this scene. The dance following Raj's exit is performed by Rita's young friend (the performer is Cuckoo, who introduced the even more famous dancer Helen to Indian cinema), wearing a white sari and black blouse. How do we read this "recognition scene" with its strange or unnatural staging of desire? Is it realistic that Raj, who has fervently resolved to be good, would now say such a thing to Rita and so cavalierly? But then he teasingly retracts the confession, playing the same Freudian game of *Fort/Da* as the film itself seems to be playing, saying now (perhaps punning on the word) that he stole it from "the stars." And Rita responds to this in the expected way, touching Raj's traumatic Real. Their conversation has now become almost ritualized repartee, highlighting Raj's willful identification with his own abjection:

> Rita: "You're such a . . ."
> Raj: "A savage [*junglee*]?"
> Rita (*smiling*): "What else? You are a savage. You buy such an expensive necklace, but you won't spring a couple of rupees for a velvet case."

Raj's insistence on "owning" *awaarapan* takes the form, as Freud would have recognized in his own psychoanalytic discourse, of reaction formation. He does, of course, wish to be loved by Rita, to be legitimized as a citizen, and to have his manhood affirmed by familial, social, institutional, legal, and state *recognition*. But, I have argued, he insists perversely on embracing the very opposite of what he desires, in mimetic citation of his denigration by the woman he loves: a form of self-contempt, brought on by his ressentiment at being unable to achieve gentleman status. His embrace of *awaarapan* also perhaps explains why he runs away like the lowest coward rather than apologize or promise to reform himself in a way that will allow him to have what he wants most of all, a life with Rita. Instead, he seems, in a gesture of abjection, to choose at that moment not to exercise the right to desire.

Conclusion: Critiquing the Social Order

The social order is not transcendentally *given;* as Hegel put it, it is *willed* or *made* by Man. This can be regarded as a radically secularist view, although Hegel also speaks of a "Divine Law" that is a "force exerted against the independence of the individual; and, *qua* actuality in general, it finds inherent in that essential being something other than the power of the state."[25] And now, at the dawn of a new social order in secular socialist Independent India, *how* the state, its normative family structure, its other institutions, its laws and executive infrastructure, its apparatuses of discipline and control, and its economy are arranged are still relatively open questions. This very openness presents an opportunity to arrange matters properly, before it is too encrusted with custom and inertia. How an *awaara* can (re)enter the socius is then a dramatic performative encapsulating the political. Full subjectivity, full citizenship, is not only a privilege to be enjoyed. It is also a responsibility, a burden that the good citizen embraces and welcomes. To be unencumbered of this burden is also to be bereft of subjectivity and citizenship. And this is the true condition in which Raj finds himself. It is a condition of unbearable lightness of being, of anomie. In the same (Idealist) philosophical tradition as Aristotle and Hegel, Kant also had something of importance to say in this connection. In the *Critique of Practical Reason* he noted that the moral law could be grounded in the subject only if we claim freedom of choice in the matter—without this freedom morality has no meaning.[26] The moral law is generated by this free subject; out of his freedom he wills the law into being. It is a moment of creation—autopoiesis, autoaffection—and not of reception. This is how, Kant might have said, we rise above being mere savages in the state of nature, were he present as Raj lashes out at Rita's playful comment about his being a "*junglee*." It is because Raj is not a full, free subject in this foundational Kantian sense that he feels irreducibly reduced to *awaarapan* or *junglee* status, and lives down to this image even when he appears to be on the verge of rising above his misfortunes through Rita's love. Love is not enough. He also needs to be recognized in a just way by the law. This is really the multilayered "mimesis" that unfolds in the film.

It would be a mistake to say that Raj *consciously* wants to be abjected from/in society, that his true desire is to reject Rita's ennobling and humanizing love, to reject the Father in either Jagga or Judge Raghunath. Raj may be an Everyman "who wants social approval and recognition."[27] At the same time, it is also true that he unconsciously desires to be outside society, to be the animal, the *awaara*, for, as he sings, "I am an *awaara*. . . . I am also a star of the heavens"—in other words, my freedom as a subject inheres in my refusing to be constrained by the received doxa of identity. He is in this specific sense not renouncing his real desire. He is merely publicly disavowing it in order to mark his exclusion from the "right to desire." Neither does he consciously wish to be punished under the law; however, his unconscious desire may be to be subjected to the Law only to undermine it by remaining true to his unconscious desire, to demonstrate (*monstrare*) the injustice of Justice in the newly Independent state, to decline acquiescence to its Law. But that de-monstration also renders him "monstrous"—a savage.

Astutely and conscientiously—if, at the deepest level, unconsciously—Raj identifies as *junglee*, as animal, *even in the final moments of the film.* He never really relinquishes his identification with/as the animal, and in his parodic performative of gentlemanliness he embodies the contradiction Derrida postulates. The presumptive identification of the human as *zoon logon echon*, separating us in fact from the animal even as it defines us as a special kind of animal and presuming to deny in the animal those traits that define us as not merely animal: "speech, reason, experience of death, mourning, culture, institutions, technics, clothing, lying, pretense of pretense [*feinte de feinte*], covering of tracks, gift, laughing, tears, respect, etc."[28]

The film submits a critique of the social order that is in the first instance a critique of the legal construction of the modern Indian as a rights-bearing subject. This critique is adjunct to the cultural critique of the construction of Indianness—mediated via the contradiction between the opposition of gentleman and *awaara/junglee*. The film imaginatively explores the meaning of a denial of the right to desire as a full citizen-subject: what happens to an Indian man when he is cut off from full citizenship? Does he lose his manhood? Does he potentially risk becoming an outlaw, being already beyond the pale of the law de facto? The implied feminization of Raj's dissent from the public discourse of Indianness that structures the surface narrative is thus very important. Partha Chatterjee reminds us that the Indian nationalist movement relegated culture to the realm of femininity—the home was the space of the woman, and it was where the national Thing could be safeguarded.[29] It was a domain adjunct to but cordoned off from the public sphere, which was the muscular realm of nationalism, the masculine domain of politics.

The eponymous *awaara* Raj is a figure of the modern, immediately postcolonial Indian subject, a figure in whom is condensed a parallax: a figure at once modeled on the Westernized, "civilized" gentleman who wears a suit *and* his alter ego, who embraces his internal precivilized or noncivilized *awaarapan*—the aspiring modern gentleman is also a thief, an *awaara*, and a "*junglee*" whom the colonizer only recently had tried to civilize. To see him as gentleman from one position and as the opposite of a gentleman from another is to see this parallax in operation: and it is in the palimpsesting of the two contradictory representations that we perceive in a stereopsis the historical depth of his construction as a subject—he is a figure produced by the specific historical formation of the modern Indian nation recently emergent from the self-contradictory nightmare of colonial cultural and politico-economic domination.

There is an unmistakably gendered (masculine) framing to this opposition, but it is counterbalanced by an attention to the figure of the modern Indian woman. Rita's success as *the other* modern Indian citizen, her impressive achievement of the position of defense lawyer, troubles the neat division of power assumed by an Aristotelian-Hegelian framework, with males in power and women in secondary roles. Can Rita then arrogate the position of the ideal citizen? Is she a model of modern Indian woman? Should Indian women in postcolonial India be encouraged to follow in her path and become independent, powerful, and like Rita pose a challenge to the law and to masculine identity itself? Clearly Rita has a higher status in every respect than Raj himself. When a male viewer "identifies" with him as a protagonist, what does Rita's challenge mean to that male spectator? It is not too much to argue that the film presents us with an Indian subjectivity that is not only emergent but also in crisis. But perhaps a more iconic counterpart to Raj as a representative of the modern Indian male, a modern female Indian postcolonial subject who could be juxtaposed as his necessary complement in the classic Hindi Social, is the anchor and pivotal figure of the film I take up in Chapter 2: *Mother India* (Mehboob Khan, 1957).

2

A Bad Son and a Good Enough Mother?

The Paradoxical Maternal Romance in Mehboob Khan's Mother India

A watershed moment in the newly independent India was the implementation of the Nehru government's first Five-Year Plan beginning in 1951, the year of the release of *Awaara,* the focus of Chapter 1. *Mother India* (Mehboob Khan, 1957), the topic of this chapter, appeared shortly after the end of that first plan and just before the beginning of the second. Even as they seem to celebrate everyday life in the new republic, both films crystallize a certain disillusionment with the project of modernity in India, a modernity that was the legacy of "Independence" and for which there could hardly be a better token than the Five-Year Plans.

Khan's film, like *Awaara,* offers up a somewhat jaded view of the state of the new nation-state, pointing up the gap between the reality of village life or the life of the urban poor—and a prosperous modernity figured as Westernized, an elite fantasy or mythology propagated by the Nehruvian state. In *Awaara*'s protagonist Raj we saw condensed a growing disenchantment with the notion of advancement toward a (Western conception of) civilization, registered in his ressentiment against the law through his perverse embrace of a "*junglee*" or savage, uncivilized ("*awaara*") ego-ideal. *Mother India* presents at best a bittersweet reenchantment with the mother nation.

Of Motherland, Moneylenders, and Mama's Boys

The film's larger project is to tell the story of a nation developing into a modern state, modeling its Five-Year Plans after the Soviet Union, the example that the postcolonial Nehruvian Indian "secular socialist" state avowedly wanted to emulate.[1] The opening shots featuring tractors and dams, otherwise so disconnected from the rest of the film (for there are few or no machines of any kind except guns prominently featured in the main story), function to signal the developmental trajectory of the new nation from that watershed political moment of freedom from colonial rule to the diegetic moment of the difficult situation of the Indian peasant. The title, *Mother India*, resonates with a range of cultural references, including an encrypted reference to a 1927 book by Katherine Mayo (Khan's film was evidently a rejoinder to Mayo's disparaging account of Indian culture, sardonically entitled *Mother India*).

There is also a not-so-veiled reference to Indira Gandhi's autoaffective identification with the sycophantic slogan coined by Dev Kant Barooah: "Indira is India. India is Indira." Mother-veneration is so constitutive a theme in popular Indian culture (including film) that it becomes a target for Salman Rushdie's spoofing in his novel *The Moor's Last Sigh*, as when a character diagnoses the mother-worship in middle-class Mumbai argot: "I'm talking *major* mother country."[2]

Writing about German cinema, Sarah Wüst observes that *Heimat*, or "homeland," in some important contexts functions as "a space of shelter from the threats of modernity, alienation and dislocation. . . . *Heimat* becomes a feminised space associated with the mother's womb and native landscapes."[3] In Wüst's formulation *Heimat* "offer[s] *imaginary* spaces on individual and collective levels," suggesting that "it can be regarded as a myth about the possibility of identity and community in the face of fragmentation, alienation and disintegration."[4] As "motherland," a feminized space, India is similarly constructed in nationalist narratives as a refuge against colonization in the past and globalization in the present; this myth of Mother India provides a touchstone for Khan's film.

The first Five-Year Plan emphasized large-scale industrial development projects, and the closing scenario of *Mother India* features one such project, a dam. From this symbolic event the story of Radha, the protagonist, is narrated in flashback, metonymically charting the sweep of recent postcolonial development toward "modernity," as well as the vicissitudes of fortune experienced by an agrarian community hanging on to what little it has. The villagers are at the mercy of unpredictable nature and predictable rapacity on the part of neofeudal moneylenders and landlords, who are if anything more unscrupulous than the former British rulers they succeeded. Thus, the contradictions of postcolonial Indian modernity are established as a frame for the representation of "Mother India" the nation *and* the woman, the diegetic character *and* the overdetermined political category.

The story turns on the struggles of the eponymous mother, Radha, recently married to Shamu, in a wedding paid for by Shamu's poor mother, who has become indebted at exorbitant rates of interest to the moneylender—the prototypical éminence grise of village India—Sukhilala (whose name, with devastating irony, connotes happiness). The resulting debt, in an economic cliché representing the lot of many poor rural people, is passed down the generations. The marriage begins promisingly, but soon the moneylender's vampiric hold on the family (requiring them to pay all but a quarter of their crop in interest) reduces them to poverty. They try to till the parched soil in a desperate attempt to eke out more from their small plot of land until Shamu loses both his arms in an accident. Shamu's unmanning is simultaneously physical and psychical: both economic powerlessness and symbolic castration. In shame, he abandons his family, symbolically wiping off the *bindi* (mark of married status) from Radha's forehead, releasing her from wifely duty. Radha becomes breadwinner, substitute paterfamilias, in the nuclear family. She is also a representative citizen in the national family, a supplement to the normatively male citizen-subject. This complicates the ostensible heroic representation of Radha as Mother India.

Radha must raise her three sons alone because the disgraced Shamu has abandoned the family. Sukhilala, recognizing Radha's vulnerability, offers to help if she marries him. Virtuously, she refuses, although when a rainstorm and ensuing flood destroy the harvest, and her youngest son dies, she is brought to the brink of surrender. Radha heroically rallies her villagers, asking them not to abandon their village and community no matter how bleak their prospects seem. Though tempted to sacrifice her honor to Sukhilala, she instead pawns her next most precious possession, her wedding bangles (*kangan*), the representation simultaneously of her marriage and wifely virtue (*pativrata dharma*). This stokes a fiery resolve in Birju, her hotheaded son, to redeem her honor by retrieving the bangles at any cost. Ultimately they will cost him—and Radha—everything.

Several years on, Birju and his older and docile brother, Ramu, are still trying to free the family from Sukhilala's clutches. Ramu marries and begins to settle down, devoted to his mother to the point of being almost a substitute for Radha's absent husband (as his name obliquely suggests, since Ram/Ramu is a cognate of Shyam/Shamu). Birju is a much more explosive mama's boy, full of resentment and aggressivity—an aggressivity often visited on Rupa, Sukhilala's nubile daughter, who nonetheless has a soft spot for the bad boy. But Rupa is betrothed to someone else, and on her wedding day Birju, having joined a gang of bandits, rides in on a horse to repossess the bangles and disrupt Sukhilala's daughter's wedding. But before he can have his revenge, his mother steps in to protect Rupa, and the village, from Birju: she shoots him. He dies in her arms.

This reaffirmation of the mother nation over even biological family takes on a certain piquancy in an era in which the "postnational" has become fashionable. As I have suggested, in anticolonial discourse, as in the public sphere discourse following Independence, it is possible to trace the feminization of the nation as Mother India. Yet the film emphasizes that Radha is co-opted by the modernist state for its own ideological purposes. Though asked to inaugurate a modern dam serving the village's irrigation needs, she has earned this honor precisely by proving herself an ideal mother through a bitter irony: she demonstrates her willingness to sacrifice her own son for the good of the community and conventional values, including the "honor" of women, traditional family values, and so on.

This constitutes the sharp edge of an *instrumentalist* "realism." The mother is not just being honored by her community for setting a good example. She is being *reified* in the sense Fredric Jameson specifies: she is commodified, the intrinsic and specific value of her suffering discounted as she becomes a means to an ideological end, the reaffirmation of the nation.[5] The film's problematic "conclusion" simultaneously privileges the national over the maternal *and sentimentalizes*/reifies motherhood. It conscripts Radha into the service of paying tribute to an attenuated national utopia, providing a free public service advertisement for the Five-Year Plan. Yet the *conclusion* should be distinguished from the film's *crisis,* which occurs earlier, with inexorable but unsettling force when Radha kills Birju.

This paradoxical typology of the sacrificing mother can be mapped onto the opposition between realism and fantasy, but in a specific way. The paradox is justified by the imperative to subordinate the personal and the familial to the collective and the national, and by her son's descent into evil, from protector of his mother's virtue to an insupportable threat against the virtue of her oppressor's (the moneylender Sukhilala's) daughter. What is more, Radha's renunciation of motherly love is *inverted, rationalized as* exemplary civic virtue exhibited in maternal filicide—finding ironic recompense in that virtue. This double session of critical interpretation is crystallized in *Mother India*'s initial image: the film's opening sequence presents Radha's face as that of an older woman, its creases and furrows evoking parched earth and what will be revealed to be the somaticization of a difficult life of (not untested) wifely fidelity and the horror of filicide she cannot *not* commit, contrasting with the honor that is being conferred on her as a model Indian woman and citizen. Put differently, Radha's face condenses the paradoxes of an Indian nation rent by contradictory impulses: tradition versus modernity.

Radha is caught between two roles: representative citizen and virtuous Indian mother/faithful wife (albeit sans husband). Radha is a role model, faithful despite temptation to the husband who left her *and* shouldering the burden of ensuring the viability of the community. The literalism of this imagery is taken to an almost absurd degree, as if beholden to the pieties of realist representation in manically ritual detail. The film often shows Radha's face smeared with the soil of the Indian motherland (and, during the deluge, nearly drowning in its mud), making the body of the citizen and nation materially one, soil itself becoming a haptic interface between nation and body. In more mundane struggle, Radha is also shown engaged in tilling the poor soil that is her only sustenance. What is the upshot of these associations of the "Mother" and "India"? In a word, a simultaneous conjoining and contradiction: the symbolic worth of the soil is yoked, as it were, in a ground state of contradiction, to its very infertility, its failure to be worthy of its primary use, the production of food and wealth for an overwhelmingly agrarian population lurching toward modernity.[6] The image of Radha's earth-smeared body and face is simultaneously a somaticization and a corporeal inscription: a writing of "India" on this mother's very body, but at the same time the most intimate con-figuration and mapping imaginable of the body of the Mother as the body of (the category) Woman.

Radha bears the burden not only of her children's welfare but also ultimately the honor of her community and nation: the iconic image of the film is Radha shouldering the plow like a (Christian?) cross. To some degree this burden is imposed on her. This nonmythic Radha's husband is called Shamu or Shyam, a possible variant of "Krishna," a version of the Rama figure of mythology: Radha, Krishna, and Rama are universally recognizable mythic prototypes for Indian audiences everywhere. Vijay Mishra sees the Nargis character Radha as simultaneously Mother and avenging Goddess Kali/Durga. (At other moments, Radha occupies the positions of Parvati, Saraswati, or even, ironically, of Lakshmi, the household goddess of wealth.) As Mother, a woman might for instance be praised for allowing her son to risk or lose his life in a war, or in some other noble struggle. But Radha's sacrifice, although it clearly safeguards the community's honor by protecting the *izzat* (honor, virtue) of one of its women through the sacrifice of her own son, is far less *plausible* and palatable as a virtuous option for any real mother. Within the confines of mainstream Indian society, her sacrifice takes on the character of social contradiction. It is only an idealized mother who must redeem the family if the males betray their proper roles.

Shamu, as I argued above, is symbolically unmanned in the film, and his sons, especially Birju, function as his surrogates. Birju becomes Radha's self-appointed protector, to a fault. Ramu, her older son, becomes, even more strangely, a near-substitute for Shamu, and this strange substitution is represented in several "fantasy" sequences in which Radha's confusion of husband and son are visually dramatized. Mishra highlights the "unstable sexual politics" of the film, remarking the symbolic castration of Shamu and Radha's ineffectual elder son Ramu (perhaps this symbolic castration is also a displacement of their socioeconomic emasculation?).[7] The film's condensation of the ideal of motherhood in Radha is thus idealistic but self-divided.

Salman Rushdie's narrator in *The Moor's Last Sigh*, referring to this film, observes that "the Indian peasant woman is idealised as bride, mother, and producer of sons and as long-suffering, stoical, loving, redemptive, and conservatively wedded to the maintenance of the social status quo"; yet Radha herself assumes the "image of an aggressive, treacherous, annihilating mother who haunts the fantasy of Indian males."[8] What is more, the idealization of women solicits its own deconstruction: the lecher Sukhilala's own daughter is, in Dwyer's characterization, "lustful," and Shamu's widowed mother, who borrows money from Sukhilala, precipitating the family's ruin, is "foolish."[9]

Besides, the symbolic as well as nomenclatural proximity of Shamu with Rama, the mythological consort of Sita, is overdetermined in the film. The elder and more obedient son is named Ramu, indicating by his one degree of separation the proximate "presence" of the paragon of manhood in the Indian epic in the film's conceptual universe. But that proximate presence is felt the more powerfully if more spectrally in a moment of fantasy, when through a double exposure the filmmaker shows how Radha literally if momentarily confuses Ramu with Shamu—son with husband! One is tempted to invoke the Oedipal structure in reading this cinematic and psychic blurring. Ramu takes the place of the missing husband in Radha's mind, yet it is the younger son, Birju, who aspires to fulfill, in his twisted way, the offices of his absented father—wanting to provide for Radha and to protect her honor as wife *and* mother. He fails, just as Rama in the *Ramayan* betrayed Sita. This overdetermined fantasmatic confusion of the roles of Shamu, Ramu, and Birju problematizes Indian manhood by dramatizing its aphanisis or perversion (even its *père-version*, in the Lacanian lexicon). That the film accesses—and rationalizes—such a grotesque fantasy by embedding it in the sentimentalized discourse of the family is remarkable indeed.

Maternal Romance

The film gives fresh if paradoxical meanings to the formula of "maternal romance." The mother and the older son at one point are represented in an extreme close-up in a two-shot, in what Ravi Vasudevan might describe as a tableau framing.[10] This tableau recalls an earlier extreme close-up two-shot of a cringeworthy embrace, in which the mother places her head on the bare, sweaty chest of her younger son exclaiming that she cannot live without him. This mother/son tableau (drawing attention to the displacement of the father) is an almost too blatant Indian variation on the Oedipal triangle, condensing contradictory dimensions of the "Mother India" cultural meme. Of course, one cannot invoke the Oedipal structure in this connection without entering some necessary caveats. Sudhir Kakar reminds us that the Indian male is not psychically governed by "castration" and does not have the same orientation to femininity.[11] Still, by now it has become somewhat pedantic or passé to object to Western psychoanalytic language in analysis of Hindi cinema; many prominent students of Indian cinema, including Vijay Mishra, Lalitha Gopalan, Ravi Vasudevan, Madhava Prasad, and Jyotika Virdi, have regularly invoked Western high theory including psychoanalysis.

The Oedipal model is productive even as analogy, if we palimpsest the biographical onto the fictional—highlighting the real-life romance between Nargis (who plays the lead female role of the mother, Radha) and Sunil Dutt (who plays her younger and difficult if devoted son Birju), not to mention the fact that Nargis's eldest daughter married the son of Rajendra Kumar, who plays Radha's husband, Shamu, in *Mother India*. Hindi film stars "frequently" subvert Indian social codes in ways that would be "scandalous" in any other context, yet "are represented as finely balancing their transgressions with personifications of ideal behaviour especially in the domains of kinship and sexuality."[12] Nargis's off-screen relationship with Dutt complicates our reception of her on-screen performance. And Birju's (unconscious) desire for his mother is readable as an echo of Dutt's conscious desire for Nargis: but again the interesting question is how the off-screen relationship between the actors conditions the *spectator's* reception of Birju's on-screen obsession with his mother and her unthinkable, idealized filicide. We therefore may read this film in a double session, as representing a visual ambiguity that in Mishra's phrase "turns a lack into something more, into a nonlack, into a sign of such foreboding and relentless negativity that it disrupts the dominant (Western) narrative of the Oedipal triangle"—a triangle that ejects the Father but then re-presents him spectrally as the fantasized Shamu or the dangerous would-be father in Sukhilala (who after all proposes to make Radha his wife and thus supplant Shamu).[13]

Bombay films often represent the Mother as renouncing "everything for the sake of her husband or son," Mishra observes. "Conversely, however, when a Mother renounces her own son (which is rare) or her husband (which is rarer still . . .) the sheer emotional weight of her act is enormous."[14] What even Mishra fails to emphasize is that there is something *contra naturam*, not just impressive but *perverse/père-verse*, about the mother's actions. The exceptionality of her act is not that it entails a sacrifice, but that it risks eliciting moral horror from the audience. Any mother willing to sacrifice her own child, however bad, killing him to preserve the "honor" of the daughter of even her oppressor, is not exactly an ideal mother. Radha's relationship with her son Birju highlights the contradictions between "sanctity" and "scandal," in Rosie Thomas's terms. Thomas argues that the film is "an arena within which a number of discourses around female chastity, modern nationalism, and, more broadly, morality, intersect and feed on each other, with significant political effects," and ultimately offers only an "illusory coherence."[15] My account diverges from Thomas's in emphasizing the film's periodization in the immediate postcolonial context and highlighting the profoundly contradictory valences of *Mother India*'s representation of Indianness.

When first released in India, *Mother India* ran for a whole year at the Liberty Cinema in Bombay to rave reviews, becoming the film most often dubbed and subtitled. It made Khan and Nargis international stars. A Muslim, Nargis was born Fatima Rashida to a mother who was a dancer and singer, an occupation associated with the oldest and conventionally least respectable profession. As an adult, Nargis became the embodiment of cosmopolitan elegance (she was called Baby Rani, or Little Queen) and a modern and sexually emancipated "new woman," ironically cast here as a peasant.[16] The fact that a Muslim woman could be so revered as a star so soon after Independence, and act in such a problematic and ideologically precarious role, is remarkable. That she nevertheless identified in some essential way with this role is indicated by the fact that she retired from acting after she made the film, dedicating herself to social causes, serving the country in a way consistent with the image of Mother India. When M. F. Husain painted Indira Gandhi's portrait in 1975, he said he had Nargis in mind as his model. Many stars in the recent past (Dilip Kumar, Meena Kumari, and Madhubala, among many others) have disguised their Muslim identities by taking on Hindu names, but in their milieu Nargis and Mehboob Khan were exceptional in refusing such masquerade.

Social Realism *and* Fantasy

Dwyer observes that *Mother India* has been widely acknowledged to be a (cinematic) "national epic."[17] It was the first Indian film to be nominated for an Oscar, in 1958, for Best Foreign Film. By the time it was shown on Britain's Channel 4 in 1983, it was being described in the former colonial center as the "foundational" standard for all Bombay cinema.[18] The most recognizable poster of the film shows Radha carrying that cross-like plow, iconic in a primarily agricultural country. But even visually this national icon is fissured by contradictions. In this image Radha's face is in what can only be called agony. This transcultural Christian iconography is not adventitious; the theme of "passion" is a conjunctural ideologeme resonant with the Indian trope of the suffering mother, metonym for a national agony, but also an index to its international appeal. Interestingly, the film's publicity brochure confirms its international address by including a telling quotation from one of the most famous Western Indologists, Max Mueller: "If I were to look over the whole world to find out the country most richly endowed with all the wealth, power, and beauty that nature can [bestow]—I should point to India."[19] The film evokes the travails of a still largely feudal, agricultural society, though newly sovereign after two centuries under British colonial rule.

Radha's "passion" can be articulated simultaneously within discourses of an idealized Indianness and within a transnational, Judeo-Christian tropology. For it can be rendered intelligible within Subcontinental typologies that will resonate at once with illiterate farmers and middle-class spectators as specifically Indian (Radha's is not just a personal agony; it is suffering shared with all the villagers), while also readable as a universal idiom of social realism *and* evocative of the aforementioned Judeo-Christian meme of bearing a cross. Though a milestone of social realism from Hindi cinema's Golden Age, this film is by no means pristinely "realist," but thoroughly infiltrated by almost hyperreal, schematic, and fantasmatic modalities.[20] Released only two years after Satyajit Ray's landmark film *Pather Panchali,* it presents quite a contrast to that classic of realist cinema, which has an even more elevated international reputation. Nargis herself had made caustic remarks about Ray's high-minded "realism" as pandering to the West's predilection for images of Third World poverty: this was, she opined, "not a correct image" of India or Indianness. For Nargis, postcolonial Indianness implied a modern sensibility, including a sensibility attuned to industrial modernity.[21]

The film reiterates a now-standard social realist script: the tyranny of the persisting feudal system, the vicious cycle of inherited debt, the exploitation of the poor, the steady progress of "primitive accumulation" that progressively weakens the hold of the peasant on the means of production on which he or she depends. Radha's family, like others in the village, falls deeper into debt not only because she is at the mercy of the lecherous and mealy-mouthed moneylender but also because she cannot read or write. For these real problems there was at

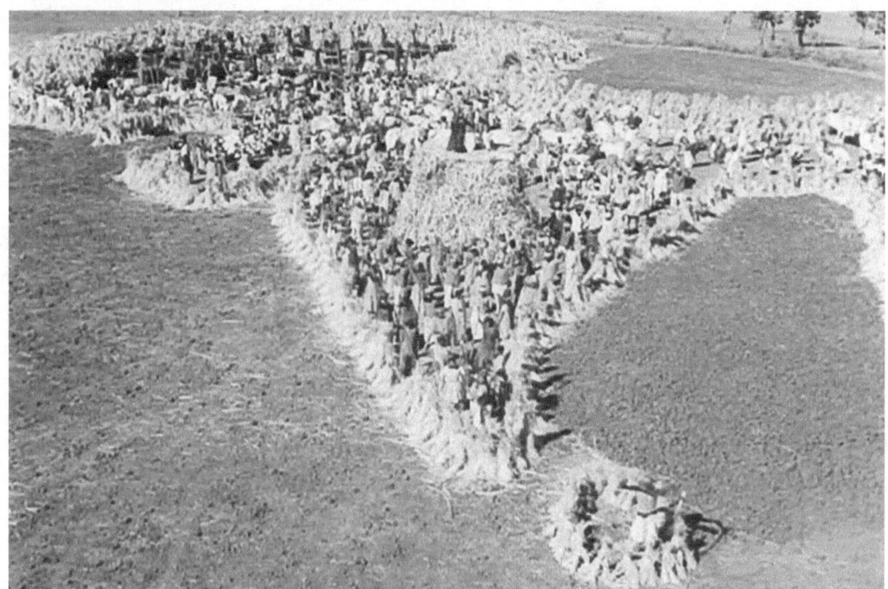

Figure 2.1. Peasants arranged in the shape of India in *Mother India* (dir. Mehboob Khan, 1957).

the time scant institutional remedy, and government policies did not promise succor. When Prime Minister Indira Gandhi's government began the campaign of bank nationalization in 1969, Vijay Prashad writes, the "rhetoric of socialism came alongside a set of policies designed to maintain the unequal political economy."[22] This contradiction was *constitutive* of the Congress Party's Realpolitik. It emerges in *Mother India* too, particularly in representing the stark reality of modernization combined with a neotraditionalist nationalism, a form of agrarian capitalism characterized by primitive accumulation (the moneylender grabbing land from the increasingly landless sharecroppers, who have little as collateral), and the entrenchment of power structures of feudalism.

Even the weather is all too real an obstacle. When the rain finally arrives, it pours: an overwhelming deluge washes away the fields. The villagers resolve to abandon their devastated fields, but Radha stops them, rallying them to rebuild their lives. They return to thresh their harvested grain, saving the community from collapse. Here, counter to its predominant idiom of realism, the film also weaves a (socialist) fantasy of peasant solidarity (Radha joining with the villagers in celebrating communal peasant life on a plot of land surreally configured in the shape of India itself—see Figure 2.1).

This mise-en-scène is as much a collectivist fantasy as plausible reality. The toiling peasants contrive to arrange themselves into a kind of cartographic bas-relief in the shape of the Subcontinent. Sumathi Ramaswamy designates this convergence between the form of the Mother/Goddess and the mapped form of the nation the production of a "geo-body."[23] This "geo-body" is an image simultaneously of a political and fantasmatic disavowal. Ten years after Independence and Partition, and in a kind of dyschronic hallucination, the image negates the splitting of the nation into independent "India," West Pakistan, and East Pakistan (which would finally become Bangladesh in 1971). So in this sense the disavowal of Partition actually expresses a desire that cannot be articulated logically in the main diegetic space of the film.[24] It is also odd that this image should insist on including the independent island nation of Sri Lanka in its visual field.[25]

Fantasy also operates in a more familiar sense: as choreographed "fantasy sequence." The fantasmatic subtext foregrounds the irresolvable contradiction of the image. Radha sings imploringly, "Please don't leave," her plea augmented by playback singing by Lata Mangeshkar, a practice inaugurated in the 1940s.[26]

Mangeshkar, born in 1929 and making her first song recording in 1942, became the preeminent playback singer of postcolonial Indian cinema, recording six thousand songs in eighteen languages—*the* voice for three generations of spectators. There were other luminaries: Mangeshkar's younger sister Asha Bhonsle, Mohammed Rafi, Mukesh, Kishore Kumar, and others, singing almost all of the Hindi film songs composed until the 1990s.[27] It is important to appreciate what is special about Mangeshkar's voice—the simple clarity of her falsetto betokened ideal Indian womanhood: virginal purity, perennial youth, romantic yearning sans lust.[28] The idea of India itself seemed to coincide with the "idea of Lata Mangeshkar," as Srivastava puts it, echoing Partha Chatterjee's suggestion that women's bodies—and here voice—became the embodiments of tradition, of the national Thing.[29] Mangeshkar's voice functioned as the partial object supporting national fantasy; choreography and mise-en-scène were equally important. Ironically, this idealized femininity also homogenized it, undermining alternative expressions and "purifying—Hinduising and gentrifying—the figure of the ideal Indian woman."[30] Mangeshkar was also able to "represent Muslim characters while musically erasing their religious identity."[31] This convenient erasure too is an ingredient in the national fantasy.

It would be a mistake, however, to negate the negation at the heart of this contradictory psychoaffective parable: the film is a dream machine, producing a counterfactual truth. It remains undeniable that the cartographic map of India on-screen speaks volumes, but in a language, as Tom Conley puts it, "of its own that does not pertain to the linguist's field of study." Maps and films work "through a welter of impressions" about information received by the reader of the map or film *as well as* "his or her own fantasies and pieces of past or anticipated memory in dialogue with the names, places, and forms on the map."[32] Hindi cinema, both mirror and lamp, reflects official constructions of Indian identity but also limns the contours of an "Indianness" conjured from figments of imagination, fantasies.

Mishra appositely highlights the multiple ways *Mother India* may be read in context: in terms of "female 'peasant heroinism,'" as a "project aimed at strengthening the nation-state" in the wake of the material and psychic depredations of colonial subjugation; as pre-text for the appropriation of the figure of Mother India by Indira Gandhi, the once prime minister with the trademark cowlick of white hair (she was infamous for her imposition of the "Emergency" on India in 1975–1976 and for her hubristic slogan "India is Indira"); and as encoding, via Nargis and director Mehboob Khan, the problematic of Muslimness, indexing the "hyphenated Hindu-Muslim nature of Bombay Cinema discourses, production practices, and indeed its very ideology." The film is thus "quite defiantly, not a religious, but a secular epic of the new, modern India where a universal moral principle transcending religious and caste differences is the dominant dharma."[33] Dwyer also highlights what she regards as the film's faux secularism—"the implicit Hindu nature of much of independent India's 'secular' mythology," silencing "any Islamic component of the new nation."[34] The question of secularism in defining national identity is a problematic I take up in Chapter 4, on terrorism cinema.

The film was a remake of a black-and-white film called *Aurat* (Woman) that Khan had made seventeen years before, in 1940—and that earlier film had been inspired by Vsevolod Pudovkin's Soviet "socialist realist cinematic adaptation of Maxim Gorky's *Mother*," published in 1927.[35] As Khan himself acknowledged, the remake of *Aurat* is a recuperation of the image of the "true Indian woman"—a revamping of Indianness gendered feminine. In the original film the woman's virtue lay in the "fact that the true Indian woman enters her husband's home when she marries and leaves it only when she dies, that she will never sell her chastity for any price on earth"; today "times have changed and life is different. . . . But the main character has not changed: the Indian woman . . . is one with the land she works on."[36] This Eternal Feminine, identified with the sacred clod, is a pretty fiction, of course. Still, celebrating a socialist utopia, the film was a huge hit in the then USSR. Not only a nod to Pudovkin's adaptation of Gorky's *Mother*, the film also constitutes a celluloid riposte against Mayo's book *Mother India* (1927), a scurrilous and racially prejudiced discussion of sexual politics in India. There are other intertextual references worth noting as well, such as a melodramatic film by the name of *Mother India* (1938) by the maker of India's first talkie, *Alam Ara* (The Light of the World, Ardeshir Irani, 1931); Khan may have borrowed some of Irani's emphases. There is also a dense cluster of associations around the two terms that are conjoined in the film's title, which is thus raised to the level of a "transcendental signifier."[37] It would seem, then, that the film is reflexively hyperaware of the multiple valences of its title and subject matter.

There are other, generic or formal, reasons to notice the intertextuality, such as the conventional melodramatic quality of Khan's film, counterposed to the more politically critical subtexts I highlight below.[38] This "maternal melodrama" is also complicatedly situated as a national cinema. As Jyotika Virdi suggests, national cinema not only privileges tradition over modernity but, in the Indian instance, also "naturaliz[es] and idealiz[es]" the imagined community under the category, often reified or essentialized, of "Indianness." There is no doubt that "powerful nationalist rhetoric dominates everything from the public sphere to individual subjectivities—our very personal identity," Virdi suggests. Popular Hindi films, she observes, locate the "fractures within the nation by projecting a national edifice *and* the rumblings against it."[39] *Mother India* is so fissured a social text that it problematizes the very notion of a "national cinema."[40]

Among the film's key contradictions is the *individual* citizen-subject's emergent psychic life, the unruly non-identification, the circulation of fantasy around the space carved out by dominant narratives. Besides, the fantasy often exceeds the frame of the film. Chapter 1 discussed the excessive quality of individual fantasy in *Awaara,* where Raj's "essential dissension" from the dominant—his "*awaaradom*" or "*jungleeness*"—is not necessarily domesticated at the conclusion, and that excess is critical. As a national narrative, similarly, *Mother India* re-constructs a specific, split form of Indianness from the outset, when Radha holds up to her face a clod of Indian earth. We are immediately ushered into a recognizably Indian mode of melodrama, overdetermined by mythology and accretions of a widely recognized and shared storehouse of images, one of whose primary functions is to reflect, as a national mirror, an image of the national identity, here specifically the image of the ideal woman:

> One can . . . connect *matṛbhūmī,* mother earth, with the figure of Sita, the heroine of the *Rāmāyaṇa,* the *dhīram bhāryam* (the steadfast wife) who, in the North Indian popular imaginary, is one of the mythic/religious prototypes of "Mother India." "Sita" means "of the furrow" and indicates via this name her autochthonic origins. In this respect "Mother India" is a way of talking about Sita, . . . really a stand-in for India.[41]

But the film also performs a second, vital, function, to construct or re-present a national, collective image of Indian identity and a (universal or "representative") image of *individual* Indianness. At both collective and individual scales, the film is a "mediated form of national consciousness" *and* suggests that the question of Indianness is not yet settled.[42] Even if not "a study of culture in conflict with itself," the film asks, what *kind* of idea is India?[43]

This *generically* identitarian question about Indianness is modulated, as we have seen, into the more general interrogation of *gender.* In one nationalist trope a woman is the repository of the national essence. What is an Indian *woman,* imagined as such a repository of the national Thing? What is a *mother,* or what is a good mother? Can a good "Mother India" still be good if she is willing to kill her own son? These are themselves conduits to other gendered questions about the nature of Indian *manhood,* and are relayed through a congeries of crucial questions about feudal structures that persist beyond the moment of Independence. The film's visual language poses questions about a transitional agrarian society into which modernity and modern technology (heavy farm machinery such as modern tractors, engineered irrigation canals, dams, and so on) have begun to make inroads, transforming it albeit slowly.

Besides, interpretation must not only address social realist representation but also recognize the remarkably resonant and complicating psychoaffective parables conveyed in the film's nonrealistic or fantasmatic subtexts. At the end of *Mother India,* for example, the water flowing through the irrigation canal that betokens the advent of modern agricultural technology is imbued with a sinister red color. This is not, of course, "*realism*"—social or otherwise—but a hallucinatory *fantasy.* The real water of the dam turns red with the fantasized blood Radha has recently spilled. In this encounter the spectator, like Radha, experiences a stereoptic "resolution" of a parallax between the *Real* dimension of her own filicide and the *real* aspect of the diegesis, while simultaneously rendering nugatory the honor her village and through it the state now confers on her as an exemplary citizen-subject in inviting her to inaugurate the new irrigation system.

The name Radha is important in Hindu mythology, and when it is invoked, mythology operates *as a register of fantasy* in Hindi cinema; its potency is hard to exaggerate: characters and entire films are patterned on the mythological urtexts or templates. The mythical Radha appears in the *Mahabharat,* the *Bhagavata Purana,* and the *Gita Govinda* of Vaishnavite Hindu tradition as Krishna's lover. In *Mother India* Radha's love for *her* Krishna is perhaps more transgressive. In the myth the lovers do not live happily ever after because Krishna marries someone else. Besides, in one version of the tale, Radha too is already married. But it is a deep and true love, and that is the dramatic irony of the myth. There will be occasion to revisit the significance of the name Radha in Chapter 5, which discusses *Lagaan: Once upon a Time in India* (Ashutosh Gowariker, 2001), and in Chapter 6, which examines *Fire* (Deepa Mehta, 1996). The name appears in many other popular Hindi films too, as metonym of the most cherished (unconscious) desires that animate the stories. And it is this psychic life that is often overlooked in many readings. I have attempted to show how this inner psychic life, fantasy, runs counter to the straight (and often straitened) realist narrative of the surface diegesis.

Radha is not only the "Lover" aspect of the transcendental Sita figure mentioned above. Indeed, she seems to inhabit, if transitionally, a range of aspects of the Goddess.[44] Besides inhabiting the form of Sita within the film, Radha takes the form of the Goddess in the House, or Lakshmi. Birju goes "bad" because he is obsessed with safeguarding her honor (*lāj*), in her assumption of the aspects of both Lakshmi, the goddess of domestic wealth, and Draupadi, the virtuous wife who must be protected against dishonor. Birju's indecent behavior with the village girls is really the figural obverse of an overdeveloped sense of moral outrage or shame—*lāj,* the word used in the film, can mean both honor and shame. Radha as a new bride, on learning that her own mother-in-law mortgaged her land to pay for her son's marriage to Radha, and fearing that this bodes ill, says sotto voce, "*Bhagvan lāj rakhna*" ("God protect my honor"). In the *Mahābhārat* Draupadi becomes a pawn in a bet, and when she is lost, the winner of the bet tries to disrobe her, but through divine intervention her sari is extended infinitely and so her virtue remains secure. To defend his mother as a Lakshmi and even more as a Draupadi figure, Birju is prepared to commit murder—to kill Sukhilala, the lecherous and extortionist moneylender who has in Birju's eyes been the reason that Radha had to sacrifice her gold bracelets to support the family as it is crushed under disabling and unjust debt.

Ultimately Birju goes too far, threatening the feudal fabric of the village by radically challenging its financial and power orthodoxies. So he has to be sacrificed as an antisocial element, and who better to complete the purge than . . . Mother India herself? This time, Radha is cast in the guise of a Kali or Durga figure—fearsome female aspects of the transcendental Goddess, whose function is to destroy evil (men) and thereby to restore social order.

The gender conventions of the weepies, the maternal melodrama, and men's gangster/action films "collapse in Hindi films," notes Virdi. She observes that in *Mother India* as in other films such as *Aradhana* (Prayer, 1969), *Trishul* (Trident, 1978), and *Deewaar* (Wall, Yash Chopra, 1975), which I discuss in Chapter 3, there is an irrepressible desire on the part of a son to redeem his mother's honor or protect her. The mother needs protection against some significant crisis, threat, or humiliation by the father (and by would-be surrogates for that father). Virdi admits some exceptions to the pattern, in which "the hero's search for his mother is attenuated by a narrative that includes the father, such as in films like *Zanjeer* (Chain, 1973) or *Yaadon Ki Baraat* (Procession of Memories, 1973)."[45]

Yet Birju's case is more complicated than Virdi's classification allows. Her account does not capture the paradigm-breaking representation of *this* (fatal) mother-son relationship. The tragic, Oedipal subtext remains obdurately in the margins of Radha's "sacrifice." If these films "project masculinity" in an "idealized" grammar, as Virdi suggests,[46] then it is surely a very problematic masculinity, not one to sustain a paradigmatic nationalist narrative.

When Birju goes beyond the pale, threatening to carry off the moneylender's daughter on her wedding day, Radha, as the protector of Indian womanhood, must place the virtue of the Indian woman above maternal scruple, even if it means violating the sacred law of the mother's unconditional love for her child; a "transcendence of motherhood."[47] The sacrifice is in the interest of the *patriarchal* structure, more important than even maternal love. The bad mother is the good Mother. The good son is a bad citizen-subject: Sunil Dutt himself opined that while the Mother was rebelling against society in a Gandhian way, Birju rebels like a Bhagat Singh.[48]

There are other, especially political, complications to acknowledge. As noted earlier, it is a film made by a Muslim director. That marginal perspective complicates Mehboob's leftist sympathies. Despite adopting the hammer and sickle as the emblem of his Mehboob Production Company, he felt he had to *disavow* his socialist sympathies to appeal broadly to Indian audiences. The voice-over at the outset intones the most banal pieties undergirding the national narrative, including religious bromides ("Only that can happen which is God's will").

Dwyer observes that "one of the attractions of *Mother India* is that it eschews clear-cut answers, allowing the audience to experience the pleasures of its ambiguities."[49] Still, Dwyer underestimates the contradictions I propose are crucial in the film, which tries to have it both ways: to show how unjust the existing postcolonial social order is, and yet ultimately to renege on this too-radical socialist critique, perhaps because the developing social arrangements in India are unready. There is something courageous about making a film that addresses so many difficult issues. A reading attentive to the fragmenting and contradictory ecology of contradictions and fissures offers us a richer grammar for interpretation. In this chapter and throughout this book, this remains a diacritic of the kind of readings I offer.

3

Sexploitation or Consciousness Raising?

The Angry Man, the Avenging Woman, and the Law

The Angry Man and the Avenging Woman have become tokens of Hindi film subgenres that emerged from the mid-1970s through the 1980s. In them we see condensed a powerful sociopolitical dissatisfaction with institutions and frustration with the status quo. This chapter tracks the telling continuities and contrasts between the two subgenres: both present motivated critiques reflecting a righteous anger about the sociopolitical moment; both crystallize class- and gender-inflected social crises as *conjuncturally specific condensations*. Angry Man films index a class-inflected crisis of masculinity specific to its historical moment. Avenging Woman cinema in turn marks the overdetermined resurgence of the Woman Question in the 1980s: suspended (for the 1980s was considered the lost decade of cinema) between pre-Emergency cinema and the post-liberalization cinema of the 1990s, reflecting a synergistic convergence of state television (Doordarshan), a development narrative linked to an emergent consumerism, and a heightened political (feminist) consciousness spurred by the global discourse of feminism.[1] These subgenres are productive sites, stereoptically rendering the parallax between political (realist) accounts of the offending conditions and cinematic (imaginative) representations, significantly involving an element of fantasy. Both subgenres provoke the question whether the responses they dramatize are viable—or wishful thinking.

Historical Contexts of "Anger"

From the early 1970s through the late 1980s and 1990s, Indian political economy and culture experienced important, even paradigm-changing transformations, and these shifts were reflected and reconstructed in Hindi-language cinema.

Defining events of the period included the war for the liberation of East Pakistan (today's Bangladesh) in 1971, the draconian International Monetary Fund loans of 1974 (a year marked by labor unrest), but most importantly Indira Gandhi's highly controversial Emergency (1975–1977). In the first section of this chapter, I focus on *Deewaar* (The Wall, Yash Chopra, 1975) and *Sholay* (Embers, Ramesh Sippy, 1975), films registering a crisis of faith in governmental and legal institutions and an associated crisis of masculinity. The Avenging Woman films followed closely on the heels of the Angry Man films. The second section focuses on the "rape/revenge" narratives animating Avenging Woman films, such as *Insaaf Ka Tarazu* (Scales of Justice, B. R. Chopra 1980) and *Zakhmi Aurat* (Wounded Woman, Avtar Bhogal, 1988); they refract a righteous anger about the treatment of Indian women. Since my goal is to identify conjunctural condensations rather than merely close-read a few iconic films, I also introduce more recent films in both sections of the chapter to offer evidence for my argument and to suggest that the actual causes provoking anger or vengeance have not entirely disappeared.

The Emergency of 1975–1977 was the edict of Indira Gandhi, elected prime minister by some accounts *because* she was perceived as a weak leader.[2] Disappointing expectations, she grew obdurate in responding to increasing social unrest; this adamantine posture drew the accolade from the president of the Indian National Congress, Dev Kant Barooah ("Indira is India, and India is Indira"). On June 26, 1975, she declared a twenty-one-month state of emergency, under Article 352 of the Constitution, until March 21, 1977, suspending elections and civil liberties. The Emergency, rationalized as a response to growing social unrest and chaos, "made the trains run on time," imposing a draconian state and police apparatus. The benefits of the Emergency's efficiencies were enjoyed primarily by the elites; ordinary citizens felt the lash of harsh rule from the center—widespread abuses of state power, torture, legal (but *illegitimate*) violence, and police brutality.

Popular and political opposition to the Emergency was vigorous, "for the first time since independence" coming from peasants, lower castes, and coalitions of the marginalized.[3] The historian Sudipta Kaviraj describes widespread resentment against Gandhi's personal accumulation of power, particularly at the cost of citizens' rights and artists' (including filmmakers') creative freedom. A metonymic instance of the reaction was the (Maoist) Naxalite uprising, which had emerged in the 1960s but intensified in the 1970s; four thousand young Communist Party of India (Marxist-Leninist) supporters were killed in police crackdowns under the colonial Bengal Suppression of Terrorist Outrages Act of 1936 (replaced in 1970 by the Prevention of Violent Activities Bill), "even as 'police informers, scabs, professional assassins and various other sorts of bodyguards of private property stalked around bullying the citizens. . . . Streets were littered with bodies of young men riddled with bullets.'"[4]

The Naxalites had a significant impact on cinema, producing important filmmakers including the still very active Anand Patwardhan. Film was also generated by the "fragmented left," including Satyajit Ray's *Pratidwandi* (The Adversary, 1970) and *Jana Aranya* (The Middleman, 1975), directly referencing Naxalite ideology and critiquing state censorship. Yet overtly political filmmaking was rare: "Most New Cinema discussions on dominant political topics remained . . . relatively marginal, and, in turn, few of the political films" of Mrinal Sen, Buddhadeb Dasgupta, or Shyam Benegal "suffered political persecution." This meant, however, the cinematic marginalization of "the overdetermined . . . issues of the day."[5]

Ray himself lambasted the New Cinema auteurs, especially Kumar Shahani, for their avant-gardism, obscurantism, and unjustifiable experimentalism, insisting on the "need for a conventional story, for a well worked-out scenario, a modicum of craftsmanship," and "a psychological-realist textual reading of the cinema," as Rajadhyaksha points out; for Shahani himself, "the conventions of objectivity and realism . . . were discredited beyond use by the Emergency's perversion of this apparatus [and] dissolution of the cinema into a form of 'mass media.'"[6] Popular cinema of the mid-1970s through the 1980s condensed popular frustrations; not ideologically or aesthetically committed to realism exclusively, it unleashed potent fantasies of empowerment, of justice meted out, of the triumph of the Everyman and woman, (over)compensating for actual powerlessness.

The Star, the Buddy, and the Brother

By around 1975, popular Hindi cinema was already crystallizing general political frustration with the nation-state, articulating cinematic idioms of resistance. Madhava Prasad highlights the *representation* of an upwelling righteous violence in Hindi films of the 1970s, the icon being the subaltern "Angry Man" persona of Amitabh Bachchan in films such as *Deewaar* and *Sholay.* Both appeared in 1975, the year the Emergency was declared. Though other Angry Man films also secured Bachchan's preeminence, especially *Zanjeer* (Chains, Prakash Mehra, 1973), *Deewaar* and *Sholay* condensed a non-elite class solidarity and shared sense of disenfranchisement by an authoritarian but ineffectual government.[7] Implicitly these Angry Man films acknowledge that resistance is ultimately fabulism. But this makes it imperative to take these utopic fantasies seriously. *Pace* commentators like Farid Kazmi who identify a "myth of rebellion" driving these films, I suggest they offer not just *myths* but antiauthoritarian *fantasies* of resistance that feed, and feed on, audiences' emotional/psychic needs—they are empowering *e-motive (dream) machines,* "moving" pictures in both senses.[8]

They are simultaneously vehicles for a singular star—Bachchan—and fables of literal, symbolic, and even homosocial brotherhood, a theme powerfully resonant given India's codified sexual segregation. If the lightning rod for the Angry Man films' current of *sociopolitical* frustration in the 1970s and 1980s was Indira Gandhi, the éminence grise behind the Emergency, Bachchan's silver-screen preeminence offered a populist antithesis. Besting such luminaries as Humphrey Bogart, Laurence Olivier, and Marlon Brando, Bachchan was voted "Star of the Millennium" in an online BBC poll; he has international name recognition, even a statue at Madame Tussaud's. Although elected Member of Parliament in 1984, he was never more ascendant in the *filmi* firmament than when he fell ill or needed prayers when facing surgery. In 1982, during shooting for *Coolie* (Manmohan Desai, 1983), he was injured; there were "nationwide prayers cutting across language, religion and region . . . a phenomenon never seen before in India."[9] I witnessed similar mass veneration in Mumbai in 2005, after Bachchan's bowel surgery and in 2012 after "abdominal surgery."

But it was especially his on-screen presence, his body image, that solicited mass cathexis.[10] Cool and reserved, Bachchan exuded elegance and self-assurance, his body presented in long shot and through zooms but very few close-ups. Bachchan's lapidary and laconic "dialogue delivery, sense of timing and . . . [physical] restraint" ushered in a new but symptomatic anger on the screen, notes Ranjani Mazumdar. The "projection" of the 'Angry Man's interiority" is enhanced, Mazumdar asserts, "through a filmic strategy (long shot to zoom in) symbolizing an order of dialogue where the 'outside' and the 'inside' are interlocked." The transfer of subjectivity to the camera also induces an *epistemological* problematic: "Multiple articulations of the perceived body, operating as the mask required for a magnified subjectification, pose limits on the exploration of 'interiority.'"[11] On the other hand, Bachchan is sui generis. His body "seems to generate its own dynamic . . . walking with the posture of an aristocrat."[12] Bachchan's body laminates two contradictory images: populist "Angry Man/Everyman" and aristocratic exception. This doubled performative suspends Bachchan between socioeconomic positionalities, inviting cathexis simultaneously from middle-class and lower-class male spectators.

Bachchan's "presence" confirms the realist theorist André Bazin's intuition that cinema can (re)present a body at the "middle stage between presence and absence," for at this "*ontological*" level the screen puts us "'in the presence of' the actor" in the "same way as a mirror . . . with a delayed reflection, the tin foil of which retains the image." This "pseudopresence," Bazin suggests, is asymmetrical: the spectator cathects onto the actor's body but encounters no reciprocal demand—the spectator's "imaginary" body image need not compete with the image on-screen, so the spectator can identify with it "in the dark," without risking embarrassment.[13] This screen body is asymmetrical in several senses: physically (Bachchan is much taller than average), cinematically (by virtue of projection on-screen), and psychologically (as image of idealized masculinity, an *Ideal Ich*, in the Freudian lexicon).

Yet Bachchan's body leaves a persistent remainder precisely because of the asymmetry of its pseudopresence: a spectral, fantasmatic excess or stain. Bachchan's cinematic figuration of "anger" is thus problematically indexical—an affect simultaneously symptomatic of a widespread public frustration yet exceeding any correspondent referent of Indian masculinity. Indeed, that "absent" referent functions as Jacques Derrida's "trace" or Giorgio Agamben's "singularity," a *hapax legomenon,* exemplary *and* unrepresentative. Bachchan's muscular elegance, with his ectomorphic body and hybrid but elite affect, can only be aspirational, belonging to a fabulous and fabulist manhood, in reality inaccessible to most spectators. Although other hypermasculine stars, from Shah Rukh Khan to Aamir Khan, Salman Khan, and Hritik Roshan, have succeeded him, they have not quite dislodged Bachchan from his pride of place as a nonrepresentative representation of Indian masculinity.

In *Deewaar* Bachchan plays Vijay Verma, antiheroic and yet more charismatic than most other heroes of Hindi cinema. From the male spectator he solicits ambivalent identification rather than condemnation, envy, or resentment, which might have happened if this were theater, or indeed reality. His counterpart, and "good" brother, is Ravi. Both are fighting or highlighting social *injustice,* albeit from opposite directions: Ravi as a policeman and Vijay initially as a worker brutalized by an unjust system the law protects and is protected by, and later as a feckless capitalist exploiting that system. They are blood brothers fated to become mortal enemies. Their father, Anand, a trade union leader, is their synthesis; fighting for coal miners' rights, he runs afoul of the capitalist boss, who blackmails him into betraying the workers. Disgraced, Anand leaves village and family forever. In retaliation, some workers catch the young Vijay returning from school and tattoo the phrase "My father is a thief" on his forearm. The tattoo becomes the token—Mazumdar says "scar"—of a trauma commemorating his disgraced father, and Vijay spends his adult career avenging Anand's unmanning. It is a token of "marginality and social displacement . . . taking [him] beyond the pale of the family."[14] It is also a stigma marking Vijay as outlaw, "Angry Man."

Primary reasons for *Deewaar*'s success and significance include its "realist" representation of political and social frustrations of the historical moment and its reconceptualization of how public space can be inhabited and reformed by (even marginal) citizen-subjects to challenge received legal, religio-cultural, and moral doxa. Another reason is its innovative representation of *urban* space: the Angry Man stands Janus-faced at the crossroads between traditionalist and modernist conceptions of the city; the city "loses its fundamentally diabolical character, becoming a space where the hopes and yearnings unleashed by the promise of nationalism are either fulfilled or dashed. *Deewaar* thus generates viewer-identification with the smuggler, Bachchan."[15] But a fourth, and perhaps the most important, reason is simply that Bachchan's Angry Man offered scripts for imagining—condensing—new masculinities, through fantasies cathected onto Bachchan's body.

Vijay determinedly routes his victory through the defiles of crime, becoming a highly successful smuggler; Ravi stumbles into his calling as a policeman only after much floundering. Inevitably he is confronted by his duty—to bring Vijay to justice. Ravi is Vijay's foil and prototypic antithesis, as Abel was Cain's. But this Indian fratricidal tale evokes a more proximate parallel—the *Bhagavad Gita,* part of the epic *Mahabharat.* The germane episode presents the Pandava prince Arjuna paralyzed by a crisis of conscience in midbattle. In an almost cinematic freeze-frame, Arjuna turns to his charioteer, Krishna, for advice on how to conduct himself in the fratricidal war: does the call of duty to conduct potentially mortal combat override moral duty to enemies who are family? Krishna's advice, based on Upanishadic doctrine, has become the classic deontology of mortality/morality: Arjuna must do his duty without regard to the consequences (*nishkama karma*), realizing it is not he who kills.

In *Deewaar* Ravi's boss performs the charioteer's role, reminding Ravi of his duty, yet ultimately the permission to kill his own brother is provided by their mother, which melodramatically evacuates Ravi's ethico-familial dilemma. Vijay's character is more complex. He belongs not exclusively to the *Gita*'s moralized landscape but to a broader, *conjunctural* force-field recasting the social and political moment allegorically. And this cinematic fantasy has not entirely renounced realism: Vijay is modeled on the real and notorious smuggler Haji Mastan. The film concludes melodramatically. Mortally wounded by his brother, Vijay dies in his mother's arms in the temple where she worships and which he had boycotted, convinced that its deity had spurned her supplications.

The etiology of the "anger" in *Sholay* is more institutional, condensing the pain of legal exile and social marginalization—criminalization—as an abstract complaint against the system that interpellates the individual as citizen-subject and is therefore nominally the latter's protector. This film also features two antiheroic buddies or brothers-outlaws, paralleling Vijay and Ravi in *Deewaar*. Veeru and Jaidev ("Jai," meaning "victory," synonymous with "Vijay") are riding in a train under armed guard, their wrists manacled. The train is attacked by bandits. They persuade their guard to let them join the fight against the attackers. Defeating the "dacoits," they arrive at Ramgarh, where they have been summoned by Thakur Baldev Singh. Though nominally representing the law, Thakur, now retired, wants to conscript the outlaws in his personal, extralegal, vendetta: retribution against the notorious bandit Gabbar, who had decimated the Thakur's family, attacking their homestead while Thakur was away on duty because he had tried to punish Gabbar under the law. Gabbar killed almost everyone except Thakur's daughter-in-law, Radha (Jaya Bhaduri, who became Bachchan's real-life wife). Thakur pursues Gabbar, but Gabbar turns the tables on him, perversely hacking off Thakur's arms as if to mock the "long arm of the law." Now, concealing his amputations from Veeru and Jai, Thakur persuades them to accept the commission to bring Gabbar to heel: thus Veeru and Jai become prosthetic surrogates, outlaw extensions of the law. Thakur takes the view that "to bow one's head in front of an oppressor is not [Gandhian] *ahimsa* but cowardliness" and "it is iron that cuts iron [*loha lohe ko katatha hai*]." Through the surrogacy of Veeru and Jai, the film offers a fantasy subversive agency, humorously paradoxical in its commentary on the law, countering the frustration and powerlessness felt by many under the powerful but inefficient and corrupt state—especially the inept police.

Sholay's critique of the state is metonymically embodied in Thakur's literal disarming. This somaticized impotence is jocularly mirrored by the body of the

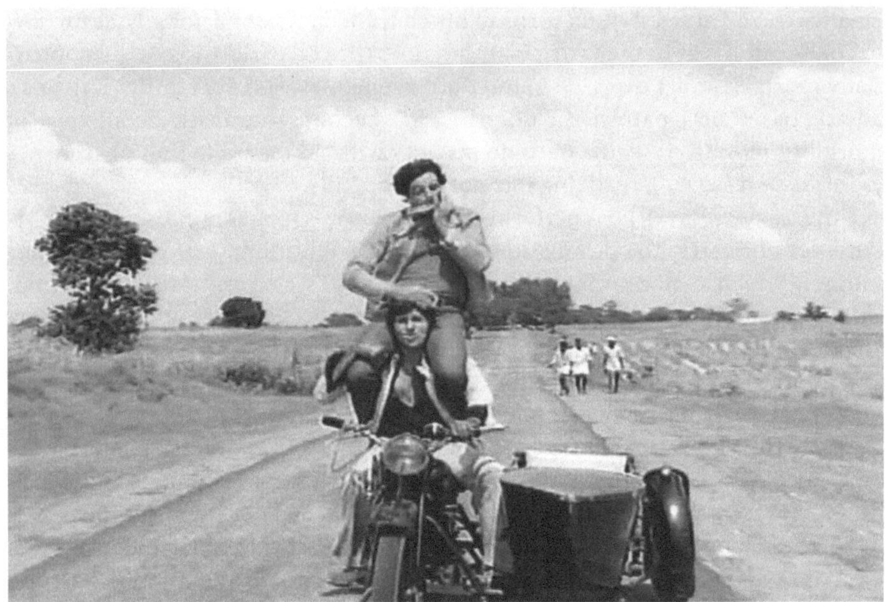

Figure 3.1. Jai (Amitabh Bachchan) and Veeru (Dharmendra) in *Sholay* (dir. Ramesh Sippy, 1975).

chief warden of a jail, a caricature hybrid of the colonial *babu* and Hitler, modeled on Charlie Chaplin but intertextually invoking Raj Kapoor's performative hommage to Chaplin in *Shree 420* (Raj Kapoor, 1955) and *Awaara,* as Chapter 1 discussed. Though ridiculous, the jailer is a figure mediating between the colonial British legacy of the common law and the state of Indira Gandhi's time.

A popular film must provide love interest. Veeru finds his match in Basanti, who drives a horse cart as a taxi service and is even more verbose than he. Jai finds Radha, Thakur's reclusive daughter-in-law, in mourning for her murdered husband. These romantic subplots are only concessions to melodramatic (and realist) convention, consistent with the hybrid style of this "curry-" and "Eastern Western"/buddy film. The crucial and multivalent pairing/bonding is between the buddies, graphically captured in the image of their motorcycle ride together (see Figure 3.1).

The heteronormative subplots ironically subtend a crypto-homoerotic subtext parallel and adjunct to the Angry Man text. *Sholay,* like *Deewaar,* reflects and condenses the "anger" defining the 1970s, producing two interlinked manifestations: the obvious one is a crisis of *citizenship,* but it is imbricated with a crisis of Indian *masculinity* encoded in the cryptotext of homoerotic "bromance" *avant la lettre.* The complex etiology of this double crisis incorporates the residual trauma and humiliation of colonization, complicated by the advent of contemporary glocalization. Its expression is routed through borrowed ("glocalized") idioms of the buddy film—with a (cultural) difference.

The cryptotext however remains encrypted: Veeru and Jai's extraordinary same-sex intimacy (*dosti*) displaces but is sublated within conventional heterosexual romance. However, their expressed intimacy, extremely unconventional for its time, should be read not anachronistically but through a specific historicization sensitive to the contextual risks and reigning cultural codes, even as it bends convention: a gay subtext cannot be presented except as a fantasy—it cannot be permitted to "condense." The brinkmanship of the narrative, negotiating among the hybrid genres within which it unfolds, explains to some degree how the film nevertheless came to be appropriated by the LGBTIQ (Lesbian, Gay, Bisexual, Transgender, Intersex, and Queer) community as the iconic queer "sleeper" hit produced by the Indian film industry—faute de mieux. Embraced as cinematic urtext of the "bhai-sexual" subgenre (blending brotherhood, displaced homoeroticism, and homosocial buddy-dom), this film presaged others, such as *Lage Raho Munna Bhai* (Carry On, Munna Bhai, Rajkumar Hirani, 2006), which features tender "brotherhood" between soulmates Munna Bhai and his sidekick/buddy Circuit, about which I have written elsewhere.[16] In *Rang De Basanti* (Color Me Saffron, Rakeysh Omprakash Mehra, 2006) Aamir Khan forms bonds beyond comradeship with his "bro" friend group. The overlay of mawkish political solidarism to the point of self-sacrifice in the second half is presented as redeeming the young men from their jejune homosocial *dosti* presented in the first, but the film consequently suffers from a thematic and stylistic schizophrenia, even if interpreted within culturally specific "*rasa*" terms.

Thomas Waugh identifies "profuse and rigidly ambiguous indigenous male-male sexual iconographies" surfacing in buddy-film fantasies, reconfiguring publicly sanctioned male-male friendships and hyperencoding—alternative—homosocial spaces.[17] These queer fantasies are increasingly cathected onto ripped male bodies such as those of Salman Khan and Hritik Roshan.[18] Such reconfigurations leave their lexical trace on-screen in the language of "*khel*" (play), and "*yaari*"/*dosti*" (friendship)—innocuous words that are today irreducibly tinctured by their reinscription of masculine performativity within globalized LGBTIQ discourses. As with the logic of "homosociality" articulated by Eve Kosofsky Sedgwick, the code of *dosti* (or *yaari*) "takes precedence over that of heterosexual love."[19]

The Angry Man film may be exploitation—even "sexploitation"—cinema, indexing many viewers' affective hyperinvestment in Bachchan's eroticized body *and* simultaneous disavowal of homoerotic desire. This maps onto Jameson's dialectical conceptualization of realism ("destiny versus the eternal present"), in which affect resists linguistic expression. The experience of homoerotic desire (affect, in Jameson's terms) *cannot be named* as such (condensed); it must be displaced into sanitized feelings of *dosti,* or friendship.[20]

Sholay attempts to compensate for such an "antinomic" realism through recourse to fantasy. Bachchan's body is eroticized as pure affect (affection) that dares not speak its name and is thus relegated to a covert fantasy blending identification with envy and in some cases desire. Yet the contours of this eroticization are blurred: it is unclear *for whom* this body is eroticized—women? Male heterosexual spectators? LGBTIQ viewers? The film scuttles the heteronormative possibilities of its main narrative, suggesting that the strength of the *dosti* between Jai and Veeru supersedes a heteronormative happy ending in which each pairs off with a woman. But Jay and Veeru cannot settle together into companionable non-hetero bliss, riding off together on their motorcycle into the sunset. The film presents an oblique allegory; realism and fantasy enact a dialectical romance yet disable the conventionally satisfying synthesis of a "happy ending."

The mission to capture Gabbar goes wrong. Veeru is captured by Gabbar; Basanti is made to dance on shards of glass. Gabbar perversely decrees that as long as she can sustain her performance (like Scheherazade), Veeru lives. Jai manages to rescue them but is wounded as they flee, pursued by Gabbar's men. The duo resist but, running out of bullets, decide one of them must go back to the village, taking Basanti, to get ammunition. Jai and Veeru have always made decisions by the toss of a (special) coin, kept by Jai in his pocket. Once more Jai tosses the coin to see who will go to the village for more ammunition. As always, Jai wins and stays to fight Gabbar, which is to say he magnanimously loses, favoring his buddy.

Veeru returns with supplies but finds Jai near death, still fighting; only then does he discover that the coin was a fake (*khota*), with two identical faces. Eventually Veeru rides off with Basanti on a train, but this is a non-conclusion—like the talismanic fake coin, it provides a fake "resolution." Jai's death also marks the irresolution of the more important quandary: he can live neither with Veeru nor with Radha (heterosexually domesticated). Introducing and then scuppering the bourgeois heterosexual narrative, the film subtly accommodates the erotic alternative, short-circuiting the customary denouements and blandishments of popular cinema. Exclusion from the legal norm licenses these outlaw buddies' self-exception from bourgeois domesticity too: male-male *dosti* is potentially more satisfying. Yet while *Sholay*'s core masculinist/homoerotic fantasy is a response to anxiety and frustration about sanctioned institutions (such as marriage) and the state's apparatuses (such as the police), the film leaves the fantasy smoldering in its "embers" and does not follow through on its implied arguments about other kinds of felt injustice, marginalization, oppression, and discrimination against women and LGBTIQ subjects.

Avenging Woman Films: The Reality of Rape, the Fantasy of Revenge

After its Golden Age, Hindi cinema became less adventurous in representing women characters. Sedimented gendered narratives grew increasingly inadequate at representing modern women's experience. Recently, new, provocative expressions of female subjectivity have begun to condense in popular cinema, often registering a protest against gendered injustice—for example, in films by Mira Nair and Deepa Mehta.

In dominant (anticolonial) narratives of Indian nationalism, the Woman was the repository of the national Thing—the *condensate*—of Indianness, her sexual purity fetishized as guaranteeing the integrity and superiority of Indian culture.[21] Yet this was an idealized Woman, not actual women. The home in cinema too was represented as a haven from everyday humiliations under colonial rule, a counterpoint to (Western) modernity. In a more recent conjuncture, during the 1970s, the ideal Indian woman was contrasted with the vamp, and more recently still with the modern woman, "almost always portrayed as decadent and punished for it."[22] It is now a commonplace that the disappearance of the vamp signaled a paradigm shift in representations of women. Similarly the fantasy sequence as the only context for expression of female sexuality is now supplemented by more "realist" scripts of female self-affirmation.

In the 1980s especially, Avenging Woman cinema crystallized narratives of self-assertion against a creeping culture of misogyny, even violence. But why were so many made by *male* directors, and why during this period? These apparently women-centered films made by men may be suspected of exploiting "feminist" consciousness via a *masquerade,* a faux sexually "correct" politics that actually sustains male scopophilic fantasy. Besides, the profit motive may coexist with righteous critique of legal or juridical institutions and a commitment to social justice.

As for why now, Lalitha Gopalan elaborates a "new 'formula'" for recent Hindi cinema in which women are represented as modern but "hardened, cynical, vengeful creatures." Citing Maithili Rao, she identifies the Avenging Woman genre as centered on a conventional (nuclear) Indian family in which the paternal authority figure is absent or debilitated. The female protagonist is a professional, modern woman—who becomes the target of rape.[23] Eventually, after tribulations, she achieves a measure of retribution, in extreme cases achieved through violent revenge. My argument, however, suggests that the films' conclusions are often *ambivalent* and additionally raise the question of the very viability of exacting such retribution or revenge.

A paradox emerges as modernity in these films' narratives is embodied in women constructed as "angry." Even though they are counterposed to narratives requiring women to abjure a suspect ("un-Indian") modernity, these films sometimes fall back to defending the very traditional "values" that underlie women's structural oppression. This (antimodern) reversion potentially undermines the legitimacy or viability of narratives of feminine anger.

One question, then, is whether these films are genuinely feminist films, "exploitation" cinema, or something else. Another is how to understand the conjuncture in which this anger emerges in films produced between the 1970s and the 1990s. Sundar Kaali (writing about Tamil cinema) suggests that in the mid-1970s the hero was invariably portrayed as asserting his "phallic triumph over the urbanity of the modern woman."[24] Is this a species of "glocalization," spurred by feminist conscientization via second-wave globalizing (Western) feminism? Is it an antimodern affirmation of autochthonous (male) identity?[25] Phallic triumphalism, manifested as the disciplining of female bodies and unruly sexualities, yoked to conceptions of the citizen-subject, is inversely readable through the performative of the Avenging Woman. A third question is whether "modern" women in these films are actually liberated from conservative tradition. Even in recent years, such allegedly modern women in general society have been targeted by female Hindu militant activists from the Right, quite apart from facing a backlash from the general public.[26]

What provoked the anger portrayed in Avenging Woman films is not hard to find today. Naila Kabeer suggests that despite many advancements, "an age-old patriarchal system [still] regards women as inferior to men" and exhibits "toxic interaction with the new global culture of consumerism" and "relentless sexualisation of women's bodies."[27] Reports of rape, as Kabeer notes, are legion: the widely reported brutal, fatal rape of a young Delhi woman on December 16, 2012, is only one spectacular recent example. Despite widespread protests, many further cases of rape and torture across the Subcontinent, including of a five-year-old, have emerged since. On December 21, a week after the Delhi case, fourteen-year-old Yasmin was raped and killed in Bangladesh. Other recent cases include those of Pakistani Mukhtaran Mai, gang-raped on the orders of a council of village elders; Seema, picked up by policemen and kept in "safe custody" in the police station only to be gang-raped by four policemen, and who died a few days later; Sima, a young college student sexually harassed in her neighborhood, who committed suicide to spare her family shame; thirteen-year-old Kainat Somroo, gang-raped by local villagers; Naseema Lubano, raped by the local landlord; Mathura, a sixteen-year-old Indian tribal girl gang-raped in the police station while her relatives waited outside to file a complaint; and Maya Tyagi, returning from a wedding with her husband, arrested by plain-clothes policemen, stripped and paraded naked through the city bazaar, then raped in the police station. Ashish Rajadhyaksha and Paul Willemen underscore the "growing feminist activism in India after the Mathura and Maya Tyagi rape cases" followed by "the amendment to the Rape Law and the impact of, e.g. The Forum against Rape which offered legal assistance to rape victims."[28] In the case of Bhanwari Devi, a lower-caste woman gang-raped by upper-caste men for challenging the practice of child marriage, the judge trying the case queried, "How can a Dalit woman be raped?"[29]

This overwhelming record of infamy is nevertheless, in Kabeer's phrase, "the tip of a very ugly iceberg."[30] Members of the business class, Ruchira Gupta asserts, are seen patronizing "paid escorts, hosting rave parties, consuming porn, and saving their sons from the consequences of molesting girls."[31] Rapes have increased by 873 percent since Independence in 1947. "Budget allocations to successive Ministries of Women and Child have been reduced."[32] It is not just a matter of passing the Sexual Harassment in the Workplace Bill or punishing offenders and especially rapists with castration or death but of changing the "culture of rape" and addressing ancillary social, economic, and legal issues.[33]

Institutionally, the most prominent and relevant case remains the Mathura rape case; it changed rape law in India and highlighted continuities between the conditions in the 1970s and today. It came before a sessions court in June 1974; the defendants were exonerated on the grounds that this was not rape but consensual sex, the warrant being that Mathura was "habituated to sexual intercourse." Defense appealed, and the Bombay High Court reversed the Sessions judge, found the men guilty, and sentenced one of them to one year and the other to five years. The High Court ruled that Mathura submitted under duress and such submission was not tantamount to consent. But the case took another turn when the Supreme Court of India took up the cause of the policemen and found them not guilty on the grounds that Mathura had raised no cry for help and there were neither signs of struggle nor visible injury on Mathura's person—thus the sex could not have been forcible, so was not rape.

The Supreme Court decision raised another round of protests, especially by women's groups, and their activism led to the Criminal Law Amendment Act of 1983. This act inserted a key provision in Section 114 (A) of the Evidence Act, affirming that the court shall presume lack of consent when a victim says, after the fact, that she (or he) did not consent to sex. Other laws of the Indian Penal Code were also changed after Mathura, such as Section 376 (punishment for rape). The punishment except in Subsection 2 of this law stipulates that whoever "commits rape shall be punished with imprisonment of either description for a term which shall not be less than seven years but which may be for life." In the major change to the law in 1983, additions were also made, mostly regarding the conduct of police personnel and other public servants, including Section 376, Subsections 2 (a), (b), (c), (d,) (e), (f), and (g). Subsection 2 (a) applies to a police officer who commits rape within the limits of a police station where he is stationed, or other station house not on the premises, or victimizes any woman in his or a subordinate's custody. Subsection 2 (b) applies to any other public servant who similarly abuses his position and power over a woman in his custody or that of a subordinate. Subsection 2 (c) applies to anyone in a management position or on the staff of any premises where a woman or girl is remanded. Subsection 2 (d), similarly, applies to any person who is on the staff of a hospital and abuses his position or power over a female person in that hospital. Subsection 2 (e) applies to anyone who rapes a woman whom he knows to be pregnant. Subsection 2 (f) applies to a girl under twelve. And Subsection 2 (g) applies to gang rape, the punishment for which will be at least ten years in prison and could be as long as life with a possible fine.[34]

As Sunder Rajan observes, in the wake of the Emergency, feminists have insisted that if unjust laws on sexual assault on women are the problem, then *amendments to the law are not necessarily the best way to address the problem*: "The struggle for social transformation by democratic processes requires equal attention to other sites, family, religious communities, caste relations, and, increasingly, the market, and to their connections to the state."[35] But the contemporary status of women does not inspire optimism. The right-wing BJP considers itself a protector of women's rights and made this claim a pillar of its party's bid for reelection in the May 2014 national Indian election.[36] Yet the BJP leader and chief minister Narendra Modi—who won the election to become prime minister—allegedly masterminded the use of rape, including the gang-rape of Muslim girls and women, as a weapon of communal violence after the Babri Masjid incident, in 1992 and 2002.[37]

Women sometimes feel that state institutions are so dysfunctional that they must take the law into their own hands, quite literally, exempting themselves from the law to manipulate or subvert it and seek vengeance on their male oppressors. The Avenging Woman films foreground this disenchantment with the state and its legal apparatus, and present alternative forms of redress premised on *a condition of exception.* Even if rape/revenge films are exploitative of feminist discourse and of women themselves, this assumption of a state of exception undergirds the fantasy of revenge in many of these films.

Avenging Woman films are typically structured in five segments:

- First segment
  - Initial complication (violation, rape)
  - Contradiction: Mass appeal versus Representation of Revenge against male perpetrator
- Second segment
  - Apologia for men in general or in particular, by portraying at least one sympathetic male
- Third segment
  - Establishment of second-order injustice, foregrounding failure of the law and police
  - Courtroom acquittal of particular men, including perpetrator
  - Blaming of victim: constructing the "dishonored" woman as "modern"
- Fourth segment
  - Turning point, diegetic rupture—providing a proximate cause legitimizing heroine's taking the law into her own hands
- Fifth segment
  - Conclusion without resolution

These five contrapuntally arranged segments reveal a curious logic of internal contradiction. They may appear in different sequences, some more salient than others in different films. (1) The first segment provides the initial complication (violation or rape) as immediate and legitimating cause of the woman's anger, and poses the question of appropriate response. It also produces a first contradiction: Is it necessary to indict men in general or point up the structural flaws in traditional Indian society, at the risk of alienating mainstream viewers, predominantly male, or can the woman's revenge be represented without risk of giving offense and jeopardizing box office receipts? (2) The second segment consequently provides an escape clause, however subtly: an apologia for men in general or in particular, by portraying at least one (token?) sympathetic male. (3) The third segment establishes a second-order injustice: it foregrounds not the rape itself but the failure of the law and the police. This segment usually features, in the first half of the film, a courtroom episode, producing in court *particular* men, including the accused, whom the spectators know to be guilty, only to show those men acquitted, usually through a lawyer's devious stratagem or a technicality. Often the legal proceedings entail blaming the victim, constructing the "dishonored" woman as "modern" (Westernized, promiscuous, decadent). Significantly, this segment also introduces a key institutional, legal, or structural challenge. And indeed the courtroom is a primary site in both *Insaaf ka Tarazu* and *Zakhmi Aurat,* discussed below. (4) A critical fourth segment inserts a turn in the plot.[38] This turn is precipitated by a diegetic rupture: an event that simultaneously establishes a pattern of "harms" done to women and radically breaks with the legal-institutional codes and social apparatuses. The rupture provides a *proximate cause* to legitimize the heroine's taking the law in her own hands: had this proximate cause not transpired, the heroine would not have turned into an avenging fury—for she has already come to terms with an unsuccessful appeal for redress for her own rape; what this establishes is that she is not by nature vindictive or a man-hater. (5) A fifth and final segment purports to present a "conclusion," but it is often ambiguous or ambivalent: a conclusion without resolution. This ambivalence is due to the fact that the films attempt to negotiate many competing imperatives—on the one side, imperatives of gender and sexual justice, but on the other, family values and tradition, national, cultural, religious, caste, and class belonging, but also market considerations.

Class, to take up one of these issues, is critical in *Damini* (Lightning, Rajkumar Santoshi, 1993) as a complicating factor in violence (including rape) visited on women. The eponymous female protagonist, a new bride in the grand mansion of the Gupta family, witnesses her new husband Shekhar's brother Rakesh, along with some friends, raping a servant. Being honest (and from a much humbler family), her impulse is to report the rape to the police. Shekhar and his family try to dissuade her, in the name of family "honor." The film features the standard segment of the Avenging Woman narrative in which a man is presented as sympathetic, and the segment containing the courtroom scene in which Damini is deposed—and again it is the women who are the worse for it. The Gupta lawyer discredits Damini as mentally incompetent; she is confined to an institution. Unhinged by this experience, Damini runs away and encounters a disaffected lawyer, Govind, who agrees to assist her. The segment of narrative featuring Govind corresponds to the formulaic segment providing an apologia for "good" men, insulating men from categorical calumny. The segment in which a rupture occurs is also introduced: the raped maidservant dies in custody, purportedly a suicide. This pivots Damini into retributive mode. As "outlaw" avenging fury, she is depicted hoisting a pickaxe to threaten her attackers; it takes a change of heart in her husband to tip the scales of justice in the right direction by acknowledging her. This conclusion is ambivalent: Damini attains a measure of justice, but only via her husband's intervention.

A more significant example, *Insaaf Ka Tarazu*, emerged a decade after the feminist movement established itself in India. It negotiates between globalizing feminist discourses and traditional discourses about women's roles. This remake of the Hollywood rape/revenge film *Lipstick* (Lamont Johnson, 1976) was a "notorious rape movie,"[39] but it was also a box office success, no doubt partly because it starred Zeenat Aman. Made by a male establishment director, the film offers both male and female spectators fantasy identifications, channeling male anxieties about women's increasing power *and/or* facilitating fantasy identifications with the Avenging Woman. Rape-and-revenge narratives share features with slasher films, in which Carol Clover identifies an ideological feint. While the main narrative often portrays the law's pursuit of the rapist, a counternarrative enables fantasy projections: either traumatic, sado-masochistic alignments with male victims of female vengeance/retribution or cross-gender identifications, tethered to a female agency approximating the "Final Girl."[40] Male spectators may vicariously enjoy the spectacle of the female body being denuded and molested by proxy, at least at the outset; female *and* male viewers may identify with the victim/Avenging Woman visiting rough justice on perpetrators. As the Introduction suggested, this identificatory logic is enabled by the contradictory operation of the "screen" of the cinematic apparatus itself: the male spectator is "screened" (exempt) from the moral universe of the world on-screen yet may enjoy voyeuristic *jouissance* in the spectacle.

Rape-and-revenge films may tilt more toward "rape" than "revenge," risking subjective or point-of-view (POV) shots to sanction pleasure at the site/sight of the female body commodified and reified via the molester's violation—a reactionary, covert counternarrative exploiting the very women that the overt narrative purports to empower. This contradiction is endemic to the "revenge" narrative. Acknowledgment of the channels of (masculine) masochistic identification with the "Final Girl" need not diminish the main narrative's proffered route of (feminine) identification with her. A related and equally critical question is whether this is a genuinely empowering identification or whether it inadvertently or invidiously exploits women under the pretext of offering a putatively, fashionably, "feminist" narrative for commercial gain. Could it be that even if thus ethically compromised, this cinema is able to offer critical commentary on social problems, engaging mainstream audiences where a more radical, explicit critique might alienate them?

Insaaf Ka Tarazu opens with a variation of the iconic "courtroom scene" segment. An army officer is produced in court, accused of murder. He proudly admits that he murdered the man but denies criminal guilt because he did it to defend an Indian woman's—and therefore the motherland's—honor (*izzat*). This segment is only a microcosmic prelude adumbrating the major narrative. The protagonist, Bharti Saxena, wins top prize at a fashion show and is fulsomely praised by someone we can already guess will be her aggressor—Ramesh Gupta, a rich playboy. He pursues her relentlessly, but she rejects him, being already engaged to Ashok. Angry at being spurned, he rapes her. The film employs POV shots to suture even male viewers to the female victim's perspective, particularly when Ramesh tears off her dress and the camera gazes directly at his crazed face in close-up, or when the presumably naked Bharti looks down her body at her own bound feet; in this foreshortened image, the audience sees what the victim sees.

In the courtroom segment that follows, Ramesh is summoned, and, according to pattern, acquitted. His lawyer, Chandra, submits that the sex was consensual and evidence of assault inadequate; Bharti herself is not to blame either. Despite her traditional name, evocative of the nation, she is young, beautiful—and "modern." It is modernity that is to blame, he avers, offering photographic evidence of her "modern" behavior—modeling, dancing with Ramesh—suggesting that such women are not shy violets recoiling from sexual advances but a "blemish" on Indian culture.

As the pattern dictates, a segment containing a rupturing event—her younger sister Nita's rape, by none other than Ramesh, transforms Bharti into an avenging goddess like Kali. She pursues and kills Ramesh. The ensuing courtroom trial is extraordinary. *Fantasy* reenactments reinvent the assault, imagining a much more enthusiastic and sexually receptive Bharti than the audience had seen in the "*real*" diegesis. The reenactment, however, is *realistically presented.* Bharti is shown leading Ramesh by the hand into a room with a portrait of a half-undressed woman, chest and legs exposed, wrists in chains, a chain round her neck. In this preposterous fantasy Bharti says that chains are like a woman's jewelry and asks Ramesh to "shackle me too," suggesting that sometimes a woman is helpless and at other times feigns helplessness. Reality and fantasy are blurred: in the "real" event, the portrait of bondage is prominently on display, a visual bridge between realism and fantasy. The fantasy reenactment is not the woman's but a man's (the lawyer's) reconstruction: but while watching even the *real* event as it unfolds in the main diegetic reality, the viewer cannot help feeling that it is an exceedingly discordant image for Bharti to have on her wall. It is no blooper that it is presented within the mise-en-scène during her *real* rape: when the defense counsel produces the painting of the shackled woman in court and asks whether the image of the nude was displayed in her bedroom, Bharti owns and affirms it as a work of art.

But that image is not the only one that is "really" on display in Bharti's apartment. While Bharti is showering, before meeting Ramesh, the camera captures a poster on the shower wall showing a representation of another nude woman who is having the front of her body scrubbed by a monkey holding a bristle brush. If the intention in the "real" diegetic narrative was to establish Bharti as an innocent victim, such confusion of realism and fantasy is deeply problematic.

Certainly the audience realizes that Ramesh and his lawyer are making up a convenient story blaming the victim. If so, why the *realism* (as cinematic "attack" or approach) of the fantasy reenactment? The cinematographic choice of a realistic mode risks lending a veneer of plausibility *to the fabrications* (fantasy) of the defense lawyer. Why *refilm* events if the intention is to *contrast* reality and fiction? Or is it to reduce confidence in Bharti's "original" version of events? The judge, jury, and courtroom audience are directly addressed by Ramesh: confronted with the charms and the blandishments of a woman as beautiful as Bharti ("she simply dazzles"), would they not act in the same way? Thus, like other Avenging Woman films, *Insaaf* leaves unresolved important questions about rape, structural oppression, and inadequate legal and institutional protection.

Zakhmi Aurat represents female vengeance even more graphically. Here too the Avenging Woman's anger requires a legitimation narrative, balancing the risk of alienating mainstream male viewers against endorsement of the Avenging Woman and simultaneously tapping into cross-gender fantasy or masochistic identification with male victims of castration. And while this film appears to present a "just retribution" script, along with other films such as *Supari* (Contract Killing, Padam Kumar, 2003), *Anjaam* (Consequences, Rahul Rawail, 1994), and *Bawandar* (Sandstorm, Jagmohan, 2000–2001), there remain questions about whether this is profit-driven "sexploitation" or genuinely feminist filmmaking by male directors.

The opening sequence presents a montage of newspaper clippings covering stories of female rape victims; an extradiegetic song ("*Apni raksha khud karegi/ aaj ki aurat,*" The modern woman will defend herself) provides commentary. As the opening credits roll, the protagonist, Police Inspector Kiran Dutt, is shown riding her motorbike. She is portrayed as an impressive figure in her uniform—a modern, tough professional.

This character is intended as homage to the national hero Kiran Bedi, who was the first woman to join the police force, in 1972. She later became a prominent public figure. The key point is that Kiran, like her namesake, is an independent and modern woman in Bombay. Early scenes show Kiran not dainty or helpless—she perspires, vanquishes a gang of criminals, fights hand-to-hand, handles a gun, shatters the window of a van to stop a rape in progress. Yet even she is ultimately and "essentially" vulnerable. As she returns home one night, Kiran is gang-raped, although she resists. Devastated and traumatized, Kiran likens herself to a corpse (*laash*) in darkness (*andhera*).

It is Suraj, her faithful fiancé, who supports her through trauma, reaffirming his pledge to marry her, just as Kiran had rescued Shanti from her assault in the van and then stood by her. Along with Kiran's female doctor, Asha Mehta, Suraj makes it mentally and emotionally possible for Kiran to take her rape case to court. The token "good" male comes to her defense, exonerating men as a class. Yet, consistent with segment two of the Avenging Woman film, the law betrays Kiran, acquitting her victimizer, whom the spectator knows to be culpable.

The devious defense lawyer Mahendra Nath, whose venality and outrageous mendacity are on display, makes a mockery of Kiran's putative power as a policewoman and the court's claim of dispensing justice. Manipulating the category of "modernity," Mahendra argues that modern women, like Kiran, are themselves hardly innocent; they are even capable of raping *men*, he asserts, producing newspaper clippings as "proof" (the word is in English in the film). On the strength of a single newspaper report, the judge acknowledges that "it's quite possible" (the statement is also in English) that Kiran is not blameless. The defense lawyer's performance signals that if women like Kiran are "modern," they are matched by equally modern Indian men of good society such as Mahendra and the judge. Here class, modernity, and globalization operate as subtexts these films need to negotiate in an intersectional representation. Through his twisted arguments, Mahendra vanquishes Kiran, consigning her to the status of "disgraced woman."

Let down by the legal/police system, Kiran is on the verge of resigning as policewoman. Suraj dissuades her from quitting, if not for herself then because of the example of cowardice (*kayarta*) it would set to other women. Suraj promises to honor his commitment to her even though the world may see her as dishonored, like Sita in the *Ramayan*, effectively someone else's "leftovers" (*kisi aur ki jhutan*), anathema to a prospective mother-in-law. (In a show of magnanimity, Suraj's mother will also finally accept Kiran as Suraj's bride.) Suraj is true to his name (sun) and Kiran's (ray), both representing the light of truth and justice.[41] Yet eventually, with his support, Kiran "sees the light" and seeks rough, not legal, justice as an Avenging Woman. There Suraj will not or cannot go. Though a self-congratulatory male fantasy, Suraj's support is structurally important, functioning as a pivot for Kiran, allowing her to resume the good fight as Avenging Woman. He hands her the *Bhagavad Gita* and her pistol, declaring, "*Yeh rahe vo siddhanth, aur yeh hai vo shakti*" ("This, the *Gita*, is the true law; this, the gun, is the real power"). In the Indian context his fidelity is a noble and remarkable exception, especially coming from such an eligible bachelor (he is a dutiful son and a doctor). But this meme of male support is a fond fantasy for "'heroic' liberalism, appealing to the idealistic sentiments of the very same spectator group that would disavow emulating it in the real world."[42] More insidiously, Suraj's support also serves to blunt women's complaint against a systemic, structural problem, appearing to let men as a group off the hook by individualizing rape, making it exceptional and therefore statistically unthreatening. The film seems to concede that Suraj's example demonstrates that some men *are* sympathetic, so there's no real sexual/gender issue at stake. Thus the film risks becoming mere exploitation of the rape/revenge "formula." As token male supporter, Suraj's role is chiefly to assuage collective guilt. His support is emotionally crucial but practically ineffectual.

Kiran's cause is subsumed within a feminist "conscientization" script. Her frustrated legal appeal convinces her she must exact her *revenge* (*badla*) by extrajudicial means. Besides, she comes to see that "anger" need not be just personal but may be construed as a collective grievance, requiring collective action from a community of women—and potentially rationalizing the path of violent retribution. The law is implicitly and explicitly put on trial: when the prosecution lawyer argues that Kiran, a policewoman, is "defaming" the law, she counters that she no longer feels bound by the law. The court, however, remains so. Furthermore, she invokes the *Bhagavad Gita*'s injunction to defend the truth—a higher law. Yet this rationale, perhaps echoing Antigone's defense in the Greek tragedy, does nothing to change the legal obstacles for women or the social stigma of being raped. The film ends ambiguously, without the court's—the law's—judgment being diegetically enunciated.

The question of feminist sisterhood is crucial. Material support for Kiran's cause comes from women, fellow victims. Asha Mehta, Kiran's doctor, was also a victim of sexual aggression, and Asha's young daughter Pinky was raped and killed. Kiran receives letters from many women attesting to "the cruelty of men." Her women's group agrees that castration would be sweetest revenge. Significantly, the word, being a key category, is expressed in English: castration, making a man "useless" (*bekar*), will cause a perpetrator to suffer like his victims, but without the release of death. The operation is carried out on several perpetrators; when the castrated men discover their fate, they lament in language intended to mirror that of female rape victims on-screen: "I am ruined! I am ravished" ("*Main barbad ho gaya! Main lut gaya*"). One male castrato complains of having "lost my purse [wallet]"! They cannot complain to the police, for fear of being dishonored as "eunuchs" (*namard*). Their only recourse, they proclaim, is suicide.

The trauma of the rape victims takes the form of repetition-with-a-difference: for the women, trauma's true domain is fantasy, first suffered in reality, then in psychical reality (fantasy), then in court. Kiran believes in a political purpose for their unmanning mission: visiting this sexual trauma on men might prompt meaningful change through repetition of victimization—the perpetrators this time being aggrieved women. As the news media report the castrations, those aims seem achievable: a television announcer notes that the police themselves have been requesting the Lok Sabha (the Lower House of Parliament) to make rape laws stricter. Public debate arises about whether "Eve teasers" should be castrated, whether India is a "sex-starved nation"; men finally begin to discuss rape seriously. Kiran describes herself to Suraj as angry and bitter, counterpart of the thousand-armed Ravana (a demon). This *daimonia* has made Kiran something more than a policewoman but less than a good (Indian) woman. Another female collaborator, Salma, describes herself similarly, as a bitter woman (*karvi*). Salma taunts one of her marks as he descends into a drugged stupor: "How will you play the flute when the flute is lost?" A vengeful spirit possesses the empowered but threatening women.

The film represents trauma through phantasmatic or *excessive* distortions of reality. When Sukhdev, Kiran's rapist (absurdly clad in a yellow sweatshirt bearing the logo "ladies"), is drugged by Salma to capture him for Asha's castrating knife, his vision begins to play tricks on him, and the camera reflects this kaleidoscopically. When later he puts a gun in his mouth to shoot himself, the camera cuts to a grotesque shot of a meaty, shredded mass, presumably of

Sukhdev's insides, clearly a departure from realist convention into near-Gothic hyperreal horror. Jyotika Virdi writes that rape-and-revenge films are generically reliant "on convincingly meting out vigilante revenge that must equal, or even surpass, the horror of rape." As she notes, "Visual representations of rape in Indian cinema also remind us of the authority of censorship regulations, and suggest the possibility of sadomasochistic pleasures structuring these rape scenes." Here too revenge surpasses the offense. Representational *excess* matters. For it is not just a matter of equalizing the score: the horrific nature of rape is betokened by the very *affective excess* of the retribution wreaked on the perpetrator and the *formal excess*, both of which move the representation beyond realist conventions.

Is the Avenging Woman then a positive exemplum? Only a transgressive fantasy? Do Avenging Woman films empower women? Are they "sexploitation cinema"? For Sharon Marcus, women are too often reduced to inner space, imagined as powerless, passive, vulnerable: "The rape script defines women as vulnerable, violable, penetrable and wounded. . . . The entire female body comes to be symbolized by the vagina . . . a delicate, perhaps inevitably damaged and pained inner space."[43] Consequently, Marcus proposes that women can "elude the limits of an empiricist approach by developing a politics of fantasy and representation. . . . New cultural productions and reinscriptions of our bodies and our geographies can help us begin to revise the grammar of violence and to represent ourselves in militant new ways."[44] *Zakhmi Aurat* appears to confirm Marcus's argument in deploying the revenge fantasy, but closer analysis suggests that conceptually remapping the female body might not be enough. "Revenge" may be viable only in cinema; such retributive fantasy cannot in a male-dominated society be exacted with impunity.

A revealing comparison from parallel cinema is *Ardh Satya* (Half-Truth, Govind Nihalani, 1983). The film's protagonist, Anant, is a subinspector with the Bombay police. Although his name means "the eternal," his story is a *realistically narrated* allegory of failure, and therefore an aborted or abridged critique of the police and the law it supports. He is undone at every level both professionally and personally, in his relationship with Jyotsna, and this has a deleterious effect on his psychic health: his temper flares uncontrollably, particularly when a man on a bus pinches Jyotsna. His reflex to protect the woman from sexual assault is presumptively a virtue, an apologia for good men in Indian society: this apologia conforms to segment two of the Avenging Woman narrative.

The film displays other aspects of Angry Man/Avenging Woman films. Yet, being an example of art-house filmmaking, it abjures recourse to fantasy. Instead it offers a conjoint social realist critique of what Antonio Gramsci termed political society (the police) *and* civil society (the family and gendered social relations). Frustrated that the police are in the pocket of local criminals, Anant valiantly fights corruption. Yet by degrees his principled stance is whittled down: impotent to resist Rama Shetty, don of the powerful local mafia, he ends up brutally torturing and killing a prisoner in police custody. He is fired from his police job and is forced to seek Shetty's employment, completing his humiliation. Shetty pushes his demands too far; Anant snaps and kills him. He loses what began as the good fight, and becomes a drunk and a monstrously violent person. His career and dreams of life with Jyotsna shattered, he gives himself up—ironically—to the police. The film solicits the spectator's identification, even suture, with Anant, and thereby undermines faith in social institutions: the police, the bourgeois family, heteronormative gender relations, but since this is a story of a failed quest for justice, this allegorical film's conclusion is profoundly ambivalent.

A much more unflinching sexual assault/revenge narrative, the diasporic director Shekhar Kapur's *Bandit Queen* (1994), presents an intimate portrait of a lower-caste woman. The film, an adaptation of a true story, was financed and produced in Britain (Channel Four). It mediates between transnational and statist discourses but is anchored in the narrative of the Avenging Woman. Based on Mala Sen's "biography," *Phoolan Devi,* the film stirred considerable controversy, not least because Phoolan objected to her representation in the film, and to Sen's cosmopolitan sensibility, though her expressed objections seem oddly moralistic for such a gender rebel. Moreover, the political impetus of Phoolan's objection to the film is at least in some measure post hoc and ideologically suspect. Brenda Longfellow reports that when Kapur, the director, was asked about Phoolan's "disavowal" of the film, he said, "In a country where women can only enter politics as post-menopausal asexual beings, she objects to her portrayal as a sexual being," as a woman actively pursuing her own physical pleasure, including by sitting astride her lover.[45] Kapur's cinematic representation of Phoolan's story is generally nonexploitative, so it is odd that the Bandit Queen should demur so delicately. But, of course, there are multiple rape scenes, as well as a scene in which, after a gang-rape, Phoolan is paraded naked for daring to transgress strictures of caste and gender, all of which might have been embarrassing to her. Sen admitted that she had met Phoolan only once and only "for a few minutes." Yet this is not necessarily a fatal disqualification.

Phoolan sees herself as a "middle-class" subject, not as subaltern. How should we understand the problematic manner in which the "imperious, erratic and politically motivated voice of Phoolan Devi" interrupts the film's circulation in transnational and domestic circuits?[46] This critical question is often suppressed even in the work of astute critics such as Madhu Kishwar, who too quickly takes the moral high ground by invoking Phoolan's subaltern credentials. By contrast, Longfellow insists that Phoolan's voice, "the voice of a lower-caste illiterate woman and former outlaw, only arrives through the lawyers and the high-caste political handlers that now surround her."[47]

Born into a poor peasant family, Phoolan was sold as a young girl by her father to a much older man and raped by him. She was gang-raped again as the partner of a gang leader after he was killed by a rival gang, and then a third time. Seeking vengeance, she led her gang in the 1981 Behmai massacre, killing twenty-two upper-caste villagers, including two of her rapists. Phoolan later agreed to a very public "surrender" in which the government seemed to capitulate to her demands, dropping more than thirty charges of murder or other criminal offenses in exchange for her surrender. Subsequently elected leader of a populist party, she became a successful member of Parliament. She was assassinated by a member of a rival gang, but not before gaining fame and fortune while retaining her claim to (low) caste credentials and class solidarity.

Bandit Queen conforms to the typology of the Avenging Woman, presenting Phoolan as a strong woman who exacts revenge for sexual violations of her person and achieves agency in that self-assertion. Yet it is impossible to ignore that the subject herself questioned the film's representation of reality. Negotiating conflicting issues of class, caste, nation, and caste, the film serves up an ambivalent cultural representation: both political proxy and portrait of an Avenging Woman. It is unusual for the same reason it is controversial. It presumes both to re-present a *real* story of female self-assertion and to perform a political intervention into the discourse of sexual violence intersecting with the politics of class and caste.

Fictional films, including minor instances such as *Sherni* (The Tigress, Harmesh Malhotra, 1988), typically frame narratives of successful female self-assertion *as fantasy*. In this film, Durga, rural belle and dutiful daughter, witnesses her father viciously punished by a village leader or Thakur, ironically named Dharampal ("righteous"). Durga's father is driven out of the village and joins a gang of thieves—again, as in other Avenging Woman films the point is that the law and the police are failed institutions; contraventions of the law, as consequence and contrast, constitute honorable dissent. Durga's own trajectory as a character confirms this. As Dharampal and his goons kill most of Durga's family, she watches helplessly; the police expressly decline to get involved. This is the segment presenting a rupture, when Durga is pushed into becoming an Avenging Woman. The issue here is not rape, but the gender dynamic is unmistakable: the woman must turn to a retributive violence because the patriarchal state and the police offer no meaningful recourse. The key question *Sherni* poses about Avenging Woman films is whether they constitute viable female self-affirmation and empowerment. Its answer remains ambivalent too.

Anjaam (Consequences, Rahul Rawail, 1994) raises similar questions in its representation of women disappointed by the law and the police. This film's opening is unpromising, indeed overwrought, even by the standards of mass entertainment. Vijay Agnihotri is a "spoilt richie-rich," in the words of the heroine, Shivani, a beautiful flight attendant with whom he falls in love, only to discover that Shivani does not reciprocate his sentiments. She marries a pilot, Ashok Chopra. Vijay, unable to accept this rejection, stalks Shivani, even after she gives birth to a daughter, Pinky. The film chronicles his obsession as he lives in a fantasy world of resentment and solipsistic anger—and the awakening of Shivani's avenging fury.

In an early segment, following the pattern of the Avenging Woman narrative, it is made clear that Shivani cannot bank on justice within the system.

Vijay frames her for the murder of her husband, and she is imprisoned. While Shivani is incarcerated, Vijay accidentally rams his car into her sister, killing her along with Shivani's daughter. Shivani's sister had just been thrown out of her house by her gambling- and alcohol-addicted cheating husband, just as Shivani was banished from her house by her husband before he was killed by Vijay. The accidental deaths of Shivani's sister and her innocent daughter now become the moment of rupture for her. Shivani is transformed into a Chandi, or avenging goddess, imagistically mirroring the icon of the goddess with the death-dealing discus on her index finger. She kills first her tormenting jailer (who, instead of upholding justice, pimps her charges to politicians), then her brother-in-law, who is indirectly responsible for the deaths of her sister and daughter. Next Shivani kills the policeman, Arjun Singh, Vijay's accomplice. On the warpath (which she calls *Dharmyudha*, or moral war) she discovers that Vijay, hurt in the accident that killed her sister and daughter, has become paralyzed. Conveniently, the damage sustained is psychological. Vijay's body remains unscathed.

The film follows a horror film convention, planting false "clues," one of which is that when she is on the hunt for Vijay, with a sickle in her hand, she comes upon him in his wheelchair, his unseeing eyes blankly staring out of a twisted head. She appears moved by his plight, apparently ready to abandon her avenging anger. Dutifully she wheels him around, shaves him, and even feeds him on a romantic beach with bonfire and sunset as backdrop. But it soon becomes evident that Shivani is nursing Vijay back to mental health not out of womanly pity (*rahm*) but because it would count as a "sin" to wreak revenge on someone incapacitated—and possibly because she wants him to truly experience the retribution she intends to visit on him; his being unconscious of it would rob her of satisfaction. We cannot miss the perverse, sadistic undertone prefigured in the moment when with subtle malice she bounces a ball on the floor and then off the wheelchair-bound Vijay's head. Miraculously, on the third bounce off his head, Vijay regains motor control enough to catch the ball aimed at his skull. He is cured. And ready to pay the price.

The film is riveting not only for this exquisite sadism but also for its antirealist representation of trauma. The film displaces the trauma experienced by both principals from the body to the psyche, representing Vijay as well as Shivani in the grip of excessive, transgressive *affect,* or fantasy. Vijay is an unregenerate but not simple villain: his psychological depravity has depth. The film mockingly stages the "*natak*" or theater of his recuperation. Immediately after his "recovery," in a scene tellingly staged in a temple dedicated to the terrifying goddess (Chandi), and even at the point of his death, he is still in the grip of his strange monomania: to have Shivani say, just once, that she loves him. Well in excess of melodrama, this monomania is more like a fundamental fantasy.

The hystericization of Vijay's trauma is deployed as a conscious figure for Western modernity itself, because it invokes the Freudian discourse that has defined modern consciousness in the West, with its explanatory apparatus of Oedipus, trauma, and cathexis. An ingenious bit of cathectic hystericization is enacted in the actor's body: Shah Rukh Khan, playing Vijay, incorporates a tic into his right shoulder, as if his traumatic rejection by the object of his obsessive lust were cathected into the gesture.

As for Shivani, she plainly goes beyond the pale. The conclusion cannot be content with a "Final Girl" scenario of victory. There is no way out of her monstrous fixation. In a literal cliffhanger, on the verge of falling off a high wall, Vijay grabs Shivani's ankles and she falls too, clutching the edge at the last moment. Their lives depend on her grip. Far from softening or capitulating, Shivani declares that Vijay's death (*maut*) is more important than her own survival, and saying this she releases her grip and plunges with him to her death while the extradiegetic voice-over sings, "Whoever picks a fight with Woman (*nari*) will be turned to ash." The film appears to express a militant feminist consciousness, but we must ask again, how "realistic" is the emergence of such a Chandi in patriarchal Indian society? Is this fantasy or commodifying "sexploitation"? The film's answer is ambivalent or ambiguous, once again.

Even setting aside this suicidal ending, that Shivani stabs Vijay in the temple, knocks his head with a sacred bell hanging from the ceiling of the temple, and uses a trident (*trishul*) to attack him—these are all behaviors that flout even the Avenging Woman conventions for representing righteous and justified revenge. It is one thing to contravene a personal moral imperative (such as love for a son, as in *Mother India*). It is quite another for a woman to undermine the institution of the mother within marriage, and to contravene the sacrality of the institution of the temple by using its ritualized accouterments (temple bell, *trishul*) in such a cavalier and instrumentalizing manner (as weapons).

A more compassionate Avenging Woman, despite herself, turns out to be Mamta Shekari (Huntress?) in Padam Kumar's *Supari* (2003). An underworld femme fatale, Mamta heads a mafia-like criminal organization. The hero, who bears the weighty name Aryan and calls Manhattan home, signaling his cosmopolitan credentials, effectively becomes indentured to the ironically named Mamta ("compassion"). Aryan lost a gambling bet and had no other recourse but to carry out contract hits for Mamta to avenge her underworld vendettas. Though she seems to have no compunction in killing, Mamta fastidiously obeys rituals of gangland assassination. What is more, she devoutly worships Kali, the fierce female goddess, who like Chandi is hailed for her destructive power (*shakti*). Kali kills men and drinks their blood; Mamta is shown praying to Kali on at least two occasions, once for three hours straight. Aryan must renounce everything—friends, the woman Dilnawaz, who tries to save him. Finally he realizes he must kill Mamta herself. Thus Aryan is caught between two women, the two poles of innocence/life and nihilistic violence/death. If this is an Avenging Woman film, it presents many complications and again ends ambivalently.

Mamta's violence, like Shivani's in *Anjaam*, is not quite bereft of cultural legitimacy, but, like Shivani's, her anger is so uncompromising and excessive that this legitimacy depends on both women's apostrophizing a *dea ex machina:* the goddess (Kali or Chandi) as divine sanction for the Avenging Woman. Thus we have the duplex fantasy idiom in the two films, pairing the imagery of the avenging goddess with the imagery of vernacular Gothic. Not only are their deaths violent; the camera also lingers with money-shot pornographic fascination on their just-dead bodies. Shivani was cast as a literally man-eating avenger. Mamta is presented to the (male) scopic gaze with a fleshy wound on the forehead, and over her dramatically made-up eyes is a zone inviting near-pornographic investment from three radically different camera angles: a huge red *tika* becomes a single dark line like a vertical slit between her furrowed brows, and finally a gaping hole. The sexualization of this imagery is unmistakable, suggesting that if this is an Avenging Woman film, sexploitation may be co-present with "feminist" triumphalism—and thus ambivalent.

Later films also present examples of problematic female self-assertion, and not all of them can simply be dismissed as commercial "sexploitation" cinema. In *Bawandar* (Sandstorm, Jagmohan 2000), an example of parallel cinema rather than popular film, the idyll of the peasant is interrupted by a moment of distanciation, of disidentification. A young Englishwoman, Amy, comes to a small village in Rajasthan to write about the political awakening of Sanvri, a low-caste rural woman. The film chronicles the extraordinary price Sanvri has paid, including being gang-raped, for helping to agitate for women's and girls' rights in her village. The film tracks her activism to secure justice from the state but delivers an ambivalent social commentary. For Sanvri remains relatively powerless against local forces and village "customs."

The film repeatedly destabilizes the ideological premises and discursive conventions of realist narrative. For instance, when Amy and her companion arrive at Sanvri's house, they are greeted by a boy. Amy, unlike her male companion, does not speak the Rajasthani dialect. Yet the director calculatedly has the boy reply *in English* to the question the adult companion had asked in careful local dialect. This is a significant interruption of the realist codes of the "authentic" peasant subject. Sanvri also challenges stereotypes of the village belle. She is a newly politicized female subject wrenched violently out of her abject silence in this rural society, where child marriage is a tradition.

The film resists predictable feminist or politically correct narratives, but by the same token cannot transcend ambivalence. In conformity with segment two of Avenging Woman films, Sanvri's husband is presented as her staunchest supporter; in supporting her, he risks perhaps more than even Shoba, the central government representative working with the women's group Saathin. Tellingly, Sanvri is betrayed by two *female* police officers. Further, she is hindered by her virulently conservative fellow villagers, by insensitive police officers and authorities (including female officers and wives of magistrates), and by hypocritical and opportunistic nongovernmental organization (NGO) workers. Thus at many levels *Bawandar* defeats easy stereotypy. Neither is subalternity here a conventional guarantor of moral rectitude. *Bawandar* refuses to romanticize the peasant as authentic national subject. However, this is an atypical art-house film.

To conclude, I underscore important generic continuities between these two types of films. First, Avenging Woman films manifest a family resemblance to Angry Man films even on purely formal levels, as I have shown. Second, both are structured as responses to dysfunctional social arrangements. Third, both subgenres' gender politics remain murky. Do the Angry Man films restore or complicate masculinity? Can Avenging Woman films speak for women without exploiting them? Do they merely feed male *scopic* pleasure or can they provide *visual* pleasure for female viewers too, alongside subtle sadomasochistic pleasure across the gender divides? Fourth, beyond offering the politically correct, utopian, or indeed fantasy responses to the problem of rape, both subgenres raise questions about the viability of retributive justice as a response to rape (or oppression). Even if they traffic in fantasy, we can conclude, both Angry Man and Avenging Woman films are what Foucault might call *crisis heterotopias.* As aspirationally political documents of culture, their power to reshape or recondense the prevailing discourses remains open to question.

II

REIMAGINING THE SECULAR STATE

4

Terrorism or Seduction

India is today the world's third-largest economy, with an annual growth rate averaging 8 percent, according to IMF and World Bank estimates in the year 2007.[1] By 2025 it will be 60 percent the size of the U.S. economy, and by 2035 only slightly smaller, yet larger than western Europe's.[2] In 2008 Tata Motors acquired both Jaguar and Land Rover, emblems of the former colonizer's power; the *Forbes* 2011 list of the world's richest people featured fifty-five Indian billionaires, up from twenty-three in 2006, including Tata's CEO, Ratan Tata, who in the same year gave $50 million to Harvard Business School. Harvard also received high-profile funding for the humanities from another prominent Indian industrialist, Anand Mahindra. In 2009 yet another Indian billionaire, Anil Ambani, acquired a 50 percent share of Steven Spielberg's production company, DreamWorks. Public perception in India is also bullish: nearly 90 percent of Indian respondents believe the country is set to become one of world's most powerful nations, according to an October 2010 Pew Global Attitudes survey.[3] Yet a third of the population—455 million—live in abject poverty, on less than $1.25 a day (the World Bank's subsistence threshold). Only recently, India was a Third World country, and even today this emerging economy is hobbled by enormous problems of both human security and national security: the masses remain poor, uneducated, underfed, and underserved, and there is civil and military insecurity, particularly in the matter of terror. "So which of the two stories [of India]—unprecedented success or extraordinary failure—is correct?" This is the apposite question posed by Jean Drèze and his collaborator, the Nobel Prize–winning economist Amartya Sen. Their own response is telling: "The answer is both, for they are both valid, and they are entirely compatible with each other."[4] Cannily, recent Hindi cinema condenses this doubled truth in the genre of "terrorism cinema."

Hindi terrorism cinema seems to illustrate Hippolyte-Adolphe Taine's postulation of "race, moment, and milieu" as a positivist catechism for the study of cultural documents. It crystallizes a traumatic postcolonial history into a contemporary crisis of terrorism, although the historical event, Partition, splitting the Subcontinent into three parts—India in the middle, flanked by East and West Pakistan—extends further back. Scholars such as Paul Brass, Sandria Freitag, and Gyan Pandey suggest that ethnonationalist communal identities rose to salience because of economic factors and an early form of a democratic public sphere during the British colonial period. Post-Independence India has avowedly been a "secular socialist" state. This vision, propagated by India's first prime minister, Pandit Jawaharlal Nehru, took inspiration from the Soviet model, counterposed to British and even American powers in the Great Game played out across Eurasia and South Asia. Yet the nation-state has also evolved from the originary "secular socialism" of the Nehruvian moment immediately following Independence in 1947 to the current (post)neoliberalist phase following liberalization of the economy in 1991, with foreign direct investment (FDI) at all-time highs and a GDP of 25 percent since 2011. As I argued above, India is increasingly integrated into the global economy but is actually responding to a "glocalist" call for a parallel emphasis on state intervention. Drèze and Sen suggest that it is not just that markets can be mixed with the state but that the state needs to remain strong: it must intervene to defend the values of secularism, freedom, and humanism even as it climbs onto the bandwagon of globalization. This line of thought Drèze and Sen trace beyond Nehru to a very diverse range of thinkers: Aristotle, Voltaire, Adam Smith, Marquis de Condorcet, Karl Marx, John Stuart Mill, even Friedrich Hayek.[5] They might have added Karl Polanyi, who is gaining a renewed eminence as prophet of disillusionment with the "utopian" myth of the sufficiency of a self-regulating economy. In the Indian context and in Polanyi's language, we might say that social relations are "embedded" in the economic system, and the state has a social responsibility and a crucial role in keeping a rapacious market logic in check and what Polanyi termed "*haute finance*" from rending the social fabric.[6] This view, of course, is resisted by reactionary and conservative interests, who would simultaneously weaken the state with respect to the market and strengthen the state to ensure military security at the expense of human and social security, if necessary. Fear of destabilizing intercommunal violence and panic about terrorism are vividly on view in popular cinema from the late 1980s to the early 2000s: terrorism cinema condenses those tensions regarding state and social security.

The Cauldron of Communalist Violence

On December 6, 1992, VHP and BJP activists destroyed the Babri Masjid (or mosque) at Ayodhya. Waves of violence between Hindus and Muslims ensued in various parts of the country, killing more than one thousand people. Is this not state terrorism, and is it really that different from nonstate terrorism, in philosophic and biopolitical terms, as Igor Primoratz asks rhetorically?[7] The VHP was banned, and many BJP leaders, including Prime Minister Lal Krishna Advani, were arrested for provoking hostilities. It is important to remember that as Gayatri Spivak notes, "official Indian self-representation" in the "Nehruvian atmosphere of the 1960s" was marked by a now-endangered "multiculturalism" and "the religious tolerance of the Hindu majority."[8]

From the late 1980s through the 1990s and into the 2000s, the specter of ethnonationalist terrorism, particularly between Hindus and Muslims, haunted the public sphere and kept the wound of Partition festering. Years after Ayodhya, the nation was traumatized by bombings in which Islamist terrorists attacked India—in 2005, but also July 2006, November 2008, and July 2011. Hysteria about terrorism is spectacularly on view in Hindi terrorism cinema as it emerged from this fraught matrix. The traumatizing figure of the terrorist operates as "switch point" between private and public, so that the trauma and its "strange attractions have become one way . . . of locating the violence and the erotics, the erotic violence, at the crossing point of private fantasy and collective space . . . the pathological public sphere."[9]

It is important to set against the founding ideology of secularism a reactionary construction of *Hindu* nationalism traceable to the publication of V. D. Savarkar's *Hindutva: Who Is a Hindu?* (1923), which anchors the "sense of nationality" in the territorial, bounded political entity.[10] Savarkar is the éminence grise of the Hindutvavadis, especially the Bharatiya Janata Party (BJP) and its affiliate, Rashtriya Swayamsevak Sangh (RSS), formed in 1925. The RSS vigorously opposed secularism until the BJP's defeat in general elections in 2004 and 2009. The RSS votary Nathuram Godse's assassination of Mahatma Gandhi, in the year after Independence, was an early sign of the contradictions fissuring the imagined nation's ideology of secularism. Ashutosh Varshney remarks Gandhi's exhortation that "secularism require[s] giving emotional security to the minorities."[11] But this sentiment has been mocked by reality. The conflict between Hindus and Muslims permeates everyday life.

Christophe Jaffrelot identifies an "*irrational* feeling of vulnerability in certain segments of the Hindu community," even though in the 1991 census the Hindu majority was 82 percent of the population to the Muslims' 12 percent. That irrational feeling, in Jaffrelot's account the "root cause for Hindu nationalism," was reactivated in the 1920s and 1930s and then again from the 1980s through the 1990s and into the present.[12] As this book has emphasized, cinema is a primary site for the desublimation of "irrational feelings," fears and fantasy. Terrorism cinema crystallizes what is beyond the rational—condensing contemporary antisecularist nationalism. Witness the furor ignited by the 1989 Mandal Commission's recommendation to increase reserved seats in education and employment for "scheduled castes" or "backward" classes, some Hindu students in Delhi resorting to self-immolation.

Another key instance in which secularism ran afoul of religio-nationalism was the 1985 Supreme Court of India's confirmation of the High Court of Madhya Pradesh's ruling that Shah Bano, an elderly Muslim divorcee who had been given the *talaq* (pronouncement of divorce—a long-standing practice of shari'a law) by her husband must be paid maintenance by him. As Spivak notes, after the Supreme Court ruled in Shah Bano's favor, "Muslim feminists and Muslim male intellectuals supported the Supreme Court ruling. It was overruled because opposition Muslims, speaking for the rights of the religious minority, began to say that was interference with the shari'a. And then when Hindu fundamentalists came to protect [Shah Bano] against Muslim men, she declared herself to be a Muslim rather than a woman."[13]

If we are tempted to read this as denial of agency, we might consider that Shah Bano's identification with religion over gender positionality might indicate a complex convergence of vectors including sexuality, family pressure, social constraints, religious ideology, and power hierarchies. She was hardly in a position to make a "free choice," as it is theoretically understood in Western second-generation feminism, for instance. Saba Mahmood's caution to this effect, in a discussion of secularism, is apposite.[14]

Muslim Indians motivatedly construe the ruling as indication of the enfeeblement of avowed secular principles. The Sangh Parivar explicitly derided the "pseudo-secularism" of the Congress, mobilizing against the Babri mosque in Ayodhya, destroying it on December 6, 1992, with calamitous repercussions across the country: communal riots doubled from one thousand to two thousand per year during the period coinciding with the Ayodhya incident (1990–1993). Prime Minister Rajiv Gandhi reversed the Supreme Court ruling. This extraordinary intervention was decried as appeasement and worse; Gandhi was assassinated six years later, in 1991, by a Tamil terrorist. And this would become an efficient cause for the film *Roja*, as well as perhaps *The Terrorist*, discussed below.

Secularism as legal keystone of Indianness has been in progressive discourse "aligned with the constitutional directive to opt out of a system of 'personal'/religious laws for a Uniform Civil Code [UCC], understood to be in opposition both to intransigently conservative and 'communal' or religious community-based interests." Yet the UCC has also been challenged as possibly "inherently inimical to India," as "state authoritarianism," and possibly irreconcilable with "gender justice and religious minority interests."[15]

The opposition of the religiously oriented and communalist interest groups to *the Nehruvian secular* may be mapped onto the opposition between a non-secularist, Gandhian political vision (*Ram Rajya*) and a Nehruvian socialism that took as its watchword a modernizing *process of secularization*. To highlight this second opposition is not to ignore the socialist element in Gandhi's own philosophy but to emphasize Nehru's institutional *secularist and secularizing* socialism, embodied in initiatives such as the Cooperative Farming Scheme or his large-scale Soviet-style industrialization schemes. This meant great social change over the periods of the so-called national Five-Year Plans.

Nehru may have advocated secular socialism, but it was only in 1976 that secularism was formally "inserted" into the Indian Constitution by Indira Gandhi—his daughter. The key articles of the constitution were Articles 25 and 30. The former ensured the right of all to "profess, practice and propagate religion," and the latter guaranteed equal access to educational institutions. These articles were scaffolding for the Representation of the People Act, which prohibits any appeal to religion during election campaigns: an act promoting secularism. Nehru was actually more committed to *secularization* than to *secularism*, and he had already oriented India in the preferred direction. Today what Congress is being criticized for by right-wing Hindutvavadis is not secularization but alleged "pseudo-secularism." When Sangh Parivar leaders such as Atal Behari Vajpayee endorsed a "positive secularism," they too were calumniated.

The Subgenre of Terrorism Cinema

My focus is on the burgeoning subgenre of films produced in the period beginning around the time of the war for the "liberation" of East Pakistan (today's Bangladesh) in 1971 and the crisis arising in the mid-1970s with Indira Gandhi's state of Emergency, through the 1980s and 1990s and into the 2000s. The Emergency was in large measure an attempt by the state to quell the Naxalite (Maoist) uprising, originating in West Bengal and seen as a terrorist threat. But after the Emergency, through the 1980s and 1990s, the Naxalite movement surged if anything more powerfully. Still, the Naxalites were by no means the only perceived source of terrorism. The country witnessed two major acts of what from the government's perspective looked like terrorism: the assassination of Indira Gandhi (1984) by her own Sikh bodyguards, acting in sympathy with separatists calling for a Sikh "Khalistan," and the assassination of her son Rajiv Gandhi (1991) by agents representing Tamil separatist aspirations. It is fair to say that fear of terrorism was a major element of the Zeitgeist out of which emerged terrorism cinema. On November 21, 2012, India hanged Ajmal Kasab, the lone survivor among the Pakistani terrorists, funded by Lashkar-e-Taiba, who bombed Mumbai's Taj Hotel on November 26, 2008. This bombing marked a new terrorism crisis. The threat of especially transnational terrorism has certainly not faded away, but the last two decades have witnessed a remarkable profusion of films about terrorism, providing an unsurpassed window on the resurgence of a crisis of Indian secularism, particularly with regard to the place of Muslim citizens in the world's largest democracy.

Along with films about non-Islamist terrorism, such as *The Terrorist* (Santosh Sivan, 1998), I focus on *Roja* (1992), the first in a trilogy by the Tamil director Mani Ratnam—the other films in the trilogy being *Bombay* (1995) and *Dil Se* (From the Heart, 1998). I explore the figure of terrorism in *Mission Kashmir* (Vidhu Vinod Chopra, 2000) and *Fiza* (Khalid Mohamed, 2000), as well as *Maachis* (Matches, Gulzar 1996), *Border* (J. P. Dutta, 1997), *Sarfarosh* (Traitor, John Mathew Matthan, 1999), and *Fanaa* (Annihilated by Love, Kunal Kohli,

2006)—all of them referencing Islamist terrorism to some degree. I also discuss more recent films such as *A Wednesday* (Neeraj Pandey, 2008), concluding with a brief discussion of *My Name Is Khan* (Karan Johar, 2010).

Terrorism cinema desublimates the political trauma of Partition—now almost a sedimented fantasy in the Subcontinent's unconscious, making communalism and Hindu-Muslim conflict as well as cross-border terrorism inescapable features of the Indian national imaginary through absorptive and palimpsestic inscription of that geopolitical trauma. It is a "uniquely Western trait" of history writing, argues Michel de Certeau, to render a national narrative intelligible by separating past from present, suppressing or repressing certain developments that, having been forgotten, expunged, or excluded, return, like all repressed elements. The return of that repressed, of what had "*become* unthinkable," permits resubjectivization so that "a new identity . . . *become[s]* thinkable."[16] The writing of history is, however, always already a rewriting, and entails the remaking of an other as *Gegen-stand*. Unlike (religious) tradition, history writing "assumes a gap to exist between the silent opacity of the 'reality' that it seeks to express and the place where it produces its own speech."[17]

Freud and Marx seem to concur that the genuinely history-making "event" is traumatic, rupturing the status quo. The traumatic historical event can be understood only in retrospect: there is a structural analogy with *Nachträglichkeit,* in the psychoanalytic sense. *Nachträglichkeit* is a deferral through which Freud links physical wounding to psychical trauma. J. B. Pontalis clarifies that this is a "precise transition: the movement from the external to the internal."[18] In this psychoanalytic sense but also in other, more "commonsense" ways Hindi cinema belies the absolute opposition of the real and the phantasmic, exploiting the parallax between the two perspectives.

In Indian contexts there is a diametrically opposed procedure of writing history. The new displaces the old but in a "stratified stockpiling," Louis Dumont suggests; the "'process of coexistence and reabsorption' is, on the contrary, the 'cardinal fact' of Indian history."[19] This absorptive impulse manifests itself whenever India is threatened by external powers (Mughal invaders, British colonizers, the French and Portuguese)—or terrorists. This specter of terrorism must be fought in reality, but it is also engaged as phantasmatic—reabsorbed or abjected as traumatic. This is how terrorism cinema functions as "pathological public sphere."

Terrorism cinema interpellates the terrorist as both transnational and domestic threat, thus doubly "para-sitical": a Janus-faced fantasy figure, even if palimpsested onto a real terrorist. The terrorist imag(in)ed on-screen is demonized and romanticized as object of desire and a *totem,* a parasite invading the national body from outside or infecting it from within. To continue the medical metaphor, on occasion the emergence of the terrorist from within the nation's body is re-cognized as an autoimmune disorder and the "natural" recommendation is to extirpate it. Translating this into Realpolitik has dire consequences.

To change the metaphor, in a Foucauldian idiom Jasbir Puar and Amit Rai invoke a biopolitical discourse in which "the terrorist has become both a monster to be quarantined and an individual to be corrected." Muslims in the West have long been demonized, more intensely than ever since 9/11 in the United States. The resurgence of this image of monstrosity enables "a multiform power to reinvest and reinvent the fag, the citizen, the turban, and even the nation itself in the interests of another, more docile modernity."[20]

The distinction between "good" and "bad" Muslims is a fulcrum on which narratives of terrorism cinema turn.[21] It also "render[s] the Indian Muslim as 'the undecidable,' he whose loyalty to the motherland could not be counted upon and needed to be ritually re-affirmed," as Sumita Chakravarty writes.[22]

Many "psychological" interpretations of terrorism pathologize the terrorist as acting out of "self-destructive urges, fantasies of cleanliness, disturbed emotions combined with problems with authority and the Self, and inconsistent mothering." Such interpretations coproduce the rational citizen-subject of modernity with its antitheses—the other, the *abnormal,* to invoke Foucault's term, including the insane, the criminal, the mentally deficient, the "undesirable, the vagrant, the Gypsy, the savage, the Hottentot Venus."[23] Echoing Edward Said, I would add the equally vilified caricature of the "Oriental," coproduced as anachronistic civilizational other of the rational, modern subject of Western modernity, or in terrorism cinema as the Muslim terrorist—secret sharer and abjected symptomatic other of the ultrapatriotic (Hindu) hero. A subtle doubleness obtains in the representation of the terrorist as a *compatriot* and as charismatic, sometimes even seductive. The seductive frisson of terror-with-eroticism commodifies the terrorist *and* sutures the spectator. Terrorism cinema "prob[es] the wound and explor[es] the effects of the repetition of the trauma."[24]

The abjected Muslim terrorist emerges as an excrescence or "stain"—to adapt the Lacanian notion—to both scare and reassure audiences. Terrorism cinema takes as its monitory, pedagogical, and redemptive mission to re-enfold the Muslim (presumed malicious until proven worthy of belonging) into the national body by *redressing* him or her as good citizen, removing the stain, healing the body politic. Terrorism cinema tries to have it both ways: neutralize or redeem the terrorist by undermining his or her ideological "cause," and simultaneously prove the superiority and liberality of Hindu ideology. Why else would many films present the terrorist as protagonist?

The Four Dimensions of Terrorism Cinema

As a response to the crisis of secularism, Hindi terrorism cinema can be understood as having four dimensions. First, terrorism cinema emphasizes that religious, sectarian, and communal identity politics can be divisive. Yet, and second, it highlights the state's failure to protect its citizens and the national culture against foreign or in-country terrorists. A third aspect is that as a *pedagogical* reflex, these films also subtend the fantasy of the utopian secular.

A fourth dimension of terrorism cinema is its recourse to imbricated transnational discourses of cosmopolitanism, cross-border conflict resolution, or even the discourses of international human rights or transnational diplomacy—no matter how obliquely.

These four dimensions refract cinematic terrorism narratives into debates about secularism versus ethnonationalism.[25] They map onto a distinction employed during states of war or emergency, between a casus belli or proschema (officially articulated just cause for a state-level use of force, such as self-defense) and the real, unacknowledged, or disavowed reasons. Indeed, some terrorism films problematize the opposition as a *contradiction*. Staging or inadvertently betraying the blending of realism, fiction, and fantasy, terrorism cinema produces an *excessive* vector from within the diegesis, traversing the historically grounded narrative and revealing a subtext that runs counter to the overt narrative, analogous to the way in which a casus belli/proschema runs counter to the true, perhaps inchoate, or even fantasmatic "cause." A casus belli for military intervention goes only so far; the more effective justifications may rely on cultural or affective appeals, including nationalist or patriotic sentiment or even an unreasoned fear of terrorism, ginned up through instruments of propaganda. Popular cinema can lend itself to the expression of real if unofficial rationales for "counterrorist" measures. Terrorism cinema for instance may *condense* narratives of terrorism and thus participate in the pathological public sphere, dramatizing questions of "belonging" to the motherland. Yet terrorism cinema's constructions of the "proper" or desirable citizen-subject also bind patriot to terrorist compatriot in the very logic of desire. This odd couple of modular citizen (Ideal Ego, or *Ideal Ich*) and abjected "foil" enact a pedagogical object lesson—they grapple with the representational politics driving pathological public sphere debates about secularism.

There are alternative *cultural* initiatives against terrorism, including Google Ideas' liberal-integrationist project to combat violent terrorism, but cinema's importance as a site for the presentation of complicated representations of terrorism cannot be underestimated. Thus a fantasy subtext in which the Muslim citizen is demonized as a terrorist might run counter to the overt narrative of secular, multicultural tolerance or to the dominant narrative of national security. Such contradictory presentation may be a truer and more *critical* reflection of relations between majority (Hindu) and minority (especially Muslim) communities, between narratives of statecraft and narratives of the reclamation of "the other." Terrorism cinema undertakes the task of reforming or reincorporating the other as part of a pedagogical project, reaffirming the nation's integrity and virtue and subtending a fantasy of a counterfactually unfragmented nation. Prophylactic negation of negation redeems the terrorist by undermining and domesticating oppositional ideology, so that Indianness can reemerge as inclusive and triumphantly magnanimous: this becomes the goal of the utopian secular (*fantasy*).

Terrorism cinema's dominant discourse ventriloquizes the state's voice, producing the official legitimation rationalizations—the casus belli chiefly against its rivals (classically, Pakistan). But the alleged failures of the state, *and* the utopian secular, may also find expression. The casus belli is palimpsested onto *repressed* or politically unacknowledged motives, Realpolitik ("realism") onto melodrama ("fantasy"). For example, terrorist plots are invariably intricated with romantic subplots, potential lovers divided by ideology, as in *Dil Se,* or *Roja* and *Veer Zara* (2004).

The hero in terrorism cinema is typically hyperpatriotic, often Hindu—an Everyman embodiment of reactionary nationalism. Yet a counternarrative sometimes insinuates itself into the diegesis through fantasy sequences, rendering *the terrorist* as possibly even more sympathetic and attractive (even seductive) than the hero—destabilizing the sanctioned and often reactionary dominant discourse on terrorism. Such representations of the terrorist invite psychoanalytic interpretations.

Thus *Mission Kashmir* evokes the psychoanalytic nostrum that childhood trauma can lead to homicidal pathology—and that what is therefore called for is a therapeutic reclamation of the traumatized subject: a fortiori the terrorist. Altaaf, the antiheroic protagonist of this film, is traumatized, as a child, by the violent destruction of his home and family in Kashmir. He grows up under the tutelage of Afghan militant Hilal Kohistani and is recruited for a terrorist mission by Pakistani and Saudi financiers. The film's opening sequence features an explosion that destroys a boat on a Kashmiri lake, followed by scenes in which an aerial camera presents a bird's-eye view: through stitched—albeit disorientingly canted—POV shots, the unseen terrorist is introduced in a literalized geographic establishing shot. Rai interprets the opening metaphorically, as an image of a virus (the terrorist) invading the national body.[26] The visual representation of the geographical space of Kashmir complicates the POV: is the spectator to identify with it, with the terrorist himself? Is this the "gaze" of the Other, the view from "nowhere," and the more terrifying for that? From a psychoanalytic point of view, as the Introduction to this book suggested, the screen has the double function of phenomenologically separating the world screened from the viewer and absolving that viewer from being implicated in the morally ambiguous reality screened, simultaneously permitting, for instance, the *jouissance* of identifying with the terrorist in *Mission Kashmir.* This specific *jouissance*, permitting both pain and pleasure simultaneously, is a main element of the film, even its major "attraction."

In *Roja*, similarly, the issue of perspective (or point of view) is crucial. Visually, the spectator is prepared for perspectival shifts by the very opening sequence. Soldiers of the Indian army, led by Colonel Rayappa, pursue and capture the Kashmiri Muslim terrorist Wasim Khan after a brief twilight skirmish in a densely wooded copse. Director Ratnam takes great pains with the atmospheric chiaroscuro of the scene, which subsequently yields to its counterpart landscape, pointedly in a bucolic South Indian village, and to the perspective of the simultaneously traditional and modern Rishi Kumar—English-speaking technocrat and cryptologist, with a name meant to sound "North Indian." He is driving to Sundarapandianpuram, a village in Tamil Nadu, to meet his intended. Her innocent younger sister, Roja, who is herding goats, spies on Rishi, and he, catching a glimpse of her, is charmed: the perspective constantly shifts between them. But it is not until the bride-to-be begs Rishi not to formally ask for her—because she loves someone else her parents disapprove of—that Rishi gallantly relinquishes his claim and, having recognized Roja in the throng within the household, asks for her instead.

This shockingly unorthodox request flusters the families, but after conferring, they consent. Denied a full perspective on what has transpired, Roja is nonplussed, but being in no position to question either father or new husband, weds Rishi and goes with him to Madras. Only after a long pique does Roja hear from Rishi his noble reasons for not marrying her sister. Chastened, with a radically altered perspective, Roja resolves to be a worthy wife.

Roja's conversion inaugurates a major break in the diegesis, whose focus now shifts to consolidating Rishi's image as "ideal Indian": modern techno-yuppie and unreconstructed chauvinist. Transferred to a new army post in Kashmir, the couple have begun anew in a strange (non–South Indian) environment. Roja wanders off one morning, and the concerned Rishi goes looking for her, only to be abducted by secessionist Islamist terrorists as ransom for Wasim Khan.

Bereft of her husband just when she is beginning to love him, Roja becomes a crusader for his rescue. From a "village idiot" (as Rishi affectionately calls her), unlettered and unable to speak English, she is transformed, via a fascinating *Bildung,* into a petulant and winningly naive patriot, chiding senior army officers and politicians, cannily framing her appeal in the universalizing discourse of the rights of the "ordinary" but representative citizen of the modern secular nation-state.

Colonel Rayappa is caught in the middle. Against the inconveniently "secular" pleas of an Indian wife who simultaneously invokes the sedimented apparatus of Indian mythology organized around the feminine, he can only protest ineffectually that the cost—releasing Wasim—is too high. He delivers his protest *to Roja* in private quarters, and in civilian clothes, smoking a very unmilitary cigarette: it is a performative that crystallizes the contradictions between the state's casus belli and the unofficial ruses of governmentality, and the Gramscian (contingent) antinomies of state and civil society.[27]

Put differently, Rayappa's military perspective is in direct conflict with Roja's. Her appeal to a minister condenses the contradictions between military/political and sentimental perspectives (bracketing here the conflict between masculinist and feminine perspectives). Even though she addresses the minister *in Hindi,* he replies in an idiolectal English, "What is there in *my* hands?" Roja retorts that *everything* rests in his hands. The minister negotiates Wasim's release in exchange for her husband, going over army heads and reneging on the utopian secular state's non-negotiation policy, fundamental to the state's casus belli, to which Roja's appeal is a contrapuntal perspective. *Inscribed* in the state's perspectival dilemma are the contradictions of the global discourse of counterterrorism—the enunciative matrix for the fantasy of the utopian secular. That fantasy's counterpart is the fantasy of the national "Thing," which the state would presumably reject as inadequately secular. Yet the latter fantasy is the defining perspective of the Hindutvavadi extremist "devalourization of the state vis-à-vis the nation," a "spiritual notion" linked to the old idea of *Aryavarta* (land of the Aryas), as Jaffrelot reminds us.[28]

Roja's irksome demand to respond sentimentally rather than politically to the crisis of "terrorism" ironically throws into relief the equally reprehensible machinations and mythologically rationalized "demand" of the m(O)ther nation. The contradictory aspects of the archetypal "mother nation"—its sentimental aspect *and* its obscene demand—reveal that its true *jouissance* is premised on the citizen-subject's sacrifice.

Qua aesthetic narrative, no matter how "degraded," the film offers a "fantasy bribe," to adapt Fredric Jameson's formulation, of a state beneficent and strong—even bellicose. Such narratives are symptomatic of a legitimation crisis of secular and nonsecular (Hindu) visions of the nation-state. The film's jingoistic fantasy is calculated to appeal to mainstream nationalists: when the militants try to burn the Indian flag, Rishi throws his body on it, hands handcuffed, to extinguish the flames. Thus, core values of patriotism and family are embodied, albeit in specifically gendered ways, in both the principals.

As Roja campaigns for her husband, he wages an equally ideological war: to convince the terrorist leader Liaqat Khan of the error of *his perspective*, reincorporating him into the fold of India's dominant secular (nonsectarian, non-Muslim) ideology. Rishi follows a script as gendered and bourgeois-sentimentalist as Roja's—patriotic hero proselytizing on behalf of the magnanimously multicultural mother country. Liaqat is *deterrorized* ("domesticated") as much as *deterritorialized* (being not quite "at home" in Pakistan, nor in Kashmir, yet fighting for Kashmir's secession). Rishi's opportunity to salvage him comes when Liaqat's young brother is killed—Rishi exploits Liaqat's destitution and demoralization to redirect his misguided perspective.

The real fantasmatic—even seductive—power of terrorism cinema lies in the production of the *symbolic* terrorist. Žižek emphasizes the gap between (visible) symbolic authority and the spectral presence of the "conceptual Muslim terrorist," whose uncanny doppelgänger is the "fantasmatic conceptual Jew." That spectral presence's power for me derives from "something in me more than myself"—but it is *my fantasy,* my belief, my credulity nonetheless. By extension it is collective investment in a fantasmatic national identity ("Indianness") that *constitutes* the "terrorist threat," technically "imaginary." There is a real, serious threat of terrorism, of course. But the cinematically/ideologically crucial gap is precisely between real and "fantasmatic" terrorists.

The government decides to release Wasim Khan in exchange for Rishi. Not wanting to be used as a pawn in the release of a dangerous terrorist, Rishi, with help from Liaqat's sister (who nurtures a crush on him), escapes before Liaqat can "cash in" on the exchange. Rayappa, Roja, and other army officers get to the hostage exchange spot with Wasim, but Liaqat and Rishi are nowhere to be seen. Rishi, feared dead, is then actually running from Liaqat but is recaptured at gunpoint. Already ideologically undone (salvaged) by the persuasive Rishi, however, Liaqat lets Rishi go to Roja.

Spectatorial pleasure—seduction—inheres in seeing the patriotic hero victorious without compromising the state's position, but there is also ambiguity about the film's stance on secularism, its trafficking in seductive *empathy* with Liaqat's pain and loss. Dirks is thus right to note that "*Roja* is, in the end, about loss, fantasy, and failure"; the "pleasures of the film," such as they are, "are purchased with extraordinary ambivalence."[29]

Markers of an ambivalent nationalist assertion proliferate in the film. In key moments Rishi, the iconically Indian hero, expresses himself in *English,* as when he says "I love you" in English, as if indexing a new era in the habitus of Indian life, where even sanctioned patriotic affect was being reorganized—split—in a more cosmopolitan language of gesture and emotion. While, as Madhava Prasad points out, kissing and declarations of love were traditionally regarded as "Western," the increasingly prevalent English phrase "I love you" is simultaneously a mark of class privilege and a response to the imagined desire of the Other, the state, for which modernity remains an incomplete project.[30] "Modern" forms of courtship and romance must be underwritten by discursive forms "ready-to-hand" in foreign idioms, which are then indigenized by their ritual invocation, marking the induction of the Indian subject into modernity as an *actant* in global flows, to invoke Bruno Latour's category.[31] Even Rishi must channel his declaration of love via a foreign idiom to "own" his own desire. By the same token this is also a moment threatening disidentification with *local* idioms, a reidentification with a bifocal or cosmopolitan mode, enabled by the "dangerous supplement," English. The hero's hyperpatriotism is unwittingly undermined by his almost apologetic cosmopolitanism.

This embedding of a fissive cosmopolitanism into the narrative of nationalism produces an emergent form of contemporary South Asian subjectivity. I develop the point in Chapter 7 as a new "condensation" linked to the figure of the nonresident Indian (NRI). Rishi's hybrid cosmopolitanism (evidence of a bifocal nationalism) is also betrayed by his jeans, his cigarettes, the software he writes even in the bathroom, and the way he describes his own occupation in English to the villagers as though they would know what it meant to be a "cryptologist." Tejaswini Niranjana notices this "blended" cosmopolitanism but suggests that modernity and tradition converge in it "unproblematically in/for the authentically secular new middle class (Hindu) subject."[32] Although Niranjana maintains that this cosmopolitanism is not at variance with the "newly formulated traditionalism" attributed to villagers, but depends on it, the matter is somewhat more complex.

It is widely acknowledged in cultural critique, ranging from the visual anthropology of Christopher Pinney and the cultural anthropology of Ulf Hannerz to the postcolonial analysis of Bill Ashcroft and Graham Huggan, that such convergences are increasingly part of the experience, even if not "unproblematically," of people who are far from elite or even confidently middle-class.[33] Yet a critical cosmopolitanism must be attentive to "race," gender, and class dimensions, as also to the dimension of desire and fantasy, of spectatorial pleasure. Such attention might productively situate *Roja* alongside a range of other important examples of terrorism cinema.

In *Dil Se,* for instance, the protagonist, Amar, a reporter for All India Radio (could there be a more apt echo of Benedict Anderson's thesis about how the nation is imagined?), is interviewing Kashmiris about whether Independence has been good for them. All his respondents, including the leader of a group of secessionist "freedom fighters," say no. Though engaged to a "proper" and good Hindu girl in Delhi, Amar falls in love with "Meghna," a female terrorist from the northern territories. The first duet they sing, while running from armed soldiers, is filmed against the setting of explosions. Amar is driven out by the locals, winding up in Ladakh, where he witnesses a man being shot by military police. He pursues the soldiers, asking whether this was not a violation of the man's civil rights. He finds Meghna again, and the rest of the film becomes almost exclusively a portrayal of a failed bid to salvage the terrorist through love: what is interesting is *how* it fails. Meghna is humanized, even eroticized. She is also torn between her love and her ideology. Ultimately and surprisingly, ideology wins, and in the dramatic conclusion, Meghna moves beyond any redemption, suggesting even in the final catastrophe the importance of terrorism cinema's reclamation project.

Dil Se is groundbreaking on several counts: formally for camera work by Santosh Sivan, who would go on to make *The Terrorist* (2000); for autoreferentiality in its invention of a poetic visual language; and conceptually for its complex figuration of the terrorist as condensing contrary poles of feeling—anxiety and seduction. Meghna's ideological motivations are reprehensible. Yet we may also find plausible, even persuasive, Meghna's complaint that the state oppresses minorities such as those she represents. What is more, this terrorist is also seductive. As Laura Mulvey suggests, the act of looking is as fraught with gender dynamics as the act of representation. In the case of *Dil Se, Roja,* and also *Mission Kashmir,* or *Fanaa,* normative Indianness is represented via the abjection of an "other"—specifically a (Muslim) threat to the (Hindu) nation, but the abjection is routed through a multivalent *gendered* fantasy that has this sensationalist, seductive, as well as pedagogical and redemptive, agenda simultaneously encoded within it.

Seduction invokes the contradictory logic of *desire:* the point of terrorism cinema's pedagogical drive is precisely to acknowledge that dissent from the national narrative might be attractive only to contain or quash that desire. Thus, in *Fanaa*, the Kashmiri Muslim separatist (and "parasitic" internal terrorist) Rehan—a humanized protagonist attractive enough for the Indian female lead to have fallen in love with him—is killed by his beloved, Zooni, a (good) Kashmiri Muslim. He dies at peace in her arms, but this union can be only a fantasy "heaven." Zooni mourns him with ambiguous words that are nonetheless a key to the real pedagogical message of the film: "It is easy to choose between right and wrong. But to choose the greater of two goods or the lesser of two evils . . . those are the choices of our life." This "choice" seems to invite judgment but, especially arriving late in the film, actually obscures the important issues it raises.

Such films are driven not only by an epistemological question, "What is a modern secular socialist state?" but also by a pedagogical imperative, how to teach citizens to be proper Indians. *Dil Se*'s terrorist is *simultaneously* seductive and indefensible. Opposition to the terrorist's poisonous sectarian (read "religious") ideology must come from both cosmopolitan ("secular universalist") *and* Hindu self-assertion, and this is the dual task the film undertakes. Meghna solicits and complicates intellectual condemnation, emotional sympathy, *and* erotic investment. She is also an attractive target for terrorism *cinema*'s reclamation narrative. The film projects onto this terrorist a problematized, complex *fantasy* construction.

Thus Chakravarty can insist that "it is the seductiveness of the stranger (not love of the national mainstream) that propels these films' narrative energies and photographic powers."[34] Noting the film's ambivalence, Chakravarty remarks that song-and-dance sequences "powerfully evoke the pleasures of an essentially fluid, joyful and globalised world in which viewers are invited to participate, while the world to which the terrorists belong is essentially closed and claustrophobic, rule-governed and predictable. Terrorism or separatism in these films is essentially atavistic, out of sync with a multiethnic, multicultural ethos shaped by transnational [and we might add secularist] influences."[35]

Fantasy and reality are, not surprisingly, interlinked in a complex relay in a film condensing such ambivalence. The mediating term is visual pleasure: in *Dil Se* as well as in *Bombay* or *The Terrorist,* there is an undeniable visual spectacle associated with the terrorist: they are attractive men or women (as in *Dil Se* or *Fiza*); they move in visually stunning physical settings such as beautiful Kashmir (as in *Roja*) or the lush forests of Sri Lanka (*The Terrorist*), and they interact with the good protagonist in gorgeous (often "fantasy") settings. It is convenient that, as Ella Shohat and Robert Stam put it in a passage quoted by Chakravarty, cinema's "'polymorphous projection-identifications' (Edgar Morin) on a certain level transcend the determinations of local morality, social milieu, and ethnic affiliation. Spectatorship can become a liminal space of dreams and self-fashioning. Through its psychic chameleonism, ordinary social positions, as in carnival, are temporarily bracketed."[36]

The ambivalence also indexes the fragility of the fantasy of a homogenous, integral nation. For the state to confront this would require that it consider the possibility raised by Geoffrey Galt Harpham, in response to the defining terror of our time—9/11—with reference to the United States: the chance that "the true and most terrifying terror is not just the possibility that we are finally responsible for the murderous hatred others feel for us but rather our doubts about who or what is responsible for terrorism, our indecision about whether it has a purpose or a cause, our uncertainty whether it makes sense."[37] Hindi terrorism cinema seems to have had such a moment of historical panic through the 1980s and 1990s, and terrorism cinema registers a complex response to the challenge to the concept of India as a secular nation-state.

Santosh Sivan's *The Terrorist* (1999) also offers a contrapuntal, if sympathetic, portrait of a South Asian terrorist. The film could almost be a sequel to *Dil Se*, if we were to conceptualize a narrative of genesis. For if *Dil Se* is an apologia by a Tamil filmmaker for the 1991 assassination of Rajiv Gandhi, as Dirks has suggested, *The Terrorist* is a further step in the revisionist narrative: it attempts something like a *fantasmatic* undoing of the actual assassination—making the actual no more than spectral, a horrible nightmare that the aesthetic and humanitarian imaginative act of cinematic fantasy can dispel. Indeed, Rajiv Gandhi's assassination was acknowledged by Sivan as the inspiration for the film.

For one thing, Malli the terrorist ("Dhanu," the real suicide bomber who killed Gandhi, is the model for Malli in Sivan's film) is female, played by Ayesha Dharker as an innocent yet sultry young woman, as "naturally" beautiful as the surroundings filmed in lush color. Terrorism films are remarkable, Mike Dillon argues, because they "complicate morally preferable (and politically expedient) categories of good and evil that conventionally accompany public discussions of terror. They also raise questions pertaining to how local representations of political violence are reconciled with discourses of global terrorism being determined on western, particularly American, terms."[38]

The nineteen-year-old Malli is recruited to be a suicide bomber from the ranks of the Liberation Tigers of Tamil Eelam (LTTE), militants fighting for a Tamil homeland in Sri Lanka, and placed in the care of a quirky but kind middle-aged man with a comatose wife. Malli's designated target in the film is a visiting politician representing the majoritarian Indian government. Her bedroom is separated from the wife's by only a wall with a trap window, through which she can look in on the wife. The comatose woman lies still but with eyes wide open. As an analog for the camera made all-seeing, the old woman seems perennially and preternaturally alert as she gazes straight into Malli's room and as it were into her very soul. The hyperreal quality of this gaze redirects our own to Malli's psychic reality—indeed to "the Real"—that is arguably the true subject of the film, for it traces the trajectory of Malli's emotional regeneration, or reclamation, from would-be terrorist into will-be mother. Malli develops a psychic connection with the old woman: for this connection transcends "realism."

Malli is assigned two male mentors, one an assistant who prepares the bomb belt and trains her on how to press the red trigger, and another who prepares her mentally. This gendered arrangement works well, with the steely young woman represented as a good student receiving gentle but firm male guidance. Until, that is, a phantasmagoric flashback interrupts this placid and almost domestic idyll on-screen, recounting Malli's brief sexual encounter with a dying LTTE fighter. Malli discovers that she is pregnant, and so her reality—like her loyalty—is split between the bomb and the womb. Which will she choose? Can she be reclaimed for conventional womanhood, for the mainstream values of a national and domesticated (in both senses) future? This provides the real drama in the film, again coherent with the reclamation project that I have argued is definitive of terrorism cinema. Here, however, the reclamation involves soliciting spectatorial sympathy in a discourse simultaneously of liberalism and normative femininity that reinscribes the ethical borders around an idealized woman—preserved as capable of the range of preassigned feminine virtues from seduction to motherhood. At the same time, there is an ethicopolitical abjection of the traumatic violence she also embodies: that is the horror, but the risk is that the terror itself can be seductive, or rather that she is seductive as a literal femme fatale, because she literally embodies terror. The conclusion of the film is calculatedly ambiguous, and stops at the point where the bomb ought to have been triggered.

Maachis (Matches, Gulzar, 1996) is another of the rare films that, like *The Terrorist,* sympathetically puts us in touch with the psychic reality of the terrorist, often resorting to forms of fantasy by the rerouting of the spectatorial gaze through the terrorist's point of view. Historicized by reference to the spectacular rise in the secessionist Sikh insurgency of the Khalistan movement in the 1980s, *Maachis* references the assassination of not Rajiv Gandhi but his mother, Prime Minister Indira Gandhi, by two of her Sikh bodyguards. The assassination occurred in the aftermath of the state-sponsored 1984 Operation Blue Star raid, which damaged the Akal Takht complex of the Golden Temple in Amritsar, killing many Sikhs. *Maachis* refracts collective anger and frustration against the state in the story of the sympathetic (seductive?) young Sikh protagonist, Kirpal. He and his fiancée are betrayed by the police, who had earlier falsely accused his best friend of harboring an enemy of the state, and brutalized him in custody. Kirpal joins a terrorist faction led by the ironically named Sanatan. Some spectators may hear "Satan" in the name, but in Hinduism the "Sanatan Dharma" is the Eternal Religion. The suggestion is that the reality of the Hindu state is at war with its fantasy self-image. As in other terrorism films, the failures of the secular state are highlighted, though ultimately the nation is reaffirmed pro forma. The terrorist and his fiancée die in the end, having become expendable after performing their function of raising doubts about the fantasy of a secular state: they can now be sacrificed at the altar of mainstream expectations. If the terrorist cannot be reclaimed, there is no room for him or her within the national family. The state must remain inviolate, sovereign, beyond reproach—a sentiment very different from that pervading the Angry Man and Avenging Woman films discussed in Chapter 3. Thus *Maachis* too serves the cinematic logic of Žižek's "determinate negation." Its pedagogical—reactionary or market-driven—goal is to redress the nation-state, to remind it of its "Sanatan Dharma" and thereby heal the rift between the ideological fantasy of a virtuous secular nation and the fissured reality, in which the nation-state is insecure, made anxious by both external pressures (globalization, international terror) and internally destabilizing forces (embarrassing economic problems, communalism).

Other films, such as *Sarfarosh* (Traitor, John Mathew Matthan, 1999) and *Fiza* (Khalid Mohamed, 2000) more unambiguously pathologize the terrorist. Echoing some of the insights offered by studies in counterterrorism mentioned above, they highlight the distortions of the psychological or psychic makeup of terrorists, and so present the terrorist figure as somewhat less sympathetic than in *The Terrorist* or *Maachis*. *Sarfarosh* represents terrorism cinema's frequently revisionist impulse—the effort to fashion fantasy reconstructions of the secular republic, the better, evidently, to accommodate the increasingly influential doctrinaire Hindu nationalism (Hindutva). Even the now-eclipsed "parallel cinema" was not immune to this revisionist impulse. For economic as well as Zeitgeist reasons, filmmakers of that parallel cinema, such as Mrinal Sen, Mani Kaul, Kumar Shahani, Saeed Mirza, and M. S. Sathyu, have retreated from the engaged "A" cinema for which they were famous, to purveying narratives that reconstruct in a popular idiom the long-standing crisis in India over the status of Muslims after Partition.

Sarfarosh too exhibits a pedagogical impulse to reframe secularism and simultaneously redeem the terrorist. The protagonist, Ajay Singh Rathod, poses the question of Muslim patriotic fealty to India. Having risen through the ranks to become assistant commissioner of police (ACP) in Bombay, he was a student of tactics and strategy under Inspector Salim, a Muslim. Though intense, imposing, and competent, Salim flubs an attempt to apprehend a criminal, a costly failure. Ostensibly on that account, he is removed from serving on a more important case with ACP Ajay involving a Pakistani agent who is also a ghazal singer, Gulfam Hassan, a *mohajir* leading a gun-running operation to foment an internal guerrilla insurgency, in particular by the Adivasi (tribals). Salim understands the difference between official reasons (casus belli) and the real if unavowed reasons for his demotion: as a Muslim his loyalties are suspect until proven otherwise. The film's overt ideological and pedagogical mandate is to legitimize Salim's apologia for Indian Muslims, a determinate negation of the suspicion that Muslims constitute a "fifth column" in the political arena.

Salim's model minority citizenship is contrasted with the treachery (*gaddari*) of Gulfam, introduced as an "artiste" who belongs "as much to Pakistan as to India." He self-consciously represents himself as a belated repository of a pre-Partition India, in which Muslim and Hindu traditions were still undivided. His nostalgia and ressentiment are refracted into the unhealable wound (Gulfam's terms are *ghaon* and *zakhm*) of Partition (*Batwara*). Gulfam is a man of the past, a ghost living in a timeless fantasy of the utopian secular. His spectrality is underscored by the repeated theme of his *mohajir* status: a Muslim migrant from India to Pakistan, a nowhere man. What differentiates the "good" Muslim Salim from the "bad" Muslim Gulfam is belongingness, sovereign citizenship. Films such as *Bombay* (also Mani Ratnam, 1995) similarly strive to remind the public that Indian Muslims too are equal citizens.

Salim's ostensible subaltern narrative displaces a politics of subalternity.[39] Yet the film also seeks to rescue from the overt nationalist narrative the potential of another fantasy narrative: Gulfam's utopian fantasy of reintegration of Muslim and Hindu traditions. Ironically this fantasy is potentially politically fissive. Gulfam embodies a ressentiment founded on a persistent if counterfactual fantasy shared by Indians like Seema, Ajay's love interest—and Ajay himself. This is a dream of healing the wound of Partition and resuscitating a hybrid national cultural tradition, ideally the glorious past represented by Akbar's India. This sentimental, utopian fantasy of a bifocal culture represented by Gulfam's aesthete's manner (*adab*) is the basis of his "friendship" and intense bond with Ajay, for the ACP is equally cultivated, a connoisseur of the ghazal and of *shairi,* an associated form of poetry, predicated on the poet/performer's intimate bond with an active, cultivated, and appreciative audience. Ajay shares Gulfam's cultivation in and his desire to preserve the interblended culture denied by the political reality of the Partition: but it is also—practically—a nostalgic fantasy. The pedagogical project of reclamation of the Muslim in this film is thus relayed through a sublation of the hybrid glories of pre-Partition India, and thus implicitly a contradiction of its overt chauvinism.

A much more recent film driven by the same pedagogical impulse is *A Wednesday.*[40] Following in the wake of a terrorist train bombing in Mumbai in 2005, the film features an avowedly "stupid common man" who feels compelled to take the law into his own hands, inhabiting the classic perverse scenario, as if, in Kant's terms, seeking to make a universal law of his own action. Frustrated by the state's ineffectual power, indeed its unexercised potential for justified violence against terrorists who threaten the state, this patriotic protagonist announces, "We are resilient by force, not by choice," as he plants bombs across Bombay, pointing up and protesting the Indian state's impotence, even its outright failure, to guarantee the safety (human security) of that ordinary citizen—giving new meaning to "counterterrorism." He presents himself to Police Commissioner Prakash Rathod as the Everyman who fears boarding a train or a bus because of terrorism. He describes himself in English as "a stupid common man," in absolute etymological fidelity to the classical political category of "*idiotes*" (ἰδιώτης), which in the original Greek signifies a person without any particular professional ability or landownership (to be distinguished from the later Latin, which gives us the everyday notion of a stupid person)—in other words, an individual left undefended and abandoned by the state, in the inverted nostrum noted by Lauren Berlant: that the political is the personal.[41] This rendering private/making psychical of the political can be read as the classic Lacanian relationship between the divided subject and the Other: the divided subject constantly asks himself or herself, "What does the Other want from me?" "What is the Other enjoying, through me, without my knowing it?" Thus the divided subject is "hysterical," or even in extreme cases in the grip of a "paranoid" fantasy. Žižek underscores the "inherent" link between paranoia and fantasy.[42]

So while the "stupid common man" negotiates with the commissioner, the commissioner himself turns to someone of higher authority, to whom the "common man" does not have access. Yet implicitly the common man's appeal is directed to this Other of the Other, "behind" the police and other state apparatuses. His appeal may represent a paranoid fantasy, but that doesn't mean he doesn't have a point. Seeing the whole "system" as corrupt, he seeks to go beyond the "front" men, and they oblige, suggesting that they are following orders from "higher up." But the common man here also represents a fantasy of real agency, subjectification, to resist the kind of governmentality that threatens desubjectification in fact. "In the eyes of authority," as Giorgio Agamben observes, "nothing looks more like a terrorist than the ordinary man."[43]

A key feature of *A Wednesday* is its direct and explicit challenge to the state as having failed to exercise its monopoly on state force to protect the "common man" or citizen and simultaneously to assert its sovereignty. As if to illustrate the arguments of Drèze and Sen, and the much earlier argument of Polanyi mentioned above in this chapter, the film in its populist fashion seems to exhort the state to intervene in the interest of both state/military security *and* human security (the interest of the common man): the social is embedded in the state. This failure has in turn compelled the representative, exemplary, patriotic common man to resort to force in the place of the state. This is analogous to what Jaffrelot has identified as a characteristic "Hindu" strategy of simultaneous "stigmatization and emulation": that is, "imitating those who [are] perceived as posing a threat . . . in order to resist them more efficiently."[44] The forceful protection of the nation-state's sovereignty is taken up by the citizen by "force, not by choice." This rationalization has a meretricious plausibility. It stirs nationalist sentiment while emphasizing the nation-state's failure to produce or to declare a casus belli to use just violence to quell unjust violence.

A Wednesday employs a canny turn on the meme of "stupidity": it tropes stupidity as the token of ordinariness and therefore of authenticity. As Nietzsche said, stupidity is on the side of life. In the case of the ordinary man-turned-terrorist, stupidity is certainly a plea on the side of life made necessary by a threat against it. Thus the film takes a profoundly self-contradictory stance, playing on a dangerous "logic" according to which (state) failure to deploy just violence requires the ("idiotic" and perverse) unleashing of lawless but ultimately law-preserving violence on the part of the ordinary citizen. A Derridean deconstruction seems operative here, a "reversal or complement of the Kantian transcendental formula of the 'conditions of possibility,'" in Žižek's phrase. "The 'infrastructural' condition of possibility of an entity is at the same time the condition of its impossibility, its identity-with-itself is possible only against the background of its self-relationship—of a minimal self-differentiation and self-deferment which open a gap forever hindering its full identity-with-itself." And the "same paradox is inscribed in the very heart of Hegelian dialectics. The key 'reversal' of the dialectical process takes place when we recognize in what at first appeared as a 'condition of impossibility' . . . the *condition of the possibility* of our ontological consistency." The common man dissident of *A Wednesday* conforms to this "logic," for the "real 'object of desire' of such a 'dissident' is not to defeat the adversary [here the secular state], even less to re-establish a democratic order in which the adversary would be forced to accept the role of a rival for power on an equal footing with others, but *one's own defeat*."[45] This logic not only "proves the dissident right" but also preserves his real desire, to strengthen the very state he is seeking to upbraid. For its strength is his strength, his identity.

In reality several groups within the national body have registered their complaints against the state for its failure to protect all of its citizens. One recent example comes from none other than the Naxalites—Indian Maoists—some of whom carried out an ambush against the security forces in Chhattisgarh on April 6, 2010, killing seventy-six soldiers. Another real example of the frustration of ordinary citizen-subjects is the eruption of mass anticorruption protests in September 2011 in reaction to several scandals involving prominent politicians and businessmen, such as the selling of noncompetitively priced cell-phone spectrum to favored companies and especially the corruption in government contracts to construction companies (primarily cement producers) for the 2010 Commonwealth Games in New Delhi. Out of this turmoil has emerged the figure of Anna Hazare, antigraft crusader who hews to ideas that uncannily mimic the *Shariat*, including public flogging of alcoholics and drug addicts and the cutting off of hands as punishment for corruption. Hazare went on a well-publicized hunger strike, mobilizing huge numbers of supporters who demanded that the government appoint an oversight committee to contain corruption in its ranks. This Hazare-led appeal to the state to reform its house and protect the citizenry from the most corrupt within their ranks failed officially, but Hazare himself gained enormous popularity. This flawed protagonist is an analog of the character that we see portrayed in *A Wednesday*.

The protagonist of *A Wednesday* acts alone to articulate frustration against an impotent nation-state in the name of the universal citizen. This "in the name of" inverts the figure of the Muslim as terrorist, recuperating the minority citizen-subject as the representative representation of the majority citizen-subject. The actor "representing" the Indian citizen—Naseeruddin Shah—is himself a Muslim with a long and distinguished career in both Indian theater and films, known for his intense roles in art films and parallel cinema but also in commercial films.

My focus here is on the spate of terrorism cinema that raised the specter of the (particularly Muslim) terrorist preceding the September 11, 2001, watershed. Films following that crisis have slightly different priorities, as I show below. Shah's righteous angry citizen in *A Wednesday* seems the more remarkable if we contrast this figure with a character involved in the more recent controversy featuring another Muslim "Shah"—Shah Rukh Khan ("SRK")—in the Hinglish film *My Name Is Khan* (2009). In that film SRK, one of India's best-known actors, plays an autistic young man (Khan) who wants to travel to America after 9/11 to tell the president that he is "not a terrorist." The "autism" of SRK's character, possibly a conceit borrowed from *Rain Man* (Barry Levinson, 1988), functionally parallels the "stupidity" of Naseeruddin Shah's character, and both are intended

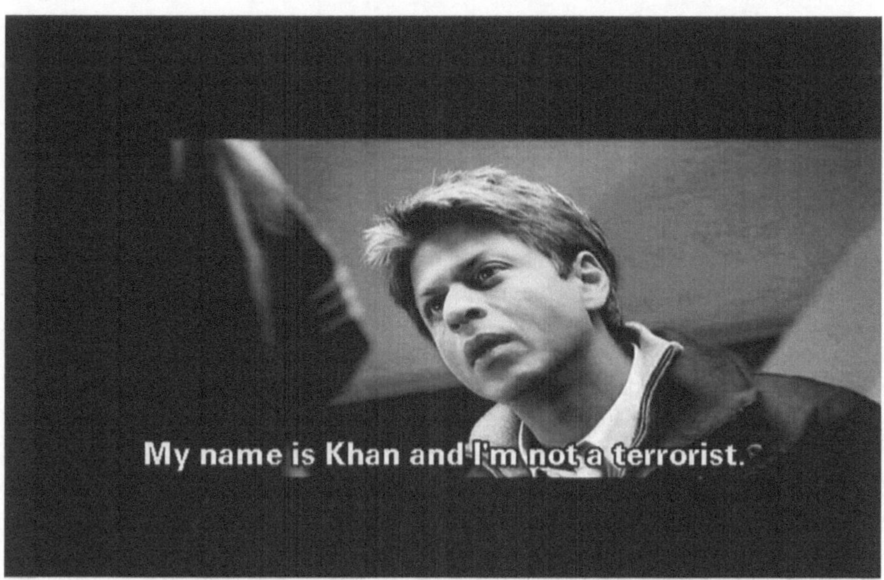

Figure 4.1. Rizvan Khan (Shah Rukh Khan) telling customs officials he is not a terrorist in *My Name Is Khan* (dir. Karan Johar, 2010).

to elicit a visceral or emotional sympathy and thereby insulate the characters in question from criticism, even as they criticize the failures of the state or substate bodies. But this strategy of "insulation" appears to have been deployed more effectively by the actor with the "common" touch in *A Wednesday.* The film was interpreted as an attempt to rehumanize Muslims (often demonized in the Indian public sphere), but it divided the public along the "secularists"-versus-"antisecularists" fault line, with many on the right expressing displeasure with the cultural icon and many on the left defending him as promoting universal secular humanist values embodied in a minority citizen doubly marginalized as autistic and as Muslim (Figure 4.1).

Despite his "handicaps"—including his unavoidably Muslim identity—Khan is motivatedly presented as an exemplary and sympathetic human being. This is a "Hinglish" film, intended to appeal to a transnational viewership. We see Khan being searched by customs officials and then declaring in English that he has a message for the president of the United States (a black man in the film). We see Khan proposing marriage to Mandira—in English. We see him selling cosmetics to women, in English again, as if to demonstrate his assimilability into consumerist American society. We see him win a minor competition on behalf of Mandira's son from an earlier marriage, and again he demonstrates his proficiency and general knowledge in English, possibly a way of flattering the self-image of diasporic Indians. We also see Mandira's son dying—and again Mandira can only express her trauma and anguish in English. A late scene presents a multicultural idyll, with the protagonist singing "We Shall Overcome

Someday" in Hindi to accompany Wilhemina's black church singing in English. In all of the scenes mentioned, the English language becomes a crucial medium to express ideas—as if there were no linguistic correlative in the native tongue. This is significant even for popular Hindi films, where English is casually interspersed into especially middle-class speech.

Shah Rukh evidently relishes playing a character whose name is clearly Muslim, but the blending of cinematic fantasy and reality mirrors SRK's real-life political travails. He stirred an even warmer controversy recently by criticizing the authorities for failing to place Pakistani cricketers on the Indian Premier League. The Shiv Sena, the Hindu right's militant wing, protested SRK's remarks vehemently, seeing them as confirming his pro-Muslim (and therefore treasonous) stance. At first SRK was defiant, most notably in a BBC interview. Ultimately, however, he capitulated under pressure. Ideological battles, even those fought in the cultural sphere, are won or lost on emotional terrain.

This film also invokes the utopian secular, identified above as characteristic of terrorism cinema. But the jingoistic film *Gadar: Ek Prem Katha* (Revolution: A Love Story, Anil Sharma, 2001) insists that the Muslim is acceptable only as abjected from the nation-state. Still, this film generates a self-consoling surface narrative that glosses over difficult issues of state-sponsored victimization of minorities and blithely promulgates a vision of India in which Muslims and other minorities can be embraced only if their difference is eliminated. Other films are less intolerant of difference, such as *Chakravyuh* (Squared Planning, Prakash Jha, 2012), which poses the question of the conflict between state "sovereignty" and "human rights" (as always, the key words are uttered in English, as if to underscore the film's "glocality"). The Indian army attacks a camp of communist Adivasis training against the government that marginalizes and fails to protect them. The motif of failure is routed, as in *A Wednesday*, through a pedagogical imperative. For if a state is unable to finesse or suppress its foundation in violence against the marginalized in favor of capitalist/ruling-class interests, it is also confronted, as Chandan Reddy argues, with a legitimation crisis.[46] Undergirding the cultural production of legitimation narratives there is a pedagogical drive to "reform" the other as well as to "subject" the citizen to the state-endorsed doxa.

Conclusion: States of/in Crisis

The state in crisis is a "lacking" state, analogous to the psychoanalytic (Lacanian) notion of the lacking Other, and it makes a *demand* on the citizen-subject; the citizen-subject seeks, to the extent that he or she is "hystericized," to respond to the demand he/she imagines or fantasizes the state making. Terrorism cinema, I have argued, is a condensation of this crisis in which the political ("real") and the psychic ("fantasmatic") converge. In *Roja* we can see that both protagonists, Rishi and Roja, respond hysterically, histrionically, to the imagined/fantasized demand of the Other/the nation-state: Rishi by saving a burning Indian flag by throwing his body on it, Roja by defending her husband as though it were sacred duty. The exemplary Indian citizen-subject seeks hysterically to replenish the lack in the Other/nation-state, in what Lacan describes as a "perverse" logic. Thus, according to the above-mentioned third aspect of terrorism cinema, these films not only project a pedagogical fantasy of the utopian secular as a better response to the perceived threat to Indianness than that of the failed state but also reinscribe the perverse scenario.

To the extent that this "pedagogical" albeit perverse logic of defining violence against the other is effected through the medium of cinema, it visits epistemic violence on the other. Terrorism cinema strips away identity anchors for minority identities: religion, ritual, custom, confession. In their place the other is required to perform a transparently "national" identity that is nevertheless normatively marked as Hindu. But this is real accession not to a new subjectivity but only to a ghostly simulacrum. The Hindu subject in turn must permit being captured (we might say captated—"head-counted" as a citizen) but also metaphorically decapitated in the pedagogy of subjectification *as a subject for the utopian secular.* For the citizen-subject must constantly perform an officially approved Indianness; there is no room, no opportunity, for true, autochthonous subjectification. The process is necessarily procrustean. The subject is hollowed out to fit the mold approved by the nation-state. In brief, to grasp the force of epistemic violence is to understand it as requiring the desubjectification of the subject followed by sanctioned resubjectification. This is consistent with Agamben's theorization of the workings of the apparatus under the regimes of capitalism: "What we are now witnessing is that processes of subjectification and processes of desubjectification seem to become reciprocally indifferent, and so they do not give rise to the new subject, except in larval or, as it were, in spectral form. In the nontruth of the subject, its own truth is no longer at stake." For Agamben, an apparatus is "literally anything that has in some way the capacity to capture, orient, determine, intercept, model, control, or secure the gestures, behaviors, opinions, or discourses of living beings."[47] Through and in the apparatus, as Michel Foucault had earlier argued, governance can be effected by disciplining biopower, by producing subjects who are simultaneously desubjectified. The true challenge of agency is to resist such *desubjectification,* to move beyond the consoling fantasies offered both by religion and by political fantasies toward *subjectivization.* That would be the inauguration of politics but also the end of the need for politics. For now, the utopian secular remains a fantasy of a society whose time is not yet. In this chapter I have sought, however, to delineate Hindi cinema's rethinking of the contours of actually existing "secularism" in a cluster of films about terrorism, in the conviction that before we can imagine the utopian secular, we must undergo such a rethinking and reevaluation of the version we have.

5

Patriot Games, Unpatriotic Fantasies

Lagaan: Once upon a Time in India (Ashutosh Gowariker, 2001) was submitted as India's 2002 entry in the Best Foreign Language Film category of the Oscars. It is a film extraordinarily rich in self-contradictory impulses, condensed in a popular idiom and concretized into the figure of a game of cricket but also reflecting social contradictions emergent between the 1990s and the 2000s: on the one hand the liberalization of the economy starting in 1991, representing the new insertion of India into the global economy, and on the other the resurgence of (hyper)nationalism. The film can be read as an example of *glocalization,* in George Ritzer's terms.[1] The film performs a revisionist patriotism, in ironic illustration of Eric Hobsbawm and Terence Ranger's argument that national traditions present themselves as reaching back to a time immemorial. In fact, traditions are *invented* through a "set of practices, of a ritual or symbolic nature which seek to inculcate certain values and norms of behavior by repetition which automatically implies continuity with a suitable historic past."[2]

In its retrospective reconstruction *Lagaan* foregrounds the constructedness—"inventedness"—of the national. The nation appears in its "Real," traumatic form, as an abreactive fantasy, enacting the splits and contradictions that produced the idealized nation out of the horror of Partition in 1947. The *cinematically imagined* nation-that-never-was reveals an anxiety about the viability of its founding principle, inclusive secular socialism, and simultaneously confirms Jacqueline Rose's observation that fantasy "plays a central, constitutive role in the modern world of states and nations."[3]

Uma Narayan reminds us that "Indian culture" was itself invented, symptomatically produced by the "historical unification of an assortment of political territories into 'British India,' a term that enabled the nationalist challenge to colonialism to emerge as 'Indian.'"[4] This chapter highlights the mutual contamination between the realist narration of the nation and fantasies enlisted in its support. Such fantasies reveal their fantasmatic grain over time, ultimately subverting their own foundational mythologies as ideological. *Lagaan* presents itself, for instance, as an *alternative*, even fairy tale "history"—after all, the subtitle of the film is "Once upon a Time in India"—but in doing so condenses contradictions between symbolic patriotic assertion and unpatriotic fantasy.

A bifocal postcolonialist critique can highlight such contradictions, between the affirmation of a patriotic credo and excessive or *fissive* desires, between reality and fantasy (*Lagaan*'s faux history—no cricket match ever unfolded quite so satisfyingly or conclusively under the British Raj, and imperial rule was not so easily subverted). A bifocal perspective precipitates the unmaking of the national narrative even as it reveals its "making," or *inventio*. It also engages with the specific romance (fantasy) offered to the spectator, revealing insights about central issues in contemporary Indian society. The film's fulcrum is a revisionist fantasy of a nation that *could have* challenged *British colonialist* fantasies of cultural superiority and of the inferiority of Indians. It is, simultaneously, a fantasy of a reconstructed nation not riven by communalist and caste divisions as contemporary India is in fact. This counterfactual fantasy, read contrapuntally, serves as commentary more about *the present* than the past. It is also a fantasy characterized by disavowal: in Judith Butler's phrase "an identification that one fears to make only because one has already made it."[5] Fantasy *interrupts* the consolidation of national(ist) narratives inherited from the past, simultaneously producing new "*objets a*," unruly desires, competing inscriptions of subjectivity, in the present. The key psychoanalytic insight is that these fantasies are subconscious, perhaps disavowed by the desiring subject. Besides, no sooner does the subject grasp the desired object than it slips away and is replaced by some other object, in a sliding chain. As Slavoj Žižek puts it, the object cause of desire is an ineradicable stain or defect in the fabric of reality. Cinematic production of conflicting desires—patriotic impulses *and* unpatriotic fantasies—is a challenge not only for cosmopolitan elite narratives in diasporic contexts but also for less mobile or "flexible" subjects.[6] *Lagaan*'s protagonist's obscure object cause of desire, I demonstrate, is disavowed in the realist diegesis even though it irrupts within "fantasy sequences."

In this Janus-faced tour de force the action returns to the colonial nineteenth century. Why go back in time? The film is organized by a parallax view, palimpsesting a social *neorealism* (emphasizing a rural life in the past made amenable to a revisionist nationalism) *and* a *fantasmic*, counterfactual present. This parallax temporality constitutes a disavowal of what Fredric Jameson terms the "time of the preterite, of events completed, over and done with, events that have entered history once and for all" through the presentation of an "inauthentic and reified temporality." This negation denies realities of actual events happening now—the trauma of communal violence, caste discrimination, and painful social transformations under globalization.[7]

And why cricket? C.L.R. James wrote that an essential "Englishness" is embodied in the game and that it is constitutively English.[8] For "underdeveloped countries" it is necessary "to go back centuries to rebuild [a national essence]."[9] I argue that in presenting a fantasy "anterior future," *Lagaan* produces a symptomatic disavowal of the actual troubled politics of caste and communalism that have continued to embarrass the secular socialist statist mythology since its inception "at the stroke of midnight" in 1947. Today internal conflicts in developing nations, not least in the Subcontinent, are "far more significant" than international violence, judging solely on the basis of numbers of people killed.[10] The film's disavowal of the actuality highlights the ideological underpinnings of its fantasmatic alternative history. Liberalization may have helped the Indian economy; it did nothing to alleviate major fractures within the polity, particularly communal divisions. It is these that the film presumes to "heal." To assume the burden, the film looks backward to a time when the peasants might have been discursively constructed as repositories of authentic Indianness, in order proleptically to imagine an Indian nation-state shriven of communal factionalism, as though "assuming the plasticity of the social world," the past could be reappropriated to produce another, counterfactual, present.[11]

Lagaan's setting, faithful to social realist formula, is the village of Champaner in the 1890s, a drought-plagued rural landscape further burdened by extortionate taxation (*lagaan*) levied by the British colonial rulers. Despite pleas conveyed via the local Rajah, the British do not ease the burden: all the more reason for anticolonial resistance. Into this matrix emerges Bhuvan, cast in a David-versus-Goliath standoff. Early in the film Bhuvan foils a hunting party led by Captain Russell by scaring off a deer: this is a metonym for resistance. The livid Russell threatens that next time *Bhuvan* will be the target. The vignette of the native's courageous and resourceful resistance against the colonizer is a framing overture to the film's central action, the cricket match.

Russell exploits every opportunity to denigrate and punish the villagers. Subordinating and humiliating the colonized subjects, including (or especially) someone such as the Rajah, who belonged to an intermediate echelon between the colonized masses and the colonizers, was de rigueur in the game of imperial power. This sport for the lower British cadres is nowhere more vividly illustrated than when Russell perversely demands that the vegetarian Rajah break his dietary vows by eating meat in exchange for a requested favor. The Montague-Chelmsford Reforms had extended voting rights to a new stratum of society by devolving power onto provincial governments. Until the turn of the nineteenth century, *rais* (local rulers such as the Rajah and others from merchant or landlord classes of neofeudal hierarchies) had enjoyed favor as intermediaries for the British.[12] But by the time of the constitutional reform in 1909 the *rais* became dispensable; the British began instead to enlist Indian National Congress (INC) mediators in regional and national politics. A decade later, fresh reforms in 1919 made the *rais* even less important to the colonialists, as politicians and other officials entirely supplanted them.[13] During the period in which *Lagaan* is set, the *rais* were still regarded as useful intermediaries and therefore colonials took satisfaction in skewering nobles such as the Rajah while seeming to protect their dominion.

It is in this spirit that Russell challenges the villagers to a cricket match: if the villagers win, their *lagaan* will be annulled for three years. If they lose, it will triple. This wager is conspicuously unfair, of course: though Bhuvan's team disparages the game as just a gussied-up version of the indigenous game "*gulli-danda*," played by village children, they are outclassed. Seeing the injustice of her brother's unsportsmanlike whim, Elizabeth, Russell's sister, offers her help to the underdogs. She is a foil to Russell, an angelic representative of the British national virtue of "fair play"—and she promptly falls in love with the Indian captain. Their union is impossible, although they themselves do not acknowledge it: there can be no such romance in such an avowedly patriotic film. Except that there is.

Revisionist History and Interracial Fantasy

The staged cricket match, centerpiece of the film, is an occasion not only to reimagine an achieved secular union in a patriotic narrative but also to titillate viewers with a fantasy of intercultural romance that runs athwart that narrative. But before we consider that romance, it is important to recognize another palimpsested and equally impossible romance: the fantasy of interethnic harmony. Bhuvan conscripts ethnically marginal figures onto the team, as if to embrace them into the fold of a nationalist narrative—a Muslim, a Sikh, a player handicapped by a speech impediment, and even an "untouchable" with a deformed wrist action. Their melodramatic victory against fantastically long odds, snatched from the jaws of defeat at the very last ball, is an object lesson to contemporary Indians divided by caste, communal background, and creed, not to mention education and class. The match culminates in the embarrassment of the British, the natives beating the imperialists at their "own game"—this last being a trope that gains significance as the film develops.

As the film closes, Amitabh Bachchan's voice-over provides the "outro," intoning that Champaner province having been dissolved, Russell is required by his own terms and by his superiors to pay triple penalty—and he is exiled to the central African desert. The *lagaan* is revoked. Having lost his wager and besmirched British honor, the blustering Russell is symbolically unmanned by the very structure of command that conferred his authority on him: a defeat more humiliating than his unsporting loss on the field, more even than betrayal by his sportsmanlike and sportive sister, who must swallow her own bitter defeat in the game of love. Elizabeth returns to England heartbroken, never to marry, holding Bhuvan's image in her heart. She became his Radha, like the mythical beloved who could never be united with the already-married Krishna, as if confirming that Elizabeth had become truly transculturated, gone native. Bhuvan's name was lost to history. The narrative thus turns on a fantasy. The film's real interest lies in the nuances and folds of the fantasy.

Throughout the film we see displaced and ultimately disavowed erotic investments on Bhuvan's part. These are significant: if read "bifocally," they illumine the contradictions that problematize the film's overt nationalism. There is the interracial erotic tension between Bhuvan and Elizabeth, but there is also a homoerotic tension between Bhuvan and Russell.

How are we to read these counterplots? They function, I argue, as fantasy subtexts, contradictory folds endemic to the filmic text. Indian masculinity was reconfigured by the Europeans as *deficient masculinity*.[14] Indian men were understandably eager to refute that reductive construction—and to convince themselves it was false. Both British and Indian performances of masculinity are on ostentatious display in *Lagaan*. Bhuvan and Russell are caught up in a double redirection of colonial violence: on one side there is a subsumption of the colonial contest into the masculinist competition of cricket, taking a "civilized" form: a game played by men, performing the masculinist tropes of nationalist resistance to British colonialism, expressed in masculine rhetoric. On the other, the aggressivity inherent in the colonial relation is rerouted through supercharged homoerotic or homosocial *sporting*, between the colonized and the colonizer.

Both their rivalry and their competitive bond of homosociality are evident when the two rivals cross each other on the field, looking at each other with exaggerated distaste that is also grudging respect. Russell's respect is in inverse proportion to his overt disdain. Bhuvan struggles against admitting to himself his admiration for Russell, but betrays his obvious desire to seem a worthy opponent. There is also the "love" triangle yoking Gouri, Bhuvan, and Elizabeth, re-presenting in an inverted form the homosocial rivalry between the male figures. Bhuvan is Russell's *match*, competitively and "homosocially." Elizabeth lends herself to this rivalry as a fantasmatic medium of exchange in the "homosocial" bond.[15]

The film is also a heterosexual love story—but confounded by ambivalence about who the beloved truly is, at least from Bhuvan's perspective. While much is conventional in the mimesis of the romance between Gouri and Bhuvan, the film resorts to improbable fantasy in representing Bhuvan's "inner," psychic confusion about his real erotic object.

In repeated fantasy sequences he romances Elizabeth, imagining her in the place of Gouri—only to renounce her, finally acknowledging Gouri, proper sanctioned love object and emblem of India, to whom he is bound at least by duty and cinematic convention if not by genuine emotional attachment. In the cricket rivalry Elizabeth is relegated to the position of a medium of exchange mediating both a heterosexual relation (hero and his sanctioned consort) *and* a homosocial relation (colonizer and colonized). Homosocial structuration almost subsumes the heterosexual relation: in the first half of the film Bhuvan seems entirely uninterested in Gouri, and her romantic interest in him is marginalized, a genuflection to cinematic reflex ("love interest"), though her faith in Bhuvan's courage (*himmat*) sustains his ego in his darkest moments, restoring his potency. And in this first half he seems only dimly aware of *Elizabeth*'s growing attachment to him. In the second half the film disavows everything but the conventional, but not before first flouting or confounding those conventions.

Along with Elizabeth, the characters Gouri and Mai (Bhuvan's mother and mentor) are relegated to choric "fantasy" spaces. From those margins they express their prescripted but conflicted desires and subjectivities mainly in song-and-dance sequences, but these complicate and enrich the film immeasurably. The important song sequence "Choote Lagaan" challenges "the widely held view of the film as a paragon of multicultural inclusiveness."[16] Elizabeth's important musical presence does not overshadow the Gouri motif in the song performed by the female choir, which enters only midway. Elizabeth's lament is a necessary prelude to Gouri's song, but it is the Indian women's powerful, rhythmic chanting that carries the theme song and, arguably, presents the most moving expression of Gouri's feelings.[17] Elizabeth's voice is for the duration relegated to the boundaries: Gouri's white rival can only be Bhuvan's partner in *his erotic fantasy*, here folded out of the *fantasy sequence*.

To another crucial fantasy song sequence ("O Re Chhori") British film audiences reacted, strangely, with laughter. In India, by contrast, the fantasy interlude was received as a fascinating hybridization of Indian folk and Western classical styles. This time, Elizabeth is *folded into* the fantasy sequence. The language of the song alternates between Hindi (when Gouri or Bhuvan sings) and English (when Elizabeth sings!), remarkably unusual even for Bollywood—especially unusual in that a white woman performs a love duet. The British audiences "missed the complex musical cues that positioned Elizabeth as the outsider in a love triangle."[18]

In the main narrative, the women function largely as appurtenances for men, conduits for the "enabling gaze" that confers and confirms masculinity.[19] *Lagaan* doesn't challenge male-centered enjoyment, or the "erotics of nationhood."[20] Still, the fantasy folded into that erotics often complicates interpretation. Even after Bhuvan for the first time (obliquely) declares his love to Gouri, he confounds this declaration in a *subsequent* "fantasy" sequence, which once again folds into the visual field an erotic ("romantic") fantasy the object of which is unequivocally Elizabeth. This treacherous fantasy is the *hero's* perhaps more than Elizabeth's, thus certainly more treacherous for the hero in this overdetermined patriotic narrative. It risks drawing audience sympathy not to the nationalist hero but to the woman who betrays her own country and blood for love, albeit in vain—indeed, the more powerfully for her sacrifice being in vain. Yet while Elizabeth transgresses racial, colonial, and gendered borders, it is only late in the film that the romance subplot is developed. She is ultimately sidelined.

Similarly it is only when the film begins to develop the competition between the two women that Gouri's character becomes salient. The film admits, almost reluctantly, that Gouri *has* cause for jealousy. Cinerotic fantasy competes with cinepatriotic fantasy in a constitutive contradiction of "the national." It is precisely such contradictions of the nationalist narrative that a bifocal postcolonialist analytic can bring into relief, and in what follows I suggest how such an analytic might unfold some of these contradictions or nuances.

In a key episode Bhuvan dangerously confuses the two women as if revealing his "real," unconscious desire. This moment activates the film's cleverest bilingual pun. When Elizabeth is late for a cricket lesson, one of the villagers asks, within earshot of Bhuvan, "*Gori kahan hai?*" meaning where is the "*gori*" (white woman)? It is *Gouri* who arrives on cue, declaring, "Here I am." The near-perfect homonymy (*gori*/Gouri) is reinforced by Bhuvan's surreal double vision represented on-screen, confusing the two women (see Figure 5.1). When Elizabeth tells him in broken Hindi that she is falling for him, English subtitles appear on screen. Yet Elizabeth's declaration of love is followed by a song in which Bhuvan declares his love to *Gouri*, and here the Hindi words are followed by English subtitles. Yet again, *their* duet is intercut when Elizabeth—wearing Rajasthani dress—is folded into what should have been only a duet, singing "I am in love," no English subtitles necessary. The viewer is bound to experience a vertiginous bifocality: For whose benefit are the English subtitles? To whom is the film addressed? To whom are Bhuvan's declarations of love actually directed? And do such questions not provoke another dimension of the film's bifocality—"crossover," transgressive affections and aspirations? Here translation and address are highly problematic categories.[21] Yet the film cannot resist *incorporating, folding in, precisely these* dangerous, fantasmatic elements into Bhuvan's otherwise exemplarily patriotic, even hyperpatriotic, performative.

Gouri is the first to volunteer to play on Bhuvan's team, but her tender act of love is patronized, and she is reduced to cheerleading on the sidelines. As for Elizabeth, she occupies the position of race traitor and betrayer of her own blood, upholder of the British cultural meme of "fair play," yet finds herself relegated to the no-(wo)man's-land, a limbo between Britain and the colony, between being the interracial lover and being the "Radha" figure for Bhuvan's Krishna. The colonizer's vulnerability is somaticized in her; it can be admitted nowhere else but in this gendered, marginal figure, insofar as she can be exempted from being a *totalized* representative of Britishness.

Elizabeth is not just an embodiment of vulnerability; her tragedy is that she is necessarily dispensable. At a celebration of the god Krishna's birthday, in a temple dedicated to him and his divine lover Radha, Bhuvan blithely explains to Elizabeth that because Radha was married to Anay, and Krishna to Rukmini, the two could never be wed though they are forever united (as "a water droplet on a lotus petal"). This unrequitable love is a deep cultural trope in Hindu religious discourse, its thwarted union also figuring the impossible hope for connection (E. M. Forster's "only connect") between colonizer and colonized. Miscegenation is impermissible; never shall East and West meet—except, that is, in fantasy.

But that is not to say Elizabeth does not represent a problematic wrinkle—or fold—in the patriotic text. In the brilliant love duet "Radha Jale" that follows the scene in the temple, Gouri sings, "*Radha kaise na jale?*" ("How could Radha

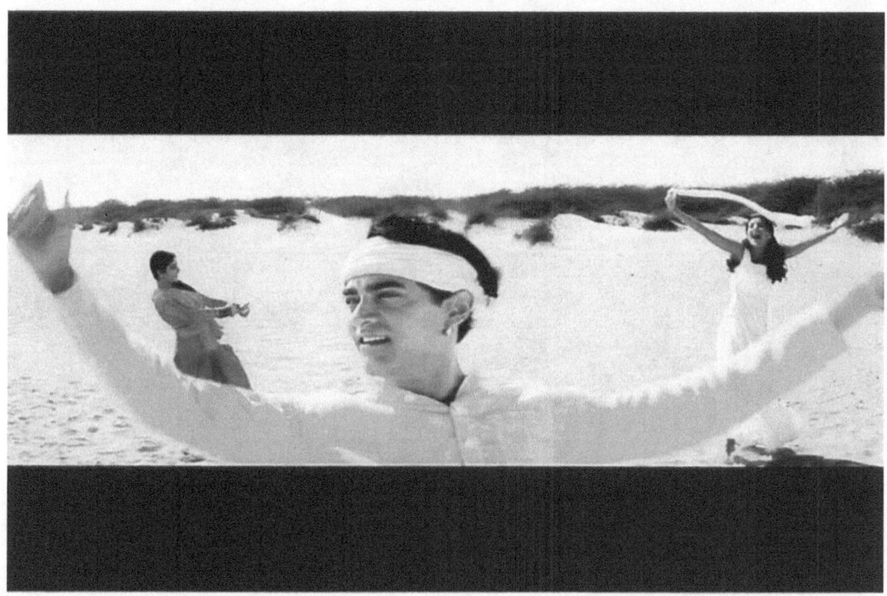

Figure 5.1. Bhuvan (Aamir Khan) in a fantasy sequence with both Gouri (Gracy Singh) and Elizabeth Russell (Rachel Shelley) in *Lagaan: Once upon a Time in India* (dir. Ashutosh Gowariker, 2001).

not burn with jealousy?"). As embodied meme for unrequitable love, "Radha" is, in the language of dance, now translated from Elizabeth's onto Gouri's body. Only in song, the realm of fantasy, can Gouri declare that her mind and her body are "on fire." Thus, in a short span of time, the *referent* for Radha has already begun to slide: who is Bhuvan's true Radha—Elizabeth or Gouri? And who is Krishna—equally the traitor Lakha (who burns for Gouri) and Bhuvan? Or also Elizabeth's English admirer, Russell's adjutant? The film then cuts back to the village, where Gouri seems to have morphed into an Indian Elizabeth-substitute. In the fantasy sequence that follows immediately, Bhuvan is shown dancing, in peasant dress, this time with Gouri—*but simultaneously fantasizing dancing with Elizabeth,* and a fair amount of surreal double-exposure footage intrudes into otherwise realistic camera work. Notably, Bhuvan is never shown dancing with Elizabeth *while fantasizing about Gouri.* The asymmetry speaks volumes about his desire. The question is, why introduce the confusion about Bhuvan's erotic object? His *conscious* commitment from the outset is emphatically (too emphatically?) on political resistance *and competition.* What is his Real (*unconscious*) object?

Critical here are *Bhuvan's* misrecognitions, resulting, of course, from the vicissitudes of his erotic fantasy. But they may also be motivated re-presentations of Elizabeth's and Gouri's fantasies. The blurring of desire challenges identity positions and settled "racial" categories. The two women's hair, faces, and bodies threaten to morph and fold, one into the other, in double-exposure

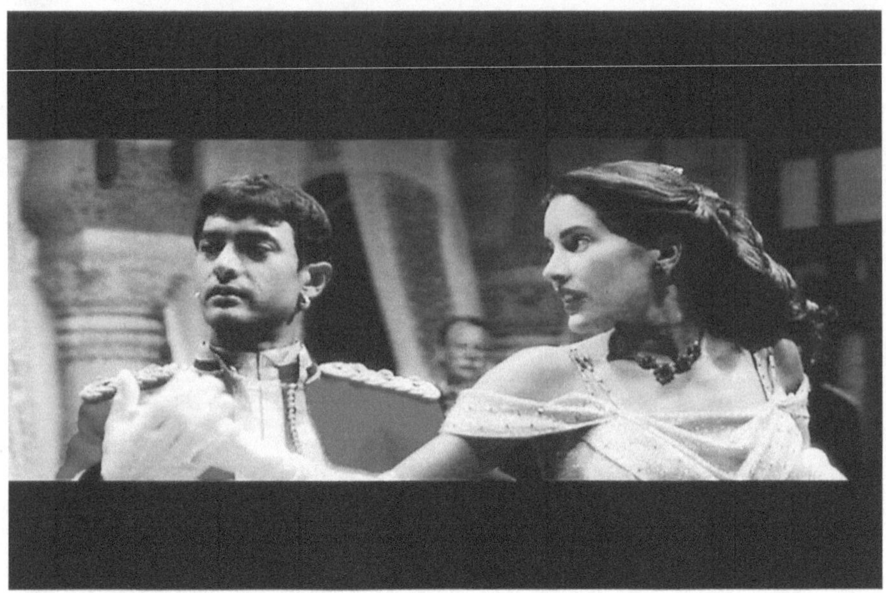

Figure 5.2. Bhuvan (Aamir Khan)—dressed in the enemy's uniform but wearing his very peasant earrings—in a fantasy sequence with Elizabeth Russell (Rachel Shelley) in *Lagaan: Once upon a Time in India* (dir. Ashutosh Gowariker, 2001).

or borderless picture-in-picture effect. This "folding" of realism and fantasy is a motivated distortion by spectacular technological manipulation of the image (see Figure 5.1).

Although the film earlier emphasized Elizabeth's difficulties with Hindi, she learns the language with incredible speed. Later, sitting in front of a mirror, she applies a *bindi* to her forehead. Does this "enculturation" suggest she could fluidly cross huge cultural chasms into the pious domestic fiction of a "good Hindu" woman and perhaps even wife? I read it as signaling an incipient cosmopolitanism, an increasingly important theme in mainstream Indian cinema—a theme developed in Chapter 7.

In another extraordinary "fantasy" scene of racial cross-dressing and star-crossed eroticism, the patriotic Indian hero, wearing a British officer's jacket, dances with Elizabeth in a ballroom, to Western music, under watchful British eyes. This scene expresses more than Bhuvan's desire for Elizabeth: it is curious that he should want to be (or fantasize being) in British costume to express it. Even more striking are the details that metonymically capture the transgressive albeit *self-contradictory* mimesis. Bhuvan's narratologically destabilizing attraction to Elizabeth is figured in micrological, *feminized*, detail: a cinephiliac obsession with the decorative and marginal.[22] Bhuvan's bold peasant earrings (vying with his cardinal-red British jacket as he dances the colonizer's dance with the white woman in the colonizers' company) pose the question, whose fantasy? It cannot be Elizabeth's alone (see Figure 5.2).[23]

Cinerotic fantasy competes with cinepatriotic fantasy, and the contradictions of Bhuvan's fantasy distort the recuperative mimesis of the heroic anticolonial struggle into a rather unbecoming if disavowed lust for the white woman. This disavowal seems stranger if set alongside his utter disregard for the Indian woman who is totally devoted to him, at least in the first half of the film. Yet mimesis rarely turns into what Irigaray and Bhabha term mimicry,[24] a subversive imitation of the colonizer in order to mock him, to take from him what he holds precious.

Interracial desire is a site of agonized ambivalence. But so are interethnic or communal divides. The film's glib "resolution" of the contradictions of religious identity, ethnicity, or caste proposes that all it takes to harmonize Hindus and Muslims is an open-hearted leader like Bhuvan, giving the lie to Lakha's resentful wager that Bhuvan will never include Ismayeel on his team because Ismayeel is a Muslim. Lakha is proved wrong, to maintain the national myth that Indians tolerate all creeds and faiths: Bhuvan welcomes Ismayeel literally with open arms.[25] Deva Singh Sodhi, a Sikh, also joins the team. Similarly, a stirring speech from Bhuvan overturns centuries-old caste prejudice against Kachra's inclusion.[26] *Lagaan*'s revisionist zeal about communal harmony elides the historical excesses of exclusivist Hindu majoritarian nationalism.[27]

The film thus offers a paradoxical fantasy "re-construction" of an always-already lost "history" of an India that never was, united through anticolonial struggle—a fantasy counterposed to imperfect actuality. But it is a richly layered fantasy, palimpsesting—folding—the desert spaces of rural India (the realist text) with the psychic terrains of interracial contest and the emotionally fraught territory of interracial romance (a subtext that often has recourse to extradiegetic fantasy). This chapter, highlighting these inter-folded erotic and historico-political fantasies, suggests that they provide the very form of the film's backward-projection into an imagined nation not yet beset by communalism and failed policies.

Bifocality

The film ventriloquizes the state's voice, addressing a transnational audience and presenting a public face for a globalizing self-presentation. This may have been a factor in the film's being submitted as India's nominee for the Best Foreign Film Oscar in 2002, over Mira Nair's *Monsoon Wedding* (like *Lagaan* released in 2001), the chief contender, made by a diasporic woman. The nationalist hero Bhuvan sustains the secular myth of the nation inclusive of all classes, creeds, religions, and sexual orientations.

Yet the film cannot be dismissed as merely a reactionary apologia for the fractious nature of the existing nation, though it is tempting to read it as extending into the cultural sphere the reigning discourse of neoliberal triumphalism, and the chauvinistic myth that "nationalism . . . arose in the 'spiritual' realm of society."[28] A bifocal perspective complicates the ventriloquized voice of the state, highlighting its ideological underpinnings and unfolding the film's contradictions. The rising tide of popular nationalism may have provided an impetus for the film's reproduction of a past that explicitly presents itself in the *realist* mode of parallel cinema but in which inconvenient truths are repressed, relegated to *fantasy,* or simply "forgotten," as Ernst Renan argued, suggesting that forgetting is constitutive of nation.[29] Progressives often express disenchantment with utopian narratives of globalization.[30] They might find this progressive position discomfitingly aligned with the film's antithetical, inward-looking "national-popular," glocalist reaction to globalization, showcasing peasants and other non-elites.

We may recall here Jameson's widely criticized suggestion that "all third-world texts are necessarily . . . allegorical," which stirred a small tempest among postcolonial critics, notably Aijaz Ahmad.[31] National allegory, thus cast in cultural stereotypy—repetitive, ritualized performatives of (Third World) culture—reinscribes the discourse of modernity as a standard against which non-European nations and subjects can only seem incomplete, "not yet" having arrived at the universalizing telos of EuroAmerican modernity.[32]

As Nissim Mannathukkaren remarks, however, "While Jameson's reading is way off the mark as far as high culture is concerned, it is not so with regard to popular culture."[33] The thesis of the "not-yet-ness" of Indian popular cinema cannot be ignored.[34] Prasad acknowledges that it is "not just a biased opinion coming from western or westernized critics, but also a thesis at work within the industry as the instrument of a drive towards change."[35] Modernity—as hegemonic EuroAmerican ideology—is inextricable from globalization. Still, it is crucial not to constrain studies of the postcolonial subject within the crudely drawn binaries of tradition versus modernity, or local versus global.

There are, undeniably, challenges of self-representation for Indian subjects in the new global conjuncture, given the deconstruction of "autochthonous identity."[36] In India the "disavowal of modernity on the ideological plane"—and the assertion of an authentic Indianness—have coexisted, writes Prasad, with "the contrary drive to modernization," in marked contrast to advanced capitalist societies.[37] But if nation-states, specifically developing or postcolonial nations, are determined simultaneously by bourgeois and precapitalist ideologies, an analysis of contemporary South Asian identity-construction and belonging requires a bifocal perspective. As Saskia Sassen writes, the national today is just not an adequate "container" for belonging.[38]

Bifocal analysis reveals contradictions structuring the allegory of the cricket match in *Lagaan* as cinematic fantasy of anticolonialist resistance after the fact. Certainly history has shown that the command of the colonizers was vulnerable to being undone by their own exercise of biopower, but the British relinquished control formally only in 1947 after an arduous political struggle—not because of cricket matches. Even the Mutiny of 1857 did not achieve a definitive victory against British rule, but rather brought the boot of colonial power down ever more firmly. In the afterglow of Independence, India's break with the colonial past has been haunted by the specter of neocolonialism, as in other recently postcolonial states in Africa and elsewhere.

Yet in 2001, a half-century after Independence, *Lagaan* offers a fantasy that evidently meets a felt need, judging from its global and local acclaim. It was listed by *Time* magazine as one of the "All-TIME 25 Best Sports Movies" and ranked in *Empire* magazine's listing of "the 100 Best Films of World Cinema"; it garnered impressive box office receipts in India, and it was nominated for an Academy Award for Best Foreign Film, the third Indian film to be so nominated after *Mother India* (discussed in Chapter 2).[39] What would a truly critical response to this phenomenon entail? At the very least, it would attend to the film's productive contradictions, ideally from a bifocal perspective not limited by a simple opposition of global and local.[40]

In the 1990s India witnessed both rapid political decentralization/economic liberalization *and* new intensifications of national feeling, a renewed emphasis on tradition as *content* and on realism as *form*. One of the early exponents of realism as form in Hindi cinema was the silent (social) realist film by V. Shantaram, *Sawkari Pash* (Indian Shylock, 1925), a critique of the moneyed classes, the villain being a moneylender, just as in *Awaara*, discussed in Chapter 1. The film's protagonist was a peasant, played by the director, like the protagonist of *Lagaan*. The realistic vector in Hindi cinema gave rise to parallel cinema, alongside the Golden Age Hindi cinema from about Independence in 1947 through the 1960s. A bifocal critique highlights continuities between those older realist films and *Lagaan* and illuminates other important films from the 1990s through the early 2000s, such as *Bandit Queen* (Shekhar Kapur, 1994); it also emphasizes specific differences in the deployment of fantasy as interruption.

Arjun Appadurai observes that "a series of social forms [cinema being one] has emerged to contest, interrogate, and reverse" the trends that have become increasingly entrenched in a Western and metropolitan discourse underwritten by corporate capitalism.[41] Here, however, I want to complicate the understanding of Indian popular cinema's access to the trope of "resistance from below," calling attention to how the overt narrative of resistance is split by the irruption of contradictory impulses. *Lagaan* manifests elective affinities with anticolonialist and anti-imperialist discourses, particularly along the vector of resistance to the British policy of "divide and rule." It appropriates and co-opts the idioms of *subalternity* yet underwrites the *majoritarian* Hindu narrative of a unified nation, here cloaked as a *realist* (rather than *melodramatic*), historically based account, complete with authentic-sounding dates and an ostentatious (and problematized) demonstration of fidelity to period costumes, architecture, settings, and dialect at the level of mise-en-scène. At the thematic level a bifocal perspective, attentive to the splitting of the surface realist patriotic narrative by competing subtexts, uncovers folds, gaps and irregularities, revealing the film as in fact melodramatic and fissured by fantasy.

The village cricket field is a landscape metaphoric of a wider *imagined* political field and metonymic of the Hindu nationalist ideology of a "big tent," presumptively inclusive of all ethnic minorities, the disabled, and the *achuth* or outcaste—the "kachra" (trash) of society. In a graphic condensation one of the most controversial recruits onto the team bears the very name Kachra. His deformed wrist endows him with a dangerous "leg spin": unsurprisingly, he proves instrumental in the team's victory. According to the historian Ramachandra Guha, Kachra is intended to evoke the image of Palwankar Baloo, India's first great Dalit cricket star.[42] Gowariker conceptualizes the peasant as the subaltern elevated to heroic status. This retrojected fantasy should be problematized by a bifocal critique: in actuality peasants have suffered terribly as India has progressed toward globalized modernity, many committing suicide since liberalization in 1991.

Class is as salient an issue in Indian society as caste—though, as David Washbrook remarks, underemphasized by postcolonial scholarship.[43] A bifocal analytic would complicate the bourgeois self-congratulation that suffuses 1990s Hindi cinema concerned primarily with elite diasporics and middle-class subjects. Bourgeois sensibility, later chapters of this book argue, is annexed to global circuits of consumption and tends, as Marx might formulate it, to subsume all human relations, all culture, to processes of commodification—except that this subsumption is never total.

While the romanticized "authentic" peasant is to be critiqued *as fantasy*, the film's project does superficially align with the celebration in cultural studies of projects of minoritarian self-affirmation that reject received and sanctioned identity constructs and bridge class and caste divides. Arguably, the project of revisionist history driving *Lagaan* squares with progressive discourses that produce subject positions that could subvert majoritarian doxa about class, caste, sexuality, and nation. Could it be that the film is not reactionary but points forward to a new, more globally cognizant (multicultural, tolerant) narrative?

Indeed, a bifocal perspective might identify a "weak" form of cosmopolitanism informing *Lagaan*. The film does index a negotiation with state forms and cultural (including religious) institutions and practices and is thus a response to "new global circumstances."[44] Globalization and modernity, projections of Western power in and after the colonial era, generate new forms of self-assertion as reaction, and the film is symptomatic: the narrative of the colonized peasants reimagined in *Lagaan* can be read as condensing a coded, glocalizing response to globalization.

Lagaan's project may also be contiguous with other progressive glocalization projects in its representation of the *indigenization* of cricket by the peasants *as a collective political practice*, a process that affirms the pan-ethnic solidarity of "Indians" irrespective of caste or creed. *Lagaan* constructs an imaginary social space reintegrating a fractured and fractious polity or *rashtra*, though several omissions betray the ideological underpinnings of the construction, notably the elision of communalist tensions and the hegemonic power of the Hindu majority. That space finds its objective correlative in a colorful rural India in which peasants manage to wear dazzlingly colorful and clean clothes in the midst of a drought—another contradiction complicating the film's premises. The social realism of the film similarly jettisons pretense of verisimilitude. It is as though the film were asking, what if we could reimagine our antecedents regardless of history?[45]

The process of glocalization is, as I have argued, cathected onto the game of cricket, although, of course, any affective dividend gained from the cathexis (in aesthetic or bodily pleasure, for instance) is strenuously denied by the players themselves. In crises, Orlando Patterson has argued, cricket can be transubstantiated into another scene of the political.[46] In *Lagaan* this transubstantiation sublimates a symbolic narrative of self-assertion half a century after Independence, the moment that haunts the national narrative. For no sooner had the nation become independent than its founding ideal of secularism began to founder: Gandhi was assassinated in 1948 by a Hindu zealot, and even today communalism braids religion and politics in volatile blends. The colonial problematic has morphed into the global and the neocolonial, and this is reflected in *Lagaan*. Appadurai suggests that the Indian commodification of cricket and other "public spectacles" seems to be the "expression of a worldwide process and thus to represent not decolonization or indigenization but recolonization by the forces of international capital."[47]

The Glocal Turn: The Vernacularization of Cricket

A diacritic of current critical discourse is that the non-West is no longer outside the West. The glocal production of knowledges, pointing up the anterior future of an imaginary India, is always imbricated with "translocal and transnational flows of capital, desire, and knowledge" and erupts in the most localized of localities.[48] This rage for an alternative modernity emerges in bizarre and arational ways within the matrix of a local material reality, as a "supplementary" fantasy.

Even a film as revisionist as *Lagaan* cannot be simplistically counterposed to the diasporic or cosmopolitan visions, for, in "fantasy sequences," the film aspires to a cosmopolitan address in a minor key—speaking sotto voce in the collective voice of a nation to "the world." The film addresses indigenous mass audiences, speaking to their sensibilities, but also pitches itself as a commodity to an extremely important market—diasporic or nonresident Indians (NRIs). This is borne out by the accolades it received from *Time* and *Empire* magazines, announcing that Indian commercial cinema had "come to symbolize an order of *psychic investment* for immigrants of Indian origin all over the world."[49] Sassen highlights "insertions of the global into the fabric of the national" as a "partial and incipient denationalization of that which historically has been constructed as the national, or, rather, of certain properties of the national."[50] But this is not exactly new: Vasudevan observes that the postcolonial Hindi cinema of the 1940s and 1950s was already complicated by a "universalizing ambition."[51]

A bifocal perspective focalizes affirmations of the local *with* this ambition: "globalization" as indexing new configurations of global capital.[52] Since the mid-sixteenth century, capitalism has been tied to the transnational exchange of commodities, labor, ideas, images, and so on, but only with the advent of print capitalism did the form of the nation emerge.[53] The contemporary orientation toward glocalization is spurred by information technology (IT) and IT-enhanced imaginaries; Hindi cinema is a contributor to such globalization from below.[54] Authentic Indianness, increasingly articulated with these new imaginaries, can no longer be anchored to a geographical "homeland" but may constitute allegiance to an "imagined" homeland. A diasporic or NRI may present a more *desirable* model of Indianness than a peasant even if she does not live in the Subcontinent. Against this background a bifocal perspective can highlight *Lagaan*'s motivated relocation of authentic Indianness within a revisionist imaginary of rural India with the peasant as modular echt Indian reinvested with cultural cachet, as counterpoint to the global. The present does not quite disappear as referent but is reperspectivized through the optic of a possible future—projected from the reimagined past.

Lagaan's "realist" mise-en-scène thus presents a reinvention of a fantasmatic "originary" India, whose objective correlative is the reinvention of cricket as an "Indian" game. Reinvention takes the form of indigenization, as if assisting in the (re)birth of what is now the nation's major sports obsession from the peduncular form of an ancient native game. *Lagaan*'s claim to a realist lineage is expressed through period costumes, props, setting, and natural lighting on the parched and sunbaked land; the "fantasy" sequences undercut or "supplement" that realist representation and at the same time destabilize the village cricket field as a zone of multivalent *contest* and *contact.*

The modern game of cricket, talisman of British cultural values ("good sportsmanship," "fair play"), is coeval with the age of colonialism and intimately related to the *mission civilisatrice.* Cricket embodied—literally propagating itself in and through the bodies of the players—core British values, to which by the alchemy of colonial hegemony even the colonized intellectual C.L.R. James swore allegiance. But it also always carried an embedded potential for denationalization and vernacularization within other cultures—its universalizability, its xenotransplantability, as James himself recognized.[55] The very projection of the West as presumptive cultural hegemon becomes, through assimilation, the means for the de-auratization of the West: it is lowered on its own petard.[56]

In postcolonial critical discourse, cricket may not have become exactly a "national allegory" but is often construed as opening an emergent space beyond the ambit of nationalist discourse.[57] The film bends this hoary trope of anticolonial resistance to unblushingly (Hindu) nationalist ends. The harshness of the ideology of Hindutva is softened precisely by its imaginary "return" to the idyllic moral and literal landscapes of nationalism's emergence. *Lagaan* thus participates in the doubled culture (or cult?) of memory that Andreas Huyssen describes as increasingly pervasive over the last three decades: revisionist history deployed in the production of reactionary futures.[58] The politics of *forgetting* as manifested in Gowariker's film are undeniably reactionary: it erases the traces of majoritarian political suppression of minority groups even as it re-members, (re-)invents, a past for the ideological purposes of the present. This faux-historical film "presents as complete, at origin, what it seeks to create."[59] Yet it undeniably imagines a more inclusive and open, even glocalized, present and future poised between a reactionary and a progressive politics. This is the contradiction at the heart of *Lagaan*. What kind of "realism" can the film then lay claim to? Is it a faux realism? Or "just" fantasy as entertainment?

While founded on an ideologically motivated forgetting (disavowal) of the reality, the film does not want us to forget that the game is a foreign form, so that it can be played and even enjoyed without risking the appearance of seduction by the foreigner's culture. It ostentatiously disavows any frivolous, aesthetic, or libidinal investment on the part of the Indian team in the game of cricket (they "play" not because they enjoy the game but because they must), even though clearly the film simultaneously appeals to the national craze for cricket among its intended audiences, which came to a crisis as India's hero Sachin Tendulkar retired from the game in 2013. This contradiction maps tellingly onto the contradictory planes of chauvinistic-and-libidinous investment embodied in the hero, Bhuvan. Ideologically, too, the film must disavow the peasants' investment in the game of cricket as generating the pleasure of (re-)creating themselves because they cannot avow that it is this transplanted, colonizer's game of cricket that lends them the sense of re-creating their identity.

Here we encounter the quandary of a meliorative trope: the colonized seek to represent and re-create themselves through the foreign game of cricket and to resist the terms set by the colonizer, as if to suggest that self-cultivation, indeed civilization itself, could be canalized only along the pathways already mapped out by the colonizer. This puts the villagers at a handicap, for then adequation to a modular culture is the best to be hoped for. At the same time, the film cannot help showing the male Indian body, in all its varieties, achieving a state of pleasure in the act of playing the game and making it his own.[60] The denial of pleasure is a defense against not only frivolity but also elitism and cosmopolitanism, since the burden of the film requires genuflection in the direction of a populist indigenism—and social realism. The imaginative regression to the moment of indigenization discussed above thus serves to highlight the drama of regenerating Indianness itself.

The film is motivated by a contemporary nationalist imperative: the desire to affirm against cosmopolitan and globalist influences the sense of self-determination, of independence, a group identity that captured the emergence of a pan-ethnic Indian "standpoint." Yet by the same token the film opens itself up to the criticism that in its eagerness to register an anticolonial victory by other means (cricket), it finesses or underestimates the real obduracy of interethnic and interclass conflict that bedevil Indian society. The film's politics are simplified rather than enriched by recourse to the popular cinematic equivalent of "standpoint theory": that a given group perspective or standpoint both enables insight and obstructs sight of features of the larger sociocultural environment of which the group is an element. The director is too eager to resolve internal differences. And while there is a gesture toward a cosmopolitan perspective, the film does not consider the kind of professionalization and transnationalization of cricket that is a direct contradiction of the kind of anterior future nationalism celebrated in *Lagaan.* So the questions I posed earlier—Why cricket, why go back in time?—are to be considered in the context of Kenneth Surin's argument that the game is "imbricated in a new conjuncture, that of an integrated world-capitalism."[61]

In *Lagaan,* vernacularization is strategically configured as (mis)appropriation: the colonizer's tools used against the colonizer, in a reversal that is the sweeter given that the Victorian colonial elite who introduced the game to the Indians were motivated by the patronizing conviction that the values encoded in cricket would improve (and incidentally help discipline and socialize) the colonial subjects.[62] Yet cricket in India never was and never could be simply a resistant "tactic"; things were more complicated—and more simple. Indians embraced it, regardless of whether any odor of colonialism still attached to it. And there were cricketers, Ranjitsinhji (1872–1933) preeminent among them, who embodied the perfect fulfillment of the colonizer's dream of making brown Englishmen—brown men English in sensibility but never quite English enough to threaten the self-image of white Englishmen.

In South Asian societies, Ashis Nandy writes, "modern political analysis has already successfully discredited [the vernacular] as soft, effeminate, immature and irrational."[63] However, Nandy can be read against the grain of his own argument as furnishing support for a bifocal framing—both outward-looking and nativist—that is furthermore a *symptom* of the very modernity that has "discredited it." Such a bifocal perspective highlights the fetishizing of the peasant in response to the perceived challenge of globalization while simultaneously identifying centrifugal drivers of contemporary cultural production, including a revival of the "complex cosmopolitanism of the Indian Ocean World," folded along with a newer cosmopolitanism; that cosmopolitanism is linked to contemporary transnational migration and intensified global dispersions of labor, capital, images, and information.[64] The film both asserts an overtly nationalist Hindi-language and Hindu-majoritarian sensibility (although it foregrounds a peasant dialect and a peasant village as representative of that sensibility) and affirms a "cosmopolitan" claim on cricket (a not-yet-indigenized cultural form) as a vehicle to affirm that sensibility. The "idea of vernacularization," as Sudipta Kaviraj writes in a different context, "indicates the near impossible paradoxicality of what we must attempt: when the western idea really enters the vernacular it must change its meaning; but we have to try to capture that fugitive meaning in English, precisely the language from which it is trying to escape."[65]

A utopianist impulse is thus encoded into the film's visual language: a synthetic cosmopolitanism that simultaneously registers an *anxiety* about the increasingly problematic status of "Indianness" in a new, global age *and* an exhilaration at the prospect of expanded possibilities for the Indian subject inhabiting a less nation-bound citizenship status. *Lagaan*'s vernacularization of cricket is routed via a visual language that does not spurn the West: Western dress, dance, manners, sport, even Western men and women as objects of desire. This visual language is a contemporary instance of (counter)modernity.[66] Perhaps the dream of the West is being used as an inoculation, maintaining the health of the nationalist fantasy—hair of the dog?

Thus vernacularization is perhaps less an appropriative *gestus* (Roland Barthes) and more an iterative self-distancing from the present in order to recuperate it *as if living it for the first time.*[67] In this act of self-distancing followed by repetition-with-a-difference, the director refashions the Indian subject as at once resisting *and* erotically drawn to the white colonizer, a subject thoroughly Indian *and* yet not entirely insulated from a global storehouse of images of the self—a Yeatsian *anima mundi*—to construct an Indianness perfected in cricket before cricket became an *Indian* sport.

The gradual indigenization of cricket in colonial India, writes Appadurai, is organized by a distinction between "hard" and "soft" cultural forms. The former imply links between value, meaning, and embodied practice difficult to break or transform. Soft cultural forms, by contrast, permit relatively easy separation of embodied performance from meaning and value, and relatively successful transformation at various levels. Cricket, a hard cultural form, changes those socialized into it "more readily than it is itself changed." But what accounts for cricket's *becoming Indian*—so integral to the Indian cultural imaginary that today it "links gender, nation, fantasy and bodily excitement"?[68] Nandy proposes that the indigenization of cricket is facilitated by preexisting mythic structures in Indian culture.[69] Appadurai suggests an alternative but compatible explanation: indigenization proceeds "through a set of complex and contradictory processes that parallel the emergence of the Indian 'nation.'"[70]

This excursus on "indigenization" explains why the game must be first characterized as non-Indian before it can be cinematically *reappropriated* to affirm a recuperated Indianness as well as underwrite the nationalist, anticolonialist narrative. As Bhuvan says to the traitor Lakha, "For the whities it's only a game. For us, it's our life." The villagers win the match despite ascribed "cultural" or moral handicaps, showing themselves also to have a "natural" ability, so that ultimately they can assert ownership of it. This is an important move in the drama of vernacularization being performed. The villagers become adepts precisely by demonstrating that there is an inherent, peduncular, "undeveloped" aptitude for the game, not despite but because of who and what they are—a species of noble savages whose culture is no less admirable than that of the "civilizing" Englishman.

This logic is underscored by the figuration of Kachra's untouchability and disability. He develops a mean spin (a "googly") precisely *because* of the awkward action of his arm, just as Arjan, another character, succeeds in outfoxing the English *because* of his unorthodox "windmill" style of bowling, which cannot be disallowed precisely because the Marquess of Queensberry rules of the game had not anticipated this unorthodox technique. Kachra's handicap becomes a refinement or hyperdevelopment of technique, and the Indian players, in besting the British players, prove themselves more civilized than the civilizer, the measure being precisely how well you play cricket. One of the umpires says there is no rule against bowling in Arjan's odd manner, but the rules would thenceforth have to be *rewritten.* Again, what is being staged is the making-Indian of the game, coding an originary moment (or more precisely originary *trace,* for the process marks its absence) projecting a future anterior.

If the film emphasizes the English origins of the game, it is to dramatize its vernacularization—anticipating audience demand for the characters' authenticity. The first Indian cricketers, Majumdar notes, were Bombay Parsis, "an educated, prosperous and westernized community," and only in the late nineteenth century did the game become popular across the country.[71] A bifocal analytic underscores the film's ambivalent articulation of traditionalism/nationalism and modernity/cosmopolitanism. As Chatterjee suggests, the "Eastern" type of nationalism could not just imitate the Western form wholesale if it wanted to preserve its own identity and self-respect.[72] It was necessary to enable a "regeneration" of a national culture that was "modern" and yet distinct. Thus the crucial ambivalence is kin to the more general rejection of some aspects of Western culture. This ambivalence is captured in *Lagaan* in moments that *cannot be* acknowledged at the surface of the narrative, again because they contradict the overt patriotic "message" of the film. They shimmer and erupt in the moments of sanctioned fantasy, particularly in the "fantasy" sequences.

Conclusion: The Unpatriotic Supplement

Lagaan's aspiration to produce—in its mimesis of a "realist" mode—a pure and self-identical narrative of an autochthonous nation-state is by its very nature as nationalist fantasy unachievable. Besides, Bhuvan's contradictory desires remind us that such hermetic fictions never succeed in censoring or papering over cracks in their facades. The film's recourse to a logic of the future anterior is made necessary precisely because the actual present does not have such a perfected Indian past to look back to in fact. So the "real" India that the realist mode presents is actually a fiction, and the fictionality of that fiction is underscored by the fact that contradictory fantasies, even produced by the protagonist (hypernationalist) hero himself, keep threatening to fissure that image of an ideal India, revealing the whole project of the film as fantasy.

Ironically, it is in the film's "fantasy sequences" that the Real threatens to break through, threatens to reverse the suspension of disbelief that supports the whole fantastic skein that is the film. The putatively realist representation of rapacious Western colonialism is spectacularly undermined by the fantasy of Bhuvan's unspeakably unpatriotic love for Elizabeth. Clearly Bhuvan is not immune to her honest, unexploitative, even selfless charms, but it is possible to read this interracial affection as a treacherous supranational or cosmopolitan desire rupturing the hypernationalist fantasy at the core of the film. That is the scandal of the film, and a bifocal perspective sets the fantasy against the reality (itself expressed as an interracial fantasy) on a global stage. For there is no outside the globalized imaginary: as Bhabha puts it, "the world" has a resonance even for very small localities.[73] Many Hindi films construct similarly hermetic fictions of nation in popular cinema. The "poetic" reconstruction of such fictions for mass consumption, however, is simultaneously deconstructed in the space-time warp of the fantasy sequences that these films cannot resist.

III

DIASPORIC CINEMA AND FANTASY SPACE

Nonresident Indian Aliens and Alienated Signifiers of Indianness

6

The Powers of the False

Fantasy Spaces for Same-Sex Love?

In a vast field of green dotted with yellow flowers (mustard?) a family luxuriates in the sun. The mother croons to her young daughter a tale of a mountain tribe: "They had never seen the sea," she says, "though they wanted to see it. . . . 'Don't be sad,' an old woman says, 'what you can't see, you can see—you just have to see without looking.'" This opening sequence of Deepa Mehta's controversial film *Fire* (1996), recalled repeatedly by the girl (Radha) as she grows up to be a woman, is as good an image of the power of fantasy as any: the power to "recall" the absent and project a future that is not, to apostrophize the impossible as possible. This image is evocative, if only at the individual level, of Walter Benjamin's reference to the Klee painting "Angelus Novus"; the angel of history is moving away from something on which his gaze is fixed, mouth agape, wings spread and caught in winds that promise the future. The past threatens to be lost before it can be assimilated, repaired. But to complicate Benjamin's reading, what if that past is no less a fantasy than the future is "impossible"?

Rosie Thomas notes that "tolerance of overt phantasy has always been high in Hindi cinema, with little need to anchor the material in what Western conventions might recognise as a discourse of 'realism,' and slippage between registers does not have to be marked or rationalised."[1] Fantasy thereby taps into what Friedrich Nietzsche and Gilles Deleuze might have called the powers of the false—to apostrophize what, like the sea in the opening image, is not.[2]

Gayatri Gopinath thematizes this potentiality of the negative in theorizing South Asian queer (female) subjectivity, "as a way of signaling the unthinkability of a queer female subject position within various mappings of nation of diaspora."[3] She theorizes the imbrication of queer and feminist critique with South Asianist scholarship and discourses. My project is rather to explore the "powers of the false" as *profilmic*—mediated by the *imaginary* or fantasy spaces embedded within popular filmic narratives from where alternatives to normative positions can be projected, or in which desire and therefore subjectivity can be produced in a "re-creative," liberatory, or subversive idiom. Fantasy produces parallel or alternative (non)places, unleashing the power of *profilmic fantasy* in the reciprocity between diasporic South Asian (DSA) and domestic cinemas.

"The queer" in South Asian diasporic cinema occupies—by election or ascription—the place of the minor. The minor insists as a resistant space, of phantasmic completeness, of possibility that takes the form of impossibility. Deleuze and Félix Guattari provocatively limn the possibilities of "impossibility" in Franz Kafka's negotiation of his own subject position vis-a-vis the German language and German national identity.[4] Yet fantasy implies compromise. The subject's specific mode of *jouissance* determines what kinds of fantasy, what compromises will sustain him "at the level of his vanishing desire."[5] As "queer," the subject's access to a viable political position is barred, rendered *structurally* "impossible." Yet because the minor cannot *not* express itself from within the dominant, it bears witness to the potentiality inscribed in its very negativity. The (non)places produced by profilmic fantasy testify to powers of the false coproduced symptomatically as the negative of the normative. Fantasy enables new, if "minor," epistemologies of self and desire, revealing contradictions in received doxa of ethnicity, nation, and gender, access to unfamiliar and unpredictable modes of being. This chapter examines a diverse cluster of films, many with a transnational span, that crystallize the fantasy of something like a Lebensraum for "ex-centric," non-heteronormative, love.

Landmark Gay-Themed Films

Same-sex love is demonized in South Asian culture, often characterized as another encroachment of the "decadent" West. Films thematizing LGBTIQ (lesbian, gay, bisexual, transgender, intersex, and queer) issues highlight the impediments to alternative sexual arrangements, channeling "supplemental" fantasies produced at the level of *directorial consciousness*—directors' visions of alternative spaces of desire.[6]

Sexuality is comparable not to a scalar dimension of identity but to a vector field of identifications, lines of flight that challenge settled and hegemonic constructions. Non-heteronormative or LGBTIQ sexuality is customarily consigned to dissident marginality, false consciousness, perversion, delusion, or a distortion of nature. Cinematic LGBTIQ fantasies challenge heteronormative constructions of cultural identity. Yet it must be acknowledged that most do not aspire to radically queer theoretical perspectives that, at least in Western psychoanalytic discourse, question the privileging of the Oedipus complex in Freud's work, rejecting its narrowly heterosexist structure as "*père*-verted," inordinately oriented to the Father. Yet in several diasporic films featuring South Asian subjects, it is possible to trace implicit dissent from a totalized

Oedipal scenario of traditional family values, with the paterfamilias at its center.

I begin with *My Beautiful Laundrette* (screenplay by Hanif Kureishi, directed by Stephen Frears, 1985), which set the standard for "gay-themed" films made by or about diasporic South Asians, though my main focus is on Deepa Mehta's *Fire* (1996), a foreign-funded film shot in India, then released to acclaim in the West before its controversial screening in India. Produced on a shoestring budget of $850,000, *Laundrette* became a classic condensation of gendered postcolonialist dissent from conventional South Asian sexual mores, dramatizing contradictions lived by racialized subjects in Britain, simultaneously indexing the legacy of colonization back "home."[7] Stuart Hall declared it "one of the most riveting and important films . . . by a black writer in recent years."[8] A sophisticated take on ethnicity, class, gender, and sexuality in the United Kingdom, it offered a vision of cross-racial connection while acknowledging it as "impossible" fantasy.

The film features Omar, a young British Pakistani youth in Thatcherite England who reunites with his childhood friend Johnny, a white gang member with little sympathy for immigrants. Johnny becomes Omar's unlikely business partner and, ultimately, lover. This ambiguous fantasy of cross-racial, same-sex attachment offsets the fantasy of socialist utopian change that Omar's father, "Papa," long nurtured but acknowledged to be impossible under Thatcher, whose neoliberal policies denied medical, educational, residential, and social services to "black citizens" unless they produced documents of legal status.[9] Papa has been driven into depression and alcoholism. As a socialist and former journalist he is "disappointed" (his word) in the working class's failure to live up to his fantasy of a utopic solidarism cutting across class, racial, national, and gender/sexual divisions.

Aimé Césaire, in his incantatory essay "Discourse on Colonialism," described capitalism as a monster that is like racism "at the end of the blind alley that is Europe."[10] Yet Omar's paternal uncle Nasser, by contrast with Omar's father and his démodé socialist ideas, has benefited unsentimentally from global capital-friendly Thatcherite policies without pledging nationalist allegiance to Britain. Nasser suggests to the wide-eyed and uncritical Omar that British South Asians must learn how to "squeeze the tits of the system," a system already deformed to suit the purposes of the upper classes to the disadvantage of the poor, including the young friends of Omar, Johnny and his gang members Genghis, Moose, Jamaican One, and Jamaican Two. Omar occupies a medial position; he embraces entrepreneurial opportunity when it knocks, but the film takes pains to establish him and Johnny as highly irregular ("queer"?) subjects of the Thatcherite nation-state: not-quite-not-Right (wing). Nasser offers Omar a job at his garage's car wash and then proposes he revive and manage two decrepit laundrettes that one of his friends has purchased as an investment.

If Nasser is irretrievably cynical in his profiteer capitalism, Omar is hardly an exponent of ethicopolitical postcoloniality. Johnny is an amoral opportunist. He has been helping Nasser extort payments from deadbeat renters on Nasser's rental properties. A member of a cryptofascist gang, he implicitly shares anti-immigration ideology scandalously expressed by the British Conservative member of Parliament Enoch Powell in his "Rivers of Blood" speech, which suggested that unless (dark-skinned) immigrants were repatriated, Britain risked being overrun by rivers of blood. In only slightly less virulent rhetoric, Thatcher also sought to drum up anti-immigrant sentiment.

Omar and his father forgive Johnny his cryptofascism, Omar out of friendship and queer desire, Papa out of idealism (fantasy). What is interesting is that Johnny chooses to forge a non-heteronormative and inter-"racial" attachment to Omar. Although the phrase "possible futures" has become a cliché of cultural studies, it is a rallying motto for progressive agendas, or for an imagined better world that today seems impossible fantasy. Omar and Johnny form a non-heteronormative attachment, which admittedly raises questions: is this a "rescue fantasy," as Jasbir Puar suggests—the fantasy of the cryptofascist rescued by gay love? Is having a brown gay lover incompatible with being a violent racist? Does this profilmic fantasy permit "a false benevolence to exist about liberal inclusion"?[11] Furthermore, it is important to interrogate the racialization of gay sexuality. It is not just Johnny who is in this fantasy "redeemed" by queering his obdurate racism. Omar too is recuperated into the fold of Britishness by the very exclusion of comparatively more denigrated non-Britishness (the unassimilable Indian immigrant), his gayness articulated to his success as immigrant assimilationist entrepreneur. In providing a job to a poor unemployed white British citizen, he establishes his credentials as member of the biopolitically defined class of "good" minorities, of an emergent and newly approved "queer subjecthood" that, in a "historical shift condoned only through a parallel process of demarcation from populations targeted for segregation, disposal or death," colludes with more mainstream doxa in a "reintensification of racialization through queerness." Omar is in Puar's terms a homosexual subject "folded into life, enabled through 'market virility' and 'regenerative productivity'" to belong on the condition of exclusion of *other* "others." This is occluded in the profilmic fantasy, as adjunct to what Puar describes as the "surprising but not fully unexpected flowering of new normativities in these queer times."[12] The *contradictory* vectors of the film subtend a progressive agenda: the powers of the false. Fantasy makes it possible to summon, at least in the imaginative space of the profilmic, the better angels of human nature. The question is, against what "real" odds and at what cost.

Profilmic fantasy serves to complicate notions of postcolonial *belonging* productively, problematizing the postcolonial diasporic's orientation to the host nation and interrogating the fantasmagorias of racism, bringing to light ugly if unacknowledged prejudices against nonwhite immigrants and diasporics. The film challenges, but also perhaps reinscribes (with a twist), received scripts of racism imbricated with nation, class, ideology, and gender. It projects a possible better future, fantasized but always worth waiting for. When Salim comes to see Omar at the laundrette but does not find him, he asks Johnny if it's worth waiting. Johnny says archly that that "Omo" (Omar the homo? homosexual desire itself?) is always worth "waiting for":

> Salim: I want to talk to Omar about business.
> Johnny: I dunno where he is.
> Salim: Is it worth waiting?
> Johnny: In my experience it's always worth waiting for Omo.

This exchange does not merely exploit an adventitious pun but plays on words to enunciate a psychic truth Johnny himself has not yet grasped. As Gopinath suggests, glossing this exchange, "the queer racialized body becomes a historical archive for both individuals and communities, one that is excavated through the very act of desiring the racial Other." For Gopinath it is homosexual desire (and explicitly not heterosexual desire), the *queer* fantasy of a possible future, that offers real hope in the film, just as its postcolonial perspective "queers" mainstream constructions of immigrants in the former colonial center. While agreeing that "discourses of sexuality" cannot be considered independently of "prior and continuing histories of colonialism, nationalism, racism and migration," my analysis diverges more generally from Gopinath's foregrounding of *female* queer diasporic desire.[13] It differs also specifically, in emphasizing that in *Laundrette* the "Omo"-sexual hope, a post-heterosexist, post-Oedipal waiting for a possible future, functions as an endless regression, a horizon of hope receding but always to be realized. Omar, of course, does come, but the *glissement* or slippage of his alter-ego signifier, "Omo," suggests something *beyond* Omar, something not yet, an ethicopolitical space beyond the erotic, raised to the level of a profilmic fantasy.

Laundrette's fantasy may be utopic but it is also ironized on this level, and also more humorously by a cinematic device that might be called resonance. While visually "realistic," portraying a gritty London, the film introduces surreal elements: Nasser's traditional Pakistani wife, spurned in favor of his white mistress, turns to "black magic" to wreak revenge on her. The sudden appearance of this fantastical element rending the otherwise realistic diegetic fabric is intentionally jarring, setting up a resonance between moments in which the narrative breaks with the actual, underscoring the potency of the hyperreal/fantasmatic. The recourse to black magic also constitutes an *imaginary* access to the hyperreal, just as homosexual desire refracts an *imagined* transcendence of actual constraints to cross-racial harmony.

Homoerotic desire presents important dilemmas and contradictions at the level of plot as well. Omar recruits Johnny, but he also enlists his cousin Salim, a drug dealer. Salim makes disparaging comments about the British working class to which Johnny and his gang belong, and contemptuously tries to run them over with his car, managing only to hurt one of them. Tania, Nasser's daughter, comes to the laundrette and propositions Johnny to run away with her. But Johnny declines, revealing to Tania and the audience, as well as to himself, his feelings for Omar. Surprised, Tania leaves on a train—effectively spurning the conventional racial, sexual, and domestic narratives imposed on DSA women. Then Salim arrives, and while he is inside the laundrette, the gang attacks his car; when he rushes out to defend it, they attack Salim himself. His loyalties divided between comradeship and his business and romantic investment in Omar, Johnny decides he must defend Salim, regardless of his personal dislike for him. His gang sees this as a betrayal and attacks Johnny savagely until he is in turn rescued by Omar.

The narrative is organized by several such unexpected resonances: this is what preserves the film's offbeat freshness today. It is out of homosexual attachment to Omar (Omo love?) that Johnny gives up everything—his old violent ways, former allegiances, friends. He allows himself to be saved by Omar's love. The beautiful laundrette washes out the stains of British multiculturalism through the surfactants of desire and fantasy—it produces not a political arena but points to the beautiful community, an "ironic utopian paradise."[14] Yet it also *queers* representations of "black" minorities in neoliberal and neocolonial Britain and counterposes an unruly and destabilizing erotic imagination against a repressive and narrowly defined Englishness.

Fire and Feminism

It is productive to juxtapose Kureishi's diasporic utopian fantasy against another diasporic's profilmic fantasy of same-sex love, this time between two very different women: *Fire* (1996), by the Canadian Indian director Deepa Mehta. The film is the first in a trilogy (the second being *Earth* [1999], a version of Bapsi Sidhwa's novel *Cracking India,* and the third *Water* [2005]) on issues affecting women in contemporary India. It also refracts anxieties about globalization's threat to tradition and about sexual identity, in particular "lesbian" identity as inimical to Indian culture. The violent reaction to the film especially by Hindu extremists poses many complex questions. If the film promotes women's freedom to follow their own desires, why is it widely seen as being at odds with feminist perspectives? Why are films about male-male relationships so much less incendiary than *Fire*?

The middle-class extended family in the film—complete with mother-in-law and sinister, Iago-like factotum, Mundu—is headed by Ashok. This paterfamilias arranges the marriage of his younger brother Jatin to Sita, a modern woman emblematic of contemporary India. Under protest, Jatin weds Sita, though he loves the Chinese Indian Julie, who wants to leave for Hong Kong because she and her family detest India and Indians. Julie does not care to be captured in marriage: she prefers "the hunt." Radha is unhappily married to Ashok, ashamed of being unable to bear children. She represses her despair by running the family's take-out business, Jatin by running the video store. Ashok fancies himself something of a renunciant, seeking "wisdom" from a guru; like Gandhi, he has withdrawn from familial responsibilities and marital duties, testing his own virtue by withholding sex from his wife while sleeping in the same bed. Ashok gives large sums of money to his guru because—this is one of many nice touches of black humor in the film—the guru "has to have an operation. . . . [O]ne of his testicles is too large for his loincloth." He is nominally devoted to his stroke-afflicted mother Biji, though it is the manservant Mundu who attends to her: Mundu is even more amoral and unscrupulous than Jatin. Ashok's hypocrisy is more straightforwardly self-delusive than either Mundu's bilious and cruel parody of piety or Jatin's supercilious and self-absorbed philandering. Radha for her part has tried to be as dutiful and loyal as her namesake, the consort of the blue god, Krishna. Sita begins her married life with Jatin in innocent expectancy, hoping for love and companionship, but finds only frustration. Neither she nor Radha receives emotional support or sexual satisfaction in marriage, so eventually they turn to each other. The film closes with Radha and Sita leaving together, but getting only as far as a Muslim holy site. On many levels, I suggest, this is a problematic "conclusion."

Though the film received fourteen international awards, Mehta was attacked for imposing "Western" ideas on Indian values, and the *New York Times* film critic Lawrence Van Gelder also accused her of smuggling an already passé feminist perspective into the Indian context.[15] The original film, to point out the obvious, is in English (as is *Laundrette*). Although the locations are Indian, it focuses only on middle-class India.

Though the Central Board of Film Certification approved *Fire* for release to the general public in November 1988 with an "adults only" certification, recommending a change of Sita's name to Nita but without making cuts, the film met with vigorous opposition. Because it cannot realistically project social acceptance of Radha's relationship with Sita within Hindu society generally, the film relegates same-sex love *to the realm of fantasy*, in which a counterfactual but possible future can nevertheless be *imagined*.

The issue was raised whether the film is complicit in construction of Muslims as somehow by definition un-Indian. Radha and Sita are indeed resoundingly hallowed names; the originals are idealizations of Indian femininity and models for the Indian wife at the center of the family, a centerpiece of popular representations of Indianness. A Hindi-dubbed version of the film was distributed with the name change. Nevertheless two Bombay theaters banned it in December 1988. A theater in New Delhi screening the film was attacked; in both instances the attackers were led by women wearing saffron clothing (a mark of the Shiv Sena, affiliated with the right-wing BJP): their protests targeted women, among whom the film was gaining cachet. The protesters waited for television news camera crews to arrive before they went on a rampage, burning posters and destroying furniture. The Shiv Sena decried the "lesbianism" depicted in the film as being inimical to *local* Indian tradition and expressed its fear that the film would "spoil" Indian women. The group subsequently changed its focus to claiming to represent a broader public objection to what it termed "western imperialism."[16] The film was also banned in Singapore and Kenya at the urging of diasporic Indians in those countries.

Gender and national identity were thus condensed in the phenomenon of the film's reception. Though pressured to reconsider its original decision to approve the film, the Central Board of Film Certification reiterated its position that the film was acceptable, and it was re-released uncensored to the public, although in areas dominated by the Shiv Sena the names of the female protagonists were changed. Civil and women's rights groups defended the film under free speech and secularist legislation, even if feminists were not universally enthralled by the film.

Certainly the film is not quite as effective in representing the constraints of compulsory heterosexuality as Pratibha Parmar's (diasporic) film *Khush* (1991) or even some of the other films I discuss in this chapter. *Fire*'s imbricated themes of sexuality, religion, politics, class, and psychology in such a complicated condensation render any simple arguments about a woman's agency, freedom, or "choice" problematic. It is surprising therefore that Mehta herself disavowed "lesbianism," saying that the film was about women having "choices."[17] Arguably the film's true project is to critique a heteronormative bourgeois Indian family arrangement, a cultural matrix suffused with a high Hindu (Gandhian) value system seen here as moralistic, oppressive, and hypocritical. That hypocritical version of Hindu values is embodied in Ashok and Biji particularly, but it is counterbalanced by the discreditably self-hating and dissolute modernity of Jatin (and Julie). Mehta's method is to set the traditionalists and the modern, younger parties (representative of a modern India, by Mehta's own account) at sixes and sevens, and so figure the contradictions of this Hinduized social matrix, shot through at once with religiosity and nonsecular discrimination. Emblematic of this central trope of the tradition-modernity binary, the two female protagonists pursue fulfillment of their thwarted desires by exiting the hetero-patriarchal nexus of the traditional, dysfunctional, Hindu family toward a future uncertain but not therefore without liberatory potential.

Many postcolonialist commentators, such as Arif Dirlik and Rob Wilson, pit the global and the local in stark opposition ("the global deforms and molests the local").[18] Yet the fantasy of "libidinal" liberation the film purveys is a condensation of the global-local conjuncture, particularly as it reinserts the discourses of postcoloniality and feminism into the Indian public sphere. Sujata Moorti proposes a less "polarized vision," writing that "the contested terrain of national identity is the focus of the debates promoted by the two sets of discourses set in motion by the opposers and supporters of the film."[19]

Mehta herself employs the dialectical relationship between realism and fantasy to reframe this contested terrain. The real, dysfunctional, marital couples of the film (Ashok/Radha and Jatin/Sita) invoke the idealized but also problematic mythological couple of Rama and Sita, from the epic *Ramayan*. The implied comparison flatters none of the couples involved, and indeed the mythological original couple is mocked on several occasions, as when Mundu masturbates to a scene from a videotaped version of the *Ramayan* as the mute, paralyzed, but scandalized Biji watches, unable to protest. Mundu's act is clearly sadistic as well as autoerotic and lubricious; it is certainly destitute of any respect for the

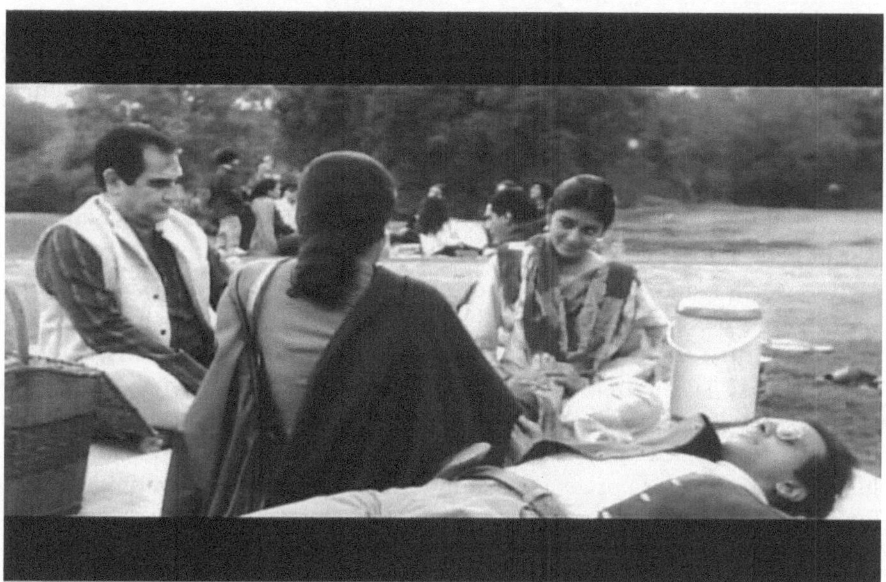

Figure 6.1. Sita (Nandita Das) and Radha (Shabana Azmi) exchanging glances, as Radha's husband, Ashok (Kulbhushan Kharbanda), looks on, in *Fire* (Deepa Mehta, 1996).

epic. Later, even when Mundu abjectly apologizes to the family, there the scene is again on the television set, as if ironizing the apology: Mundu is anything but genuinely contrite. At another moment Mundu literally fantasizes himself in the role of Rama with Sita as his consort. There is also a live street performance of the *Ramayan*'s "*agnipariksha*" (Trial by Fire) episode—by transgendered *hijras*: at the very least this subverts a traditionalist reading of the original. The familiar mythical story involves the abduction of Sita, Rama's consort, by Ravana. But Ravana does not assault Sita, despite having the opportunity. Sita is rescued, and while Rama initially accepts her, he bows to pressure, putting Sita's virtue to trial by fire. She emerges with her virtue intact. Nevertheless, the community remains skeptical and Rama banishes her. Sita, distraught, calls on the earth to open up and swallow her. Ashok and his guru witness the theatrical performance, transfixed. Clearly the profilmic representation asks us to reflect on their attitudes to women—and adumbrates an important late scene of the film, when Ashok does nothing to save Radha when her sari catches fire in the kitchen. Ashok is no Rama, but he too betrays his wife.

Perhaps the most subversive public moment of intimacy in the "lesbian narrative" central to the film occurs at a picnic attended by the entire family. Radha and Sita are beautifully dressed, clearly for each other's eyes. Sita massages Radha's feet (see Figure 6.1) in a manner that others present read as sisterly, but the women (and viewers) recognize as sensual.

Part of the erotic charge inheres in the fact that it is in a very public—and historic—place, the gardens attached to a (Muslim) mausoleum, or *dargah*. Mughal gardens are culturally coded sites, the iconic site being the gardens around the Taj Mahal, evocative of the love of Shah Jahan for his beloved Noor Jahan, in whose memory the Taj was built. In a site so dense with romantic convention, it is ironic that Radha and Sita express their scandalously unconventional eroticism. The scene of their public display adumbrates their final reunion at the Sufi shrine, Nizamuddin *dargah*, an intermediate space between the Hindu/Punjabi (at any rate non-Muslim) space of domesticity from which they have exited and (secular/civil) social space.

It is worth remarking that the foot-massage scene pointedly evokes and contrasts with two other scenes in the film. The first is the one in which Jatin gently holds his girlfriend Julie's foot as he applies nail polish to her toenails, caresses her foot, and kisses it. In this visual parallel with the scene in which Sita sensually massages Radha's foot, Jatin expresses his hopeless desire for Julie, his wish that she had married him; he goes so far as to tell her he can't live without her. Julie responds that she prefers the "hunt," her favorite word, meaning to chase for game—or kill. In other words, she states her preference for a relationship based not on the security of excitement-killing matrimony and domestic duty but on desire—at any cost. This too is a rejection of traditional Hindu family values, we should not forget, given that protesters against Mehta excoriated her for antitraditionalist provocations—though they were focused mainly on the two women's transgressive same-sex attachments and notably not on Jatin's infidelity or Ashok's hypocrisy.[20]

This scene astonishingly yields to a smash cut (without any intervening visual frame) to the second scene I referred to above. In this second parallel scene we see Ashok this time, massaging—or caressing—his guru's feet in a different though equally formulaic gesture of devotion. The guru himself drones on about nothing less than "desire night," which he insists is the world-destroying "love of power," opposed to "aspiration light." Ashok's massaging the guru's feet is a culturally specific meme, signaling a disciple's devotion to his mentor. But that is not all: Ashok is clearly caught in the grip of *erotic* fantasy; perhaps his wish to suppress his own desire is intended to be a parody, as I suggested earlier, of Gandhi's own similar "experiments in truth," a send-up of moral hypocrisy on Ashok's part. In those experiments Gandhi subjected his wife to trials of his own vows of celibacy, asking her to lie chastely in bed with him.

The three scenes are provocatively interlinked as a sustained gloss on the policing of desire by institutions such as marriage and organized religion. But they also invite a psychoanalytic interpretation. It is a central tenet of at least Lacanian psychoanalysis to never cede ground on one's desire (*jamais céder sur son désir*), because that would result in the aphanisis of the subject. The tenet should not be reduced to absurdity as recommending radical selfishness or solipsism, but understood as fundamental to subject constitution.

The "impossibility" of fantasy is registered at several levels in the film, including the crucial level of language (visual as well as lexical). At the end of the film Radha and Sita escape to reunite in a Muslim (Sufi) shrine. This is too inconclusive a deus ex machina, too utopian—which is to say too "impossible"—a visual representation of a fantasy scenario that inverts the opening image of an idyllic space of freedom, the mustard field of green and yellow, and seems to concede that they cannot hope to be truly accepted in society. Radha and Sita remain ultimately suspended in an in-between, liminal space. If the mustard field is distantiated as visible only through fantasy, the improbable idyll of lesbian love is figured as a fantasy by suspending it in a Muslim religious shrine. The film "spatially" marks impossibility in the choice the women have made to seek refuge. It is a choice that vanishes into a horizon without an endpoint: even theoretically it is not clear where the two women *could* go away *to*, except for the nonplace (*non-lieu*) of their desire that has no legal/cultural/social status within the territorial space of Indian culture. For the older Radha especially, the absence of a telos underscores the daring as well as the hopelessness of her surrender to a fantasy of an alternative future for herself with Sita. Radha, having survived a near-death in the domestic space of her marriage, is now again between two deaths—she is dead to a heteronormative world but also suspended in a nonplace with no "end."[21]

Lexically, too, the impossibility is thematized explicitly. As Sita says, "Listen, Radha, there is no word in our language that can describe what we are, how we feel about each other." In the scene where she has a close encounter with death, Radha confesses her feelings to Ashok. His words also suggest that Radha has become literally *unnameable* within the received parameters of language and culture. He asks, "What kind of woman have you become?" "Look at you, shameless *randi* [whore]. Instead of begging for forgiveness you give me lectures." Radha's own response to his vitriol is poignant: "Without desire," she tells Ashok, "I am dead."

That Ashok ironically already sees her as dead (to him) is made literal in this terrible scene where, after he pushes Radha and as she is forced backward, her sari catches fire and, dead calm, he abandons her on the point of her impending immolation, a queered *agnipariksha*. This scene will also evoke the well-publicized specter of staged "accidents" in kitchens in many Indian homes, where a recently wed woman's clothing happens to catch fire in her kitchen. Many of these "accidental" deaths turn out to be dowry-related acts of manslaughter or murder, usually over disputes about dowry or related issues—often these crimes are motivated by raw cupidity, an opportunity to secure another, perhaps a larger, dowry. In *Fire*, as Radha's sari burns, Ashok does not even feign an attempt to save her. Instead, picking Biji off the floor where she has fallen, he watches Radha burn, as if desublimating the mythological *agnipariksha*. Ashok chooses, in Biji, what he had chosen in his charlatan guru—not just his mother but a "fallen-down" and repressive traditional Indianness, out of joint with the times. Further, and worse, his is a dangerously reactionary and desperate clinging to tradition: it nearly has fatal consequences for Radha, a woman who is finally learning to be true to her own desire. This is the desire denied in the public sphere to Indian women.

Radha's near-death experience by fire has been prepared for not only by the earlier scene of a *natak* (the street theater representation, performed by *hijras*, or transvestite/transsexual performers) of the *agnipariksha* but also by the very title of Mehta's film. While Radha is no subaltern, there is an element of the structural silencing of the woman Gayatri Spivak alludes to in her essay "Can the Subaltern Speak?" particularly as her voicelessness in the dysfunctional family environment is ironically echoed in Biji's real muteness.[22] Radha was unable, before the "filmi" Sita entered her life, to speak against her own "deadening" (in her own precise terminology) confinement within a marriage bereft of desire and of/for her own desire. What Sita does is to open up an opportunity, a space, for the emergence in her of what Hegel would recognize as "self-consciousness," which "exists in and for itself by virtue of the fact that it is in and for itself for another. That is, it exists only in being recognized."[23] This recognition need not be the recognition of the relatively powerless by the relatively powerful. It can also be an affirmative recognition of another by someone who does not wish to exploit the other.

This recognition is in marked contrast with Ashok's misrecognition of Radha, his own indoctrination as a male in patriarchal Hindu society, which can see Radha only as a dutiful, self-denying wife/mother, or not at all. Since Radha cannot give Ashok children (she is unable to become pregnant but he seems to blame only her), and because she grows attached to another woman, she is indeed quite dead to Ashok, and only a *sati*-like immolation can redeem her, or so Ashok seems to think. The imagery of *sati* permeates the entire film. And the issue of *pativrata*, or a wife's unquestioning devotion to her husband, is a pillar of Hindu tradition.

The fantasy of an alternative space for non-heterosexual desire and subjectivity is offset in a parallax from the social realist elements portraying existing conditions for women. If my analysis has emphasized the emergence of an excessive, alternative space through the powers of fantasy, it is important simultaneously to ground the film's realism—its anchoring to the real histories of women's subjugation through practices such as *sati*, a crucial metonym for the plight of women over the centuries of Indian history into the present. The contradiction of the film arises at this disjunction of two spatialities: the parallax does not resolve itself in a stereopsis in which "lesbian" love can coexist with the discourse of "choice" *within* heteronormative structures. Radha and Sita cannot find a space of their own within heteronormative society, and the *film* offers no *internal* historical perspective from which the naturalness of that heteronormativity might have been interrogated.

It would be hard to find a contemporary illustration more noteworthy than the late 1980s case of Roop Kanwar. Kanwar, an eighteen-year-old, was married a scant eight months to and spent only a few weeks with Maal Singh and lived in the small town of Deorala when he died. Kanwar decided she would become a *sati* (an embodiment of truth, or *satya*) in the time-honored custom intended to demonstrate publicly and for eternity the woman's purity (*pavitrata*) as well as her devotion to her husband (*pativrata*). On September 4, 1987, dressed in her wedding attire, she walked, reportedly very calmly, to the site where her husband was to be cremated, and she was burned to death on the funeral pyre. Incidentally, it would be interesting to test the veracity of that "calmly"; sometimes women planning to be *satis* are drugged so that they don't panic and fail to go through with the culturally sanctioned but surely daunting ritual. But even if the reports are accurate, it is a good question whether any woman can truly be calm in body or mind before committing *sati*. Is it just brainwashing? Is it false consciousness? Is it just coercion?

These are not incidental or eccentric questions in the context. As Spivak describes the *sati* phenomenon, it is clear that actually desiring to be consumed by the "holy" fire is deemed the highest "proof" of a woman's virtue, since she cannot be of further service to her husband. When the Hindu widow ascends the pyre of the dead husband and immolates herself upon it, Spivak reminds us, what we are talking about is "widow sacrifice," the coercive putting to death of a woman just because she was married to a man who died before her. "The rite was not practiced universally and was not caste- or class-fixed. The abolition of this rite by the British has been generally understood as a case of 'White men saving brown women from brown men:' Against this is the Indian nativist argument, a parody of the nostalgia for lost origins: 'the women actually want to die.'"[24]

There are two contextual points to be made in connection with Spivak's formulation. In the first instance, there is the question of cui bono—who benefits from the institution of *sati?* The obvious answer is that in a male-dominated society such as India's it is mainly men who benefit, as is clearly indicated by the imperative of devotion to the husband, *pativrata*. In a discussion of the Kanwar incident Sikata Banerjee observes that "Kanwar's death . . . provides an illustration of the dangerous social consequences when a chaste woman's body literally becomes the canvas on which a community's honour and identity are depicted," discussing in particular what she calls a very male-oriented Hindu "muscular nationalism." The narrative of Sita's *agnipariksha* in the *Ramayan* has been widely disseminated in religious contexts as well as in popular fora such as the TV serialization of the *Ramayan* broadcast throughout India. The ritual in which Kanwar participated is a "representation of sexual purity and its association with Rajput (even Hindu) honour." Yet *sati* is "not an immutable fixture within Hindu society. Indeed, the origin, implication and historical frequency of sati are fiercely contested in scholarship."[25] Spivak's comment applies also to the filmmaker herself—a relatively privileged, middle-class diasporic director. Such elite postcolonial commentators on the woman's condition in India must also "unlearn" their privilege along the lines that Spivak sets down: "In seeking to learn to speak to (rather than listen to or speak for) the historically muted subject of the subaltern woman, the postcolonial intellectual systematically 'unlearns' female privilege."[26]

Sati, then, cannot be understood in a vacuum, even when we are discussing its appearance as a motif in several unconnected episodes in *Fire:* the film is firmly of its milieu and must be evaluated in a very specifically historicized and contextualized way. That being said, presented by the film, the motif of *sati* is undeniably a metonym for a long-standing Hindu world view. Mehta's film, released just over a decade after the Kanwar incident, seemed such a strong indictment of the structural conditions that would glorify *sati* that it became the focus of a violent reprisal, especially from Hindu right-wing extremists, votaries of the ideology of Hindutva. As noted earlier, members of the Shiv Sena (the so-called army of the Hindu god Shiva—the group is the Mumbai-based organization formed by Bal Thackeray in 1966, two decades after Independence, with a special regional interest in the state of Maharashtra and industry interest in Bollywood), including and indeed led by women, in particular Meena Kambli, a local leader from the subgroup Mahila Agadhi, attacked two Mumbai cinema theaters, protesting Mehta's film. Other attacks occurred in Pune, Delhi, and elsewhere, often involving other Hindu right-wing groups such as the Vishwa Hindu Parishad (VHP) and the Bajrang Dal. From the perspective of the extreme Right, films such as *Fire* have a negative influence, exposing women to unnatural and culturally alien behavior such as lesbianism. Sujata Moorti notes that if Mehta was trying to raise consciousness about women's oppression, the message was "subverted by nationalist modes of thinking developed during colonialism."[27] Yet what is often obscured in the debate is the idea that the film does not introduce lesbianism to a culture innocent of it but reflects what is suppressed by that culture, especially in its religious or nonsecular manifestations. Mehta was demonized and prohibited from proceeding with her plans to make *Water,* the third film in her then-intended trilogy (the first being *Earth*), in her preferred location, Varanasi. After many attempts to film in India, the crew was forced to shoot in Sri Lanka instead. It remains obscure whether the protesters saw too much distortion of reality (fantasy?) in the film or *too much reality.* It also remains unclear in the end what power the transgressive fantasy of Radha and Sita in each other's arms in a Muslim *dargah* really exerts, and whether that final refuge from their oppressive reality is a satisfactory conclusion. At the end of the film we are faced with not only the powers of fantasy but also its deficits—the powerlessness of fantasy.

Fire's potency as a profilmic fiction may derive from the way in which alternative spaces are opened up, not only in the fantasy unleashed by the cinematic assemblage but also as an aftereffect of cosmopolitan cultural awareness, for example, of a growing feminist conscientization of women, within the heteronormative space of marriage, within a household revealed to be dysfunctional, hypocritical, in denial. Everyone from Ashok on down, including Jatin, Biji, and Mundu, is unsympathetic, the only exceptions being the lesbians with the resoundingly mythological (Hindu) names Sita and Radha, who find a safe house only in a (Muslim) shrine (the *dargah*) rather than a Hindu temple. Yet it is telling that the two women have not really resolved anything: they have just run away from society, from their family and prior commitments, from the social itself, as if acquiescing to their "apparitional" status as women who love a woman.[28]

The power of the false is a phrase meaningful only to the extent that the false is itself not converted by the legerdemain of bad faith into a positive truth. Truths may be, as Nietzsche put it, fictions whose fictionality has been forgotten, but that is not to say the false is a truth whose fictionality may be forgotten without consequences. Fantasy, in *Fire,* is perhaps today only a mirage in the desert of the real, but it is potent because it could become reality, and if not, it is in a Platonic sense autotelic: it does not necessarily need to point beyond itself.

In the psychoanalytic lexicon, fantasy has real force in two senses. First, fantasy functions as a portal—as the hole through which the Real shows itself, tearing the fabric of the actual. It is necessary that the Real remain at bay, for if it were to take over, it would annihilate the subject. In the second sense it has a real—sociopolitical—force that is not exhausted by the psychoanalytic formulation of the fantasy. Precisely because it opens up an extimate space outside the everyday reality, it enables an access to pleasure and desire—and therefore to a regenerated subjectivity—and points to a possible future to come.

Given the disappointment or frustration of the marginalized subject in the public sphere, that subject constructs a fantasy of a reality more adequate to the subject's true desire. The fantasy allows for the expression of a desire that is more fully adequate to the subject's experience of himself or herself, more adequate in establishing the self and defining the object of desire, as well as the relation between subject and objects of desire. As Slavoj Žižek phrases the point, "*through fantasy, we learn how to desire.*"[29]

Yet *in the diegetic universe of the film itself* the "resolution" the lesbian couple arrive at is ultimately nothing more than a fantasy. It is only too easy to nurture facile claims about the power of the false to challenge entrenched regimes of thought. *Fire* is thus riven by contradictions, and while it manages to *queer* the notion of heteronormativity, it does not own—indeed the director actively *dis*avows—an LGBTIQ identification. Mehta's disavowal of lesbian identity for Radha and Sita, considered together with its unsatisfying "conclusion," may then provide a tentative answer to the question why *Fire* has not been universally embraced as a lesbian film.

The film conforms superficially to Bonnie Zimmerman's definition of a "lesbian narrative": it presents a central lesbian character (here, co-protagonists), is focused on sexual passion between women, and is read by lesbians to "affirm lesbian existence."[30] But even Zimmerman refers, in her very title, to "what has never been," something that is always yet to come. My suggestion is that the film, even despite the director herself, offers the *spectator* a fantasy, if not a utopia, yet to be actualized. As noted, Mehta herself has denied it, saying that the film is not about lesbians as much as it is a question of choices—for the two women the real issue is making a choice to be happy even if that means giving up their (bad) marriages. Radha and Sita *do not see themselves* as lesbians. Still, the film opens up avenues for "queering" patriarchal or traditional marital constellations of power. Thus I have bookended the discussion of *Fire* between more explicitly LGBTIQ-themed films.

Minor Narratives: Non-heteronormative Subtexts and Cryptotexts

On December 11, 2013, India's Supreme Court reversed the July 2009 ruling of the Delhi High Court decriminalizing same-sex relations between consenting adults in private. The decriminalizing ruling by the Delhi High Court had understandably been received with euphoria by the LGBTIQ community, many, like Sunil Mehra, former editor of the Indian edition of *Maxim*, expressing relief that they could live normal lives. The judgment by the Supreme Court came as a "shock" to many progressives and activists, who characterized the reversal as the Indian legal version of *Bowers v. Hardwick*, a 1986 ruling in which the U.S. Supreme Court upheld, in a 5–4 decision, a Georgia court's sodomy law criminalizing homosexual sex between consenting adults, denying a "fundamental right" of "homosexuals to engage in sodomy," irrespective of "the fact that homosexual conduct occurs in the privacy of the home" and regardless of whether it is "an inadequate rationale" to support the law on the basis of popular belief that sodomy is immoral.[31] This ruling was itself reversed in 2003. Progressives and other supporters of the Delhi Court ruling can only hope that the Indian Supreme Court will reverse itself in the future. Indeed, some think it is inevitable. The question is "How should we understand this most recent reversal today?"

The key legal statute is Section 377 of the Indian Penal Code (IPC), otherwise known as the Unnatural Offences Act. The section reads: "377. Unnatural offences—Whoever voluntarily has carnal intercourse against the order of nature with any man, woman or animal, shall be punished with imprisonment for life, or with imprisonment of either description for a term which may extend to ten years, and shall also be liable to fine." In the contemporary law courts, and on the basis of this construction of homosexuality, the law calls for harsh strictures against and punishment (for up to ten years) for "homosexual acts." In December 2013, the Supreme Court appeared to have reinstated the strictures against such acts. In a country famous for the *Kama Sutra* and the well-known erotic sculptures of Khajuraho, it is ironic how prudishly the space of sanctioned sexuality even behind closed doors is policed in postcolonial India.

Prima facie consideration would suggest that the main issue is morality, as Section 377's language suggests. But this may not be the whole story. There is a dimension of cultural and political sovereignty at stake as well, harking back to the era of British colonialism. After all, Section 377 of the Indian Constitution derived its language in 1860 from an archaic law of the colonial British canon characterizing homosexual acts as "unnatural." What is remarkable is that the criterion of consent between or among adults is irrelevant to considerations of legality here, and so persons engaging in such acts are punishable whether or not they enter into same-sex relationships voluntarily or out of mutual desire as adults in possession of their faculties. Although the Delhi High Court ruling of 2009 seemed to have advanced democratic rights even for sexually minoritized groups and individuals, India's secular polity now appears to have regressed to the level of states such as Iran and Saudi Arabia, not to mention Afghanistan, where "homosexuality" is regarded as perversion, punishable by imprisonment or even death.

This regressive tendency takes on additional dark undertones if considered as part of a general hostility to any change threatening compulsory heterosexuality and patriarchy, which are construed as emanations or symptoms of the "natural" social order. The case of Malala Yousafzai (the student activist for girls' and women's rights to education, and now Nobel Prize winner, who was shot in the head on October 9, 2012, by a member of the Taliban in the Swat Valley) indicates the risk borne by anyone who challenges extremely conservative sexual regimes from within. Is the recriminalization of same-sex relations under Section 377 in India equally indicative of the perceived threat to the hegemonic sexual regime? The answer to that question, I suggest, might be a "yes, but"—because there are other dimensions to the issue.

For one thing, not all "homosexual acts" are perceived to carry the same level of threat, because it is not just a matter of disturbing the order of procreative sexuality. In some of the cultures most hostile to "homosexual acts," penetration of a man (usually a younger man or boy) by another (usually older) is not itself a marker of either man's real or incipient homosexuality. It is not a homosexual act, in such cases, that defines homosexuality.

There are also other distinctions to be observed. Even more threatening to traditionalists than male-male homosexual acts are female-female same-sex acts. It is a double whammy: lesbians are doubly marginalized, as women and as non-heterosexual; even worse, if women are poor or from minority communities, class, religion, ethnicity, or caste can compound their marginalization. Among these differences is a degree of commonality. As Luce Irigaray points out, "All the systems of exchange that organize patriarchal societies and all the modalities of productive work that are recognized, valued, and rewarded in these societies are men's business."[32] Yet what is important is to avoid homogenizing all non-heteronormative behavior as counterposed to a monolithic heterosexual norm. Even in the domain of non-heteronormative sexuality, difference makes a difference.

Fire did have some political effect beyond the domain of *filmi* fantasy. The film screenings were an intervention into the public sphere and into public debate. They had material effect in breaking the silence on the oppressive tradition that denied the kinds of desire for which it admitted no name. After the controversy died down, telephone counseling centers and help lines were opened to callers seeking information, assistance, and connection with similarly inclined individuals who might not otherwise have connected. Women organized the Campaign for Lesbian Rights (CALERI) to retrieve lesbianism from the shadows of Indian society and to develop public and state recognition of the dignity and rights of lesbians. Along with the Delhi-based group Sangini and a sister organization in the United States, the South Asian Lesbian and

Gay Association (SALGA), CALERI participated in the larger struggle against discrimination.[33]

Relatedly, the Indian Lawyers Collective has argued that Section 377 is too vague. There is an important gay rights discourse that teases apart the contradictions between the sexual and the political even within Section 377. For instance, it points out that Section 377's language violates Articles 14, 15, 19, and 21 of the Indian Constitution, which guarantee equality, freedom of expression, and personal liberty to all citizens regardless of religion, creed, caste, class, and gender. A fundamental contradiction is therefore instituted in this law of the secular democracy. And there are serious implications to glossing over, or overlooking, such contradictions. Driving non-heteronormative sexual behavior back into the closet risks endangering the lives and livelihoods of people who do not follow the conventional heteronormative trajectories in terms of family, lifestyle, reproduction, and work life. Worse, it could jeopardize social support for and government funding of HIV/AIDS prevention efforts. The Naz Foundation, a gay rights NGO, petitioned to decriminalize gay sex with the Delhi High Court, arguing that law has been used to blackmail and visit violence on the bodies of sexual minorities. Besides, such law quashes any public-sphere debate about subjects made taboo artificially by decree. The controversy surrounding the film *Fire* is an instructive object lesson, illustrating the saliency of the issue even in today's Indian democracy, in a contemporary society that is proud of its progress toward modernity, even as judged on a globalized standard. Section 377 discriminates indiscriminately and criminalizes unjustly, collapsing any act that does not conform to a particular, radically traditionalist or reactionary, construction of the "natural" into the catchall category of "immoral" acts.

It is even more important, especially in a secular state, not to collapse cultural/political codes into moral codes, no matter how strong the urge. The controversy surrounding Mehta's film became a barometer of an important phase in the ongoing debate about same-sex relationships in India at least since Independence, when the British legal construction of its alleged "immorality" and "unnaturalness" has been dominant. One of the important lessons to be learned from the controversy was that questions of sexuality are imbricated with questions of nation and nationalism, and that there are continuities between perceived threats to heteronormative sexuality and imagined threats to national identity in the context of accelerated globalization.

The legal debate about the Supreme Court's reversal has been framed largely within a discourse of *morality.* Some defenders of the reversal, for instance, put it quite simply and unapologetically: "We are living in India, this is not America, and according to the morals of our society, this is a correct judgement." Another opined, "Homosexuality is a Western import—we have assimilated some good aspects of their culture but this is a bad aspect of their culture. We cannot ape the West blindly, otherwise how will we protect our culture?"[34] Many supporters of gay rights and other progressive observers decry India's slide back from a "modern" and "enlightened" view of sexuality. Yet perhaps the impression of backward motion in the world's most populous democracy has as much to do with a perceived threat to *cultural sovereignty* in the contemporary globalized conjuncture as with *sexual* morality. To focus on only the *sexual* politics misses the critical dimension of the unfolding debates in India about secularism and *sovereignty*.

As it rends the heteronormative fabric of traditional patriarchy to make space for nonprocreative female mutuality and self-sufficiency, lesbian love threatens to upset power dynamics even outside the bedroom, by redirecting primary allegiance, as Terry Castle argues, not to men but to other women.[35] A more radical threat posed by lesbianism is epistemological, as suggested by Monique Wittig's argument that a lesbian is not a woman, an ontological category derived from the category "man."[36] Lesbian epistemology does not posit the masculine as standard; it implicitly refuses the "citational performative," in Judith Butler's phrase, which requires that "woman" is always defined by reference to "man" and, by extension, to heteronormative coupling or compulsory heterosexuality.[37] It might be useful to revisit a few other important films that populate the range between the two poles of this distinction, for a fuller comparative appreciation of whether mainstream Hindi cinema can, even via the offices of fantasy, test the received doxa of Hindu heteronormativity. In a growing cluster of films minor cinematic narratives featuring non-heteronormative attachments are relegated to sub- or cryptotextual levels, able to claim only the realm of fantasy, yet they may promise political effectivity as a new horizon.

Even though South Asian films in general are far less permissive about any kind of sexuality than Western cinema of the same period, there are some notable films in which gay themes have been smuggled in, such as the classic comedy *Mera Naam Joker* (Call Me the Joker, Raj Kapoor, 1970). A female character in the film passes as Minoo Master, a male petty thug, but then she and her trusted protector, Raju, the eponymous Joker, fall in love, and it becomes an interesting question whether Raju had already developed feelings for Minoo Master before he reveals that he is a "she." One could also mention in contrast the film version of E. M. Forster's *A Passage to India*—the film, made in 1984 and directed by David Lean, was seen by Indian cinema-goers even if they had not read the book, and it pivots on the truncated homosocial bonding between a white man and a brown man falsely accused of sexual assault of a woman.

A diasporic profilmic fantasy of same-sex love that explicitly explores the idea of configuring an alternative (Indo-Guyanese) space for "impossible desires" is the South Asian Canadian Michelle Mohabeer's *Coconut/Cane & Cutlass* (1994). This short film (thirty minutes), shot in 16mm, is a classic example of alternative cinema. This is true even of its style—poetic, ruminative, non-narrative, autobiographical in some degree. It employs, for instance, lyrical authorial interventions in the form of voice-over, and complicates memory with contextual history to create a fragile fantasy through dance, archival footage, use of optical prints, front-screen projection images, and layered and episodic plot segments. Yet ultimately this very personal document seems to relinquish broader political ambitions, privatizing the important struggle to achieve a meaningful LGBTIQ identity.

More recent films seem more direct when they introduce same-sex desire, yet they tend to whisk the homoerotic away from under the spectator's nose and reinstate heteronormative desire, subsuming the gay theme in some way. This procedure is a kind of "precoital" interruption or withdrawal, a parodic and motivated incompletion (rendering un-*real*) of a lesbian or gay romance. Glimmerings of this tactic were discussed in Chapter 3 in the context of *Sholay* (1975). As I show below, another good example of this representational "bisexuality" informs *Bend It Like Beckham* (Gurinder Chadha, 2002), where the fantasy of same-sex desire is first proffered and then strategically thwarted and displaced as comedic subtext.

Bend It Like Beckham presents a young diasporic woman, Jesminder (Jess), who is more assimilated, more cosmopolitan than her immigrant parents, and who wants only to play soccer. This introduces the main conflict: as a marriageable Asian woman in an immigrant family, she is forbidden from showing her skin in football shorts. She is pressured to conform but otherwise is not really conflicted about whether to be "just British" and play on an English soccer team or honor the code of feminine modesty dictated by her Sikh "tradition." This film is an exception in its sensitivity to the range of possibilities for subject formation, including possibilities that mean breaching ethnic, sexual, and cultural barriers.

Soccer functions as a displacement of sexuality. On another level there is a more banal fantasy of female self-actualization: Jess's desire to play soccer is fulfilled via several fantasy expressions. The film opens with a cleverly executed fantasy of Jess receiving a pass from David Beckham, which she successfully heads into the goal. There are other related fantasies: of "talking to" Beckham in the privacy of her room and of "bending" the ball round a group of sari-clad women as she is taking a penalty shot (the actual defenders and soccer players are transformed by Jess's imagination in this moment of fantasy). In the final minutes of the film the fantasy object Beckham himself appears with his wife, Victoria, on an elevated gangway at the airport, just before Jess and Jules fly away to America on a soccer scholarship.

In this last scene the "fantasy" that comes true for Jess and Jules is also a literally transnational fantasy: both of them win scholarships to go to "Santa Clara University" to play soccer in America, which is imagined as offering greater opportunity. In this sanguine exceptionalist fantasy, America is a land of opportunity even for the sport of soccer, and South Asian Americans are imagined as a model minority who, in contrast with British Asians, face relatively little discrimination. This mythology (or "fantasy"), conjoint with the model minority myth circulating in the space of North American multicultural spaces, functions as an impossible aspirational narrative that ends up silencing a more "realist" account of the truth of multiculturalism in Western "receiving" countries of postcolonial immigration.

Jasbir Puar and Amit Rai describe the transnational dimension as conjugating "the gender as well as racial exceptionalism of the United States," for in America, or so the fantasy would run, Jess and Jules "can play women's soccer without compromising their heterosexuality or their homoerotic bond." So it is first a fantasy of having your cake and eating it. But it is "also the site of salvation for racial others: unlike Britain, the United States promises for Jess an acceptance of her brownness along with an escape from her conservative familial home and extended neighborhood community in Hounslow."[38] While Puar and Rai are right to point to the gender and racial exceptionalism of the film's rhetoric, their account is inadequately complex. Even in the smaller details their account misses the fact that Jules's father is on balance sympathetic with and supportive of his daughter's enthusiasm for the sport.

Puar and Rai's account underestimates the poignant complexity of the atmosphere of the "conservative familial home" of Jess's Punjabi family. Jess's father, who had suffered the slings and arrows of racialism in his own ambition to play the game of cricket as a young immigrant in Britain, is not just the paterfamilias of a traditionalist family but crucially identifies with Jess's desire to play a sport, as that might smooth her passage into more complete assimilation in white mainstream society. Significantly, he comes around at a dramatic moment to offer a moving tribute to his daughter's skill at soccer (employing the quintessential British colloquial locution, he describes it as "brilliant") and an even more touching declaration of his desire to see her succeed as a student in America on a soccer scholarship. Even during the important occasion of his older daughter's wedding, he permits Jess to leave the celebration and play her important match. So while there is a germ of truth in the authors' conclusion that "the United States symbolizes opportunity, escape, and reconciliation of the clash of cultures" and that it "purports to be a safety valve for the unyielding racism, sexism, and homophobia of other places," it is not entirely fair to cast the Bhamra home as a site simply opposed to opportunity and personal or gendered freedoms for someone such as Jess.[39] Bifocality seems to suggest itself once again as a better approach.

In even more recent films, particularly independent productions, the representation of LGBTIQ themes is growing much more explicit, even graphic—and more sophisticated. I mention a few briefly. *Sixth Happiness* (Waris Hussein, 1997), starring Firdaus Kanga, is based on Kanga's print autobiography, titled *Trying to Grow.* This is a sexual bildungsroman of a disabled diasporic South Asian British youth. Not at all apologetic about his non-heterosexual identity, Kanga embraces a gay identity with an alacrity that contrasts with anything in *Fire*, let alone in mainstream popular Hindi films. But that is also to say that *Sixth Happiness* highlights an important gap in the domestic tolerance for films with LGBTIQ themes. Another important film was the short *Summer in My Veins* (Nishit Saran, 1999), released a scant few years before the young director's death. It chronicles Saran's coming-out narrative. Because it is a poignant and unpretentious story, it has remained evocatively on the "identity politics" end of the spectrum, but speaks especially to the young person discovering his or her non-heterosexual identity.

The Hindi-language *My Brother Nikhil* (Onir, 2005) was a landmark film loosely based on the real story of Damien D'Souza, one of the most prominent AIDS activists in the country. The film is important because it looks unblinkingly at one of the important crises that struck the LGBTIQ community especially hard. Damien is represented here as a competitive swimmer (Suri) who is shunned because he is diagnosed with the HIV-AIDS virus. But his challenges and joys are presented with sensitivity, humor, and honesty.

It is crucial to attend to the fine detail in the transnational traffic of cultural memes and cultural practices at the level of the local, familial, and individual story, the everyday experience if you will, even if it is against the backdrop of larger, global, cultural transformations. Notwithstanding the emergent LGBTIQ movement in India, where a couple of NGOs are now fighting harassment and discrimination supported by Section 377, same-sex love between women remains closeted—both literally and figuratively relegated to a confined space in the shadows of society. It is against this backdrop that we might better appreciate the powers of the false that entertain the possibility of women such as *Fire*'s Radha and Sita to flout convention and find a space of their own. My contention is that even in this brave diasporic vision, we must recognize the play of fantasy, running counter to the actual prospects such women might be able to contemplate in real life. Fantasy has the potential to produce alternative zones—or queer existing ones—for agential film narratives. These zones not only *represent* but may also *be* the primary "alternative spaces" for the free expression of desire, the nurturing matrix for self-fashioning. These spaces reaffirm the power of fantasy, yet they concede that profilmic projections of such fantasy fulfillments of desire precede actual social development: they point the way to more generous vistas, more equitable spaces, possible futures that are not yet.

7

The New Cosmopolitanism and Diasporic Dilemmas

Rehabilitating the "NRI"

Globalization has transformed the global and local expressions of cosmopolitanism from the anthropological, geopolitical, and legal inflections given the term by the Enlightenment philosopher Immanuel Kant. While premised on the ethics of being a citizen of the world, cosmopolitanism often encodes a refined, perhaps even elitist, multiculturalist belief in universalism crystallizing modernity's "hidden agenda."[1] A new cosmopolitanism has also begun to infiltrate contemporary diasporic South Asian (DSA) cinema, albeit in a very rudimentary way, structurally and thematically recasting Indianness, with the figure of the diasporic, overseas, or nonresident Indian (NRI) subject at its center. This new cosmopolitanism decenters the Indian Subcontinent as the anchor of autochthonous Indianness, challenging religious and cultural discourses premised on an immemorial, originary essence. In destabilizing sociopolitical attitudes that would cast Indianness as homogeneous and sovereign, it also subtends new, increasingly centrifugal cultural identifications, including imaginary ones. The lability of signifiers of Indianness facilitates a new visual language. The local is dialectically posed against the global; hybrid, even idiolectal, "glocalization" tenders a dissonant blend of traditional markers of "Indian" culture with cosmopolitan signifiers—Westernized fashion, "Hinglish," internationalist "lifestyle choices." This dissonance registers the asymmetries of uneven development, complicating any facile universalism implied by "cosmopolitanism," and the contradictions produced by the dynamic of India's induction into the global.

Cosmopolitanism has long been an earmark of popular Bombay cinema, manifest in the cinema's ethnic, religious, class, and caste diversity, its internationalist outlook, its double consciousness representing a singular national culture on the one hand and subverting insular nationalism on the other. Indeed, absent a singular national identity, the film industry has often furnished the "primary social identity and community for most people" involved in it, writes Tejaswini Ganti.[2] The question of belonging has been especially pertinent for DSAs or NRIs—the latter acronym is a political category for overseas Indian passport holders, while the former describes anyone of South Asian descent living abroad.

Domestic opinions about Indians in Africa were traditionally different from those about Indians in the Caribbean or in the British or North American diaspora. The reputation of the North American diaspora superseded that of the British, which had enjoyed greater cachet in the decades immediately following Independence. Between the 1970s and the mid-1990s, however, a reconfigured cosmopolitanism emerged in Hindi cinema, registering unprecedented shifts in the perceptions of NRIs.

The orthodox discourse on national diasporas treats them as distinct from and peripheral to the nation-state of origin. Some advocates of postcolonial and "postnational" perspectives suggest that the nation-state form is becoming obsolete, being superseded by forms defined by global flows and porous borders. What seems unquestionable is that we need a more complex and multifaceted account of the dynamic relationship between nation-states and their diasporas. Cinematic representations of "Indianness" are shifting in concert with this changing relationship. I propose that a bifocal and transnational perspective is necessary to apprehend a condensing sensibility—a new cosmopolitanism—in DSA cinema. It would actively account for the play of identifications and disidentifications between Indian citizens "at home" in India and DSA subjects—ironizing the conventions of both the global and the local ("Indianness") but also opening new possibilities for defining Indianness in way more adequate to transformations within the global ecumene.

Indianness today is construed as simultaneously centripetal and centrifugal: anchored to both Subcontinental territorial space and diasporic/transnational contexts that can threaten to make peripheral the very category of "home"/homeland. This is the site of a critical ambivalence in DSA cinema's new cosmopolitanism. An essentialist understanding of Indianness would cast it as sovereign, primordial, timeless, integral, anchored within national boundaries; many factions are certainly trying to do just that in reaction to advancing globalization. Against this anxious, centripetal, and insular tendency I argue here and in the Conclusion that Indianness is growing more disaggregated, fragmented, increasingly "cosmopolitan," but also *nonidentical to* the sum of its fragments.[3] This is in line with what Stephen Toulmin diagnoses as a growing sense of "historical *dis*continuity" across many fields of human enquiry.[4] We must make allowances for differences in citizenship status, class, race, ethnicity, gender, and age among other accidental factors. And some of what passes for cosmopolitanism in DSA Hindi cinema is mere masquerade, covering over anxious glocalism or even abject nativism shamed into camouflage. The nativist impulse of Hindi cinema is revealed in its frequent recourse to essentialist identitarian mythologies as a defense against globalization and modernity, dissembling this essentialism under a patina of middle-class and elite tastes and fashions.

This essentialism is the inverse image of the essentialism undergirding colonial discourse, and I distinguish both from the *postcolonialist* category of "strategic essentialism" in the Conclusion. Homi Bhabha writes that "an important feature of colonial discourse is its dependence on the concept of 'fixity' in the ideological construction of otherness. Fixity, as the sign of cultural/historical/racial difference in the discourse of colonialism, is a paradoxical mode of representation: it connotes rigidity and an unchanging order as well as disorder, degeneracy and daemonic repetition."[5] Postcolonial cinematic representations in DSA films such as *Masala* (discussed below) refuse this fixity, as a sign of subordination. The issue is how representations of diasporic South Asian subject constructions and identifications mesh with domestic, including Bollywood, versions.

Contemporary DSA films characteristically pivot on the drama of individuals who aspire to some form of new cosmopolitanism but often remain caught in an intermediate position, as if unready for hybridity. New theories of hybrid cinema and cosmopolitanism provide a framework for understanding the contradictory representations of DSAs. In the 1990s, Bollywood "took note of the NRIs as cosmopolitan in mind, speaking in English or American accents, but with their heart and soul in the right place respecting all things Indian"; their plots "spanned several cities across several continents with diasporic characters taking centre stage . . . opening up affinities with audiences across the globe."[6] In the Conclusion I make a stronger if related argument, foregrounding the disaggregation of the floating signifiers of Indianness, which makes them available for incorporation into unpredictable cultural hybridizations, and performatives exogenous to Indian culture.

The "domestic abroad," writes Asha Varadharajan, is the product of two parallel processes: the "neoliberal restructuring" of the state and the "diasporic reimagination of the nation." She invokes a *Marxisant* tradition of historical materialism, highlighting the state's role in creating the transnational phenomenon of the "domestic abroad."[7] Yet to understand diasporic migrations we must move beyond purely economic issues like remittances and balance of payments, engaging with the underlying sociocultural forces; and we must move beyond class issues and attend to psychical complexities of identification and disidentification complicating reifications of *national* identity. Tracking the condensation of the new cosmopolitanism in DSA films, foregrounding their fissive potential and their power to forge transnational connections, this chapter situates cosmopolitanism within contemporary debates about nationalism, globalization, and multiculturalism.

The new cosmopolitanism is most salient in Hindi films from the mid-1980s into the early 2000s, a conjuncture decisively punctuated by the regime of neoliberalism starting around 1991, initiated by the economist Manmohan Singh, who later became prime minister. Since 2004 India's reforms have slowed considerably. Yet the new cosmopolitanism was self-contradictorily expressed in films set and/or produced *in* (or oriented *toward*) the multicultural contexts of the United Kingdom and North America. Narratives of the new cosmopolitanism often vacillate between cultures rather than celebrate a blithe or feckless *jouissance*, at home nowhere and everywhere, in Edward Said's phrase.[8] This chapter examines a group of films that can be considered exponents of this new condensation.

Debating Cosmopolitanism

In contemporary *American* debates, proponents of renewed commitment to cosmopolitanism include Martha Nussbaum, Amartya Sen, Amy Gutmann, Anthony Appiah, and Bruce Robbins; among the detractors are Benjamin Barber, Gertrude Himmelfarb, Timothy Brennan, Daniel Archibugi, and Aijaz Ahmad. Summarizing five recurrent objections to cosmopolitanism, in order to accommodate them, I suggest that a new cosmopolitanism, even though it is still emergent in Hindi cinema, can be a useful analytic category. Next I consider important examples of DSA cinema from across the Atlantic (the United Kingdom and the United States) that reveal a desire to present a regenerate Indianness informed by some aspects of the new cosmopolitanism. I conclude by noting five major challenges for DSA cinema in this regard.

Cosmopolitanism has periodically fallen in and out of favor as philosophical attitude and political orientation. The term derives from the Greek words *kosmos* ("world," "order") and *polis* ("castle" and later "city-state"); thus *kosmopolites* meant "citizen of the world." The resurgence of cosmopolitanism has been spurred by several factors: the repositioning of postcolonial nations in the global economy; the removal of important political barriers (the Berlin Wall) or the development of new border porosities (the European Union); liberalization of trade across existing borders (the North American Free Trade Agreement, or NAFTA); and intensified transnational flows of capital, labor, goods, information, and images.

Proponents argue that cosmopolitanism projects "a unifying vision for democracy and governance in a world . . . dominated by a globalizing capitalism."[9] Premised on an ethics of transnational solidarity and global justice, basic human rights and ethical business practices, the new cosmopolitanism subtends an ideal: a "global village" guaranteeing agency and citizenship in civil society. The ideal has been articulated as a critical reassessment in the contemporary conjuncture of cosmopolitanism as civic deontology, against provincialism and socioeconomic divisiveness or new transnational threats of ideological terrorism.

Yet the charge of elitism has been a common objection to cosmopolitanism—that cosmopolitanism underestimates the significance of class divides, or the ultimately social, economic, and political divisions between the global North and the global South. On the left, as Robbins observes, it is assumed that physical or imaginative travel beyond national or cultural borders is to "wallow in a privileged and irresponsible detachment."[10] Robbins underscores cosmopolitanism's contemporary resurgence.[11] What makes it new is its commitment to engaging issues of power, politics, and class and historical differences among Third World diasporas or racial minorities in the United States.[12] As Martha Nussbaum suggests, cosmopolitanism's ethical mantra is "diversity without hierarchy."[13]

Cosmopolitanism is criticized by Masao Miyoshi, Aijaz Ahmad, and Arundhati Roy as predatory opportunism—the "toxic cosmopolitanism of global markets," in Benjamin Barber's words.[14] However, cosmopolitanism *needn't* be toxic. Roy describes globalization as "a mutant variety of colonialism, remotely controlled and digitally operated"; yet she herself can be read contrapuntally as arguing for a double consciousness premised on localized politics of "resistance" *with transnational* solidarity.[15] Ritzer, too, posits "glocalization," at once globally oriented and locally rooted, as just such a reaction against globalization.[16] Such double consciousness is underwritten by Aihwa Ong's distinction between globalization in "the narrow sense of corporate strategies" and broader, cultural, transnationalism.[17] DSA cinema, I show below, is not inimical to the distinction.[18]

Cosmopolitanism has been judged guilty by association with culture-flattening globalized capitalism: witness the Greek and Cypriot economies in the first decade and a half of the twenty-first century. After the rise of the nation form in the nineteenth century, cosmopolitanism lost some of its aura. In the more radical or reactionary versions of this view, identification with presumptively modular Western forms of capitalist democracy is constructed as false consciousness, a betrayal of local ("authentic"?) cultural identity. The Introduction discussed George Ritzer's indictment of cosmopolitanism as evidence of the success of McDonaldization—globalization masked with a "human face."[19] But cosmopolitanism's proponents dismiss this as a scotomized, unenlightened world view.

A third objection, expressed by Timothy Brennan among others, concerns cosmopolitanism's blindness equally to ethnonationalist Realpolitik and postcolonial strivings for national pride. This view is congruent with arguments about the sovereignty of the nation-state.[20] For Brennan, cosmopolitanism is also questionable as "an ethic of proper intellectual work."[21]

There are also philosophical objections. Even before September 11, 2001, cosmopolitanism was deprecated by some public intellectuals, such as Richard Rorty, Sheldon Hackney, and Gertrude Himmelfarb: at best they would admit the exceptionalist American patriotism of Michael Walzer, who asks rhetorically, "Why can't I be a cosmopolitan American?"[22] But Appiah (with Amartya Sen) insists that it is precisely because the nation is distinct from the state that it is possible to be a cosmopolitan patriot. For Appiah the state, protector of minority rights, "matter[s] intrinsically" to many, guaranteeing "cultural variety" while recognizing the arbitrariness of the nation.[23]

Whether or not claims to national identity are "morally irrelevant" (in Nussbaum's words),[24] one can defend both nation-state *and* capacious cosmopolitanism. Hilary Putnam rejects the choice between nationalism and cosmopolitanism as an empty choice. He maintains that concepts of justice—premises for *ethical* cosmopolitanism—are grounded in material experience and situated personal practices. Moral principles are universals, not inimical to but conditioned by culturally specific interpretations or practices.

A fourth objection, voiced by communitarians including Amitai Etzione and Alasdair MacIntyre, privileges group identification over cosmopolitan universalist humanism. But insular and nativist communitarianism can render cosmopolitanism anorexic, constricting its natural, defining inclusiveness. Besides, the local is inextricably sutured to the global, and that too requires cosmopolitan inclusiveness.[25] Citing Diogenes's affirmative cosmopolitanism, Nussbaum argues that an "emphasis on patriotic pride is both morally dangerous and, ultimately, subversive of some of the worthy goals patriotism sets out to serve." The neo-Stoic cosmopolitan identity—*kosmou politês*—that Nussbaum endorses situates the self at the center of concentric rings of belonging: first self-world; then, encompassing it, family; then community; then nation; and finally the world. There is no conflict among these concentric circles, if properly inhabited.[26] By contrast, MacIntyre privileges immediate attachments within the individual's group. Hackney and Rorty advocate only a slightly less narrow circle of allegiance: the nation. But such views seem inadequate to the task of representing the complexities and contradictions of actual affiliations, belongings, exclusions. Here, therefore, I read DSA cinema as exploring and tentatively mapping the complexities of a more expansive Indianness.

Rorty defends multiculturalism, yet stops short at the nation's borders, as Nussbaum observes—as though that boundary were magical. "At bottom," Nussbaum writes, "nationalism and ethnocentric particularism are not alien to one another, but akin. . . . Once one has said, 'I am an Indian first, a citizen of the world second,' . . . what, indeed, will stop one from saying, . . . 'I am a Hindu first, and an Indian second,' 'I am an upper-caste landlord first, and a Hindu second'?"[27] Nussbaum would agree with Bertrand Russell that one's place of birth is an accident; it follows that religious or confessional identity too is an accident. Judith Shklar reads Montaigne as recognizing that this accidental habitus may be more enduring than ideology.[28] What makes identity politics dangerous is the murderous or suicidal cleaving to such politics—and the visiting of holy terror on people who defend other accidental ethnonational identities. People are willing not only to die to "defend" religious or ethnonational identity but also to kill for it. Cosmopolitanism subtends a preferable *ideal* against chauvinism or rabid, ideologically driven "nationalism": transnational, transcultural justice.[29]

A fifth criticism is that cosmopolitanism homogenizes cultures under utopic, monoculturally Eurocentric universalisms—undermining non-Western or local identities and particularist claims. Many do conceptualize cosmopolitanism as a monoculturally Eurocentric "invention," but Appadurai emphasizes that it is not necessary to "chronologically presuppos[e] either the authority of the Western experience or the models derived from that experience."[30] Cosmopolitans defend and celebrate cultural variety, and recognize diverse forms and origins of cosmopolitical thinking.[31] They accept the dual challenge of reconciling diversity with "cosmopolitan unity" and imagining an interculturalism in which each party risks being transformed in an identificatory encounter with the other, being "translated" to other ways of being, other imaginings, in the sense of Walter Benjamin's celebrated essay "The Task of the Translator."[32] As Said reframes it, cosmopolitanism is a principled refusal to exoticize the other, and implicitly a willingness to learn from those other ways of imagining and of being in the world—a position seconded by Gayatri Spivak.[33] There is, furthermore, an ethical responsibility not to annihilate the other in the very process of identification: "Our fascination with the native, the oppressed, the savage, and all such figures," Rey Chow suggests, masks "a desire to hold on to an unchanging certainty somewhere outside our own 'fake' experience. It is a desire for being 'non-duped,' which is a not-too-innocent desire to seize control."[34] Another, associated criticism is that cosmopolitanism colludes in a pure politics of power, subsuming cultural differences. Yet true cosmopolitanism does not endorse aestheticizing power relations; it insists on ethical responsibility across interest groups, even on the transnational scale.

The irresolution of the debate hardly amounts to condemnation of the new cosmopolitanism. Still, even theory has yet to produce a credible conception of the cosmopolitical alive to *impediments* to intellectual and material freedoms *and possibilities* for transnational solidarism. One should therefore not be too severe with Hindi cinema for its imperfect cosmopolitanism: its negotiations of relations between diaspora and "home," for instance, *can* resist globalization as a top-down, corporate, or "market-oriented" ideology and fashion unscripted subjectivizations or subject-positions.[35] James Clifford highlights an "emergent *postcolonial* cosmopolitanism," referencing Benita Parry and invoking Arnold Krupat's suggestion that Native American culture be situated within the orbits of new cosmopolitan literature—"the projection of heterodoxy not to the level of the universal, but, rather, to the level of the 'inter-national.'"[36]

Cosmopolitanism also has a wider theoretical and conceptual register: endorsements of "rooted" cosmopolitanism (Appiah, David Hollinger, and Mitchell Cohen), "vernacular cosmopolitanism" (Bhabha), and non-Western cosmopolitanisms (Aihwa Ong and Louisa Schein). Germane too is Jacques Rancière's notion of *equality* that is not *identity:* if we wish to "break out of the desperate debate between universality and identity, we must answer that the only universal in politics is [enacted] equality."[37] This equality, I would submit, is the foundation of cosmopolitan subjectivization.

Cosmopolitan subjectivity is still *nascently* imaged in DSA cinema, an often tentative *supplement* to obdurate or conventionally chauvinistic expressions of nationalism, insularism, and conservative traditionalism. Yet these contradictory tendencies animate DSA films, and so what is required is a bifocal attention—not only to what Jenny Sharpe characterizes as a vanishing traditional ("rural") India, but also simultaneously to a new cosmopolitan orientation to urban and overseas markets, where the greater "profit margin" conditions what kinds of stories are told about Indians, what versions of Indianness are projected by the dream machine of cinema.[38]

The new cosmopolitanism is entangled with *multiculturalism,* as cosmopolitanism's obverse: if cosmopolitanism's ambit is *cosmos,* then multiculturalism's domain is the nominally bounded *nation-state.* A bifocal understanding highlights diasporics' multilayered negotiations of what Appadurai describes as *global* flows, but also of multicultural *national* or *glocal* flows. Canada has a special ministry for diaspora affairs, permitting dual citizenship for diasporics. Such policies acknowledge both rights and duties of minorities, yet they do not distinguish between Rancière's logics of "identification" and "subjectivization."[39] Below I discuss several films, including British and North American DSA films, among them Srinivas Krishna's film *Masala,* set in Canada, as a good illustration of a transnational postcolonial approach to Hindi cinema that is alive to manifestations of the new cosmopolitanism. The Conclusion further develops the case for such an approach.

Cosmopolitanism in political theory and in film may seem heterogeneous discourses. Nonetheless, analyses of transnational belonging, citizenship, and subjectivization in contemporary DSA films can be revealingly framed by, and profitably draw on, political and cultural theories. For instance, Jürgen Habermas's postnational cosmopolitan rationality unconstrained by exclusivist ethnic imagination is a standard according to which contemporary Hindi cinema's engagement with cosmopolitanism can be illuminated; and Spivak's catachrestic "strategic essentialism" may offer an answer, not yet fully incorporated in the films themselves, to account for how Indianness is increasingly untethered from essentialisms in these narratives.[40]

A Critical and Transnational Cosmopolitanism

A *critical* cosmopolitanism presumes antiessentialist representation, "calling on knowledges, values and conceptual tools which are neither nativist nor rootlessly cosmopolitan."[41] It entails attentiveness to constructions of class, race, and gender, and ethical responsibility to the other while, in Walter Mignolo's formulation, "dewesternizing," "deorientalizing," and "decolonizing" citizenship (recognizing that citizenship is already marked as an eighteenth-century European concept) to rebuild "pluri-versal senses of belonging."[42] This is one reason not to fear the disaggregation of "Indianness," as I suggest in the Conclusion. DSA films must resist co-optation into the deceptively flattering category "model minority" cultural production: their new cosmopolitanism must be critical, self-reflexive, and open to otherness and interculturalism, building equality (not identity) across ethnic divides—and learning the lessons of strategic essentialism. Rancière in this spirit theorizes an emancipatory politics against the "new" racism and globalized capitalism.[43]

Such a critical new cosmopolitanism has not been perfectly achieved, but DSA cinema is not averse to aspiration. Pnina Werbner admits that overtly cosmopolitan and transgressive narratives of British DSA cinema "have had little impact on either South Asian diasporic politics or familial sexual politics and inter-generational relations."[44] This is why such cinema might benefit from a strategic essentialism; yet recent DSA films *have* been crucial to the circulation of increasingly *self-reflexive* narratives, discourses, and images of Indianness within discourses of multiculturalism and postcolonial modernity.

Not all DSAs are *évolués* aspiring to the American Dream, upper-class Britishness, or European elite culture. DSA narratives featuring new cosmopolitan attitudes tend to be fissured by "roots" nostalgia, the sting of racism, class-based exclusion. The question is whether a new cosmopolitanism can challenge elitism, sexism, racism, and classism in spite of itself, *and* offer meaningful aesthetic pleasure.

The question arises most acutely with respect to the 1.7 million NRIs in the United States.[45] They are part of an increasingly influential overseas market worldwide, but that is not to say that domestic mass audiences universally find films with diasporic themes and sensibilities appealing.[46] In the early decades after Independence NRIs were envied and resented as contributing to the treasonous "brain drain" to greener pastures in the West, such as Silicon Valley. Nehru himself insisted that overseas Indians choose between Indian and foreign citizenship. Even today persons of Indian origin residing abroad must ordinarily apply for a visa to reenter their home country.

Middle Cinema (cinema by or about middle-class filmmakers/subjects) in the 1990s began to present a new *paysage moralisé*, rehabilitating the NRI as exemplarily virtuous. The NRI was now no longer constructed as a selfish and Westernized expatriate, but recuperated as India's transnational representative, a custodian of Indianness, purer and more patriotic than the natives. Films such as *Pardes* (Subhash Ghai, 1997), while depicting the West as a potential source of corruption and vice, represented the NRI as a potentially redeemable, even exemplary, subject. Yet in *Pardes* and other 1990s Middle Cinema the on-screen NRI remained an ambivalent figure, a product of national (or Subcontinental) cultural anxieties and ideological contradictions. For instance, the domestic Indian family, prominently featuring NRIs and superficially "cosmopolitan" lifestyles, began to be reaffirmed as a bulwark in those films against encroachments of global or Western hegemonic culture and capital in films such as *Hum Aapke Hain Kaun* ([*HAHK*], Sooraj Barjatya, 1994), which grossed a record Rs. 2 billion (US$44 million); *Dilwale Dulhania Le Jayenge* (The Brave Heart Wins the Bride, Aditya Chopra, 1996); and *Kabhi Khushi Kabhie Gham* (Sometimes Happiness, Sometimes Sorrow, Karan Johar, 2001).

A critical (from the Greek *krinein*, meaning "decision" or "turning") phase in the NRI's rehabilitation occurs in *Dilwale Dulhania Le Jayenge* (hereafter

DDLJ).[47] The main characters Raj and Simran are NRIs raised in England but "essentially" Indian. Recently graduated, they separately persuade their fathers to underwrite a trip to Europe, Eurail passes in hand. Predictably, the two meet on a train and eventually fall in love. However, Simran's father, Baldev, has promised her to a family friend's son, at "home" in Punjab—the cliché "arranged marriage." Discovering her European tryst with Raj, he conveys her to India to marry as planned. Raj follows, pretending to be the scion of a rich family seeking an investment opportunity, an archetypal NRI. On the eve of Simran's planned wedding her mother contravenes tradition (and her husband) by counseling the two to elope. Yet Raj surprises everyone, demonstrating his respect for precisely that tradition by refusing to take Simran away without Baldev's paternal blessing. Eventually even the paterfamilias cannot see Simran unhappy and relents, recognizing that it was the NRI who upheld "Indian values," not the native but villainous intended groom.

Another instance of the rhetorical shift toward the rehabilitation of the NRI as redeemable or redeemed redeemer of Indianness emerges in *Kabhi Khushi Kabhie Gham* (hereafter K3G). This film features the aspirational Indian family: the wealthy Indian businessman and patriarch Yash Raichand has two sons, Rahul and Rohan, and lives on a grand scale. But there is trouble in their upper-class paradise. As a boy, Rahul learns he was adopted, but he conceals the knowledge from his younger brother. As a young man, Rahul falls in love with the working-class beauty Anjali; Yash had arranged Rahul's marriage to his closest friend's daughter, so he is angered to discover Rahul's presumption. A "good" and obedient son, Rahul promises to renounce Anjali, but when her father dies unexpectedly he breaks that promise to save her further anguish. Yash disowns him, so Rahul and Anjali go into exile in London. Rahul becomes a rich NRI, but remains a model of modern Indianness, faithfully staying true to the cultural traditions of the homeland. Ten years on, Rohan finds out about Rahul's adoption and excommunication. He vows to reunite the family and, aided by a sentimental narrative device, succeeds. The film simultaneously rehabilitates the NRI, offering audiences vistas of a new, cosmopolitanized Indianness, *and* ultimately reaffirms core conservative values: nation, tradition, family.

These ambivalent representations of NRIs solicit a bifocal perspective. Purnima Mankekar endorses a differently conceived bifocal perspective than mine, gesturing to a "politics of solidarity with and accountability to communities of struggle" in the United States and India, "problematizing binaries of home versus diaspora."[48] By contrast, I invoke "bifocality" to highlight DSAs' negotiation of competing pulls—national feeling *and* diaspora, multiculturalism *and* cosmopolitanism—precisely because Indianness itself is undergoing a paradigmatic transformation, which has begun to make Indians themselves more ambivalent about what constitutes the national identity.

An important motive for the rehabilitation of NRIs is their increased *financial power* and significance as *cultural prostheses* of Indianness. On January 9, 2003, Prime Minister Atal Behari Vajpayee inaugurated the first "Pravasi

Bharatiya Divas" (Day of Indians Abroad), a celebration ostensibly to strengthen linkages between domestic and diasporic Indians. Special concessional tax regimes under Chapter XIIA, Sections 115C–115I, of the Indian Income Tax Act targeted the "Pravasi Bharatiya." Under then deputy prime minister L. K. Advani, NRI remittances to and foreign direct investment in India rose dramatically; transnational boosterism became a lucrative minor industry in the United Kingdom and the United States. Yet the outreach to wealthier NRIs has a sinister aspect: *in India,* it has helped the Vishva Hindu Parishad (VHP, established 1970, registered in New York State in 1974) bankroll Hindutva anti-Muslim militants, including the Rashtriya Swayamsevak Sangh (RSS).

Class difference is an unavoidable fault line of the new cosmopolitanism. And one can hardly exaggerate the implications of the post-1991 neoliberal reforms for how "Indianness" is differentially construed across socioeconomic strata. Conservative commentators insist that GDP has risen since liberalization (by 4.4 percent in the period 1992–1998) and poverty has declined (by 7.1 percent for the same period). Stark inequalities persist, however, paralleling asymmetries elsewhere under global capitalism. Technocratic liberalization has disproportionately helped the middle and upper classes, and has hurt others. Between 2002 and 2006 more than 17,500 poor farmers in Andhra Pradesh, Maharashtra, Karnataka, Kerala, and Punjab committed suicide, protesting their worsening lot.[49] Not even the National Crime Records Bureau could avert its eyes; it officially confirmed the suicides. Small-budget films have appeared representing the plight of such farmers: *Summer 2007* (Suhail Tatari, 2008), *Kissan* (Puneet Sira, 2009), Marathi-language *Jhing Chik Jhing* (Nitin Nandan, 2010), *The Dying Fields* (Fred de Sam Lazaro, 2007), and *Peepli Live* (Anusha Rizvi, 2010). Directors Sira and Sam Lazaro are DSAs. Such films suggest popular cinema *can* engage progressive agendas, even if mediated via DSA circuits.

A survey of DSA films might begin with two touchstone films by the British director Stephen Frears from the Thatcher years that offer representations of DSAs in multicultural Britain. Sexual identity is a key axis along which DSA cinema expresses its cosmopolitan inclinations. Frears's *My Beautiful Laundrette* (1985), also discussed in Chapter 6, offers a proto-cosmopolitan hope through the unlikely business and sexual partnership of British Pakistani Omar—young, entrepreneurial, unlike his bitter socialist father—and his school friend Johnny, a white street tough fond of "unscrewing" people if they fail to make payments to Nasser, for whom he works. Omar sets up a laundromat business with Nasser's help, recruiting Johnny, who is thus redeemed from his British National Party cryptofascism by a miscegenating and homosexual eros. Queer sexuality as recipe for racial rapprochement? This improbable partnership, thematizing (albeit ambivalently) openness to cross-racial and anti-heteronormative cooperation, illustrates some of the contradictions animating DSA cinema's crystallization of the new cosmopolitanism.

In Frears's *Sammy and Rosie Get Laid* (1987) everybody, not only Sammy and Rosie, gets screwed. The couple's bohemian lives are deranged by Sammy's father's visit, which uncovers British racism and classism. A male black British character named "Victoria" fingers Thatcherite neoliberalism for causing Britain's political turn away from cosmopolitan openness. The film is an early if anomalous model for the new cosmopolitan DSA sensibility, challenging ideological, sexual, racialist, and other bromides on film.

My Son the Fanatic (Hanif Kureishi, 1998) expresses more self-conscious pleading for cosmopolitanism. Contradictions of sexuality, race, class, religion, and the generational gap are dramatized within the film's DSA family, which is struggling to define its place within British multiculturalism. Pervez, a taxi driver, tries to redeem his son Farid from a misogynist, "antidemocratic and anti-Jewish" fundamentalism. Unfaithful to both wife and religion, Pervez seeks unsanctioned tenderness from a white prostitute, comfort from forbidden whiskey, and pleasure from Louis Armstrong. The film does not condemn Pervez for availing himself of this cosmopolitan smorgasbord; ironically, it presents the younger generation as less cosmopolitan, seduced by provincial fundamentalism. Farid delivers a critique of "immorality" and capitalist democracy, but the film unequivocally privileges cosmopolitan civilization and civility against Farid's radicalism.

New cosmopolitan attitudes are key to Ayub Khan-Din's film *East Is East* (2000), which purveys the idioms of individual self-determination modulated primarily through sexually liberal attitudes. The film is set in 1971, a quarter century after Indian Independence and Partition—also the year of Bangladesh's "War of Liberation," aided by India, out of the secession of East Pakistan, "the most dramatic manifestation of the tussle between a centralized and undemocratic state structure and the forces of regionalism."[50] The film features a South Asian immigrant to Britain, George Khan, whose time in Britain coincides with the period in which the Empire began to reverse the colonizer's trajectory: George came to England, we are told, "from Pakistan" in 1937 and married Ela, a white Christian Englishwoman. While the anachronism is a forgivable lapse (Pakistan did not exist in 1937), the film produces more telling contradictions: George's split emotional attachments reflect the conflicted postcolonial British DSA experience. Marginalized in Britain, George curses at news of the Mukti Bahini (Bangladesh's Freedom Force) achieving victories with India's help (in 1971). He is caught *entre deux guerres*—between racist violence "here" in England and military violence "there," at "home" that is no longer home. But he cannot find it in himself to reach for a more cosmopolitan existence.

Anti-immigrant white anxieties are metonymized in the spectral presence of Enoch Powell, éminence grise of the 1970s, warning against the "alien wedge," recommending their "assisted repatriation."[51] Images of Powell appear on a television screen broadcasting the "Rivers of Blood" speech, giving vent to what Stuart Hall calls the "authoritarian populist" orthodoxy of the 1960s, and on a poster taped to a windowpane that Meenah, George's daughter, expertly shatters by kicking a soccer ball through it. By the 1980s Powell's doctrine had (over)ripened into the conservative dogma enshrined by Thatcher.

George is a parody of the postcolonial fantasy luridly expressed in Tayeb Salih's novel *Season of Migration to the North*—avenging colonization by sexual conquest of the colonizer's woman. But George cannot tolerate the repetition of a similar profane conquest by one of his sons, who wants to marry a white woman too, "just like my dad," as that son puts it. George insists on marrying two other sons to South Asian brides, however unappealing. In the grip of a hypocritical anticosmopolitan superego, George cannot allow himself to enjoy the unholy pleasures his children celebrate: sausages, bacon, clubbing. His parochial religiosity is satirized in his obsession with Sajid's uncircumcised "tickle tackle," his traditionalism mocked by Saleem's art project, a model of a vagina with luxuriant pubic hair. Even at his most endearing, George is grotesque, an incompletely civilized/assimilated immigrant "dis-oriented" in the multicultural metropole.

The Khans live in nominally cosmopolitan spaces. We see George enjoying himself at the movies, watching traditional Indian films. Yet none of the spaces in which he moves—mosque, chip shop, his own strict home—is strictly speaking "new cosmopolitan": these zones are coded as ethnic, marginal within a peculiarly British environment, hostile to syncretism or pluriversality.

Yet despite its implied critique of anti-immigrant sentiment, the film is inadequately reflexive in thematizing legacies of British colonialism and immigration; it does not meet the challenge of pluriversal citizenship, though superficially endorsing a new cosmopolitanism. Cloaked in the mantle of subversive minority (if not "minor" or "Third") cinema, it falls short of challenging the white, capitalist, conservative status quo. Because its focus is narrowly on individual, and youthful, self-determination, it concedes too much on larger issues. Certainly the younger generation is generally more cosmopolitan, with the possible exceptions of Maneer and perhaps Sajid: generally the other children are "modern," smart, and well adapted. Ian Aspinall, playing Nazir, commented that the film was "not afraid to cross all the barriers—it goes to the edge in humor, drama, and subject matter."[52] Ultimately it falls short of *critical* cosmopolitanism.

DSA filmmakers risk denigrating South Asian traditions in underwriting cosmopolitanism. Khan-Din's film, pitting Meenah and Nazir against their grotesque father, courts inverse xenophobia or self-hatred, reinscribing Western modernity as modular and superior to non-Western; "new" cosmopolitanism becomes a weapon to batter conservative "old" Islam. Reviewers often gloss over these contradictions. Writing in *The Nation*, Stuart Klawans observes that "the allure of assimilation gives the movie its conflict; and yet assimilation has already occurred."[53] Has it really, even for DSA youth born in Britain, still often second-class citizens? What would it mean to "dewesternize, deorientalize, decolonize" citizenship in response to Mignolo's exhortations or Étienne Balibar's call for an emancipatory politics in which identity is distinguished from equality, and universalism respects particular histories?[54]

In Khan-Din's film, as in other DSA films, the political is mediated by the complications of sexual identity, class difference, and intergenerational conflict.

Questions arise about the filmmaker's own political self-reflexivity. In one funny but troubling scene an overweight girl and an older woman are made objects of a large dog's "amorous" attentions. Other women are diminished in various ways. Ela remains a dutiful if battered wife to the end, as if reinscribing conservative roles for women. Her toleration of George's physical abuse might have drawn complaints from antiracists had Ela been Muslim, but pairing George with Ela functions, disturbingly, almost to license Khan-Din's portrayal of domestic abuse as a statement about the *South Asian* family, discouraging a *gender-focused and intersectional* critique. This "brown-on-white" violence appears to tell a universal story of a man abusing a woman but it really speaks of the abuse by *(Muslim) immigrant men.* Ironically Khan-Din appears to align himself with a white racist othering of the "Paki." Yet the film simultaneously displaces *ethnographic* critique: Ela's abuse is framed as a particular instance of domestic violence, not as general critique of Muslim culture. The film seems oblivious to postcolonialist critique of the rapid globalization of multicultural cities and "large tracts" of the postcolonial world, which were already made "diasporic" by colonialism in the 1970s.[55]

In the matter of sexual self-determination, DSA films could be more progressive, drawing on insights about complex, "pluriversal" identifications of British DSA women, studied for example by Kim Knott and Sadja Khokher. Unlike their parents, these female subjects *situationally* chose "religious" or "ethnic" identifications, or rejected them, identifying instead with Britishness.[56] Somewhat more successful examples of the new cosmopolitan outlook in terms of sexual self-determination include Gurinder Chadha's *Bhaji on the Beach* (1993), a lighthearted portrait of gendered intergenerational conflicts. In *Bhaji* the "Saheli Asian Women's Group" goes on a jaunt to Blackpool for a beach escape "from patriarchy," and Chadha deftly introduces the women's sense of differentiated community and collective political self-awareness, unusual in DSA cinema. In *Bend It Like Beckham* (2001), discussed in Chapter 6, Chadha invokes a more individualistic, but equally "new cosmopolitan" vision of South Asian female sexual identity/identification.

Not all DSA films, however, offer what Paul Gilroy describes as "new and unpredictable forms of identification and cultural affinity between groups that dwell far apart."[57] It is instructive to contrast British DSA films with their North American counterparts. Two examples are *Masala* (Srinivas Krishna, 1991) and *Mississippi Masala* (Mira Nair, 1991). The fortuitous reciprocal echo of their titles intimates shared motifs; their contemporaneity is equally revealing. Like *East Is East,* both films reference 1971–1972, a watershed phase in DSA history. In 1972 Uganda's dictator Idi Amin expelled Asians. This was a historic failure of multicultural and cosmopolitical possibilities. Though the exiles had roots in the Subcontinent, many went to Britain as members of the British Commonwealth. Some went to North America, occasionally via Britain. Canada, which had in 1971 adopted a policy of "official multiculturalism," following recommendations of the Canadian Royal Commission on Bilingualism and Biculturalism, accepted seven thousand Indian expatriates from Uganda. That influx, and the simultaneous doubling of the number of immigrants from India in the 1970s, reignited the debate over immigration, "identity politics," and multiculturalism in Canada. A similar backlash occurred after the 1965 U.S. Hart-Celler Immigration Act loosened restrictions, more than doubling the number of South Asians in North America between 1965 and 1975. The backlash carried over to the 1980s in the United States ("Dot Busting") and Britain ("Paki-bashing"), and was reignited after September 11, 2001.

Following Canada's 1993 federal elections, cultural conflicts in metropolitan Toronto and Vancouver suggested "that the laudable ideal of multiculturalism has neither prevented racism nor helped English Canadians establish an identity."[58] Prime Minister Pierre Trudeau spoke in 1971 in the Canadian Parliament House of Commons on the occasion of the government's adoption of multiculturalism, saying, "National unity if it is to mean anything in the deeply personal sense must be founded on confidence in one's own individual identity; out of this can grow respect for that of others." Trudeau's words highlight the conflict between individualism and universalism—even as they make the two categories complementary. In Canada, "ethnic or religious groups may appear as relatively isolated minorities, but when expanded into the global framework, their relationships must be understood as part of an international network"—a "*Verbindungsnetzschaft*."[59] As Will Kymlicka and Wayne Norman add, from a political theory standpoint this is a natural evolution because "citizenship is intimately linked to ideas of individual entitlement on the one hand and of attachment to a particular community on the other."[60]

Krishna's film coarticulates the discourses of multiculturalism and cosmopolitanism. Its premise seems to be that Canada's official multiculturalism has not succeeded in creating a "pluriversal" new cosmopolitan polity, if the test for the new cosmopolitanism is that a state promotes equality not as bland universalism but in an encouragement of even dissensual pluriversalism. *Masala*'s protagonist seems caught in a valley between legal citizenship and nominal inclusion of the foreigner under official multiculturalism, or, even less optimistically, between homogenizing universalism and monocultural and mononational rootedness.

The film opens with a reimagined (refantasized) disaster. On June 23, 1985, the Montreal-London-Delhi Air India flight 182 was attacked by terrorists. It exploded over the Atlantic, killing 329, including 280 Canadian citizens, most of them of Indian descent. This is a personal trauma for the protagonist, also named Krishna, who feels guilt for having escaped that fate: he had stood up his immigrant Indian parents and brother, with whom he was to return to India on that flight. He is haunted by fantasies of airplane explosions "caused" by the equally fantasmatic middle-aged god in gaudy blue facepaint like that of the Hindu god named . . . Krishna. This multilayered tragicomic fantasy reflects the verve and irreverence of the youthful filmmaker, all of twenty-five when he made the film. The young protagonist is predictably and terminally hip, perhaps too arch an inversion of "coolie cool." Jobless, Krishna turns to drugs to assuage his guilt, although he believes his parents lacked the "toughness" required of immigrants in multicultural white-majority culture. They were "losers." Krishna is constantly besieged by the accusation that he is a "fuck-up"—an underachiever in the brave new world of official multiculturalism, destitute even of the excuse employed by underachievers in other multicultural settings: that they fail because they are hindered by prejudice. The central plot is the narrative of Krishna's failure—and his *embrace of underachievement* as a bitterly pyrrhic triumph over conformist assimilationism: yet this aesthetic pose of underachievement, I argue below, is intended to mark assimilation as a failure of cosmopolitical imagination on the part of the multicultural nation-state.

As the film opens, Krishna has just emerged from a detoxification program. He arrives at an ex-girlfriend's apartment hoping to collect eight hundred dollars she owes him, but her new boyfriend threatens Krishna. Krishna pulls out a knife and slashes the boyfriend's chest superficially; the boyfriend fires a handgun at him. The scene serves to establish Krishna's street-cred, his tough pose registering a dissenting or self-assertive multicultural citizenship in contradistinction to his parents' "loser" attitude, but expressed as chic, new cosmopolitan underachievement.

Fantasy assumes a plethora of forms in the film. Krishna is an equal-opportunity fantasist: sometimes his fantasy object is Lallu Bhai's desperate housewife bending lewdly while performing calisthenics; sometimes it is Rita, Tikkoo's daughter, who herself is angling for Krishna, intending to save him from downward mobility. Krishna's aestheticization of failure refuses all such ministrations.

Krishna does have some extended family support, including from Mr. Tikkoo, played by Saeed Jaffrey. Krishna is also the beneficiary of the intercession of "Lord Krishna," a kind of guardian deity manqué for Krishna, also played campily by Jaffrey in gaudy blue paint and glossy red lipstick. Most directly, he receives advice and assistance from his sharp-tongued and successful uncle Lallu Bhai Solanki (once again, played by Jaffrey), intent on cornering the diasporic—and international—sari market in Toronto. He is not above supporting the secessionist struggle in Punjab for Khalistan, here represented as terrorism challenging the "tolerance" of official Canadian multiculturalism. Lallu Bhai is a disillusioned opportunist who is banking, quite literally, on favorable intersections between *official* multiculturalism and *commercial* cosmopolitanism (another avatar of globalizing capitalism). But what alternatives does the film offer? Even read as a disillusioned cosmopolitan take on official Canadian multiculturalism, a rejection of the cliché "model minority" myth into which South Asian diasporics are induced, the film offers no concrete recommendations. It is not even clear whether the director would support an exit from Canadian multiculturalism into a species of critical cosmpolitanism. Should marginal citizens then embrace an aesthetic of underachievement, resist official multiculturalism, adopt the attitude of a new, *disillusioned* cosmopolitanism?

Linda Basch, Nina Glick Schiller, and Cristina Szanton Blanc note that "world systems theorists . . . reduce migration to labor migration and immigrants to workers, eliminating all discussion of the many different racial, ethnic, or national identities which shape people's actions and consciousness" and their role as political and social agents.[61] Bereft of meaningful agency, Krishna perversely cultivates an aesthetic of underachievement as the inverse image of alienation from society, particularly from meaningful labor. Karl Marx wrote in the *Grundrisse* that "labour is the living, form-giving fire . . . the transitoriness of things, their temporality, as their formation by living time."[62] Following Marx, Michael Hardt and Antonio Negri argue that labor is joy invested in things. This film captures the theft of that joy through denial of meaningful opportunity to labor, while enjoining every citizen, and especially immigrants and minorities, to contribute to the gross national product (GNP)—and to official multiculturalism. But Krishna is a "bad boy" rebel without readily identifiable cause, except to dissent from the state's harnessing of multiculturalist "tolerance" the better to exploit labor. The protagonist embodies his mythological namesake's virtue of irreverence, or "*lila*," akin to the Dionysiac spirit championed by Hardt and Negri: "powers that subvert and pose a radical alternative to the State's elaborate practical and theoretical apparatuses of control and exploitation."[63] Krishna embodies the exhaustion of the singular in resistance to the state-form, which is why Hardt and Negri invoke the "becoming-common" of labor in collective, multitudinous—and necessarily global, cosmopolitical—resistance. Krishna cannot imagine or even fantasize such a collective critical cosmopolitanism as an answer to the impasse in whose defiles he is stymied: but its necessity might be what the viewer should take away from the film.

Fantasy has an important role in communicating the film's negative utopianism. As Oskar Negt and Alexander Kluge write, "Fantasy has a tendency to distance itself from the alienated labor process and to translate itself into timeless and ahistorical forms of production that 'do not and cannot exist.'" The worker is prevented "from advocating for his interests in reality."[64] Krishna too is alienated in this sense, and also clearly in the grip of a kind of psychic blockage: he cannot traverse his fundamental fantasy and thereby position himself in a new relationship to the Other, as Lacan would have it, though he may register a vague dissent. So he perversely construes labor as antithetical, regressive, choosing instead defiant underachievement, a species of ressentiment. Thus the sole posture available to Krishna appears to be, regrettably, his adolescent pout, his quasi-subversive "attitude" that can only take the form of a fantasy street-smart leather jacket chic, making a facilely cosmopolitan virtue out of rejecting official multiculturalism.

Many contemporary nation-state policies of official multiculturalism (in contrast with historical multicultural regimes such as the Hellenistic, Roman, or Hapsburg empires) abjure the requirement of assimilation—the United States being an exception. Canada, like Australia, another former settler colony, even regards assimilationism as undesirable, although Keith Spicer, Canada's first commissioner of official languages and later head of the 1987 Spicer Commission, argued vehemently *for* assimilationism.[65] Krishna's aesthetic of failure is a posture that negotiates between—and evenhandedly deprecates—naive or abject survivalism like that of his parents and the cynical capitalism of Lallu Bhai, but doesn't manage to negotiate his way out of that valley, or dilemma.

The director relays his own skepticism about official multiculturalism through the Minister's remark to Shashi (Krishna's uncle): "You can come to Canada, set up an immigrant women's collective, build temples, have your processions, keep your identity," but if you don't play by the rules, the Minister says candidly, you may be criminalized. As if responding, the god Krishna wonders rhetorically, "What happens to Indians when they travel to foreign lands?" His answer: Indians lose their cultural anchoring, their "grace, their composure, and they're constantly pestering me for explanations. They should be spending more time worshiping." One of his (self-imposed) duties is overseeing the Rath Yatra planned by the city's Hindu community. Against the backdrop of Subcontinental Hindutva politics and the successful efforts of the VHP to drum up material support in the diaspora, this procession is hardly an innocent celebration of culture.[66] This raises the nice question: should viewers identify with the Canadian state or with Krishna and the other immigrants?

Observers point out that "the Canadian state, by embracing and managing multiculturalism, has . . . co-opted political space available to minority groups for mobilization of resistance along ethnic and racial lines."[67] Many Canadians are suspicious about official multiculturalism and would prefer a more nativist ideology.[68] There is also a *class* element to this suspicion. Krishna may not be one of the deterritorialized *elite* cosmopolitan DSAs. But neither is he quite proletarian. He is a "nowhere" man, with no future or true home: cosmopolitan in the bad sense.

Krishna's rootless cosmopolitanism is also *racialized.* Belonging remains a problem for nonwhite immigrants despite official Canadian multiculturalism. Greed and market values have distorted the meaning of citizenship in the New Right vision of citizenship. Tests of citizenship are applied asymmetrically across racial or ethnic groupings, even in officially multicultural contexts where assimilationist ideology prefers passive citizenship. But as Kymlicka and Norman observe, we need to redress this "passive citizenship" by a countervailing stress on "active multiculturalism," reconceptualizing citizenship for an increasingly pluralistic society.[69] *Masala* presents Krishna as torn between desiring Canadian citizenship as merely legal status and "good" citizenship, between wholehearted commitment to Canadian citizenship and returning "home" to India. His double refusal infantilizes him: his aesthetic of underachievement boils down to a refusal of a mature commitment to either nation or cosmopolis. All Krishna can do is offer a cinematic mimesis of dissensual citizenship.

For all its cynical parody, however, the film raises important questions about contemporary multiculturalism and cosmopolitanism. Krishna the bad boy remains only a boy—he cannot grow up. Krishna had armed himself with a knife, resolved never to be as defenseless as he had been when his uncle Tikkoo was attacked on the street or as abject as his parents had been. Though he makes a final heroic stand in defense of another little boy being bullied on the street, it is he who is stabbed and killed, ironically, at the very moment he attains a modicum of moral agency.

If Krishna leaves us with an offbeat but compelling account of thwarted cosmopolitan potential, Mira Nair's *Mississippi Masala* (1991) offers a comparison text (providentially repeating the word "masala," rich in associations for Bollywood aficionados). Here *masala* references a "miscegenating" love between Demetrius, an African American, and Mina, an Indian immigrant. The film is a commentary on race, ethnicity, and marginality, displacement and "pluriversal belonging." Mina is the daughter of Indian migrants thrown out of Uganda in 1972 by the dictator Idi Amin because Indians became too powerful a business presence, provoking resentment from natives. From their exile in Britain, Mina's family relocates a second time to Greenwood, Mississippi. There they live in a motel owned by an Indian family with the irretrievably stereotyped name of Patel. Mina cleans toilets at the motel, where she meets Demetrius, proprietor of a small carpet-cleaning business.

The film suggests that their love promises a new cosmopolitan transcendence of traditional taboos and racist prejudices impeding solidarity and community among people of color. Yet it has been criticized by bell hooks and Anuradha Dingwaney for recycling stereotypes, failing to offer real interaction between Asians and blacks, and propagating the fantasy that love might overcome "racial" and ethnic divisions in multicultural America.[70] Their suggestion that the couple's elopement is a "self-chosen" homelessness seems unwarranted.[71] For this parable of a *necessary,* difficult exile thematizes, however tentatively, a new cosmopolitan hope.

While Demetrius's family receives Mina with enthusiasm and admiration, Mina's family is ambivalent about Demetrius. Mina's father, Jay, ought to abhor racism as a refugee from Amin's ethnonationalist Uganda. Jay had told his Ugandan friend Okelo in Africa that he felt "African first and Indian second." Okelo had retorted that Africa was "for Africans—Black Africans." Now, in one revealing scene, he rebuffs Demetrius, saying he does not want his daughter to struggle on account of association with a black man. Demetrius retorts pointedly: "Struggle? Struggle? Look, I'm a black man born and raised in Mississippi. Not a damn thing you can tell me about struggle. You and your folks can come down here from God knows where and be 'bout as black as the ace of spades, and soon as you get here you start acting white and treating us like we your doormats." Pointing to his own face, he continues, "I know that you and your daughter ain't but a few shades from this right here. That, I know." He denounces Jay as an anticosmopolitan, insularist racist, yet he and Minu can do no better than elope. This is not achieved "post-racialism." Nonetheless, *Mississippi Masala* is clearly inspired by the ideal of new cosmopolitanism.

This ideal also informs Nair's later film *Monsoon Wedding* (2001). Lalit Verma's "upper-middle-class" family is preparing for Lalit's daughter Aditi's arranged marriage to Hemant, a DSA living in Texas. Aditi herself is still uncommitted. One night she steals away to be with her lover. The tryst ends disastrously when, as they are kissing in a rain shower, the police show up to harass them; Aditi drives away in the car, abandoning her lover to the police. Later Aditi confesses her affair to Hemant, who displays his "new cosmopolitanism" in accepting her anyway, admitting that he too is not perfect. But the family has darker secrets behind the colorful spectacle of their four-day wedding, including pedophilia/incest perpetrated by the family's DSA benefactor. Usually such darkness remains hidden in Bollywood melodrama, which pretends to commonsense "realism" according to which Lalit's family's cosmopolitan lifestyle is so elite as to be a fantasy for most Indians. It was precisely against such anorexic realism that Nair made the film—and to reflect her own experience as not exclusively elite.[72] Nair's films are examples of new cosmopolitan sensibility: subsuming traditional sexual values into a more honest acceptance of the complexities of familial, sexual, and social relationships, rejecting cultural insularism and "race-" or nation-fetishism.

Monsoon Wedding features middle-class diasporics for whom English is as familiar as Hindi; other DSA films are actually set in Western locales where English is the main language. In Krutin Patel's *ABCD* (2000) the title refers to the phrase "American Born Confused Desi," a reference to a hapless kind of DSA, a misfit in a multicultural American culture, torn between Indian and Western values. The protagonist, Nina, is angry, compulsive, promiscuous, but also a new cosmopolitan. Her foil is her brother, the equally compulsive but workaholic and conformist Raj. The tension between them captures defining dilemmas of sexual, professional, and cultural identity among young DSAs.

As if suggesting that DSAs cannot be pale imitations of modular white citizen subjects, Piyush Pandya's *American Desi* (2001) stages a subtler cosmopolitanism. Krishna Reddy prefers to be called "Kris" and deprecates his Indian heritage. An ersatz "new cosmopolitan," he is a true "ABCD." Ironically, Kris's white American friend is more comfortable with hybridity than Kris himself: he plays a recording of "Mera Juta Hai Japani," the iconic song about hybridity from *Shree 420* (see Chapter 2). His Indian friend Ajay affects a black vernacular argot, in apparently genuine cross-ethnic *identification*. Kris's contrasting disidentification with his "native culture" is simultaneously presented as a *distorted* cosmopolitanism and mocked as self-hatred.

Kris's cosmopolitan pretensions, juxtaposed to Ajay's apparent cross-racial identification, are illuminated by Sunaina Maira's study of young "*desis*" who adopt black styles but not in genuine long-term solidarity with black experience. These young DSAs, themselves caught in capitalism's power structures, distinguish themselves from their parents' generation through these cool cross-racial identifications only to jettison their faux rebellions when the time comes to enter the "real" (corporate) world.[73] The film implicitly recommends that *desis* embrace their ethnic, Indian, identity in the West, as *rooted* new cosmopolitans, honoring *desi*ness without sacrificing the blandishments of model minority mobility. The *évolué,* "cool" cosmopolitan, like Nina Shah, knows enough to embrace cosmopolitanism not as a "confused" ABCD, craving assimilation, but as a new cosmopolitan DSA. Kris's false consciousness is represented as inferior to the confident new cosmopolitanism Nina embodies. She looks, walks, and talks like any young American, but she also speaks Hindi with idiomatic relish. She dances the traditional *garba,* actively participates in the Indian students' association, is not ashamed of her "*desi*ness." It is in a process of "reverse assimilation"—embracing his Indian heritage (a path to *desi*ness he embarks on primarily to woo Nina)—that Kris discovers that he too can become a new DSA cosmopolitan.[74] Indianness, however, remains the indelible marker of Nina's *difference:* she reinscribes the "model minority" stereotype.

Pandya fails to address broader questions about multicultural life. *American Desi* glamorizes the DSA, trafficking in the fantasy that you can have your cake and eat it. For instance, it underappreciates that South Asians do not have the freedom that white Americans enjoy electively to render irrelevant, transparent, their ethnic difference. Thus the stand-up comedian Jay Chandrasekhar, who directed *Super Troopers* (1996), can cast himself as relegated to an epidermal limbo: "Where are the good roles for actors who are neither white nor black?"[75]

Diasporic South Asian Cinema's Dilemmas

DSA cinema falls short of engaging a developed progressive and democratic cosmopolitanism, beyond individual emancipation of DSA subjects. Yet this cinema implicitly poses a challenge: is it possible to see in diasporic dilemmas an opportunity for a more ambitious reimagining of Indianness?

One crucial dilemma is that between rootedness and the new cosmopolitanism. Can this dilemma be "resolved" by a bifocal perspective imbricating multiculturalism and cosmopolitanism? A mature DSA cinema might take seriously the difficult social and political material challenge of double consciousness facing South Asian migrants: anxieties about belonging, fragmentation of identity, cultural confusions, widening generational and class divides, loss of heritage.

This is where the fantasy of "imaginary homelands" conjured by the cinematic apparatus becomes productive. DSA cinema's bifocal orientation might acknowledge the desirability of rootedness while also problematizing *all* homelands as constructed by the offices of fantasy. What might it mean then to reimagine Indianness in such perspective, indexed to Indian culture without fetishizing rootedness or a national essence? And how might this transform Hindi cinema?

Seen from the other side of that bifocal lens, one of the critical challenges for DSA cinema is how to (re)imagine the home nation itself. Some films tend to become either facilely or ideologically anticosmopolitan: Ashish Rajadhyaksha notes that populist nostalgia has proliferated in "the rhetoric of an Asian diaspora."[76] New cosmopolitan solidarisms or transnational political agency may be thwarted by constricting mythologies of the "homeland." Emergent cosmopolitan identities, even if "thin" identities, present what Rushdie calls "a new angle" for entering the contemporary conjunctures of multicultural and cosmopolitan flows, or relations of contiguity and tension between cosmopolitanism and nationalism. Yet DSA cinema can also project a future in which South Asians can mine and mind the gap, as I have argued elsewhere, between partial belonging and inappropriate/inappropriated citizenship, between residence within the host nation and exclusion from it.[77]

A bifocal perspective has wider implications. South Asian Americans have been simultaneously "abjected" and commodified as "model minority citizens." A bifocal critical perspective might challenge such stereotypy. Karen Shimakawa writes that "Asian Americanness . . . occupies a role both necessary to and mutually constitutive of national subject formation"; DSA cinema can contribute to constructions of DSA subjectivity that do not reify *"an Asian American subject or even an Asian American object."*[78] Yet this does not mean disabling political agency. Contemporary DSA cinema is curiously transitional, symptomatically mirroring the suspension of South Asians between marginalization and ascribed model minority status, between traditionalist/parochial and modern/cosmopolitan mentalities.[79] These identities subtend continual, processual, *becomings—temporary and transitional condensations*—that defy a unipolar allegiance to "America" or "Asia."

DSA cinema also offers up varieties of anticosmopolitanism (glocalization): the desire "for origins . . . at the very heart of the attempt at new identity formations on the part of displaced peoples."[80] This desire also invokes the realm of *fantasy, if on the inverse track.* The desire for pure cosmopolitan lability is a fantasy; the desire for rootedness is equally chimerical, relying on selective memory, idealization, nostalgia for utopically reinvented homelands. The new cosmopolitanism can promote self-reflexivity about such fantasies. For example, in *Aa Ab Laut Chalen* (Let's Return Home, Rishi Kapoor, 1999), two NRI lovers, having found themselves and each other, believe they can finally return "home," as adumbrated in the title.[81] The film reasserts the fantasy of Indian moral/cultural superiority; the "real" Indian homeland is reduced to a spectral prosthesis, the country's real-world problems held in abeyance. Here the film might have done better to be more self-conscious about those problems and to explore what setting such national self-assertion in the United States implies.

This suggests another dilemma for DSA cinema. Many DSA films elide class issues, almost exclusively featuring young people with money, fine clothes, fast cars, beautiful bodies. Yet second- and third-generation South Asians in North America have been more invested in negotiating their place in the Generation X and Generation Y lifestyles than in committing themselves to defining their South Asianness in narrow, parochial terms. Their cosmopolitan politics—and aesthetics—of "forgetting" one's ethnic, national, or cultural roots are as important as any commitment to ethnicized identity.[82] Sometimes the issue is less class than the techno-managerialization and cultural mainstreaming of young South

Asians *across* class and community. DSA films can explore such matters much more subtly than they have in general managed to do.

Cosmopolitanism has traditionally been associated with elites: yet the new cosmopolitanism concerns non-elites as well. In Europe or the United States cosmopolitanism is more often associated in its positive aspects with people of white or EuroAmerican extraction, and cosmopolitanism of the bad variety (rootlessness, wandering) with those from elsewhere: the *sans papiers*, the burdensome refugees, the dissenting "bad subjects" such as Krishna in *Masala*. In the United States this rootlessness can signify the rudderless downward or lateral mobility of the migrant worker, the kind of shiftless (shifty?) wanderings of idle rich scions of wealthy non-Western fortunes. Still, cosmopolitanism in DSA films may facilitate new, flexible subjectivities and fresh opportunities for reimagining agency and solidarity across ethnic, class, and national borders.

We cannot ignore the variety of "actually existing cosmopolitanisms"; the challenge is *understanding* their contemporary forms and possibilities.[83] Postcolonial analysis needs a discourse of cosmopolitanism in DSA cinema that more adequately accounts for how DSA subjects negotiate Indianness in multicultural and transnational idioms. An evolved diasporic cinema would probably be more attuned to the fine grain of South Asian life, less tentative about its politics. Foregrounding a new cosmopolitanism can trouble the simple bifurcation of West and non-West and be alive to emergent identities, identity positions, and identifications.[84] Similarly, cultural identity is often mistakenly conceived in terms of a monolithic, timeless, shared culture. In fact cultural identities "have histories" and come "from somewhere," although those histories and origins are dynamic and not fixed, so it is never a question of recovering a core self but rather of a "politics of position" with all the interactions of "history, culture and power" that implies.[85]

A third challenge facing DSA cinema is the fixation on *individual* achievement, without collective responsibility or answerability to a larger community. DSA cinema often privatizes the struggle for agency and self-affirmation. The challenge is to imagine solidarity in the struggle for a civil society, in solidarity with other minority or oppressed groups.

This is not to say that an emphasis on the individual subject is misguided. It is at the level of the citizen-subject that the most crucial problematics of cultural identity manifest themselves: learning to "think and feel beyond the nation," learning true openness to the cultural other. Moreover, for a diasporic, the question of cosmopolitan sensibility poses itself in a specific form. Said's praise of Erich Auerbach's cosmopolitanism is apposite and instructive. Auerbach had cited Hugo of St. Victor as a kind of shibboleth: "The man who finds his homeland sweet is still a tender beginner; he to whom every soil is as his native one is already strong; but he is perfect to whom the entire world is as a foreign land. The tender soul has fixed his love on one spot in the world; the strong man has extended his love to all places; the perfect man has extinguished his."[86] Said, of course, is careful to remind us, in an echo of Adorno, that this is not mere elitism: the "perfect man's" exile is to be regarded not as a privilege but as "an alternative to the mass institutions that dominate modern life." Especially in the wake of the September 11 attacks, such an elegant and nuanced paean to cosmopolitanism may *seem* indulgently solipsistic, but for Said, most people "are principally aware of one culture, one setting, one home; exiles are aware of at least two, and this plurality of vision gives rise to an awareness of simultaneous dimensions, an awareness that . . . is *contrapuntal*."[87] While one might demur at the word "exiles," the new cosmopolitanism is another name for a contrapuntal sensibility, a dream worth dreaming.

One could even argue therefore that the new cosmopolitanism entails an ethical duty as well, an imperative to be receptive to the stranger, the other. If cosmopolitanism is to mean something more than the desire to make the world one's oyster, it should mean that our pursuit of our interest is not at the expense of people in other countries. The "compassion" one feels for one's kith and kin is really inimical to the ideal of cosmopolitanism if it breeds such a parochial love of one's own and cauterizes us to the pain of the other, especially the foreigner. After 9/11 this dangerous aspect of compassion, tied to an upwelling of patriotic and insular fervor, betrays the ideals of cosmopolitanism. This line of reasoning is at the heart of Nussbaum's description of a Stoic cosmopolitanism.[88] DSA cinema may not yet have undertaken the ethical burden of a mature cultural aesthetics, but it *is* in a state of emergence.

A fourth dilemma for DSA cinema is representing sexuality and gender with greater nuance and sophistication without alienating loyal audiences or allowing the gender politics to be domesticated as "generational conflict." When queer sexualities are focalized, they are cast as exceptions, reinscribing heteronormative paradigms. Sexuality itself superficially treated, often trivializing complex sex and gender issues. The sexual politics of DSA cinema also remain nascent or inadequately self-reflexive about how globalization has changed the nature of sexual arrangements; Dennis Altman makes a related argument in *Global Sex*.[89] The challenge here is to imagine a new erotics that isn't simply ironic or parodic, but mature and self-reflexive. Some smaller films—like those discussed in Chapter 6—do rise to the challenge.

A fifth dilemma is representing "race" or ethnicity in multicultural contexts without glossing over thorny issues of racism, assimilationism, or indeed the ideological trap of the "model minority" syndrome. In mainstream American culture South Asians are produced either as undesirable citizens or as model minority subjects commodified and conscripted to denigrate other minorities. The new DSA cosmopolitanism *can* resist this invidious polarization.[90] It can actively intervene in the representationalist project of recoding not only South Asian identities but also the form of civil society itself.

Perhaps an idealized new cosmopolitanism would include imagining a moral community of the sort Nussbaum envisions, a global ecumene (*oikumene*, inhabited world) where every human being is recognized as being of equal worth but of *different* talents and varying material circumstances and fortunes.

Can DSA cinema offer a new cosmopolitanism that takes seriously the idea of democratic citizenship?

Arguing for a new role for the imagination in the globalized era, Appadurai recommends that even academic research strive toward greater—and more "critical"—internationalism.[91] Can DSA cinema's new cosmopolitanism aspire to such critical internationalism? Can it revalorize imagination, even fantasy, moving beyond fixities of nation and sedimented identities, so the dialectic of the individual and the collective, the national and the transnational, the particular and the universal, remains vital? If cosmopolitanism is a "view from above," a universalist perspective that addresses the relationship of citizen to state and the global ecumene, a heightened, critical vigilance about transnationalism and internationalism is made imperative today by corporatized globalization. Some, like Robbins, provocatively imagine cosmopolitanism as a view from the "bombsight," as it were, as one flies above those whom one could harm. Indeed, it is when one can do harm but does none, to paraphrase Shakespeare, that one's cosmopolitical humanity is most meaningfully affirmed. The question of harm is critical in connection with terrorism, war, environmental degradation, pollution, epidemic disease, famine, drought, and labor and capital migration—and debating harms makes a cosmopolitan perspective indispensable.

Too often the new cosmopolitanism, in DSA films as well as in philosophical debates that frame my own discussion, remains rather thin, not yet substantively transcultural. Sissela Bok recommends we be patriots first and cosmopolitan second, that we proceed "from part to whole."[92] A more compelling goal is to reimagine ways of affirming moral and emotional allegiance beyond familiar parochialisms of nationalism while respecting local commitments—an interminable *dialectic* between globalism and cosmopolitanism from below.

8

Poverty Porn and Mediated Fantasy in Danny Boyle's *Slumdog Millionaire*

In May 2009, reports began emerging that two child stars of Danny Boyle's smash hit *Slumdog Millionaire* (2008) had had their slum dwellings bulldozed, rendering them homeless. This cruel reality calls into question the fantasy in which they had been conscripted: Boyle's film. Certainly mainstream cinema projects illusions—private as well as public fantasies—onto screens. Yet there is something different about the fantasy purveyed in *Slumdog*—witness the hype and controversy accompanying its release. Boyle's film offers an ebulliently melodramatic narrative approximating popular Hindi cinema, and dialectically blends an updated social realism with orders of fantasy, all while being ethico-politically provocative. For the film punctuates a moment of India's modernity in which the metropolis (Mumbai) became the face of the neoliberal state's projected image; the slum of the title becomes its unspeakable obverse. Presumably it takes a foreigner to make an "Indian" movie that speaks the truth of the contradiction. The film drew mixed reviews from various interest groups across the political divides of neoliberal India—both praise for depicting a slumdog who by his own wits succeeds in becoming a "millionaire" *and* resentment from slum dwellers who felt insulted by the representation of "slumdog" squalor; both praise from liberals for raising awareness about the dark side of the neoliberal state's policies *and* criticism from conservatives who saw Boyle's film as airing the country's dirty laundry as an insider would never have done, interrupting the dominant neoliberal national narrative: "India Shining." This chapter tracks some of the controversies provoked by the film, which injected into Hindi film culture an aesthetics both unaccustomed and nonetheless thoroughly recognizable to Indians themselves. It was even embraced *as* an Oscar-winning *Indian film,* though the director himself declared he had made a British film for British audiences. Is Boyle's film a revealing interruption of neoliberal state fantasy or just a neocolonial gesture? Is Boyle just slumming?

Adaptation, Interculturalism, and Intertextualism

The film is a *British* adaptation of the 2005 novel *Q&A*, by the Indian diplomat Vikas Swarup, and its adaptation introduces a formal or generic problematic of *the postcolonial intercultural,* as it relates to Hindi cinema, which this chapter explores. The problematic was raised in Chapter 7, a consideration of the "new cosmopolitanism" in a cluster of films produced not strictly within the Hindi film industry but outside it, often in English and by diasporic or even non-Indian filmmakers. Here I extend that consideration by exploring *a particular case* of a film that, while troubling the category of Indianness, also presents a "new cosmopolitan" perspective on India, condensing issues important to my broader argument in this book.

The plot revolves around Jamal Malik's coming of age in a largely Muslim Mumbai slum, Dharavi. Resourceful and enterprising (he even takes a plunge into an outhouse pit of human excrement in order to obtain the signature of the famous actor Amitabh Bachchan), he finds a job at a call center and later becomes an unlikely contestant and winner of a major televised game show. His story is intimately tied to that of Latika, a young girl who grew up with Jamal and his brother Salim. She survives, through the brothers' help, an attack on the slum by a Hindu fundamentalist mob, only to end up sexually enslaved to Maman, a gangland boss unscrupulous enough to maim and blind slum children in order to conscript them into a begging scheme like Mack the Knife in Bertolt Brecht's *The Threepenny Opera,* itself a kind of adaptation of John Gay's *The Beggar's Opera.* The three young escapees are "rescued" by Maman, who blandly offers them a cold Coke as a first enticement. When they learn that Maman is disfiguring children in order to force them to beg for his racket, the brothers escape a second time, by jumping onto a train. Latika, lagging behind, is offered a hand by Salim—only to be betrayed at the last minute. Left to Maman's clutches, Latika is forced into becoming his sex slave. The brothers fend for themselves: they sell goods on trains, hitch rides on train car roofs, become self-appointed "guides" at the Taj Mahal, and prey on tourists. But Jamal has not forgotten Latika and persuades Salim to join him in returning to Mumbai to find her and rescue her once again.

They succeed in rescuing Latika and killing Maman; but Salim joins forces with Javed, a rival gangland boss, and demands that Latika become his property, threatening Jamal with the gun that killed Maman. Jamal leaves and ultimately ends up working at a call center. There he acquires technological and other skills, which he uses to find Salim online and trace Latika. Jamal fights with his brother, who seems repentant; he reveals to Jamal that Latika is at Javed's house and provides the address. Jamal impersonates a repairman and works his way into Javed's kitchen, where Latika is unhappily reduced to cooking and serving

Javed's needs. Jamal declares that he loves Latika, asking her to come away with him, but she suggests bitterly that he forget those feelings: there is no escaping Javed. Though he cannot attempt the rescue at that moment because Javed comes in, treating Latika boorishly, Jamal promises to wait for her daily at the railway station. Somehow Latika manages to make it out one evening, but before they can get away, Salim and others in Javed's gang recapture her, slashing her face. Once again Jamal is estranged from Latika. His appearance on the game show, *Kaun Banega Crorepati,* becomes his last hope of contacting her, for he knows that she is a regular viewer.

Even though he makes it onto the show, he is framed by the corrupt host Prem Kumar and delivered into the hands of the police, who brutalize Jamal to extract a confession from him about cheating on the answers. Which raises the film's key epistemic question: how could Jamal know the answers to the questions posed to him without cheating? The torturous police interrogation, with which the film opens, concludes that he is plausible and innocent of fraud, and so he is allowed to return to the game show's final round, which Latika happens to watch at Javed's new house outside Mumbai, where she is newly imprisoned. Salim, now grown remorseful about keeping the two lovers apart, helps her escape to find Jamal again, giving her car keys and a cell phone. As luck would have it, the final question posed to Jamal is about the third musketeer in Alexandre Dumas's *The Three Musketeers.* Although Salim, Jamal, and Latika, when they were young, called themselves the three musketeers, Jamal doesn't know the answer. Figuring his brother would know, he uses his lifeline phone call to call Salim's cell phone, now in Latika's possession. She answers the call, but she doesn't know the answer either. Jamal "luckily" chooses the right answer. Meanwhile Javed discovers Salim's treachery, and tracks him down, locked in the bathroom, sitting in the tub. As Javed breaks in, Salim uses his gun to kill Javed but then is himself shot. He dies saying "Allahu Akbar" (God is great). After his big win Jamal waits as usual for Latika, and this time their love finds no impediment. As the credits roll, the reunited couple perform a dance on the platform to the now-famous song "Jai Ho"—arguably the Hindu equivalent of "Allahu Akbar."

The film structures itself around the Indian game show that is an adaptation of the originally British show *Who Wants to Be a Millionaire?* But the structural "logic" of intertextuality or adaptation also reveals itself in other important segmentations of the plot. For instance, I observed above that the story of Maman and his troupe of maimed and blinded beggar children was an adaptation of Brecht's *Threepenny Opera* and through that play of Gay's *Beggar's Opera.* (One might equally invoke other touchstones, including Charles Dickens's Industrial Age children's nightmare, *Oliver Twist.*) The subplot of child abuse is thus not a gratuitously violent device, as some have suggested; nor is it "unrealistic" literary conceit, merely a nightmarish fantasy of sadism. Such abusive exploitation of children is only too visible in major Indian cities like Mumbai, and all too real. My point is rather that "adaptation" is an important intertextual and intercultural analytic category, troubling the category of *Hindi* cinema but thereby justifying consideration in this book.

As I have also suggested above, the game show *Kaun Banega Crorepati* frames/enables the improbable victory of protagonist Jamal. The frame provides scaffolding for the plot, but it also poses the epistemic problematic that drives or structures the unfolding of the story: how could Jamal *know* the answers to questions posed to him on the game show? Further, it raises a question about the film's implicit truth claims—in other words about *realism*. How credible is it that a slumdog could become a millionaire in this way?

Experience versus Knowledge: Interculturalist Utopianism

The film is thus organized by a simple diegetic device: it sequentially furnishes more or less credible scenarios (in flashback), rationalizing Jamal's recollection of either (primarily) direct experience or (in some cases) indirect but experience-mediated knowledge of the random questions arising on the show. In the progression of what might be called "anamnesis scenarios" the film legitimizes its interculturalist utopianism, its message that even a slum dweller can become a millionaire—with the assistance of hope and luck.

Yet rationalization by anamnesis is simultaneously undercut, *supplemented*, in the deconstructive sense, by a competing "logic" of *luck*. In a culture as fatalistic as India's, this is a significant aspect of the profilmic "form": audiences are more likely to be persuaded by the convergence of fated events as adequate legitimation or explanation of Jamal's success than they would be by the rationalization of his success by experience. The film in other words sells an optimistic *fantasy*, cruel albeit life-affirming: a hopeless hope, as I argue below. This consoling fantasy may have had something to do with its being nominated for ten Academy Awards in 2009 and winning eight Oscars, including Best Director and Best Picture.

The flashback technique is a staple of Hindi cinema; here it presents the succession of anamnesis scenarios. Each scenario is associated with a quiz question and also introduces the stories of other characters, especially Latika and Salim. Each flashback presents a key episode rationalizing *how* Jamal, who has grown up without benefit of a decent education, could know the answers and win the competition. The truth claim is consistent in privileging direct experience or indirect witness over abstract (and implicitly elite, cosmopolitan) knowledge.

The episodic structure therefore invites reflection on questions of form but also of social issues in Hindi cinema. The film's *generic* significance consists as much in its pastiche of a Bollywood aesthetic turning on flashback, melodrama, and coincidence as in its recourse to a more "Hindi Social" aesthetic, parlaying a dialectic between realism and fantasy to crystallize a critical commentary on important social issues: poverty and class; sexual and other kinds of exploitation of children and women; education, religion, intercommunal conflict, gangland violence; housing and the geographic or geopolitical significance of the metropolitan slum; liberalization/modernization; and even the IT revolution. The film approximates but also interculturally and intertextually comments on popular forms of Hindi cinema, troubling nativist and essentialist definitions of "authentic" Hindi popular cinema, presumed to be inaccessible to cultural outsiders. Equally important, the film condenses important ethicopolitical issues animating the contemporary transnational public sphere: the quandaries of globalization, the clash between modernization and tradition, the representation of torture, graphic violence, and the quasi-pornographic wallowing in neocolonial schadenfreude—poverty porn.

The film's heart is in the right place. It works against the imputation that a slumdog who does not succeed simply lacks gumption or initiative; it contests the classist and neocolonialist stereotype of the indolent and unambitious Third World native subaltern. Yet if Boyle seeks to present Jamal as a hero to cheer for, all the film manages to do is show that Jamal succeeds because he gets lucky—all the quiz show questions fortuitously mirror his "experience." This preserves the optimistic possibility: that other slumdogs will take heart and hope from the film, rather than being disheartened to think that Jamal is so much more knowledgeable than they could ever hope to be. For someone whose life chances are as straitened by circumstance as Jamal's, only Lady Luck tenders hope. Yet if she smiles on Jamal, the message to the ordinary slumdog must be ambiguous: All slumdogs, rejoice, for luck may smile on you too, just as it did on this slumdog! All slumdogs, abandon hope, for the chances of your getting *this* lucky are vanishingly remote! Truly reliable guarantors of material success in life are actually family connections and inherited wealth, social support systems, access to institutions and education—though there too luck helps. That reliable route to success, however, is the long way up, and very few can take heart from the slow progress of the occasional subaltern such as a Mayavati or a Laloo Prasad Yadav, both of whom rose to political power despite extreme poverty and caste disadvantage. Cinema sells *fantasy.*

The narratological conceit that this one slumdog, who has no education or means, just got "lucky" is also a sop to the consciences of those who have an interest in maintaining the status quo, which in fact ensures that it is extremely difficult for *ordinary* citizens to win riches and fame through education, knowledge, and hard work. Katherine Boo adds that privileged viewers who see the film only as an upbeat story of a poor young man's triumph do so not only because the film had a happy ending but also because they are permitted to soothe any pangs of conscience by buying into the fantasy that Jamal's suffering "had been part of the solution."[1]

Interestingly, the film implicitly and explicitly acknowledges Jamal's *unreadiness* to be a contestant on a game show that purportedly rewards broad—even a global—cultural literacy. Jamal finds work as a low-level tea caddy in an Indian call center, a locus classicus of glocalization under conditions of IT-enabled globalization. On one occasion he is asked by a friend to step in for him to enable the friend to abandon his work station to watch the game show in progress on a television monitor in an adjacent room, with co-workers. Jamal reluctantly puts on the headset and fields a call from a client in Scotland; he may be clever, but he is certainly not clever enough to fake his way plausibly through even this short interaction. This is a cliché about call center workers and their thin disguises, but it reveals a critical contradiction in that while it shows Jamal to be highly unlikely to be able to compete in the kind of wide-ranging quiz show that requires global—cosmopolitan—cultural knowledge, we are asked simultaneously to believe that Jamal can win millions of rupees by acing almost all the questions posed to him.

To get around the disconnect, *Slumdog,* as already noted, deploys flashback scenarios to make plausible Jamal's ability to repeatedly come up with the right answers to the quiz questions, but it also prepares the ground with minor narrative excursions in the present, including the scene depicting his attempt to come up with a "Scottish accent" when speaking to the call center client; while the caller is clearly not fooled, the episode suggests that Jamal has some indirect knowledge of the British Isles, making it just barely plausible that he might be able to answer the game show question about where Oxford Circus lies. Yet sometimes the device is imperfect. The spectator is asked to believe that Jamal "knows" the name of the American statesman whose portrait appears on a $100 bill (Benjamin Franklin), even though he does not know the name of the great leader whose image graces the *Indian* currency's Rs. 1000 bill (Mahatma Gandhi), just because his friend Arvind, blinded by Maman and now begging in the subway, is able to identify the $100 bill by identifying the person whose image is printed there through Jamal's description of him (an "old man" who "looks like a girl"). How exactly would Arvind, who was blinded as a very young slum dweller, have known this?

I have suggested above that the film concedes, if only unwittingly, that it is *improbable* that someone like Jamal could win the game show contest. Instead, it makes a different claim: that it is *possible* that Jamal knows the answer to *just* those questions that happened by sheer good luck to come his way. The contradiction is important: the *mode* by which the film presents its truth claim (realism) is calculated to demonstrate *plausibility.* Yet it apostrophizes fate and just dumb luck, which is to say the diegetic content acknowledges statistical *implausibility.* Ultimately this is even in the film's own terms a *fantasy.*

Instead of imputing to Jamal a broad cultural literacy, general cultural competence, the film enacts an epistemological displacement, substituting particular, accidental, personal, and experiential "knowledge." What Jamal knows is merely what happens to have happened to him, no more, no less. Yet this radically accidental and individualized knowledge also has a class subtext, because this kind of knowing is non-elite—and requires only luck. The film's driver is blind hope, made a cruel fantasy because its chief "consumers," as with much Hindi cinema, are mass audiences. It is interesting, then, that expressing surprise at the film's enthusiastic North American reception, and as if unapologetic about Britain's colonial past or unconscious of the neo-Orientalist overtones of his statement, Boyle said he had originally intended the film for *British* audiences because "the British understand more of India than other people."[2]

An Auteurist Film

Boyle brings a distinctly British *auteur*'s eyes, and a particular style, to the film. This raises a host of questions, such as whether his is a *biased* perspective despite his declared intention to make a film with "universal" appeal. This makes the film provocative for a *critical* postcolonial studies. The film's reception, as noted above, has been deeply controversial, especially regarding its proclivity for luxuriating in unpleasant realities of slum life in India—"slumming" in the slums, trafficking in "poverty porn," luring viewers to "gawk at the squalor," and indulging in a phantasmagoria of filth and violence, in voyeuristic schadenfreude.[3] As in Chapter 3, dealing with "sexploitation" cinema, I argue here that it is important to ask whether there is an exploitative dimension to this film *about* exploitation.

Boyle brings to the project the brio that animated his film *Trainspotting* (1996), another occasion on which he portrayed a city (Edinburgh) as decaying, its youth in dire economic straits but somehow vibrantly alive. To some extent this protects him from calumny. *Slumdog*'s Indian setting is, furthermore, integral to its "realist" mise-en-scène, indexed to its programmatic framing of social problems, such as the beggar mafia or religious and ethnic conflict between Hindus and Muslims.

Such social problems precipitated similarly in "Golden Age" Hindi cinema: *Slumdog* invites and complicates comparison. The parallels indicate Boyle's incorporation of both national and transnational idioms admixed with a self-reflexivity about genre and style. His low-budget (just $14 million) film blends popular entertainment—an appealing romantic subplot—with a focus on characters representing important social issues. Boyle's brisk editing style, more typical of a post-MTV aesthetic, is aided by upbeat music. His dynamic cutting, dolly shots, and mobile camera work often violate codes of realist mise-en-scène, as in an early chase scene in which young slumdogs are running from policemen, like the one near the beginning of Boyle's *Trainspotting* or in domestic Indian films such as *Satya* (Ram Gopal Verma, 1988). His ebullient exposition in settings steeped in squalor remains true to his trademark style: deliberately unconventional, frank, iconoclastic, cool.

This style is an intercultural and intertextual linking trait among contemporary directors such as Pedro Almodóvar, Alejandro González Iñárritu, Alfonso Cuarón, Mathieu Kassovitz, Tom Tykwer, Baz Luhrmann, Stephen Frears, Gurinder Chadha, and Mira Nair, to name just a few. *Slumdog*, like *Trainspotting*, places Boyle within this cohort, sharing not only a style but also a cool sensibility and an interest in intercultural contact. Boyle's effervescent style may be a crucial factor in making the appeal of its optimistic fantasy universal. Many younger Indian directors are also adopting domestic versions of this hip style: not only Ram Gopal Varma but also Nagesh Kukunoor, Kaizad Gustad, Dev Benegal, Santosh Sivan, and Mani Ratnam. Stylistically and in other ways "Hindi" cinema is an increasingly capacious category, reflecting a more general disaggregation of the signifiers of Indianness. The phenomenon is related to the increasing maturity of other media platforms, particularly the television industry.

Today TV in India has come a long way from what it was in the days of black-and-white, with its single state-controlled channel, Doordarshan. The new aesthetics of contemporary TV programming available in the country reflects aesthetic values shared by contemporary producers, including Boyle and some of the other aforementioned contemporary filmmakers, of cultural products. These aesthetic values respond to *and shape* new spectatorial expectations from Hindi cinema—a new globalized visual taste itself a product of transnational, transcultural circulation of competing media platforms, including television, MTV, Google, YouTube, Facebook, Twitter, Vimeo, Hulu, and so on. To take just one example, *Slumdog* concludes, after the ending of the film proper (as the credits roll), with a dance ("Jai Ho") clearly influenced by the post-MTV global traffic of music videos.

The importance of this changing aesthetic cannot be overstated. The new audience expectations of cinema reflect a hyperawareness about India's ascendancy in software design and its "move toward media convergence enabled by digital technologies"; films in India, especially Hindi films, now rely on "the glossy visuals and rapid editing associated with Hong Kong cinema, American music videos, and global advertising."[4] By the same token the industry must be alert to whether its "products" are competitive on the global entertainment market; even among elite classes, there are "resurfacing worries of backwardness . . . in the middle of a resurgent economy," which "point to persistent anxieties . . . dating back to the colonial era."[5] In 1976 the *New York Times Magazine* featured Indian journalist Khushwant Singh's blunt assessment that India's movie industry "makes the worst films in the world—and the Indians love them."[6] That was many years ago; Hindi cinema today finds itself in the difficult position of having to appeal to a *national* audience schooled in the currency of a *transnational* cinematic idiom while still drawing undereducated mass audiences denied exposure to globalized cultural circulations. Making bad films in the old style is no longer an option. As I have suggested, the increasingly common "adaptation" or remake has been one (problematic) response: *Chachi 420* (Kamal Hasan, 1998), an unblushing remake of *Mrs. Doubtfire* (Chris Columbus, 1993); *Kaante* (Thorns, Sanjay Gupta, 2002), lifting style and plot from Quentin Tarantino's *Reservoir Dogs* (1992); Vishal Bharadwaj's *Maqbool* (2003) and *Omkara* (2006), transposing Shakespeare's *Macbeth* and *Othello,* respectively, hybridizing an intercultural cosmopolitan style and formulaic characteristics and indigenous settings, languages, cultural references, and values. The aesthetic idioms employed in Hindi cinema are increasingly hybrid, intertextual, and intercultural, with the result that signifiers of Indianness are increasingly disaggregated and labile. This is a point I return to in the Conclusion.

A striking example of intercultural style in Boyle's film is the interpolation of Spanish lyrics into the song-and-dance routine seen at the end, after Jamal and Latika's final kiss. This may seem only a flourish, but it carries a semiotic trace of the film's ambition to a cinematic and musical global lingua franca. Furthermore, this hybridizing sensibility has an ethicopolitical motive: breaching customary cultural divides. Boyle's interest is not stylistic innovation just for the sake of innovation or marketing. Any discussion of the film ought to ask which markets, which spectators, are addressed and how, and so provide a more adequate account of the geopolitical, historical, and socioeconomic vectors that condition reception.

The Hindi Socials were models of social realism blended with popular entertainment—including fantasy; Boyle's film approximates this blended social realism. The surface "melodrama" of his film conceals a critical *agalma,* a secret ambition transcending mere gestural homage. Boyle seeks to enter an intercultural and intertextual conversation, and to *intervene* into the mediatic public sphere by pointing up social truths many Indian directors shy away from.

This underscores the irony that what Boyle's film leaves us with is the *improbability* of its sustaining fantasy. Boyle's is a cinematic Mumbai where wonders can happen even to a slumdog as he goes from rags to millions of rupees: a space at once real and fantastical, a cultural crossroads both global and local, bringing together themes, agents, ideas, and cinematic styles. By the same token it is a nonplace, not so much postmodern or supermodern as a space outside, before, or alongside modernity. The Mumbai slum, in particular, is not a nonspace in the sense of being devoid of the relationality among collective identities that Marc Augé assigns to "anthropological space" or in the postmodern sense of being a space of translation only—on the contrary, it is constituted as *permanently impermanent yet rooted,* a place where people work and live, miracles happen, and slumdogs are transmogrified into millionaires. The film is neither British nor truly Bollywood; the slum is both utopic and dystopic: a space where *realism converges with fantasy.*

Still, it is remarkable that while an Indian filmmaker would probably not make such a film, *Slumdog* was embraced by many in India *as an Indian film.* One reason for this was its success at the Oscars; foreign recognition conditioned domestic acknowledgment. Bhaskar Sarkar notes that "contemporary Bollywood's heightened desire for an Oscar constitutes nothing less than a national aspiration in the arena of global media; and this appetite was surely sharpened by the failure of so many previous attempts": *Mother India* (1957), *Lagaan* (2001), *Devdas* (2002), *Shwaas* (2004), *Paheli* (2005), and *Rang De Basanti* (2006).[7]

Chapter 7 discussed the idea that the "new cosmopolitanism" of diasporic South Asian cinema is largely an elite or middle-class phenomenon. Boyle's film, though not blind to the suffering of real slum dwellers, is remarkable in identifying an *emergent* cosmopolitanism within even these poorest corners of Mumbai. Still, many details require sober analysis: what does it mean for a British film almost entirely in English to be celebrated as an Indian film? Being largely in

English certainly no longer *disqualifies* a film from inclusion and categorization as "Indian"—indeed, this book discusses several films in English, including *Fire, Masala, Mississippi Masala, East Is East, My Son the Fanatic*, and *Bend It Like Beckham*, with substantial impact on India's film industry, displacing the formerly dominant "role of Hindustani/Urdu" as "the metalanguage of Hindi cinema's ideological work. . . . English provides the ideological coordinates of the new world of the Hindi film."[8] That dominant role was already complicated: Hindustani and Urdu are morphologically identical but graphically and semantically divergent. On billboards advertising Hindi films, Hindi/Hindustani is transliterated in roman letters; a similar practice is common in online communications. Hindi is a dominant language; Urdu is increasingly minoritized as "foreign." Boyle's film seeks to insinuate itself into the Indian cinematic landscape as a British film that may be considered an "Indian" film.

One might say the film is *cross-dressed as an Indian film*. But that leads to another question: How do we understand the film's "address" simultaneously to domestic, diasporic, and Western audiences? The answer is complicated. The film's defenders can be divided into progressives and neoliberals. Many progressives celebrate its unflinching presentation of unpleasant realities. Defenders of Boyle's film admire it for shaming pusillanimous Indian filmmakers (who propagate pretty fantasies) by boldly presenting uncomfortable realities; neoliberals laud its narrative of individualist gumption, which exempts institutions, governments, corporate interests, and the rich from shouldering any responsibility for the welfare of the poor. A corresponding division among detractors is between the new middle-class, who resent the film's implicit challenge to their cocooned world view, and cosmopolitan and NRI critics, who find the film insulting to their vision of an emergent, "shining India."[9]

Besides, since the issue of "realism" in this film turns on how the *slum* is represented, it is well to remember that the slum is not only a real place but a conceptual category, important for understanding Indian modernity, even a nonplace combining real and imaginary representations. The film is not an objective documentary. The point is not always appreciated even by theorists of modernization. Ashis Nandy affirms popular cinema as valuable precisely for providing "the slum's point of view of Indian politics and society and, for that matter, the world."[10]

A Range of Responses

In the dominant paradigm of film criticism originating in the 1950s (Chidananda Das Gupta through Ashis Nandy), Vasudevan observes, "the spectator of the popular film emerges as an immature, indeed infantile, figure . . . bereft of the rationalist imperatives required for the Nehru era's project of national construction." However, both those critical of commercial films and their audiences for their "lack of reality orientation" and those who "valorize Indian culture's resistance to modern forms of consciousness" often fail to grasp the complexities of spectatorial address.[11] Boyle's film evidently appeals to audiences internationally and across class divides, including to the all-important diaspora.[12] Diasporic markets generate up to 65 percent of total takings, not to mention creating "buzz" and lending some transnational credibility to certain films that subsequently get screened in India and draw more attention than they would have done if they had opened in India first—*Fire* being a prime example. In the United Kingdom "Bollywood releases routinely enter the weekly box-office top ten and score high screen averages. For example, in a U.K. box-office chart for a week in August 2003, the Bollywood hit *Koi Mil Gaya,* playing on just thirty-six screens, [had] the second best screen average after *Terminator 3* . . . in its second running week and showing in 477 theatres."[13]

The film also responds to growing transcultural interest in *India as a globalizing economy.* If colonial misadventures generated voyeuristic and biopolitical interest in Orientalist knowledge of the non-West, globalization and the rise of India have renewed transcultural interest in Indian dance, theater, fiction, and films. Recent filmic representations of intercultural contact include the Oscar nominee *Lagaan* (Ashutosh Gowariker, 2001), discussed in Chapter 5, *The Royal Tenenbaums* (Wes Anderson, 2001), *Outsourced* (John Jeffcoat, 2006), *The Darjeeling Limited* (Wes Anderson, 2007), and even *The Best Exotic Marigold Hotel* (John Madden, 2011), which features in the lead role Dev Patel, the actor playing the slumdog in Boyle's film. Earlier I had also mentioned in this connection theatrical productions such as *Moulin Rouge* (Baz Luhrmann, 2001) and *Bombay Dreams* (Andrew Lloyd Webber, 2002).

Slumdog may be a British film, nominated for an Oscar *as a British film,* with dialogue mainly in English, but it was shot in India and featured mainly Indian actors. The question of *Slumdog*'s curiously divided identity arises not only in the matter of audience reception but also in the matter of the casting. It is revealing that Boyle, though avowedly committed to telling the truth about the slum, turned to a British Asian actor, clearly not from the Dharavi slum, to play the adult lead (the younger children were cast from among real slum dwellers: that bar was considerably lower). This casting certainly compromises the film's implicit claim to realistic representation—it appears to concede that it was not possible to find a real slumdog even to play the role of a fantasized slumdog who could succeed on the game show—it constitutes an admission that the story is a fantasy and highlights the chasm between Boyle's own consoling rags-to-riches tale and the hard reality. It is a fantasy of class-overcoming offered to mass audiences about a subaltern played by a middle-class NRI. Or perhaps the fantasy is a salve, peddling the neoliberal mantra that success accrues to those who simply want it enough. Overseas Indians praise the film for being devoid of "liberal guilt," even *(mis-)recognizing* its fundamental fantasy: "a fundamentally *American* story—the individual triumphs, good people win in the end, hard work, savvy, and luck are richly rewarded. Of course, this is nowhere near the truth."[14] And if "telling it like it is" is the claim of "realism," then Boyle also undermines the warrant for his own claim, reinscribing his outsiderness in the very act of seeking to make plausible a fantastical tale of a slumdog becoming a millionaire.

If this seems unfair, consider that Amitabh Bachchan himself excoriated *Slumdog*, provoking sympathetic protest among his enormous fan base. Bachchan is not just an icon of the movie industry but a demigod. As I demonstrated in Chapter 3, his appearances in a string of culturally significant films elevated him to a status on a par with spiritual leaders and saints. It is a cinematic irony that the film features a *darsana*, or visitation, by Bachchan, in a cameo by proxy. It is in the scene in which young Jamal takes a dip in a cesspool beneath an outhouse to get an autograph from the demigod, who descends to earth by helicopter. Many Bachchan fans saw this scene as disrespectful.

Bachchan proved a harsh critic of the film. He derided precisely its presumptive claim to *realism*, the claim of representing uncomfortable truths about India. He suggested that Boyle was pandering to self-flattering, neocolonial Western prejudices—like Satyajit Ray, India's best-known film director. As *The Guardian* put it, Bachchan "rubbished" the film, throwing brickbats at it rather than the bouquets the West showered on it.[15] On his popular blog Bachchan excoriated Boyle for presenting India as a "third-world, dirty, underbelly developing nation," suggesting that the film's popularity was owing to its having been made by a Westerner.[16] Later Bachchan recanted, but the demigod had already spoken, and fans would hold to his lapidary word. Nor was Bachchan the sole celebrity critic. The Bollywood star Preity Zinta and Shilpa Shetty (no stranger to controversy) of the hit show *The Big Boss* protested that *Slumdog* presented India too negatively, distorting the reality.[17] A "media-mad politician," emphatically not a slumdog, sued to have the title changed to *Slum Dash Millionaire*. Upper-echelon Indians disliked the film, too: "They thought it slighted the increasing affluence and prominence of their country."[18]

Boyle could be defended on the grounds that he is an equal-opportunity connoisseur of metropolitan underbellies, whether Western or non-Western. The successful *Trainspotting*, grossing nearly $17 million within a year in the United States and nearly £13 million in Britain, rubbed the audience's noses in Edinburgh's urban blight—while still striking a chord with savagely antinationalistic political wit and ironic energy. The negative portrayal of Edinburgh and Scottish society was not gratuitous, many fans of the film insisted, but an indicator of political sophistication and postmodern and postnational urbanity. But Boyle was making a film about his own country then, and even those who identified with the characters in *Trainspotting* could presume a baseline identificatory, national sympathy that cannot be presumed in *Slumdog*.

So the question arises, how did the Indian slum dwellers themselves receive *Slumdog*? Katherine Boo, writing in the *New Yorker*, observes that in Bihar, slum dwellers threatened to burn fifty-six effigies of Boyle because the very title bestialized them, equating them to dogs. Although some actual residents of the Dharavi slum represented in Boyle's film were similarly and more immediately offended, others cheered the film as finally putting them in the global spotlight and for taking up their cause during and after filmmaking.

Indisputably, the film gave slum dwellers a voice and a forum that *indigenous* popular culture has not always afforded them.[19] And Boyle's crew supported the young actors and their family to some extent after the film was completed—the nine-year-old Azharuddin Ismail, who also played the young Salim in the film, was sponsored at his school by Boyle and his crew. It was not enough. Since the release of Boyle's film, many people have made videos and written articles about "the real slumdogs" who didn't, and don't, make it. Ismail was evicted from the slum.

An ethical defense of the film's (social) realism, as I suggested above, is that its heart is in the right place. But it is not exactly Third Cinema: it purveys a crowd-pleasing and neoliberal fantasy under the guise of social realism. We cannot simply dismiss one side or the other in the controversy about *Slumdog*'s claim to "realism." It is noteworthy that the slums have been seen as a positive model not within the country but by outsiders—not least by Prince Charles of England, creator of the Foundation for the Built Environment, who was favorably impressed in 2003 when he visited the Dharavi slum on which the film is based. In a recent speech Prince Charles praised the slum for its "underlying, intuitive 'grammar of design,'" as well as for "the timeless quality and resilience of vernacular settlements"; he predicted that "in a few years' time such communities will be perceived as best equipped to face the challenges that confront us because they have built-in resilience and genuinely durable ways of living."[20] It is possible to interpret Prince Charles's tribute to the slum as a counternarrative to neoliberal ideology, affirming the possibility of inhabiting a parallel economy and way of life sufficient unto itself, connected to but not enfolded within the dominant capitalist narrative endorsed by globalization—even if not escaping the regime of capital itself. On the face of it, this view is progressive, championing the subaltern slum dwellers. But as Arundhati Roy insists, the film "allows real-life villains to take credit for its cinematic achievements because it lets them off the hook. It points no fingers, it holds nobody responsible. Everyone can feel good. And that's what I feel bad about." Roy concedes that the film is well made. But she also avers that it ultimately fails the test of "realism."[21]

The alleged idealization—fantasy—of the slum as a model of a metropolitan parallel community or of an alternative possibility of living a satisfactory life does not sit well with the propertied wealthy and the neoliberal ideologues. From their perspective slums reduce property values and are a blot on the face of "shining India." Shyamal Sengupta, a Mumbai film professor, dismisses Boyle's representation as cultural tourism, a "white man's imagined [fantasy?] India."[22] Yet it remains true that few Bollywood films focus on slum dwellers; it cannot surprise us that there is a hunger among lower-class fans for films that provide occasions for such recognition. They understandably crave seeing themselves represented in both senses detailed by Gayatri Spivak: *Vertretung* (proxy, or political representation) and *Darstellung* (portrait).[23] In psychoanalytic terms, these representations, structured by the dialectic of realism and fantasy, offer forms of "suture" unavailable to them elsewhere: it is for them the closest thing to a public sphere, where their concerns can be aired.

This cinematic public sphere involves multiplex dimensions of fan participation, including negotiations of class struggle. Fan culture cannot be reduced to a monolithic, singular perspective; nor can it be said to reflect an undifferentiated "mass" appetite in film spectatorship. Fans belong to different social strata, and they are "part rowdy, part *rasika* [connoisseur], part pirate, part copyright-enforcer."[24] Lower-class film viewers, Sara Dickey writes, are "sharply aware of their social and cultural distance from the upper class," and use fan club membership "to address and redress that distance."[25] However, class stratification remains largely uninterrogated even in films featuring non-elite citizens. It would be unrealistic, even unfair, to expect Boyle's film to deliver a universally satisfactory representation of Mumbai—social realism untrammeled by fantasy.

Critics such as Roy would not be satisfied with anything less than a systemic, progressive remedy for the social ills the film indexes—poverty and the dearth of educational and job opportunities, exploitation of socially marginalized children and women, violence and torture by law enforcement and other authorities, weak institutions, and a nation-state made weaker under conditions of globalized capitalism. But what would a realistic solution to the problems of slum dwellers look like? The Peruvian Nobel laureate in economics Hernando de Soto, who grew up in Switzerland, notes that it had been a very poor country in nineteenth-century Europe until the jurist Eugen Huber drafted its civil code and thereby consolidated small, dispersed property holdings, upsetting the status quo but also giving power to the people. Huber's code became the seed of a major revolution in Swiss society, transforming it into the extraordinarily successful economy we know today. Similar benefits could accrue, de Soto maintains, to other poor countries such as Peru and India if comparable legal and institutional access were made available to ordinary citizens. A truly "realistic" response to the conditions portrayed in *Slumdog* would have to include such structural changes, including changes in the distribution of wealth and in the availability of a truly global-era education to the poor as well as the rich. But such realism is too onerous to contemplate. Humankind cannot bear very much reality—or realism. Thus the seductive fantasy of getting rich overnight, preferably by dint of *individual* initiative or sheer luck. Who doesn't want to be an instant millionaire? Yet, to paraphrase W. B. Yeats, this is the kind of seductive fantasy we nurture in our hearts at the risk of our brutalization.

A more systemic reason to object to such fantasy as the film purveys is that it allows the state to disappear, to disavow its responsibility to the citizen-subject that it necessarily produces in its legal and institutional fictions. The contemporary reign of neoliberal discourse (since liberalization reforms were instituted in 1991) has devolved responsibility ever more onto individuals, exonerating the state from being responsible for the individual's welfare and from holding big business accountable. This discourse also occludes, behind the veil of fantasies, the process of the production of seductive fantasies such as those at the heart of *Slumdog*.[26] I argue in what follows that this production depends on the form of melodrama.

Melodrama as Hinge between Realism and Fantasy

Boyle adapts melodrama, arguably giving a fresh spin to the dialectic between realistic and fantasy modes familiar from Hindi films since Independence. This is practically a native cinematic idiom, blending *forms* of social realism, song-and-dance routines, romance, sentimentalism, fantasy, mythological elements, comedy, coincidence, exaggerated affect, and extradiegetic fantasy routines as elaborations of inexpressible desire.[27] Boyle's film does not merely mimic melodramatic *themes:* moralization, *simplification* of affect, predilection for stark *dualities* of good versus evil, the Manichaeism of tradition versus modernity, and valorization of tradition despite modernity's blandishments. It complicates melodrama's *disinclination* to engage in psychological exploration; it does not privilege family and society over the individual. Melodrama upholds middle-class aspirations and values and the dream of property ownership. *Slumdog* offers only a pastiche of melodramatic fantasies, encoded in the very title of the game show "*Kaun Banega Crorepati?*" ("Who Wants to Be a Millionaire?"), initially hosted by none other than Amitabh Bachchan. Yet precisely in this complicated relationship with Hindi melodrama, Boyle's film sheds light on Hindi cinema's sedimented conventions.

For instance, the significance of bourgeois class aspirations for melodrama can hardly be exaggerated, but in *Slumdog*, they are *ironized* on the one side by the fantasy of overnight success (the game show) and assailed on the other by the reality of the truly poor (the slum).[28] The nuclear family is conspicuous by its absence in Boyle's film. This exclusion highlights and problematizes a *functional* principle of melodrama. Classic melodrama provides the emotionally wrenching logic for the ultimate resolution of the central difficulty, namely, noncoincidence between the *fantasy* of romantic love and the social *reality* that separates the focal couple. This couple might indulge themselves in a song-and-dance episode—temporarily suspending social customs, discovering a "separate peace." Yet they reemerge into "reality" as though untouched by the *jouissance* they enjoyed during the fantasy.[29] Within melodrama, fantasy often is the pivotal point where the "romance plot" and the *enargeia* of "eros" are most powerfully expressed. In many commercial films fantasy affords momentary exit from the realist narrative, even if ultimately collapsing back into diegetic realism.[30] The main realist narrative in *Slumdog* is by contrast thoroughly infiltrated by fantasy, and not just in "fantasy sequences."

Similarly, a *structural* feature of classical melodrama is the privileging of chance and coincidence—often obeying the logic of not the reality principle but wish fulfillment. *Slumdog* (perhaps unwittingly) complicates this structural principle by *rationalizing* Jamal's ability to come up with the right answers, "screening" what Freud would have identified as *Wunsch*.[31] The film reperspectivizes fantasy not as realism's opposite but its obverse.

In *Slumdog* melodrama functions as a hinge articulating the harsh reality of the slums with aspirational fantasy—magical thinking, a fantasy lure—belying its pretensions to addressing real social issues (slums, poverty, violence against children). But this does not seem to undermine its appeal: it is what moves the audience emotionally. Salim sacrifices himself for Jamal so he can be reunited with his beloved Latika and dies in a gunfight coincidentally at the moment of Jamal's victory, proclaiming "God is great"—a melodramatic parody of the Muslim credo unfortunately made familiar to many in the West only as the fatal words of suicide terrorists. This parody should give us pause.

There are other melodramatic moments—provoking sentimental or excessive affect in the viewer. Jamal's mother is brutally murdered even as she tries to save him and his brother: his friend Arvind suffers a vicious blinding, in possibly the most graphic scene of the film. Jamal's beloved Latika is raped, scarred, indentured to a cruel gangland boss; he himself has to endure torture by the police. The "excessive," graphic representation of these heinous acts is calculated to elicit heightened sympathy for the characters. All the heartbreak, blending happiness and sadness, success and loss, is characteristic of melodrama, generating contradiction or suspense/suspension that can be overcome only by fantasy. When effective, the logic of suture fuses identification in the symbolic and the imaginary registers: the spectator is sutured into the melodramatic narrative of becoming rich overnight (and getting lucky in love!) while *simultaneously acknowledging* the improbability.

Thus Jamal's story as a *contradictory* melodrama *supports rather than defeats* the identificatory fantasy crucial to suture. Spectators want to win as Jamal does in the great game show of life; they want to be reassured that street smarts are all you really need to succeed. That is also why the poor, who have little *realistic* hope of getting rich otherwise, invest in the lottery far more often than those in higher social strata—despite the impossibly long odds.

In *Beyond the Pleasure Principle* Freud writes that unpleasurable realities can be mastered by ludic or otherwise fantasmatic reconstructions of reality, or transmuted into a happier outcome.[32] The abject conditions of the slum are thus made a necessary pretext for Jamal's success and therefore for the aspirant spectators' hope against hope, for permission to allow fantasy to trump reality, even though they *know* better. Is this not the central insight encapsulated in the psychoanalytic formula of disavowal expressed by Octave Mannoni and developed by Jacques Lacan and Slavoj Žižek, for persisting in a *belief* or *fantasy* when one intellectually *knows* perfectly that it is false? *Je sais bien, mais quand même* (I know very well, but nonetheless . . .).[33]

A further point is that it is one's avowed or unavowed political ideology that determines whether the reality principle or the fantasy (pleasure principle) wins out. This operation of ideology explains some of the otherwise odd divergences in the film's reception history—they have as much to do with ideology as with

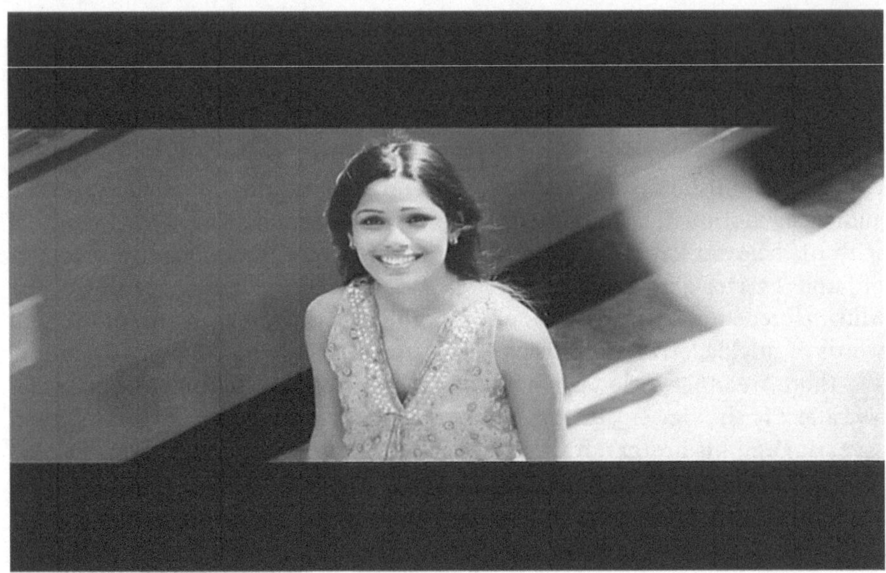

Figure 8.1. Freida Pinto, whose casting as Latika raises many questions of representation, in *Slumdog Millionaire* (dir. Danny Boyle, 2008).

an innate enclitic tendency to lean more toward the reality principle or toward the pleasure principle. How *much* reality a human being can bear is relative. No wonder that so many people loved *Slumdog*. As I suggested above, meaningfully addressing the slum's problems would require long-term structural reforms in education, social programs, massive redistribution of wealth, a sea change in public attitudes, and a reversal of neoliberal policies. These smack too much of the reality principle: they are hopelessly unromantic, hardly the stuff of Bollywood dreams and *filmi* fantasy.

Boyle's implicit claim to social realism is also to be questioned in terms of his representation of differentiative categories of "race," ethnicity, or phenotype. For instance, given the conflicted significations of skin color within South Asian society, the casting of Freida Pinto as the adult Latika is as problematic as the casting of the Britisher Dev Patel as Jamal. The child Latika is, tellingly, played by Rubina Ali, a darker Muslim, but the young adult is played by Freida Pinto, a lighter-skinned Christian of Portuguese extraction who in 2010 was the model for L'Oréal in the United States (see Figure 8.1). Her casting is thus a complicated issue in a nation where skin tone intersects with caste prejudices and creed hierarchies.

Another dimension in which Boyle's avowed fealty to realism is to be reevaluated is his decision to depict a Muslim slum in which an episode of communal violence is staged; *during* this violent episode Jamal and his brother Salim witness the horrific murder of their mother and the apparition of a "Hindu" god. How is it that such violence can happen in the same social environment in which the Muslim protagonist is elevated to the status of universal hero of non-elite Indians, both Hindu and Muslim—can the very people who would kill a Muslim in his slum cheer for him as their representative hero on a game show? Is the film suggesting that Mumbai is a city in which being Muslim matters or in which it finally does not matter? It is as though a Muslim overcomes his communal, inherited stigma only through the grace of material success/celebrity status. The neoliberal *fantasy* of overnight material success supersedes and occludes the *reality* of communal division.

Boyle's film plays with conventions of realism and fantasy in other provocative ways, stylishly blurring conventional *distinctions* between realism and fantasy. On the one hand, Boyle *follows* realistic conventions, committed to rendering "authentic" Indian sensibilities and social conditions, sometimes seeming to rub our noses in gritty reality—the camera makes nearly hyperreal the filth, violence, crime, poverty, the rot that is everywhere in the slum. On the other hand, the film's implied claim to social realism begs the question of whether the representation is fair and true: is Boyle trafficking in poverty porn, for Western eyes? Katherine Boo, in her *New Yorker* piece, admits that "the West did seem to make a fetish of the Indian poor, even as the official poverty rate was falling: from thirty-six to twenty-seven per cent in a decade." This is what sticks in the craw of many Indians—that it selectively emphasizes the "underbelly" of the Miracle of Mumbai, the uglier reality of India, ignoring more positive realities. They argued that Boyle is an outsider, with no real stake in how Mumbai or its "slumdogs" are represented; Indian directors would not serve up the slum for the frisson of voyeuristic horror quite so blithely.

These detractors also point to an ethicopolitical problem: Boyle's film may be operating under the thinly disguised presumption of educating Indians about a reality that is disavowed or not seen by Indians themselves. Is this a return of the *mission civilisatrice*, promising to bring enlightenment to benighted natives in metaphorical darkness? Boyle's realism, in this view, is covert Western post-imperialist presumption, supposing itself to be fearlessly uncovering Mumbai's corruption, vice, prostitution, filth, and most melodramatically (criminal and police) violence against slum children. Although the film might be regarded as extending the narrative genre that links Gay's *The Beggar's Opera*, Brecht's *Threepenny Opera*, and Charles Dickens's *Oliver Twist*, a genre featuring often violent organized exploitation of children in *Western* societies, *Slumdog* offends sensibilities as itself a neo-Orientalist or neocolonialist fantasy construction. It is one thing for Boyle to present Edinburgh's squalor in *Trainspotting*—that was, as argued above, an inside job—and quite another to represent Mumbai's squalor as an outsider.

If on the one hand Boyle aspires to a social realism with a conscience, on the other hand he *flouts* realism's generic, cultural, ideological, structural, and stylistic conventions through intercultural and intertextual references. Ironically this contravention is partly responsible for the film's "crossover appeal." (Con)-fusing reality and fantasy, *Slumdog* engages in ideologically motivated magical thinking, suggesting that all that India's slum dwellers need is the fundamental aspirational fantasy. Fantasy is not opposed to reality but participates in its construction.

There is evidence among those involved in this film project of self-awareness about the dialectical relationship between realism and fantasy. The renowned composer A. R. Rahman, who won two (of the film's eight) Oscars in 2009 for *Slumdog*'s music, especially the closing "Jai Ho," affirmed the film's "optimism and the power of hope." He accepted his Oscars in uplifting words: "All my life, I've had a choice of hate and love. . . . I chose love, and I'm here."[34] If only choosing love could transform reality for everybody. Optimism may not constitute pathology, but fabricating a counterfactual response to harsh reality can "blind people to a genuinely, actively lived life" and is therefore "cruel optimism."[35] I would, however, agree with Lauren Berlant's Nietszchean thesis that "even when it turns out to involve a cruel relation, it would be wrong to see optimism's negativity as a symptom of an error, a perversion. . . . [O]ptimism is, instead, a scene of negotiated sustenance that makes life bearable as it presents itself ambivalently, unevenly, incoherently."[36]

Many in the West, including diasporic Indians, may have thrilled at the optimism of the film. Besides, it puts India on the cultural map. It also shows ordinary Indians, including non-elites, as nurturing the same dreams that drive the NRIs and Westerners. It shows that even poor people in the slums can be successful through their own abilities, without inflicting inconvenient demands on the rich and powerful; it shows India as ultimately not that different a place from the West, complete with game shows. Should this be celebrated as a revalorization of the ordinary Indian individual and his or her experience? If it does, it conforms to Peter Brooks's characterization of melodrama as *stupid:* a somewhat craven effort to redeem the stupidity of everyday life by infusing the experience of *loss* felt by ordinary people with meaning, bringing into "the drama of man's quotidian existence the higher drama of moral forces."[37]

The film does ideological work in deconstructing any relation of "success" with knowledge, what Avital Ronell, drawing on Nietzsche and Maurice Blanchot, but differing from Brooks's notion mentioned above, diagnoses as "stupidity." Stupidity, Ronell suggests, is not straightforwardly opposed to knowledge or wisdom, but is for Nietzsche "on the side of life, discipline and education" and perhaps even the premise of a settled cultural life.[38] It may be precisely because the film disconnects Jamal's success from "knowledge" and formal education that it connects him to the masses. But, to quote the Beatles, What's wrong with that?

Representation and Standpoint

There is another ethicopolitical question of representation: whether the film's representation of exploitation is itself exploitative. The film may implicitly rationalize its representation of squalor in the slums as part of a social realist project of conscientization—raising awareness. But it presents images that seem to many viewers sensationalist, even pornographic: some question whether it was necessary to represent Jamal being tortured by investigators to beat a "confession" of fraud out of him—apart from whether they had just cause to be suspicious that this slumdog could have "experienced" the right answers.

But perhaps the most vivid example of a question regarding the ethics of representation is raised by the film's representation of violence against slum children on screen. Maman's "beggar mafia" maim and exploit slum children as beggars in the city. The most controversial moment occurs when Arvind has his eyes burned out by hot oil: a blind boy tugs more powerfully at heart- and purse strings. The depiction of the maiming may be graphic, but it is not unrealistic. The question is whether it is unethical visual sensationalism: poverty porn.

It is precisely Boyle's outsider *vantage* that other observers see as his *advantage*, his license to film: it is his "distance" from India that allows him to be a reliable and ethical presenter of "dirty laundry" that cultural insiders avoid. Boyle's outsider perspective reveals a "truth" to which insiders blind themselves—or is too traumatically "Real" not to be recognizable to them. Boo points to this traumatic Real by retailing the story of another slum boy, Sunil, who might have recognized in Boyle's fiction the violence meted out to his fellow slum dweller Deepak by security guards of a walled compound into which Deepak had entered to pilfer scraps to sell. To teach a lesson, the guards "gouged out his eyes, put a sickle in his asshole. . . . They ripped a cut, like a smile. The children [of the slum where he and Sunil lived] saw his body after it was tossed back over the wall. The police had no record of the murder."[39] Is Boo's description exploitative? Is *it* poverty porn? Perhaps no more definitive answer can be given to such a question than to say it is a matter of standpoint ethics. One can judge the ethics of the representation only from where one lives.

Even if we register the many unassailable criticisms of the film, it is impossible to deny the positive reaction of so many viewers. The film does have the virtue of being available as a mass *fantasy*—and Boyle manages to out-Bollywoodize Bollywood itself. We cannot deny that Boyle wins the hearts and emotions of mass audiences whose dream, in the words of Latika, played by the luminous Freida Pinto, is to get rich quick (see Figure 8.1).

The gender and class dimensions of the representation are critical to understanding the film's appeal. The romantic subplot (Jamal/Latika) turns on a *male* fantasy appealing to the largest sector of the Indian film-going public, single young men. Unlike in Mira Nair's *Salaam Bombay* (1988), we get almost no insight into the female experience of the lower class slum dwellers "represented" here by Latika. Is she an entirely passive or helpless victim? The class narrative is crucial too and is tied to the ethnic narrative also at the heart of the film. Ultimately all of these narratives are yoked into a narrative about the *nation*. So in a very real sense, Boyle is painting a portrait not only of a city's slum but of the city, and not just of a city but of Indian culture. This is why the offense, or at least the controversy, provoked by the film is so intense, but its ethicopolitical credentials ultimately can be adjudged only in a standpoint ethics, not as a question of fact, of veridical truth in representation—in other words only by the standard of *realism*.

The class and ethnic narratives emerge at other levels of fantasy too, as *imaginary* engagements with the huge problem of communalism in India. The film's representation of these class and ethnic narratives as connected with communal strife in the city would seem to militate against the film's claims to "telling it like it is"—its claim to unadorned realism. Remarkably, one of the first of Jamal's correct answers is based *not* on a plausible or actual experience but on a completely implausible apparition. In the horrific episode of the attack on the Muslim *basti,* or slum, Jamal's mother is killed gruesomely. As Jamal and Salim run away, they are stopped in their tracks by a vision of a child (or the Hindu god Rama) painted blue and carrying a bow and arrow in his right hand. This apparition enables Jamal, sitting in the contestant's chair at *Who Wants to Be a Millionaire,* to answer the question "What does the god Rama carry in his right hand?"

This apparition emerges nonrealistically into the midst of all the mayhem. What is the child doing there? Is he an escapee from a grand Hindu pageant? A *darsana* of the actual godhead? A Hindu figurehead for the murderous riot inflicted by Hindus on Muslims? If it is a fantasy, it is not to be easily dismissed as merely a decorative or a fanciful distraction. If it is a fantasy, it perhaps corresponds to Freud's notion that the fulfillment of wishes is "brought about in a hallucinatory manner by dreams [or fantasy], and under the dominance of the pleasure principle this has become their function."[40]

There is also a fundamental contradiction here at the level of representation. As a fantasmatic *representation* of interethnic or communal tension, there is something incongruous about the way the shock cut intervenes into the diegetic universe of the film. Certainly it represents the *reality* of Hindu-Muslim tensions, and Hindu nationalism infects almost every domain of Indian public life, representing "a dense cluster of ideologies of primordialism, many of which were developed during processes of vernacular and regional elite formation in colonial India during the second half of the nineteenth century."[41] In this context the image seems particularly jarring because it insinuates a fantastical apparition of Hindu nationalism incongruously into the *otherwise* realistic diegesis.

There are yet more dramatic moments at which the illusion of verisimilitude/realism is shattered, such as when the angry adult Jamal confronts his brother Salim at a construction site. In an interstitial fantasy moment interrupting the realistic narrative, he imagines attacking Salim and both of them fly out of the unfinished building into space, as though they had been transported into *The Matrix*'s "desert of the real." But this fantasy is immediately supplanted by a rather tamer clutch in which, as we return to the actuality, Jamal manages only to wrestle Salim to the floor and rather feebly punch him. Perhaps the interruption was just a stylistic hiccup. But Boyle has shown that he is not above playing with "reality," destabilizing it just for a lark.

The illusion of realism is also sundered somewhat by the final dance sequence, "Jai Ho." After girl has been reunited with boy and has sealed the reunion with a kiss and an embrace, the film "ends," only to pick up again with the dance at the railway station. This looks like a parody of the song-and-dance routine that characterizes the dominant mode of many Bollywood films. But if the typical Bollywood film contrapuntally poses fantasy sequences against realist sequences in part to establish a dialectical relationship between these spaces and times, those sequences are also interruptive—they disrupt the linearity of narration and the unities of place. Boyle achieves some of these spatiotemporal dislocations by using flashbacks in the process of what I have described as a logic of establishing plausibility.

I underscore Boyle's access to melodrama and fantasy precisely because he intends *Slumdog* to approximate contemporary "Bollywood" production in some measure. Yet Boyle also seeks to establish continuities in form and substance with other, iconic, Hindi films. Comparison with such films can provide antecedents for some of the motifs and themes taken up by Boyle's film, and can highlight some important *differences* in the ways melodrama mediates the dialectic of reality and fantasy as presented in those films and in *Slumdog Millionaire.* It is productive to contextualize—or rather to *inter*textualize—this film in a relational matrix. Amitava Kumar attempts just such a contextualization in a brief article in *Vanity Fair,* situating Boyle's film within a matrix of Bollywood films, at least three of which Boyle himself acknowledges as having influenced *Slumdog Millionaire.* Kumar's article is an annotated listing of influences and antecedents for *Slumdog*'s representation of life in Mumbai, such as *Black Friday (*Anurag Kashyap, 2004), especially *Slumdog*'s twelve-minute police chase through the crowded Dharavi slum, with slum kids substituted for *Black Friday*'s militants. But such a chase scene could just as easily be an homage to Varma's *Satya,* which features a chase that itself seems to echo something from *The French Connection* (William Friedkin, 1971). Varma's *The Company* (2002) is a model too, as Kumar notes: "Both offer slick, often mesmerizing portrayals of the Mumbai underworld." Kumar also mentions the landmark film *Deewaar* (The Wall, 1975), likewise set in Bombay, featuring bandit gangs and a gang leader based on the actual gangster Haji Mastan, who is battled by Amitabh Bachchan— whose autograph Jamal, the eponymous slumdog, obtains at the cost of having to take a dip in a public outhouse toilet.

Given its engrossing portrait of a woman who lived outside the law and middle-class domesticity, *Bandit Queen* (Shekhar Kapur, 1994, discussed in Chapter 3) is a possible precedent for Boyle's film, as is the gangster thriller *Parinda* (The Bird, Vidhu Vinod Chopra, 1989). Raj Kapoor's *Shree 420* (1955) is also a landmark of the outsider tradition within which *Slumdog*'s subaltern hero can be placed. Boyle's effervescent tonalities evoke most particularly Mira Nair's *Monsoon Wedding* (2001). Kumar mentions this film as an influence, but Nair could just as easily have been influenced by Boyle. Kumar also mentions other films, less plausibly, such as *Guide* (Vijay Anand, 1965) and *Maqbool* (Vishal Bharadwaj, 2003); these are interesting as representing the film's transcultural *intertextuality.*

Kumar cites Suketu Mehta, the author of *Maximum City* (a novel about Mumbai), to the effect that 14 million Indians see a movie daily in one of India's thirteen thousand theaters, and worldwide a billion others a year see Indian movies. In making this film Boyle is paying intertextual homage, from his own standpoint. For the author whose book is the basis for the film, it is Boyle's own standpoint that redeems the film's focus on the society's underbelly: the diplomat Vikas Swarup, author of the 2003 novel *Q&A* that inspired the film, rejected the notion that the film was a negative portrayal of Bombay—on the grounds that it was simultaneously a realist and an aspirational construction (fantasy).

Can Bachchan have been wrong to criticize the film? The film admittedly presents a fantasy, a melodrama, that is little more than an exercise in *filmi* wish-fulfillment, fluttering the fig leaf of cinematic "realism." Yet it is also life-affirming. At the social level this is the fantasy of autopoiesis: the underdog/slumdog makes himself into the image of a success, a self-made modern Indian and global citizen—and gets the girl. And it is all pulled off with calculatedly offhanded brio. Who *wouldn't* want to be a Mumbai millionaire slumdog?

Conclusion

Transnational Translations

Mobile Indianness

If Hindi cinema is both mirror and lamp, it is also a medium for the construction as well as the deconstruction of Indianness. Building on my earlier discussion of diaspora, I want to conclude this book by emphasizing that to track Hindi cinema's ongoing development, we need not only a bifocal perspective but also a transnational analytic. For this is a cinema simultaneously produced in and about the Subcontinent *and* generated by and oriented to people of Indian extraction living outside the national borders. NRIs and diasporics are financially as well as culturally important, a "fifth sector" of the market for Hindi cinema. This conclusion also describes the dynamics of a disaggregation of Indianness in the face of advancing globalization. Indianness is—to marry images from Joseph Conrad and Virginia Woolf—not like a kernel inviolate "within the shell of a cracked nut," but rather a "halo," an effect of representations in which realism interacts dialectically with imaginary or fantasy projections, revealing it to be a more or less self-conscious artifice.

Apposite too is Gayatri Spivak's skeptical rejection of any singular Indianness—for her, Indianness is always already a catachrestical aggregation:

> "India," for people like me, is not really a place with which they can form a national identity, because it has always been an artificial construct. 'India' is a bit like saying 'Europe.' . . . And "Indianness" is not a thing that exists. . . . India is not just Hindu. That "Indic" stuff is not India. The name India was given by Alexander the Great by mistake. The name Hindustan was given by Islamic conquerors. The name Bharat . . . commemorates a mythic kind. So it isn't a place that we Indians can think

> of as anything, unless we are trying to present a reactive front, against another kind of argument.[1]

Hindi cinema turns on this important paradox: Indianness is not "a thing that exists"—it has meaning only as a reactive formation. The more Hindi cinema is charged with reinscribing the national self-image, core Indian values, or the national "Thing" (*das Ding*, in the psychoanalytic lexicon), the more that Thing slips its grasp, dissolving like a fantasy, and this aphanisis itself provokes anxious repetition.

This repetition is linked to a *recursion* of the cosmopolitanism many scholars, such as Tejaswini Ganti, have identified as endemic to the Bombay film industry, and which I foregrounded earlier as becoming an increasingly salient *cinematic trope* (though cosmopolitanism hardly represents the *experience* of most Indians still living in poverty). A classic example is the parallax relationship between nativism and cosmopolitanism captured in the famous image of the Chaplinesque tramp in Raj Kapoor's *Shree 420* (1955). The tramp, played by Kapoor, sings, "My shoes are Japanese / My trousers English. / On my head is a Russian hat / But my heart is Indian for all that." While Indianness is reaffirmed, the affirmation is relayed through the cosmopolitan: the national is hybridized and displaced through reference to signifiers of foreignness. Kapoor seems to be asking viewers to rethink absolutist chauvinism.

The processes of globalization have given the lie to the fiction of a primordial, singular, and bounded national identity—and Indianness is not exempt; they have also decentralized power and redistributed wealth, albeit asymmetrically. The United States is no longer the global hegemon; India is vying with China to fill the vacuum. When hegemony in some global regions such as the EuroAmerican West declines, power, capital, and cultural influence are redistributed to new regions. For hegemony itself, Fernand Braudel has argued, is constantly shifting, from one geographical region to another.[2] Cultural flows confound the notion of cultural property—what is *proper* to a given culture.

This is why cosmopolitanism has been a key issue in my discussion. In "Perpetual Peace" Immanuel Kant articulates the ideal, not a matter for national or international law to adjudicate but one *guaranteed* by Nature itself (*natura daedala rerum*).[3] This "universal *cosmopolitan existence*" cements the "perfect civil union of mankind."[4] Only a world political community, a "universal federal state" (*allgemeine Volkerstaat*), could make claim to a universal cosmopolitan right.[5] Such claims do not presume anchoring to a territorial nation. Rather Kant's ideal is an attachment to and investment in a collectivity broader than a nation-state.[6] Cosmopolitanism does not imply rejection of membership to groups defined by issues, territory, or ethnicity. It suggests only that subjectivity or agency is not limited to or by those anchors.

This has implications for what I have described as the "new cosmopolitanism" of Hindi cinema. Some cinematic expressions of this new cosmopolitanism unleash what, borrowing from Deleuze, I have termed the powers of the false.[7] Freeing up alternative fantasy spaces of non-heteronormative desire and unprecedented modes for imagining cultural life, these images of Indianness could challenge received doxa about national culture. Fantasy's imaginative energy can be associated with the arational, Dionysiac "mania" that was for the ancient Greeks a necessary supplement to Apollonian reason in the pursuit of wisdom and *arête*.

Globalization today has less to do with the dematerialization suggested by Marx and Engels's formulation, "All that is solid melts into air," and more with the culturalist apprehension that the presumptive solidity of cultural identity, of social facts, is always already mediated, dematerialized. It is only in the light of subsequent knowledge and experience that we understand and "invent" the tradition that endows experience with meaning *and* unmasks it as invention. This constructionist thesis resolves the apparent epistemological contradiction William Mazzarella posits between "reflexivity" and "mediation," that a medium of representation cannot be both reflexive and constitutive of subjectivity.[8] For we *can* reflect on the discourse that constitutes us: Hindi cinema dialectically weaves together reality and fantasy constructions of Indianness but simultaneously invites critical self-reflection. This is a diacritic, after all, of my book's project.

The portrayal of the young slum dwellers in the film *Slumdog Millionaire* furnishes an illustration of how representation and reflection are co-enabling. The representation of the slum dwellers spurred a great deal of public self-reflection and reportage, including an account highlighting the opinion of many young slum dwellers that they are not mere victims or subalterns but *more cosmopolitan* or worldly-wise than their counterparts in earlier generations.[9] Clearly cosmopolitanism is no mere bourgeois fantasy.

How then to resist the pull of the fantasy of originary (pre-globalization, prelapsarian) plenitude, which, as Chapter 5 suggested, was evidently a motivation for making *Lagaan: Once upon a Time in India?* Can the national narrative acknowledge the *elasticity* of imagination even as it pivots on, into, fantasy? The fantasy of primordial sovereignty of the nation has not entirely waned in the international public sphere any more than it has vanished from the anxious politics of the Hindu right, in the ascendant again with the return to power of the right-wing Hindu nationalist Bharatiya Janata Party under Narendra Modi in the 2014 elections. The nation is "always conceived as a deep, horizontal comradeship," as Benedict Anderson put it,[10] but transnational links facilitated by global "culturescapes" should not be discounted, even if they seem utopic fantasies. "Indianness" is analogous to Eric Hobsbawm's "tradition," a tradition whose *invention* is motivated by a need to legitimize and imbue political and social thought, practices, and action with meaning. I suggest here that the (re)invention of Indianness is also proceeding apace, in concert with intensifying economic and cultural globalization. This has implications for the "new cosmopolitanism" of Hindi cinema. Some cinematic expressions of this new cosmopolitanism unleash, via a process analogous to Freud's *Nachträglichkeit*, or "belatedness," the powers of fantasy.[11]

The inventedness of traditions indicates a fundamental entropic potential, the fungibility of cultural identities. The assertion of national identity betrays insecurity; such assertion pervades Hindi cinema. And while both domestic and diasporic or nonresident Indians (NRIs) often have strong attachments to the idea of India or Indianness as anchoring *molar* cultural identity, it is getting harder to "fix" an essentialized, sovereign Indian identity. New narratives, confected out of fragmentary signifiers of Indianness, are continually, dynamically, being produced by popular culture, including Hindi cinema, and participate in new "worldings." Such fragments can be, to borrow W.J.T. Mitchell's formulation, a physical object (an image or an element of a visual or verbal work of art, an acoustic image) or a mental and imaginary entity, a "psychological *imago,* the visual content of dreams, memories and perception"; what is interesting is how the fragments take on a life of their own, "flowing from one part of the globe to another."[12] Such fragments are embodiments of material culture deposited in sites of cultural memory or self-apprehension, fragments themselves not coherently articulated into a molar *whole* but rendered *molecular.* Mitchell elsewhere suggests that this migrancy, what I call motility/mobility, contributes to the irresistible disarticulation of the whole: "The difficulty of containing or censoring the migration of images is a well-established fact."[13]

This disaggregation effect may not impinge on the everyday lives particularly of rural and non-elite classes, whose members have more immediate concerns. The point pertains mainly to the problematic of representation itself, and as such addresses primarily the middle and upper-middle classes or metropolitan and global elites. Political experience shows, however, that even for non-elites, Indianness asserts itself as communalist identity or patriotic reflex—Spivak's "reactive front"—in contexts of internal political tensions or against incursions of globalization. A case in point is the meme that India remains India no matter what outside influences enter its ambit; Indianness has proved itself over its long history of being capacious, absorbing all foreign incursions—invaders, colonizers, fragments, objects, images. This meme is articulated in the locus classicus, the aforementioned tramp's song from *Shree 420.* But its inverse image, the global dispersion of signifiers of Indianness, may be traced even in Hollywood cinema, Western hip-hop, and diasporic punk culture. Aswin Punathambekar suggests that we need to engage with the "transitive logic" of transnational and critical postcolonial analysis of the "complex interactions among a) the diaspora, b) Bollywood, and c) India" while recognizing that the tokens of Indianness are becoming increasingly mobile, available for discrepant appropriations by different audiences and in different contexts.[14]

Contemporary Hindi cinema thus mediates traffic between diasporic and nationally produced cinemas, and fantasy is an important currency. Some fantasies are banal, products of consumerist culture such as advertising; others are politically incendiary. But occasionally fantasies make available interstitial, alternative spaces, equivalents of Gilles Deleuze's "virtual," which passes into the actual and out again into the "pure past." They are unstable *spaces,* yet may provide a matrix for a more fulfilling psychic life, conduits for new identities and identifications not anchored to geographical *places.*

Witness the way diasporic and immigrant groups conceptualize their location in multicultural polities: young Asian (including Indian) Americans call attention to the fungibility of identitarian categories when asked to identify themselves on censuses or when competing for admission to selective American universities, or debate whether to identify themselves as Asian or "white." Jasmine Zhuang, a Yale junior whose parents were both born in Taiwan, did not check the box for "Asian" on the application form for the Ivy League school, despite her last name and even though her application essay was about Asian American identity. As she put it, "Identity is malleable."[15] This malleability is somewhat exaggeratedly formulated by Douglas Kellner: "Identity today," he writes, is "a freely chosen game, a theatrical presentation of the self, in which one is able to present oneself in a variety of roles, images, and activities, relatively unconcerned about shifts, transformations, and dramatic changes."[16] The situation is certainly different for global underclasses and non-elites, and varies by nation, age, gender, and other existential historical and material conditions. Because it theorizes some of these differences, Spivak's thesis of "strategic essentialism" is more persuasive.[17]

Many South Asian Americans regard the "Asian" box on college application forms as not a guarantee of admission but a liability and so don't check it. Yet the novelist Bharati Mukherjee's refusal to be categorized as an Indian American novelist provoked great controversy among South Asians. Diasporic or immigrant Asians do not necessarily fetishize stable or fixed national identity, although they appreciate the importance of passports: there is a parallax between cultural identity and national identity. Is this a form of cosmopolitanism? Contemporary Hindi cinema also explores questions of belonging, transforming the category "Indianness" by dramatizing the relationship between and among diasporics and native subjects "at home." But even within the Subcontinent the question of belonging is hardly a settled matter, given the tensions between vocal Hindu majorities and internal minorities, particularly Indian Muslims—a question more vexed (as Chapter 4 shows) in the wake of recent terrorism in India attributed to Muslim extremists.

While Indianness is increasingly being literally and theoretically *displaced* from "India," this unmooring or denaturing has the potential to foster new and unpredictable discourses of postcolonial identity construction, making a *bricoleur*'s use of fragments (images, objects, signifiers) of "Indianness." Hindi cinema often experiments with a broader register for identity construction, animated by common concerns, shared aspirations, solidarisms of various kinds. But even individual fantasy, as I argued in the Introduction contra Ernst Bloch, ought not be discounted as disengaged abstraction or "false reconciliation."[18]

A Bifocal Postcolonial Perspective

Hindi cinema is best understood as a bifocal postcolonial perspective that construes Indianness in a stereopsis but ultimately also allows us to deconstruct mythologies of the nation in larger historico-social frameworks of reference. Such an analytic articulates Indianness through a "transnational lens at once located in the nation, but also out of the nation in its provenance, orientation and outreach."[19] It foregrounds how "modernity," historical agency, and appeals to the divine were mutually intricated motifs in the construction of Indianness in the 1990s.[20] Dipesh Chakrabarty relatedly demonstrates how Indianness has from the outset been routed through "transnational" memory making, hitched to a *traumatic* national memory: Partition. Chakrabarty emphasizes the distinction between a historical event susceptible to historical explanation and a traumatic event, which resists explanation, fracturing narrative.[21]

One could say that liberalization in 1991 was a historical event that became an important narratological influence on subsequent Hindi-language Middle Cinema, particularly Hinglish films featuring diasporics. Hinglish cinema addresses and represents *diasporics and particularly NRIs.* Among the most notable examples of this new generation of Hinglish films are *Diwale Dulhania Le Jayenge* (The Brave-Hearted Will Win the Bride, Aditya Chopra, 1995), *Pardes* (Foreign Land, Subhash Ghai, 1997), *Hum Tum* (Me and You, Kunal Kohli, 2004), and *My Name Is Khan* (Karan Johar, 2010).[22] Straddling the domestic and the diasporic markets, Hinglish films tellingly condense the ambivalence and anxiety encoded into identity construction, especially with regard to their use of language. They have acquired cachet worldwide, marking a reconfiguration of Indianness. Simultaneously there have been forces that discompose and deconstruct it, sometimes unwittingly. For example, my bifocal analysis of *Lagaan* in Chapter 5 emphasizes a double consciousness in its *mediation* of Indianness, showing how the patriotic assertion of Indianness that supposedly drives that film is irreducibly fissured by "unpatriotic" fantasies.

A broader argument for the value of a bifocal postcolonial analytic would make the case that it can provide a frame for understanding the rise of Hinglish cinema against the "rapid spread of American English worldwide in recent decades, due partly to the ubiquity of American films, television, popular music, and new media."[23] In many countries English has become increasingly prominent in cultural production, admixed with the local languages: Hinglish cinema, blending Hindi and English, is similarly generating bifocal narratives of geographical and imaginative cultural (dis)location. These are potential contact zones for cultural translatability.

Hinglish cinema belongs to the subcategory of Middle Cinema, given its class-based division between contemporary characters resorting frequently to Hinglish and characters speaking Hindi or Hindustani exclusively. Yet the mixing of Hindi with occasional words in English familiar to Indian audiences occurs across socioeconomic classes—and it is certainly not a new phenomenon.

Given India's experience with colonial domination and colonial education, the Indian legal code and the entire educational system have been indelibly marked by the language of English common law and the infiltration of the English language (via British literature). These were extensions of the "civilizing mission." Macaulay's infamous "Minute on Indian Education" argued for education in English literature, culture, and language in order to create "a class of persons Indian in blood and colour, but English in tastes, in opinions, in morals and in intellect."[24] The results were mixed, as reflected in the blending of Hindi and English recorded in *Hobson-Jobson* (1886), a glossary of "colloquial Anglo-Indian words and phrases."[25] "Babu English" earned notoriety especially among the middle classes. The language of Hindi cinema today is no "purer"; usually it is Hindustani, a hybrid of Hindi, Urdu, and Persian, with words derived from Persian and Turkic languages, written in Devanagiri script.[26]

Because Hinglish cinema appeals simultaneously to NRI and domestic audiences, it equivocates between cosmopolitan and nationalist sensibilities. This equivocation reflects especially the values of India's middle class, a significant market segment. The diaspora is an equally important sector—and Hinglish films often seek to represent diasporic contexts, in which racism and xenophobia may be key elements of the social environment, especially after 9/11.

Hinglish cinema is characterized by "code mixing" and is growing more transnational, cosmopolitan, NRI-oriented. The Hindu right is resistant to such cultural production, being unsurprisingly anxious about cultural sovereignty and the loss of "enjoyment" of the national Thing, fearing that something essentially Indian is in peril as globalization advances. Yet its economic programs implicitly acknowledge globalization to be potentially beneficial to some sectors of the economy. In a kind of schizo-nationalist buyer's remorse, the Hindu nationalist party (BJP) expresses a fidelity to echt Indianness while embracing modernity in its public self-representations and investment policies, signaling its cultural relevance and political sophistication. Bhaskar Sarkar diagnoses this schizo-nationalist syndrome as "mourning the nation";[27] I would emend the diagnosis slightly to "mourning the *sign* of the national," for this is a symbolic battle. Yet such ambivalence is not expressed *only* among the ranks of the reactionary. In his book *Monolingualism of the Other,* Jacques Derrida also expresses an ambivalence, especially as a philosopher, about his "impure" desire for purity in the French language.[28]

Rationales for a Transnational Postcolonial Studies Approach

A bifocal postcolonial transnational analysis can highlight the contradictions of Indianness, whether it be in diasporic or domestic cinema—in films such as *Moulin Rouge* or *Slumdog Millionaire*—or within theatrical productions emerging from a country that once colonized India such as *Bombay Dreams.* We need a transnational postcolonial analytic to recognize not only the quandaries of early postcolonial Hindi cinema but also the contradictions of films made in the contemporary conjuncture. Arjun Appadurai suggests we think Indianness as "fundamentally fractal, that is, as possessing no Euclidean boundaries, structures, or regularities." This fractal metaphor indexes the multiplicity of identifications Judith Brown points to, but it also invites a "polythetic account of their overlaps and resemblances."[29]

Appadurai's discussion highlights global flows—the constitution of large-scale conjunctures routed through disjunctures.[30] My argument is that the transnational analytic must be bifocally articulated with a focus on the production of the local. Peter Geschiere theorizes this bifocal transnationalism, defining "autochthony" as "the global return to the local."[31] This discourse of "locality" is a culturalist category emerging out of a revolutionary period in Western democracies: the 1960s and 1970s, the crucial year being 1968. Vidar Helgesen suggests that South Africa's anti-apartheid movement, Indonesia's 1990s *reformasi* process reacting to the Asian financial crisis and government atrocities committed in East Timor, and the color revolutions in Georgia and Ukraine (which, though "supported financially and politically by the west—and with a strong Russian pushback," were popular self-assertions of the local) also reinscribed a global ideological conception of democracy in the Age of the Citizen.[32] The Arab Spring protests of 2011 were another example of such glocalism. In India the critique of imperialism and the critique of "modernity" came to the fore following Independence in 1947; "the local" became a shibboleth for the refusal of presumptively modular Western-oriented conceptions of modernity.

Such glocal self-assertions are definitions of citizenship and belonging—not so much engagements in participative democracy as ongoing engagements in self-construction. They can certainly constitute *direct* citizenship, challenging the status quo. There are also more *indirect,* less glamorously political glocalist affirmations in Hinglish cinema, and Hindi cinema more generally. These may function as a forum where ambivalent self-constructions are imagined against more global forms: a resurgent impulse to affirm the continuing viability and purity of local, in this case Indian, culture while also inscribing a more cosmopolitan cultural identity.

Appadurai points out that the challenge is to think the conjunctural routed through disjunctures.[33] However, the sense of the lost local has a specific cultural significance (signification/*signifiance*) in films discussed in this book. The anxiety to affirm a lost, autochthonous local Indianness while recognizing the deconstruction of the category of Indianness is offset by experimentation with *new or reimagined* forms of Indianness, new instantiations of "fractal" and fragmentary constructions of identity.

This co-production of local and cosmopolitan representations of Indianness is important, for example, in *Slumdog Millionaire,* which tests the category of "Hindi cinema," and there is increasing traffic between Bollywood and Hollywood cinematic aesthetics and filmic language. Financing models for the Indian film industry are shifting away from "black" money or state sponsorship to private funding. The state *has* increased funding for cinema and permitted private investment, particularly from diasporics and NRIs, and readjusted entertainment taxation policy. In brief, there is a growing acknowledgment of the need for a bifocal transnational understanding of Hindi cinema. One might offer several rationales for such an approach.

First, the transnational mediation and mimesis of Indianness make this approach necessary: in the age of a mass-mediated "Empire," à la Michael Hardt and Antonio Negri, Indianness qua cultural identity circulates increasingly in transnational media, rather than being generated exclusively on native soil. Second, such an approach reveals the *newness* of contemporary constructions of Indianness: new forms of sovereignty produced through the decentralization of global power, *new* transcultural instantiations of citizenship. Young filmmakers challenge the orthopraxy and pieties of Indian culture, document emergent and unaccustomed identity positions and identifications, or reimagine the contours of everyday experience. Third, it may be time, as Appadurai puts it, to "rethink monopatriotism . . . directed exclusively to the hyphen between nation and state, and to allow the material problems we face—the deficit, the environment, abortion, race, drugs, and jobs—to define those social groups and ideas for which we would be willing to live, and die. . . . [M]any of these new sovereignties are inherently postnational."[34]

Fourth, new forms of intercultural contact are being represented in Hindi cinema, including erotic and culinary, or as products of alternative formations of capital, such as transnational criminal circuits. Films such as Nagesh Kukunoor's *Hyderabad Blues* (1998), Kaizad Gustad's *Bombay Boys* (1998), Gurinder Chadha's *What's Cooking?* (2000), and Nisha Ganatra's *Chutney Popcorn* (2002) present transnational cultural displacements and fragmentations of accustomed sexual, moral, and culinary practices, and Ram Gopal Varma's gangland cinema features a transnational criminal network, with Mumbai as a node in a new transregional flow. As I have shown, even the locus classicus of the Indian village is problematized in a film such as *Lagaan* by a *transnationalist* fantasy.

A fifth rationale for a transnational postcolonial perspective is the *travel of globalizing discourses* and "cosmopolitan knowledges."[35] This proliferation directly influences how "Indianness" is being *problematized* in recent Indian cinema both at home and abroad. The transnational traffic in discourses about citizenship, class, power, race and ethnicity, social justice, governmentality, religion, and especially gender has transformed identitarian discourses in India too.[36] Transnational feminist and LGBTIQ discourses productively complicate and interrogate images of gender in mainstream films.[37] Even mainstream, straight female stars have undergone a remarkable makeover into a "transnational" style. Gone, most remarkably, is the vamp, antithesis of the "good Indian woman," fulcrum of an earlier paradigm of the Indian family. She has been replaced by a "modern" woman in whom modernity is not necessarily inimical to tradition, in whom a glamorous consumerism and sexiness can coexist with virtuous domesticity, transnational appeal, and cosmopolitan sensibilities.

As female stars' cinematic profile has changed, so has their ability to command salaries more in line with global standards. Salaries of A-grade female film stars such as Aishwarya Rai have doubled to around $800,000.[38] Rai, voted most beautiful woman in the world, vied with *Slumdog Millionaire*'s Freida Pinto for that crown and to be the next Bond girl. Pinto became the face of L'Oréal, explicitly crediting her successful appearance in Boyle's film.[39]

For some it is frustrating that Indianness is becoming more dispersed and deterritorialized; others are suspicious of flexible *diasporic* challenges to rooted cultural identity. Diaspora is a useful category, Avtar Brah writes, for analyzing the "economic, political and cultural modalities of historically specific forms of migrancy."[40] But diasporics don't define themselves by pledging allegiance to a homeland; neither do they assimilate totally into host societies: their ambivalent belonging has always been an important issue for race theory in both Britain and the United States. Indians were not included in the broad U.S. census categories: Caucasian, Negro, and Oriental. Indians tended to be categorized differently in different contexts, including as Aryans. As far back as in the 1923 case of *U.S. v. Bhagat Singh Thind* the question of the precise status of South Asians was a legal issue.[41] Today a bifocal transnational framing of diaspora seems indispensable, not least to posit "unhomed" possibilities for identity positions, or identifications. This, then, is a sixth reason for a bifocal, transnational analysis.

As I have noted with respect to Stephen Frears's *My Beautiful Laundrette* and Srinivas Krishna's *Masala*, many DSA films depict the challenge of defining "belongingness" in British or North American contexts. Customarily in Hindi cinema the West was only "*vilayet*," site of a sojourn, a detour from which to *turn* and return. This hyperinvested motif of "return" is represented archetypally in iconic films such as *Purab aur Paschim* (East and West, Manoj Kumar, 1970), *Dilwale Dulhania Le Jayenge* (The Brave-Hearted Will Win the Bride, Aditya Chopra, 1995), *Pardes* (Foreign Land, Subhash Ghai, 1997), *Kuch Kuch Hota Hai* (Something Happens, Karan Johar 1998), or *Aa Ab Laut Chalen* (Let's Return Home, Rishi Kapoor, 1999). In *Bend It Like Beckham*, by marked contrast, *the West* is "home" as the imaginary homeland in the East can no longer be; this film inaugurated a new wave of films including *Kal Ho Na Ho* (There May Be No Tomorrow, Nikhil Advani, 2003), in which transnationalism is a more salient vector for the fantasy of desire-fulfillment.[42]

Diasporic filmmakers have challenged the Right's reactionary constructions (and fantasies) of a racialized, gendered, and class-specific Indianness. In addition to films like *Fire*, there are small-budget indie films, made by diasporic directors, focused on "cultural displacement" across transnational divides.[43] Here novelists might have an edge, however. Following V. S. Naipaul's notion of "a million mutinies now" as defining the Indian cultural experience, Tarun Tejpal's 2009 novel *The Story of My Assassins* describes Indianness as "polyphonic," riven by "faultlines." Similarly, Manil Suri's *The City of Devi* (2013) irreverently troubles conventional constructions of Indianness: the novel features the character Ijaz ("the Jazter"), self-consciously cosmopolitan but also a homosexual predator.

Sunaina Maira's ethnographic analysis suggests that second-generation diasporic South Asian youth in North America are not deeply invested in a reified Indianness permanently and essentially at home in the "home country." Rather they seem to cobble together identities built on "very particular elements" of Indian culture that are themselves fragments exported to the new soil of North America and in the process often denatured, as Maira notes. She also detects a cultural nostalgia, however: "The notion of being 'truly' or 'really' Indian involved possession of certain knowledge or participation in certain activities. . . . The ideology of nostalgia . . . is the ethnicized flip side to a notion of subcultural 'cool' based on American youth culture." Indianness at home is at the same time being transformed, and does not necessarily mirror the development of diasporic Indian identity formations.[44] These are illustrations of a *disaggregation* of Indianness also identifiable in other forms of cultural production.

A bifocal transnational analytic can highlight the problematic of South Asian diasporic self-presentation and representation, and therefore of Indians' self-understanding more generally. In the United States diasporic Indians have done extremely well. Despite constituting only 1 percent of the U.S. population, Indian Americans are 3 percent of the country's engineers, 7 percent of its information technology workers and entrepreneurs, and 8 percent of its medical professionals, physicians, and surgeons. Indian Americans became an official minority in the 1980s, and since then their reputation for contributing to the IT sector has if anything enhanced their model minority status. Big-budget diasporic films rarely focus on poor migrant Indians or interrogate the construction of South Asians as model minority. This category is, despite its surface approbation, in fact a stereotype that harms minority relations. Not only is the approbation intended to consolidate mainstream values and therefore enable majoritarian interests to re-entrench their hegemony, but also the stereotype of the model minority is—through the implied contrast with other, less admired minorities—used to browbeat the latter precisely by the backhanded compliment to the former, and is "predominantly a reference to economic exceptionalism, upward class mobility, and educational excellence"; it reinforces "specific gendered, racialized, and national components of difference."[45]

A transnational postcolonial analytic focalizes the increasing deterritorialization and dehiscence of traditional anchor points of identity and culture in the diasporic films I have discussed as exponents of a "new cosmopolitanism": *ABCD, American Desi, American Chai,* and *Bend It Like Beckham. Kal Ho Na Ho* is a landmark Hinglish film, set entirely in the United States. The film problematizes NRI life, highlighting regional and language divides between Gujarati and Hindi speakers, complicating gender politics in the diaspora and, in a radical innovation, presenting an older couple in love—a widow and a widower, no less. Yet this film also presents a consumerist fantasy of Indianness seamlessly woven into the equally fantasy-driven warp and woof of America's consumer culture.

A seventh reason for a transnational perspective is the *symbolic* deterritorialization and disaggregation of the constitutive elements of notional "Indianness." Indianness as category, image, ideal, or *fantasy* is also being disarticulated and detached from Subcontinental *cultural* moorings—in the negative sense denoting the failure of the attempt to fix the national "Thing," and in the positive sense approximating what Engin Isin and Patricia Wood call a postnational "cosmopolitan citizenship."[46]

An eighth and final rationale for a bifocal prospective and a transnational postcolonial analytic is the financial, social, and cultural ascendancy in recent decades of NRIs and diasporics. Today they play an increasingly conspicuous role diegetically (on screen) as well as extradiegetically (as financiers and movie theater patrons).

Overseas Indians: A Fifth Sector

NRIs are said to constitute a "fifth sector" (perhaps unwittingly echoing the fact that they were once regarded as a kind of cultural "fifth column," responsible for the damaging "brain drain" from the country) for the film industry. For NRIs have not always been regarded as benign actors by Indians and the Indian state. In the 1970s, domestic attitudes to NRIs were at best mixed. British Indians were perceived to be less enviable than the comparatively affluent North American NRIs.[47] At home, emigrants were initially regarded as having abandoned the country for more profitable climes, contributing to a "brain drain." *Purab aur Paschim* rendered a stirring portrait of this ambivalence, tinged with envy. India in the 1970s was chafing against Indira Gandhi's infamous state of "Emergency" (1975–1977), which curtailed civil liberties even though it "made the trains run on time." The Emergency illustrates what Giorgio Agamben, following Carl Schmitt, theorized as the most ominous implication of all politically motivated states of emergency, that the state of emergency becomes a justificatory norm.[48] It is to this process that the Angry Man films of the mid-1970s and 1980s were responding.

The Congress Party, elected in 1990, revolutionized economic policy: in 1991 Manmohan Singh's government broke with a long tradition of secular socialism and mixed economy inaugurated by Nehru, inviting foreign direct investment after decades of "nationalization." This conceptual realignment with globalization's discourse of "efficiency" promulgated by the International Monetary Fund (IMF) was also a response to the breakup of the Soviet Union, India's model and avowed economic and strategic ally immediately following Independence.[49] One notable effect of the neoliberal transition was that NRIs began to be offered Persons of Indian Origin (PIO) or Overseas Citizen of India (OCI) cards for frequent business travelers and tax incentives for sending remittances of foreign currency to India, or investing in domestic real estate, heavy industry (particularly steel), call centers, or the film industry. Since liberalization, NRIs and diasporics have contributed nearly 25 percent of foreign direct investment in India.[50] *Diasporic* Indianness has become ever more intimately tied to the workings of liberalization and neoliberalism *in India*, although it has to be noted that since 2004 the economy seems to have stalled. This has been partly responsible for the return to power in the recent election of the Hindu nationalist BJP party under Narendra Modi.

Diasporic and overseas Indians are hyperconscious about the projected image of "Indianness" and have demonstrated a desire to control conditions of production. Even Coca-Cola and Pepsi (the latter incidentally headed in the United States by an NRI, Indira Nooyi) have endorsed and been endorsed by major Indian stars, including Aishwarya Rai and Shah Rukh Khan. Management of India's public image has also increasingly become a state priority, witness the government's widely distributed "Global Indian" and "India Shining" publicity campaigns. The latter, one of the best-known nationalist advertisements (and mentioned earlier in this book), was represented by a video distributed online, on television, and in cinema theaters, featuring Amitabh Bachchan intoning the virtues of "India Shining," suggesting that there are "two Indias in this country." One is "straining at the leash . . . and the other *is* the leash." The video promotes an India "poised" to come into its own, "pulsating" and full of dynamism. "It's time to fly"—the alternative is not tradition but antiquated nostalgia for an already vanishing Indianness.

The changing profile of NRIs has had a major economic and cultural effect on Indian cinema, even inaugurating a New Wave influenced by younger American and European as well as Asian filmmakers, and new stylistic influences ranging from Hong Kong cinema (the influence is evident in Varma's gangland films or in *Gangs of Wasseypur I* and *II* [Anurag Kashyap, 2012]) through European and British cinema to Hollywood (as in the case of Anurag Basu's *Kites* [2010]). "The pendulum is swinging the other way as well," Sudesh Mishra reminds us. Baz Luhrmann's *Moulin Rouge* (2001) reveals the influence of Bollywood music aesthetics on Western filmmakers. In 2008 the Mumbai billionaire Anil Ambani entered Hollywood, purchasing two hundred cinema houses in the United States under the aegis of Reliance Big Entertainment and linking up with several small production companies, including Nicholas Cage's Saturn Productions, George Clooney's Smokehouse Productions, Tom Hanks's Playtone Productions, Brad Pitt's Plan B Entertainment, and Jim Carrey's JC 23 Entertainment, to coproduce films in Hollywood. Mishra also points to the 2009 $1.5 billion partnership between Ambani and Steven Spielberg to set up a film studio in Hollywood with the aim of shooting thirty films in the following five years.[51]

Liquid Indianness: Interculturalism, Hybridity, and Disaggregation

The nation-state seems an increasingly inadequate container for possible identity positions and imaginary identifications, given the exponentially broader physical, professional, and cultural mobility of individuals of all backgrounds and the increasing lability of signifiers of identity. Besides, as Sheldon Wolin argues, the modern state tends to calcify into bureaucracy: "Everyday political power no longer rests with the citizens, but takes place among the *self-perpetuating power structures* apparently disconnected from the activity of ordinary people."[52]

Hindi cinema is a rich site for enunciation of emergent identities composed of fragments available as partial objects for identification or transcultural borrowing—including, or especially, in imaginative and fantasmatic constructions of self-images not necessarily constitutive of an originary, preexisting whole. Hybrid, imaginary, and fantasy constructions of Indianness appear also in the work of novelists of the diasporic experience. In the Indo-Caribbean writer Shani Mootoo's *Out on Main Street and Other Stories*, for example, diasporic characters find themselves in potentially embarrassing situations and environments where they must *perform* "authentic" Indianness—along several interlinked axes such as ethnicity, religion, sumptuary or culinary practices, and sexuality.[53] Often they "fail" to be "authentic" in any traditionally recognizable register. Crucially Mootoo refuses to apologize for her "imperfectly Indian" diasporic characters, rejecting the implication that diasporic performatives of Indianness are derivative and therefore deficient self-presentations.

The polemic makes a broader argument: modern Indianness is refigured as a fluid agglomeration of signifiers, emblematic of Zygmunt Bauman's "liquid modernity," in which "patterns and configurations" of modernity and its cultural practices are "no longer 'given,' let alone 'self-evident'"; they "have changed their nature and have been accordingly reclassified: as items in the inventory of individual tasks." Rather than "preceding life-politics and framing its future course," they are "to follow it (follow *from it*), to be shaped and reshaped by its twists and turns. The liquidizing powers have moved from the 'system' to 'society.'"[54] Indianness as a "pattern" for sovereign culture is undergoing a similar process of liquidization. On the one hand this process signals a breakdown of imagined integrity of national identity (the national Thing). On the other hand Indianness may assume eccentric, unpredictable, and hybrid forms, temporary *condensations*.

This shape-shifting "Indianness" appears adapted, remixed in popular cultural sites including in hybrid musics (British *bhangra*, American hip-hop), a particular example being signifiers of sexual identity among second-generation Indian Americans. Maira has documented that "the sexualising of ethnic identities imbues them with a moral charge, enabling the enforcement of notions of cultural purity in the second generation, or *conversely their disruption*"; the language of sexuality as laminated to the "rhetoric of ethnic authenticity" reflects complicated negotiations of identity along axes of signification and embodiment.[55]

Relatedly, Ulrich Beck diagnoses a progressive *denationalization* (*Entstaatlichung*) as an effect of contemporary globalization, of "welfare state and the retirement pension system, of public benefits and community politics, of infrastructure policy, the organized power of the unions, the interfirm negotiation system of free collective bargaining as well as public expenditures, the tax system and 'tax practice'—everything melts into political expectations of organizability under the new desert sun of globalization."[56] What needs to be added to this account of statist denationalization is *cultural* disaggregation. Culture is a "leading indicator" for India—it cannot escape denationalization *or* analogous processes of disaggregation: the national Thing is unmasked as only a national *fantasy,* and the evidence is condensing in contemporary Hindi cinema.

Indianness as cultural identity can be grasped only at the horizon of its vanishing. It is not plenitude even in its locus classicus, "at home." Although reactionary or conservative interests contest this disaggregation, it is not experienced universally as an impediment to imaginary identifications but rather its opposite: as license to entertain unscripted and unprecedented identifications or performatives of identity, mainly for middle-class and elite Indians and diasporics, but at least aspirationally for subjects from lower echelons. This is the "elasticity" I emphasized in the Introduction, in my strategic misprision of Benedict Anderson's argument that "even the largest of [nations, as imagined communities], encompassing perhaps a billion human beings, has finite, if *elastic* boundaries, beyond which lie other nations."[57] Cosmopolitanism is not just the opportunistic "flexible" citizenship chosen by the well-heeled elites of the world,[58] but being "at home" electively is not guaranteed either.[59]

Even the most humble citizens of India cannot be sequestered against globalizing "modernity": for example, many from fairly modest backgrounds have taken advantage of new opportunities described by Hartmut Rosa as the "digital" revolution forced by the Internet and the "buildup of satellite TV," and the "mobile" revolution that "enabled microelectronic communicative availability unbound by location."[60] I have also argued elsewhere that it is precisely for nonelites that the "outsourcing" boom in a city such as Bangalore has occasioned a fundamental transformation in self-image, defying traditional notions of rooted Indianness.[61] As Rosa notes, globally we are witnessing today a "*nonintegrated form of parallel processing that leads to fragmentation and a loss of steering, intelligibility, and malleability* (Gestaltbarkeit) *on the individual as well as the sociopolitical level.*"[62]

Hindi cinema reflects how metonyms and fragmentary signifiers of Indianness are repurposed and often denatured in a process of cultural hybridization.[63] There is rarely any presumption of an authentic provenance for those fragments: what once might have seemed "rigid signifiers" of Indianness now seem only "floating" signifiers, in Stuart Hall's phrase. This reveals an underemphasized implication of Hall's identification of a "new politics of representation," premised on "cultural diasporization"—a process of "unsettling, recombination, hybridisation and 'cut-and-mix.'"[64] The fragments are partial objects of identification or metonyms available for transcultural bricolage, not only to Indians, confirming Gilles Deleuze and Félix Guattari's disillusionment with the "myth of the existence of fragments that, like pieces of an antique statue, are merely waiting for the last one to be turned up, so that they may all be glued back together to create a unity that is precisely the same as the original unity. We no longer believe in a primordial totality that once existed, or in a final totality that awaits us at some future date."[65] There is no telos of integral, unified Indianness. This is something Spivak, referring to the North American context, wrote of the term "Indian"—that "subterfuges of nomenclature that are by now standard have almost (though not completely) obliterated the fact that that name lost some specificity in the first American genocide."[66]

Observers emphasize the complexity of circuits of intercultural borrowing, mixing, and catachrestic appropriation and reappropriation in Western multicultural environments since *bhangra* emerged in Britain in the 1980s, nourished by the black music scene. Cultural productions and practices involving hybridization and sampling are fueled by the global interest in Hindi film music, together with reggae, dub, and soul. In the United States, cross-fertilizations and borrowings have been equally complex. Performers such as Missy Elliott, Jay-Z, and Dr. Dre borrow metonyms from Indian culture (alongside others), motivated by a desire to open up a "Thirdspace," or to highlight issues of concern to themselves.

Interestingly, Dr. Dre's borrowing in a song called "Addictive" (which debuted at number four on the Top R&B/Hip Hop charts in 2002) drew a lawsuit for "cultural imperialism" in a U.S. federal court from the Bollywood composer Bappi Lahiri. The suit alleged that Dr. Dre sampled four minutes of the song "Thoda Resham Lagta Hai," composed by Lahiri with vocals by the Bollywood diva Lata Mangeshkar, without acknowledgment. These hybridizations of Indianness are sometimes criticized as neo-Orientalist distortions, appropriations, and misappropriations of Indian culture, bastardizations of authentic forms, or insulting to Indians and contributing to the disaggregation of Indianness. The politics of Lahiri's suit were complicated by the fact that Lahiri himself has been accused of incorporating hits from all over the world into his Hindi-language productions.

The legal suits may have been motivated less by the instinct of cultural preservation than by cupidity. However, my intention in noting these hybridizations and repurposings of cultural fragments is not to endorse or criticize. More important is that they embody an everyday form of "cosmopolitanism." The "borrowings" at issue here and in songs such as Eric Sermon's "React" are part of larger circulations, and these require from transnational postcolonial critique a critical cosmopolitanism: not a celebration of identity politics but a recognition that culture is hybrid and depends on circulations of ideas, images, goods, and people, activated by "actants" caught up in cultural flows transcending conscious agency.

Indianness then is best conceptualized as an actant in a network, in the terms of Bruno Latour, responding to circulations of culture, goods, and capital, as well as images and other information.[67] Diasporic "actants" sometimes reconstellate Indianness in ways irreconcilable with traditional identity positions; such dissonant appropriations suggest that immigrant culture is no longer segregated from the mainstream culture nor wholly anchored to the home culture. The "coolie" is finally cool, one more instance of the fashion for global heterophilia and forms of extraterritorial elective affinity under conditions of late capitalism. Even within the Subcontinent, globalization entails rethinking the orthodoxies of Indian morality, personal virtue, and implications of modernity.

Many signifiers are hybridized to the point of nonrecognizability. One striking case in point is Lil' Kim's controversial cover photo of the pointedly titled *One World* magazine wearing something that could be a signifier of "South Asian" or generically "Muslim" clothing, with its sexualized burqa-clad brown-skinned woman with blue-gray eyes. But what is interesting is how the image is politicized, hybridized beyond clear anchoring to any specific culture. In that sense such a performative could be invoked in critically cosmopolitan interventions on Thirdspace issues.

This image may have been miscalculated in its political ambitions, especially given some contemporary reactions (including the *Charlie Hebdo* killings in Paris in January 2015) from Islamicist extremists to representations of Muslim cultural signifiers. It would not have been hard for Russell Simmons, the magazine's owner, to have predicted that even in 2003 some Muslims would take umbrage. Remarks Lil' Kim herself made in the issue ("F*** Afghanistan") surely could not have helped. Still, it is recognizable if not excusable as an example of *parody* (not just Fredric Jameson's postmodernist "*pastiche*"). My interest is in the fact that even as parody, such political commentary is being mediated in publicly circulated images, and traffics between and among minority spaces, appropriating fragmentary signifiers of cultural difference in a process facilitated by intensified transnational flows.

And it is not only Lil' Kim. Lady Gaga also appeared in something like a veil and tight-fitting dress. And what are we to make of Burka Barbie, the burka-clad icon of American consumer culture sold as a toy for girls: a joke at the expense of Muslims? How are we to read performances as disjunctive as those of South Asian performance artist MIA and Lady Gaga, both of whom repurpose fragments of South Asianness? Gaga wears the same provocative bra when she pays homage to Deepak Chopra, the New Age Indian guru, and when performing in her music video as she destroys her "bad romance."

In the U.S. context the representation of the Asian other in the music of a "South Asian" group such as the Taqwacores has a different diasporic "feel" than the appropriation of the South Asian other in Missy Elliott's "Get Ur Freak On" and different again from Jay-Z's appropriation of Punjabi MC's "Mundian Tu Bach Ke" *bhangra* beat. Here, as Nabeel Zuberi notes, "the mobility and mutability of sonic information in an environment of digital reproducibility" circulates fragments and traces of Indianness; their role as "actants" in reassembling identity performatives "complicates any simple equation between forms of music and the racial or ethnic [or national] body." It is noteworthy that Zuberi too invokes a notion of Latour's I have referred to above: "By following circulations we can get more than by defining entities, essence or provinces."[68]

The issues of appropriation and expropriation—of feckless xenophilia—are unavoidable. While authenticity may be irrelevant to Dr. Dre or Lady Gaga, it remains important to interrogate possible issues of neo-Orientalist commodification of the metonyms and fragments of "Indianness." The anxiety about the disaggregation of Indianness and claims of authenticity remain flashpoint issues in terms of who gets to represent Indianness. Does a white Western woman such as Nina Paley, who received death threats for distributing a cartoon "movie" about Sita called *Sita Sings the Blues*, have a right to narrate a story from the iconic Indian narrative the *Ramayan*?[69]

Questions of authenticity of Indianness and of Indianness as cultural property posed by the Paley affair are crystallized by a diasporic respondent's quip that NRI should actually mean Not Really Indian.[70] Similarly Parag Khanna's rant, "You are not an Indian," questions the claim of NRIs to being truly Indian.[71] He insists vigorously that there is a difference between "desis" and NRIs, and NRIs must honestly acknowledge that they really do not have a direct connection with the homeland. Khanna's acerbic commentary, it could be argued, is aimed at a nostalgic attempt to reclaim an always already lost homeland, and is thus analogous to Hamid Naficy's conceptualization of nostalgia as involving a desire to return to the homeland.[72] We should also mine the contradictions, the gaps, between resemblance and identity, and we should recognize that nostalgia is not only predicated on this gap but also "enamored of distance, not of the referent itself."[73]

Examples can be multiplied. Spike Lee too has, without attribution, quoted, borrowed, fragments of Indian culture, notably from A. R. Rahman's super hit song sequence, "Chhaiyya Chhaiyya," originally from Mani Ratnam's *Dil Se* (1998). This obliviousness to markers of Indianness points up their lability, not their "universality." Deformations of these fragments are not necessarily meant as insults; they signal an opening up of a symbolic marketplace where national identity circulates as consumable brand. The voices of the preeminent Indian playback singers Lata Mangeshkar and Asha Bhonsle have been sampled into many Middle Eastern and black hip-hop musical remixes. The Kronos Quartet collaborated with Bhonsle in 2005 to produce a hybrid album titled *You've Stolen My Heart* (after the famous song "Chura Liya Hai Tumne Jo Dil Ko"), on which they perform R. D. Burman compositions. The musical *Bombay Dreams* was a hit in London and Broadway. South Asian groups such as Corner Shop, Fun^Da^Mental, or the Taqwacores hybridize their own cultural metonyms—Islam with punk rock—appropriating images such as the Union Jack and the Statue of Liberty precisely to denature them and frustrate any reductive representations of South Asian performativity.[74] Even within India itself, events such as the controversy surrounding the defunct Star TV Plus show *Nikki Tonight* explicitly challenge what is authentically Indian and "authenticity" itself. The challenge in the case of *Nikki Tonight* was not just the "non-Indian appearance" of the show's host ("a blonde woman who claims to be an Indian,"), who insulted Gandhi, effectively forcing the show's termination. Indeed, Nikki was in general irreverent in her disposition toward Indianness, dismissing it as meaningless.

Of course, cultural mixture per se is not a new phenomenon, and it is certainly not limited to the contemporary silver screen. Consider the ballet *La Bayadère,* which was recently revived in major cities in the United States; it was first performed in 1877, representing Indian themes and characters but in white faces and white bodies dressed in faux Indian costumes and makeup, performing orientalized body language. A comparable appropriation is the opera *Lakme.* Edward Said wrote compellingly about a different cross-cultural appropriation, in Verdi's *Aida.* Thus the process of disaggregation of cultural signifiers and fragments is intensified and ramified in several contexts, so that Asians themselves often have recourse to fragmentary signifiers of Western culture incorporated—through quotation or citation—into their own performatives of identity. If this is postmodern interculturalism, it is postmodernism with a "difference."

I present these exempla as interventions in—even ambushes of—the politics of identity and representation. At their most subversive these acts of culture resist essentializing narratives of Indianness or finalized interpretations of cultural truths and teloi. Yet they also open out onto ambiguous possibilizations offered by fantasy and aspiration, risky intercultural negotiations of signifiers denoting or connoting "Indian" and "non-Indian." As Iain Chambers puts it, late modern identities are *performed* in such negotiations: "You constantly shift where you stand, you subdivide your life into separate areas and into differences, you construct your lifestyle in a mobile way. You consciously make decisions about how you will appear in this moment, how you will present yourself."[75] These performatives have the potential to unlock borderless vistas of unfamiliarly defined aesthetic systems of valuation, making imaginable unregulated refractions and recodings of objects, looks, concepts, commodities, and even bodies.

The logic of subversion informing these reworkings of cultural property and the "proper" recognizes and exploits the ambivalence of power Bhabha highlights: "The work of regulation, appropriation, or authorization requires another kind of risky, indeterminate mimetic process whereby the discourse of authority has to 'project' its paradigm onto adjacent and antagonistic fields of meaning and events." Every affirmation of the authentically Indian opens itself to its own hybridization, to its own splitting or "barring." Actively hybridizing—subversive—cultural production seeks to point up the dissemination, dispersal, and disaggregation of Indianness, the disruption of the axiomatic link between ontology and topology: what is "dislocated . . . is therefore, a sense of ontology, of the essentiality or inevitability of being-and-belonging by virtue of the nation, a mode of experience and existence that Derrida calls a *national ontopology.*"[76]

For Hindi cinema as a whole the disaggregation of Indianness signals that new, increasingly globalized, cultural and historical conjunctures are redefining the domain of representation, though not necessarily in the everyday lives of rural and non-elite populations. The future of Hindi cinema is as rich with possibilities as Indianness itself, precisely by virtue of its becoming less rigidly anchored in fixed tradition or immutable essence. The issue of who gets to represent Indianness must be set alongside instances in which "Bollywood," fragmented into partial objects or metonyms—"detachable attractions"—becomes labile, or at least mobile. When signifiers of Bollywood travel to Nigeria, where Hausa youth appropriate Bollywood film music for their Sufi songs in the hybrid genre known as *bandiri,* or when partial objects appropriated from Hindi cinema are incorporated into a parodic send-up purporting to explain the invention of the mullet in a Bollywood song-and-dance sequence while insinuating images of the Absolut bottle, we are witnessing a kind of cultural hybridity and cultural mobility that disaggregates "Indianness."[77] What needs to be focalized is the site of enunciation. The location of enunciation may be more critical than the enunciated token or performative of "Indianness." The "disaggregation" of Indianness then is not necessarily cause for alarm, and it is not as though Indian culture is about to disappear. Rather it is going to continue to be enunciated from possibly unanticipated and unpredictable sites, and the important question is no longer whether the enunciation has anterior license, or "authentic" authority.

This book has been about a process of enunciation of different aspects of what it means to be "Indian," a process of cultural "storytelling." It has tried to highlight the potential of Hindi cinema to convey its story to Indians and to others—to transmit Indianness, as Bhabha (drawing on Walter Benjamin) might put it, without fully translating itself, to represent in the middle voice. Here it is well to remember Benjamin's caution not to confuse information and story, just as it is important not to translate "translation" too facilely. For the translation of signifiers is merely spatial or geographical circulation of fungible signifiers that may permit decontextualization, the unhinging of the signifiers from "authentic belongings" and "organic filiations." By contrast the transmission of storytelling would require the grasp and conveyance of a totality of truths, what Benjamin would call a bank of "explanations."

The imaginary we call "Indianness" is best framed within a transnational postcolonial analytic as part of a larger process, not eternally immured in an immutable tradition, but living in localized practices, changing beliefs, demotic figurations of self. Under globalization, cultural and political identities have been realigned significantly, including shifting from the Nehruvian socialist-secular alignment of the economy with the model of the Soviet Union or anchoring to an immemorial past defined by spirituality, primordialist mythology, traditional and patriarchal ethics, and feudal sociopolitical arrangements, toward more cosmopolitan, globalized cultural flows, more oriented to the balance of world economies, whether in the United States and western Europe or in China.

Some see this as not just disaggregation but deracination of national culture. Yet roots and geography "are no longer the clear supports of our identity," as David Morley and Kevin Robins put it; recent Hindi cinema registers but perhaps also contributes to disaggregation of what constitutes identity precisely because it is a possible source of freedom, transformation—and *enjoyment.*[78] Daphne Berdahl, discussing the nostalgia associated with commodities from the former German Democratic Republic, notes that nostalgia is "about the production of a present rather than the reproduction of a past."[79] Any study of the phenomenon of Hindi cinema must attend not only to the "textual" condensations of Indianness in the films themselves but also to the *con*textual meanings of the historical moment and milieu in which "Indianness" is continually renegotiated. In these condensations may also lie the potential for (re)imagining Indianness anew. In popular forums such as Hindi cinema a cinephiliac production of *partial* objects of identification and desire may facilitate circulations of "unhomed" political and cultural performatives of identity—and pleasure in the potential for self-transformation. Hindi cinema can enable the kind of genuine "intimate revolt" Julia Kristeva speaks of as antidote to the new maladies of the soul in the contemporary society of the spectacle, of consumerist fantasy—an antidote that would require genuine self-questioning (*se quaerere*, going in search of oneself), a continual rethinking of "Indianness."[80] Hindi cinema registers hybridity and disaggregation as painful and not always feckless cosmopolitanism.[81] Yet it also tenders the possibility of new, unpredictable, intimately revolutionary identity positions and identifications, condensations of unscripted, radical imagination that, as Cornelius Castoriadis theorizes following Freud's conception of psychical reality, "brings itself into being, makes be that which exists nowhere else and which, for us, is the condition for anything at all to be able to exist"; it is radical also in that it is open to a radical self-othering.[82]

Wolin emphasizes that postmoderns are "not alone in being indifferent to boundaries; the state, modern technology, market activity, lawyers, financiers, administrators, economists, actors, musicians and contemporary artists, scholars and intellectuals are also cosmopolitan, multinational operatives, and for them the nation as *domus* is only a "home base of operations," but not a bounded identity.[83] My project similarly highlights disaggregation. But this is also to indicate the *possibility* of the political that does not presume reified Indianness or settled boundaries of the nation (*domus*), domesticating the citizen and taming her (*domitus*). The political is also the moment of the deconstruction of categories of identity such as *nation* and *citizen*—in being deployed in the agon of politics, these categories are vulnerable to being radically analyzed and undone, possibly to be reconstructed ad hoc, as dictated by social, political, or ethical demand. It is in this spirit that Spivak conceptualizes a practical but groundless "politics of the open end"; and Achille Mbembe similarly endeavors to interpret an African formation and temporality as "precisely the moment when different forms of absence become mixed together: absence of those presences that are no longer so and that one remembers (the past), the absence of those others that are yet to come and are anticipated (the future)."[84] This book has sought to identify in cinema a vernacular idiom acknowledging the idea of Indianness less as a mimetic representation of a preexisting and immemorial cultural identity than a perpetually unstable demotic imaginary that may be the groundless ground from which to build possible futures—and a potential source of *pleasure* produced by the very disaggregation of cultural identity.

Notes

INTRODUCTION

1. The term "Bollywood" is certainly derivative, as Prasad explains. He routes its etymology through the description of the Tollygunge studios in Calcutta as "Tollywood"; "Bollywood" was the term therefore applied to the film industry associated with the studios in Bombay and Pune. See M. Madhava Prasad, "This Thing Called Bollywood," available at http://www.india-seminar.com/2003/525/525%20madhava%20prasad.htm.

2. Lalitha Gopalan, *Cinema of Interruptions: Action Genres in Contemporary Indian Cinema* (London: British Film Institute, 2002), 24.

3. In this cohort we might place critics such as Ashis Nandy, *The Intimate Enemy: Loss and Recovery of Self under Colonialism* (New Delhi: Oxford University Press, 1983); Sumita Chakravarty, *National Identity in Indian Popular Cinema, 1947–1987* (Austin: University of Texas Press, 1993); M. Madhava Prasad, *Ideology of the Hindi Film: A Historical Construction* (Delhi: Oxford University Press, 1998); Nasreen Munni Kabir, *Bollywood: The Indian Cinema Story* (London: Channel 4 Books, 2001); Ravi Vasudevan, *Making Meaning in Indian Cinema* (New Delhi: Oxford University Press, 2000).

4. See Rachel Dwyer, *All You Want Is Money, All You Need Is Love: Sex and Romance in Modern India* (London: Cassell, 2000); Jyotika Virdi, *The Cinematic Imagination: Indian Popular Film as Social History* (New Brunswick, NJ: Rutgers University Press, 2003); Vijay Mishra, *Bollywood Cinema: Temples of Desire* (New York: Routledge, 2002); Ashish Rajadhyaksha, *Indian Cinema in the Time of Celluloid: From Bollywood to the Emergency* (Bloomington: Indiana University Press, 2009); K. Moti Gokulsing and Wimal Dissanayake, Indian Popular Cinema: A Narrative of Cultural Change (Stoke-on-Trent, UK: Trentham Books, 2004); Raminder Kaur and Ajay J. Sinha, *Bollyworld: Popular Indian Cinema through a Transnational Lens* (New Delhi: Sage, 2005); Rajinder Kumar Dudrah, *Bollywood: Sociology Goes to the Movies* (New Delhi: Sage, 2006); Shakuntala Rao, "The Globalization of Bollywood: An Ethnography of Non-elite Audiences in India," *Communication Review* 10, no. 1 (2007); Anandam Kavoori and

Aswin Punathambekar, eds., *Global Bollywood* (New York: New York University Press, 2008); Sangita Gopal and Sujata Moorti, eds., *Global Bollywood: Travels of Hindi Song and Dance* (Minneapolis: University of Minnesota Press, 2008); and Bhaskar Sarkar, *Mourning the Nation: Indian Cinema in the Wake of Partition* (Durham, NC: Duke University Press, 2009).

5. Stanley Cavell, *The World Viewed: Reflections on the Ontology of Film* (Cambridge, MA: Harvard University Press, 1979 [1971]), 23–25.

6. Bordwell, "Space in the Classical Film," 56; André Bazin, "The Ontology of the Photographic Image," in *Film Theory and Criticism: Introductory Readings*, 6th ed., ed. Leo Braudy and Marshall Cohen (New York: Oxford University Press, 2004), 195–199, esp. 199.

7. Warren Buckland, *Teach Yourself Film Studies* (London: Hodder and Stoughton, 2003 [1988]), 23–24.

8. Cavell, *World Viewed*, 166.

9. Mary Ann Doane, "The Indexical and the Concept of Medium Specificity," *Differences: A Journal of Feminist Cultural Studies* 18, no. 1 (2007): 130–131.

10. Susan Hayward, *Cinema Studies: The Key Concepts*, 3rd ed. (London: Routledge, 2006 [1996]), 334.

11. George Ritzer, *The Globalization of Nothing 2* (Thousand Oaks, CA: Pine Forge, 2007), 36.

12. Ernst Bloch, *The Spirit of Utopia* (Stanford, CA: Stanford University Press, 2000 [1964]), 2.

13. Cornelius Castoriadis, *The Imaginary Institution of Society*, trans. Kathleen Blamey (Cambridge, MA: MIT Press, 1987), 292.

14. Slavoj Žižek, *Demanding the Impossible*, ed. Yong-june Park (Cambridge, UK: Polity Press, 2013), 32.

15. Ashish Rajadhyaksha, *Indian Cinema in the Time of Celluloid: From Bollywood to the Emergency* (Bloomington: Indiana University Press, 2009), 6; emphasis original.

16. Gyan Pandey, "In Defense of the Fragment: Writing about Hindu-Muslim Riots in India Today," *Economic and Political Weekly* 26, nos. 11–12 (March 1991): 559–572, esp. 560.

17. Sheila J. Nayar, "The Values of Fantasy: Indian Popular Cinema through Western Scripts," *Journal of Popular Culture* 31, no. 1 (Summer 1997): 73–90, esp. 76–77.

18. Rajadhyaksha, *Indian Cinema*, 249n29.

19. Eric J. Hobsbawm, "Introduction: Inventing Traditions," in *The Invention of Tradition*, ed. Hobsbawm and Terrence O. Ranger (New York: Cambridge University Press, 1983), 1–14.

20. Joan W. Scott, "Fantasy Echo: History and the Construction of Identity," *Critical Inquiry* 27, no. 2 (Winter 2001): 284–304, esp. 286, 284.

21. Benedict R. Anderson, *Imagined Communities: Reflections on the Origin and Spread of Nationalism* (London: Verso, 1991 [1983]), 224.

22. Diana Fuss, *Identification Papers: Readings in Psychoanalysis* (New York: Routledge, 1995), 2–3; emphasis mine.

23. Judith Butler, *Bodies That Matter: On the Discursive Limits of "Sex"* (New York: Routledge, 1993), 112.

24. Julia Kristeva, *This Incredible Need to Believe*, trans. Beverly Bie Brahic (New York: Columbia University Press, 2009 [2006]), vii; emphasis original.

25. Fredric Jameson, *The Antinomies of Realism* (London: Verso, 2013), 18.

26. Bachchan was featured in a video in which he described India as "poised" between

two visions, one backward-looking and one future-oriented; available at http://www.youtube.com/watch?v=wP-TwHwLc98.

27. André Bazin, "Theater and Cinema," in *Film Theory and Criticism: Introductory Readings,* 6th ed., ed. Leo Braudy and Marshall Cohen (New York: Oxford University Press, 2004), 418–428, esp. 419.

28. Roy Armes, *Third World Film Making and the West* (Berkeley: University of California Press, 1987), 110–111.

29. See Chakravarty, *National Identity,* 4.

30. Salman Rushdie, *The Satanic Verses* (New York: Picador, 1988), 16.

31. Eric Barnouw and S. Krishnaswamy, *Indian Film* (New York: Oxford University Press, 1980), 69.

32. One exception to the rule is Bengali cinema, most prominently represented by the films of Satyajit Ray. See Kironmoy Raha, "Bengal in the Forefront," in *Frames of Mind: Reflections on Indian Cinema*, ed. Aruna Vasudev (New Delhi: UBS, 1995), 69–78, esp. 70.

33. Wimal Dissanayake, "Rethinking Indian Popular Cinema: Towards Newer Frames of Understanding," in *Rethinking Third Cinema*, ed. Anthony R. Guneratne and Wimal Dissanayake (New York: Routledge, 2003), 206; see also Vijay Mishra, "Towards a Theoretical Critique of Bombay Cinema," *Screen* 6, nos. 3–4 (1985): 133–146.

34. Samir Dayal, "The Modern Reader's Dilemma: Something Old, Something New. . . , Review Essay on Simona Sawhney's *The Modernity of Sanskrit* (Minneapolis: University of Minnesota Press, 2010)," *Twentieth-Century Literature* 56, no. 2 (Summer 2010): 245–253.

35. See Dissanayake, "Rethinking Indian Popular Cinema," 208–210.

36. Ibid., 208.

37. K. A. Abbas, qtd. in Chakravarty, *National Identity*, 42.

38. Sumita S. Chakravarty, "Fragmenting the Nation: Images of Terrorism in Indian Popular Cinema," in *Cinema and Nation*, ed. Mette Hjort and Scott MacKenzie (London: Routledge, 2000), 222–237, esp. 228.

39. J. Macgregor, "Bollywood Seduces the West," available at www.netribution.co.uk/2/content/view/283/182/, originally published online on March 19, 2006.

40. Prasad, *Ideology of the Hindi Film,* 30, 42, 51.

41. Ashish Rajadhyaksha, "India: Filming the Nation," in *The Oxford History of World Cinema*, ed. Geoffrey Nowell-Smith (Oxford: Oxford University Press, 1996), 678–689, esp. 679.

42. See Aamir Mufti, *Enlightenment in the Colony: The Jewish Question and the Crisis of Postcolonial Culture* (Princeton, NJ: Princeton University Press, 2007), 244. Equally important, Hinglish cinema is a complex and context-specific blending of Hindi with English, as I discuss in this book.

43. Kavoori and Punathambekar, *Global Bollywood*, 1–3.

44. Zygmunt Bauman, *Liquid Modernity* (London: Polity Press, 2000).

45. Sandhya Rajendra Shukla, *India Abroad: Diasporic Cultures of Postwar America and England* (Princeton, NJ: Princeton University Press, 2003), 2.

46. Nayar, "Values of Fantasy," 75.

47. See Rogers Brubaker and Frederick Cooper, "Beyond 'Identity,'" *Theory and Society* 29 (2000): 1–47. I thank Andrea O'Reilly Herrera for bringing this essay to my attention and for conversation on the topic on the occasion of a keynote presentation I made at Warsaw University, Poland, in May 2010.

48. Ajanta Sircar, "Of 'Metaphorical' Politics: Bombay Films and Indian Society," *Modern Asian Studies* 29, no. 2 (1995): 325–335, esp. 326.

49. Bruno Latour, "On Recalling ANT," in *Actor Network Theory and After*, ed. J. Law and J. Hassard (Oxford: Blackwell, 1999), 15–25, esp. 20.

50. Kuan-Hsing Chen, *Asia as Method: Toward Deimperialization* (Durham, NC: Duke University Press, 2010), 3.

51. Planning Commission, India, *First Five Year Plan*, 1951, chap. 8, available at http://planningcommission.nic.in/plans/planrel/fiveyr/1st/1planch8.html.

52. See Arvind Sharma, "On Hindu, Hindustan, Hinduism and Hindutva," *Numen* 49, no. 1 (2002): 1–36.

53. Valentina Vitali and Paul Willemen, eds., *Theorising National Cinema* (London: British Film Institute, 2008), 4–5n4.

54. Chakravarty, *National Identity*, 228.

55. Shyam Benegal, "Secularism and Popular Indian Cinema," in *The Crisis of Secularism in India*, ed. Anuradha Dingwaney Needham and Rajeswari Sunder Rajan (Durham, NC: Duke University Press, 2007), 225–238, esp. 226.

56. Seyla Benhabib, *The Rights of Others: Aliens, Residents and Citizens* (Cambridge, UK: Cambridge University Press, 2004), 219.

57. Priya Jha, "Lyrical Nationalism: Gender, Friendship, and Excess in 1970s Hindi Cinema," *Velvet Light Trap* 51 (Spring 2003): 43–53, esp. 43.

58. Fredric Jameson, "Third World Literature in the Era of Multinational Capitalism," *Social Text* 15 (Fall 1986): 65–88, esp. 65. See also Aijaz Ahmad, "Jameson's Rhetoric of Otherness and the 'National Allegory,'" *Social Text* 17 (Autumn 1987): 3–25.

59. Akbar S. Ahmed, "Bombay Films: The Cinema as Metaphor for Indian Society and Politics," *Modern Asian Studies* 26, no. 2 (1992): 289.

60. Ravi Vasudevan, "Film Studies: New Cultural History and Experience of Modernity," *Economic and Political Weekly* 30, no. 44 (November 4, 1995): 2809–2814.

61. Ernest Gellner, *Nations and Nationalism* (Oxford: Blackwell, 1983).

62. Perry Anderson, ctd. in Vitali and Willemen, *Theorising National Cinema*, 5.

63. Slavoj Žižek, *Tarrying with the Negative: Kant, Hegel, and the Critique of Ideology* (Durham, NC: Duke University Press, 1993), 203.

64. Ravi Vasudevan, "Cinema in Urban Space," Seminar 525, *Unsettling Cinema: A Symposium on the Place of Cinema in India*, available at http://www.india-seminar.com/2003/525/525%20ravi%20vasudevan.htm (accessed July 29, 2011).

65. Aswin Punathambekar, "We're Online, Not on the Streets," in Kavoori and Punathambekar, *Global Bollywood*, 282–299, esp. 291.

66. Purnima Mankekar, *Screening Culture, Viewing Politics: An Ethnography of Television, Womanhood, and Nation in Postcolonial India* (Durham, NC: Duke University Press, 1999), 165.

67. Shanti Kumar, *Gandhi Meets Primetime: Globalization and Nationalism in Indian Television* (Urbana: University of Illinois Press, 2006), 52.

68. Ibid., 28.

69. Durga Das Basu, *Introduction to the Constitution of India*, 18th ed. (Nagpur: Wadhwa, 1999), qtd. in Kumar, *Gandhi Meets Primetime*, 29.

70. Arvind Rajagopal, "The Rise of National Programming: The Case of Indian Television," *Media, Culture, and Society* 15 (1993): 91–131, esp. 92.

71. M. K. Raghavendra, "Local Resistance to Global Bangalore: Reading Minority Indian Cinema," in *Popular Culture in a Globalised India*, ed. K. Moti Gokulsing and Wimal Dissanayake (London: Routledge, 2009), 15–27, esp. 15.

72. Doane, "Indexical," 141.

73. Michael Hardt and Antonio Negri, *Empire* (Cambridge, MA: Harvard University Press, 2000), 45.

74. Rajadhyaksha, *Indian Cinema*, 8.

75. See Bernard Stiegler, *Technics and Time, 3: Cinematic Time and the Question of Malaise* (Stanford, CA: Stanford University Press, 2011), 1.

76. Slavoj Žižek, *Looking Awry: An Introduction to Jacques Lacan through Popular Culture* (Cambridge, MA: MIT Press, 1992), 163–164.

77. Jürgen Habermas, *The Structural Transformations of the Public Sphere: An Inquiry into a Category of Bourgeois Society*, trans. Thomas Burger and Frederick Lawrence (Cambridge, MA: MIT Press, 1991). See also Oskar Negt and Alexander Kluge, *Public Sphere and Experience: Toward an Analysis of the Bourgeois and Proletarian Public Sphere*, trans. Peter Labanyi, Jamie Owen Daniel, and Assenka Oksiloff (Minneapolis: University of Minnesota Press, 1993).

78. Kavita Daiya, *Violent Belongings: Partition, Gender, and National Culture in Postcolonial India* (Philadelphia: Temple University Press, 2008), 12–14.

79. Immanuel Kant, "An Answer to the Question, 'What Is Enlightenment?'" in *Kant: Political Writings*, ed. Hans Reiss, trans. H. B. Nisbet, 2nd ed. (Cambridge: Cambridge University Press, 1992 [1970]), 54–63, esp. 55.

80. Guy Debord, *The Society of the Spectacle*, trans. Donald Nicholson-Smith (New York: Zone Books, 1994 [1967]).

81. Ravi S. Vasudevan, "The Melodramatic Mode and Commercial Hindi Cinema," *Screen* 30, no. 3 (1989): 29–50, esp. 39.

82. Pramod K. Nayar, *Seeing Stars: Spectacle, Society and Celebrity Culture* (New Delhi: Sage, 2009), 161.

83. Sudhir Kakar, "East Meets West: The Psychohistory of Sudhir Kakar," interview with Paul H. Elovitz, *Clio's Psyche: Psychological and Historical Insights without Jargon*, 5, no. 3 (December 1998): 100–104, available at http://www.cliospsyche.org/.

84. Sudhir Kakar, *Intimate Relations: Exploring Indian Sexuality* (Chicago: University of Chicago Press, 1989), 27.

85. See Dinesh Bhugra and Susham Gupta, "Psychoanalysis and the Hindi Cinema," *International Review of Psychiatry* 21, no. 3 (June 2009): 234–240.

86. Samir Dayal, "Managing Ecstasy: A Subaltern Performative of Resistance," Special Issue, "Subaltern Affect," *Angelaki: Theoretical Journal of the Humanities* 6, no. 3 (2001): 75–90.

87. See Gayatri Chakravorty Spivak, *Other Asias* (Malden, MA: Blackwell, 2008), 186. See Homi Bhabha's Foreword to Frantz Fanon's *Black Skin, White Masks* (London: Pluto Press, 1986), rpt. in *Colonial Discourse and Post-colonial Theory: A Reader*, ed. Patrick Williams and Laura Chrisman (New York: Columbia University Press, 1994), esp. 116. I have written in a similar vein about Fanon. See Samir Dayal, "Ethical Antihumanism in Frantz Fanon," in *Edward Said and Jacques Derrida: Reconstellating Humanism and the Global Hybrid*, ed. Mina Karavanta and Nina Morgan (Newcastle, UK: Cambridge Scholars, 2009), 220–249.

88. Gayatri Chakravorty Spivak, "The Politics of Translation," in *Outside in the Teaching Machine* (New York: Routledge, 1993), 179–200, esp. 180–183. See also Peter Geschiere, *The Perils of Belonging: Autochthony, Citizenship, and Exclusion in Africa and Europe* (Chicago: University of Chicago Press, 2009): 1, 27, 61, 214.

89. See Nayar, *Seeing Stars*, 158–159.

90. Spivak, *Other Asias,* 189.

91. See especially the response by Jeffrey Sconce to Barton Scott's discussion of the style of *Love Story 2050* (Harry Baweja, 2008), a film about nonresident aliens of South Asian descent living in Australia and imagining a futuristic Mumbai, available at http://tinyurl.com/6aodt2t (accessed July 3, 2011).

92. Arjun Appadurai, *Modernity at Large: Cultural Dimensions of Globalization* (Minneapolis: University of Minnesota Press, 1996), 35.

93. Rai, *Untimely Bollywood,* 83.

94. Partha Chatterjee, "When Melody Ruled the Day," in Vasudev, *Frames of Mind,* 51–65, esp. 57.

95. Sharmila Rudrappa, *Ethnic Routes to Becoming American: Indian Immigrants and the Cultures of Citizenship* (New Brunswick, NJ: Rutgers University Press, 2004), 117.

96. Tejaswini Ganti, *Bollywood: A Guidebook to Popular Hindi Cinema* (London: Routledge, 2004), 80.

97. Gopalan, *Cinema of Interruptions,* 22.

98. Nayar, *Seeing Stars,* esp. 160, 157–159.

99. Udayan Patel, interview, in Kabir, *Bollywood,* 15.

100. See Sugata Bose and Ayesha Jalal, *Modern South Asia: History, Culture, Political Economy* (London: Routledge Press, 1997), 168, 169, 176.

101. This is the informed opinion of Kavita Krishnamurthy, playback singer for none other than Aishwarya Rai, in some polls voted the most beautiful woman in world cinema. See Kabir, *Bollywood,* 167.

102. Gopalan, *Cinema of Interruptions,* 21; emphasis original.

103. Ibid., 25; emphasis original.

104. Jean Laplanche and Jean-Bertrand Pontalis, "Fantasy and the Origins of Sexuality," in *Formations of Fantasy,* ed. Victor Burgin, James Donald, and Cora Kaplan (London: Routledge, 1986), 5–34.

105. Gayatri Gopinath, *Impossible Desires: Queer Diasporas and South Asian Public Cultures* (Durham, NC: Duke University Press, 2005). For a critical appreciation of Desai's book *Beyond Bollywood,* see Corey Creekmur, "Review of Jigna Desai, *Beyond Bollywood: The Cultural Politics of South Asian Diasporic Film,*" *Film Quarterly* 59, no. 1 (Fall 2005): 49–51, esp. 50.

106. Sandhya Shukla, *India Abroad: Diasporic Cultures of Postwar America and England* (Princeton, NJ: Princeton University Press, 2003), 5.

107. György Lukács, "The Classical Form of the Historical Novel," from *The Historical Novel,* in *The Norton Anthology of Theory and Criticism,* 2nd ed., ed. Vincent B. Leitch (New York: W. W. Norton, 2010 [2001]), 909–921, esp. 918.

108. Michel Foucault, "Nietzsche, Genealogy, History," in *Language, Counter-Memory, Practice: Selected Essays and Interviews by Michel Foucault,* ed. D. Bouchard (Ithaca, NY: Cornell University Press, 1977), 148.

109. See Gopalan, *Cinema of Interruptions.*

110. Slavoj Žižek, *Living in the End Times* (London: Verso, 2010), 28.

111. Ibid., 7.

112. Geschiere, *Perils of Belonging,* 22, 223. See also Amit S. Rai, *Untimely Bollywood: Globalization and India's New Media Assemblage* (Durham, NC: Duke University Press, 2009), 81.

113. Dissanayake, "Rethinking Indian Popular Cinema," 202–225, esp. 214, 217.

114. Marshall Berman, *All That Is Solid Melts into Air: The Experience of Modernity*

(London: Verso, 1983). See Samir Dayal, "Blackness as Symptom: Josephine Baker and European Identity," in *Blackening Europe,* ed. Heike Raphael-Hernandez (New York: Routledge Press, 2004), 35–53.

CHAPTER 1

1. Wimal Dissanayake, "Critical Approaches to World Cinema," in *The Oxford Guide to Film Studies,* ed. John Hill and Pamela Church Gibson (New York: Oxford University Press, 1998), 530.

2. Ravi Vasudevan, "Shifting Codes, Dissolving Identities: The Hindi Social Film of the 1950s as Popular Culture," in *Making Meaning in Indian Cinema,* ed. Ravi Vasudevan (New Delhi: Oxford University Press, 2000), 99–121.

3. Ibid., 102.

4. Gayatri Chatterjee, *Awara* (New Delhi: Wiley Eastern, 1992), 18–19.

5. Behroze Gandhy and Rosie Thomas, "Three Indian Film Stars," in *Stardom: Industry of Desire,* ed. Christine Gledhill (London: Routledge, 1991), 107–131, esp. 108; Rachel Dwyer, *All You Want Is Money, All You Need Is Love: Sex and Romance in Modern India* (London: Cassell, 2000), 130.

6. Iqbal Masud, "The Great Four of the Golden Fifties," in *Frames of Mind: Reflections on Indian Cinema,* ed. Aruna Vasudev (New Delhi: UBS, 1995), 29–41, esp. 39.

7. See Chatterjee, *Awara,* 19, 33.

8. G.W.F. Hegel, *The Phenomenology of Mind,* trans. J. B. Baillie (New York: Harper Torchbooks, 1967 [1910]), 468; emphasis original.

9. Ibid., 467.

10. Chatterjee, *Awara,* 18.

11. Slavoj Žižek, *Looking Awry: An Introduction to Jacques Lacan through Popular Culture* (Cambridge, MA: MIT Press, 1992), 163–164.

12. Jean Laplanche and Jean-Bertrand Pontalis, "Fantasy and the Origins of Sexuality," in *Formations of Fantasy,* ed. Victor Burgin, James Donald, and Cora Kaplan (London: Methuen, 1986), 5–34, esp. 24–25, 26–27.

13. J. Donald, *Fantasy and the Cinema* (London: British Film Institute, 1989), 136.

14. See Sangita Gopal and Sujata Moorti, *Global Bollywood: Travels of Hindi Song and Dance* (Minneapolis: University of Minnesota Press, 2008), 16.

15. Ibid., 16; see also Vasudevan, "Shifting Codes," 105.

16. Dana Polan, "Review of *Cinema 1: L'Image-Mouvement,* by Gilles Deleuze," *Film Quarterly* 38, no. 1 (Autumn 1984): 50–52, esp. 51.

17. See M. Madhava Prasad, *Ideology of the Hindi Film: A Historical Construction* (New Delhi: Oxford University Press, 2001).

18. Vasudevan, "Shifting Codes," 102; emphasis mine.

19. Ibid., 105.

20. Jacques Derrida glosses autoaffection in the following way: "If autoposition, the *automonstrative autotely* of the 'I,' even in the human, implies the 'I' to be an other that must welcome within itself some irreducible hetero-affection . . . then this autonomy of the 'I' can be neither pure nor rigorous; it would not be able to form the basis for a simple and linear differentiation of the human from the animal" (see Derrida, *The Animal That Therefore I Am,* ed. Marie-Louise Mallet, trans. David Wills [New York: Fordham University Press, 2008], 95; emphasis original). Thinking the "I's" relationality to the other, Derrida is saying here, is also thinking the "I"—autoaffection in this sense is just what is occur-

ring in Raj's address, introjection, and identification with the dog, not only at a superficial analogical level ("I am like the dog") but also at the level of fantasmatic, unconscious re-cognition of the self in terms of the relation with the other ("I unconsciously imagine myself in terms of my similarity and intimate—existential—relationship to the dog").

21. Jacques Lacan, *Écrits: A Selection,* trans. Alan Sheridan (New York: W. W. Norton, 1977), 322.

22. Žižek, *Looking Awry,* 163–164.

23. Ibid., 167.

24. Ibid.

25. Hegel, *Phenomenology of Mind,* 467.

26. Immanuel Kant, *Critique of Practical Reason,* trans. L. W. Beck (Indianapolis: Bobbs-Merrill, 1956), 89.

27. Chatterjee, *Awara,* 20.

28. Derrida, *Animal,* 135.

29. Partha Chatterjee, *Nationalist Thought and the Colonial World: A Derivative Discourse?* (London: Zed Books for the United Nations University, 1986).

CHAPTER 2

1. Reports of the Planning Commission, available at http://planningcommission.nic.in/plans/planrel/fiveyr/welcome.html (accessed January 4, 2011).

2. Salman Rushdie, *The Moor's Last Sigh* (London: Jonathan Cape, 1995), 137.

3. Sarah Wüst, "Young German Heimatfilm: Negotiations of a Powerful Myth," *Austausch* 1, no. 1 (April 2011): 76–94, esp. 78.

4. Ibid., 80; emphasis mine.

5. Fredric Jameson, "Reification and Utopia in Mass Culture," in Jameson, *Signatures of the Visible* (New York: Routledge, 1992), 10, 11.

6. Even after the liberalization of the 1990s, India remains a primarily agrarian nation. And although the FICCI (Federation of Indian Chambers of Commerce and Industry) anticipates a steady growth in manufacturing, the country still lags China in the manufacture of items such as leather, textiles, chemicals, and other goods.

7. Vijay Mishra, *Bollywood Cinema: Temples of Desire* (London: Routledge, 2002), 79.

8. Rushdie, *Moor's Last Sigh,* 138–139.

9. Rachel Dwyer, *All You Want Is Money, All You Need Is Love: Sex and Romance in Modern India* (London: Cassell, 2000), 133.

10. Ravi Vasudevan, "Shifting Codes, Dissolving Identities: The Hindi Social Film of the 1950s as Popular Culture," in *Making Meaning in Indian Cinema,* ed. Ravi Vasudevan (New Delhi: Oxford University Press, 2000), 99–121, esp. 107.

11. Sudhir Kakar, *Intimate Relations: Exploring Indian Sexuality* (Chicago: University of Chicago Press, 1989), 129–130.

12. Behroze Gandhy and Rosie Thomas, qtd. from "Three Indian Film Stars," in *Stardom: Industry of Desire,* ed. Christine Gledhill (London: Routledge, 1991), 108, by Dwyer, *All You Want Is Money,* 136

13. Mishra, *Bollywood Cinema,* 81.

14. Ibid., 7.

15. Rosie Thomas, "Sanctity and Scandal: The Mythologization of Mother India," *Quarterly Review of Film and Video* 11 (1989): 11–30, esp. 13.

16. Gayatri Chatterjee, *Mother India* (London: British Film Institute, 2002).

17. Rachel Dwyer, *Filming the Gods* (London: Routledge, 2006), 101, 148.

18. Mishra, *Bollywood Cinema*, 61–62, and Rushdie, *Moor's Last Sigh*, 138. For an example of an unpersuaded critic, see B. D. Garga, "The Turbulent Thirties," in *Frames of Mind: Reflections on Indian Cinema*, ed. Aruna Vasudev (New Delhi: UBS Publishers, 1995), 17–28, esp. 22.

19. Quoted from Gayatri Chatterjee's *Mother India* by Sumathi Ramaswamy, *The Goddess and the Nation: Mapping Mother India* (Durham, NC: Duke University Press, 2010), 243.

20. See M. Madhava Prasad on state-sponsored realism in *Ideology of the Hindi Film: A Historical Construction* (New Delhi: Oxford University Press, 1998).

21. See Dwyer, *All You Want Is Money*, 137.

22. Vijay Prashad, *The Darker Nations: A People's History of the Third World* (New York: New Press, 2007), 215–216.

23. Ramaswamy, *Goddess and the Nation*, 8.

24. See Mishra, *Bollywood Cinema*, 64.

25. Ramaswamy, *Goddess and the Nation*, 8–9.

26. Sanjay Srivastava, "Voice, Gender and Space in Time of Five-Year Plans: The Idea of Lata Mangeshkar," *Economic and Political Weekly*, May 15, 2004, available at http://www.epw.org.in/showArticles.php?root=2004&leaf=05&filename=7189&filetype=html (accessed November 10, 2012).

27. Pavitra Sundar, "Meri Awaaz Suno: Women, Vocality, and Nation in Hindi Cinema," *Meridians: Feminism, Race, Transnationalism* 8, no. 1 (2007): 147.

28. See Neepa Majumdar, "The Embodied Voice: Song Sequences and Stardom in Popular Hindi Cinema," in *Soundtrack Available: Essays on Film and Popular Music*, ed. Pamela Robertson Wojcik and Arthur Knight (Durham, NC: Duke University Press, 2001), 170.

29. Srivastava, "Voice"; see Partha Chatterjee, "The Nationalist Resolution of the Women's Question," in *Recasting Women: Essays in Colonial History*, ed. Kumkum Sangari and Sudesh Vaid (New Delhi: Kali for Women, 1993).

30. Srivastava, "Voice."

31. Ibid.

32. Tom Conley, *Cartographic Cinema* (Minneapolis: University of Minnesota Press, 2007), 1–2.

33. Mishra, *Bollywood Cinema*, 62, 77.

34. Dwyer, *All You Want Is Money*, 131–132, 133.

35. Mishra, *Bollywood Cinema*, 66.

36. Mehboob Khan, qtd. in Dwyer, *All You Want Is Money*, 132.

37. Mishra, *Bollywood Cinema*, 68.

38. Timothy Corrigan and Patricia White, *The Film Experience*, 2nd ed. (New York: St. Martin's Press, 2008), 304–305.

39. Jyotika Virdi, *The Cinematic ImagiNation: Indian Popular Films as Social History* (New Brunswick, NJ: Rutgers University Press, 2003), 94.

40. Ibid., 206.

41. Mishra, *Bollywood Cinema*, 68.

42. See Sumita S. Chakravarty, *National Identity in Indian Popular Cinema, 1947–1987* (Austin: University of Texas Press, 1993), 8, 3–4.

43. Iqbal Masud, "The Great Four of the Golden Fifties," in *Frames of Mind: Reflections on Indian Cinema*, ed. Aruna Vasudev (New Delhi: UBS, 1995), 29–41, esp. 32.

44. See Ramaswamy, *Goddess and the Nation*. Ramaswamy observes that the "glorious goddess of the Indian nationalist imagination makes absolutely no appearance at

all in the film" (243). While this is technically true, it is important to remember that the typology of the Radha/Shamu, Radha/Krishna, Rita/Ram, and other such resonant pairings are embedded in the film's fantasmatic subtexts: it is certainly not entirely accidental that the names of the characters recall this familiar typology in which each name evokes its "consort" or opposite number.

45. Virdi, *Cinematic ImagiNation*, 91.

46. Ibid., 91, 92.

47. Rajeswari Sunder Rajan, *Real and Imagined Women: Gender, Culture and Postcolonialism* (London: Routledge, 1993), 105.

48. Qtd. in Mishra, *Bollywood Cinema*, 85.

49. Dwyer, *All You Want Is Money*, 134.

CHAPTER 3

1. I have benefited on this point from Sangita Gopal's talk "Between State and Capital: Women Make Movies," presented at the "Imperfect Futures" conference at Brandeis University, May 7–8, 2014.

2. Sudipta Kaviraj, "Indira Gandhi and Indian Politics," *Economic and Political Weekly* 21 (1986): 1697–1708.

3. Ashish Rajadhyaksha, *Indian Cinema in the Time of Celluloid: From Bollywood to the Emergency* (Bloomington: Indiana University Press, 2009), 238; Rajadhyaksha is drawing on Rajni Kothari's analysis.

4. Kaviraj, "Indira Gandhi," 1699–1700.

5. Rajadhyaksha, *Indian Cinema*, 238–239.

6. Ibid., 239.

7. Lalitha Gopalan, "Avenging Women in Indian Cinema," *Screen* 38, no. 1 (Spring 1997): 42–59.

8. Farid Kazmi, "How Angry Is the Angry Man?" in *The Secret Politics of Our Desires: Innocence, Culpability and Indian Popular Cinema*, ed. Ashis Nandy (London: Zed Books, 1998), 134–155.

9. Pramod K. Nayar, *Seeing Stars: Spectacle, Society and Celebrity Culture* (New Delhi: Sage, 2009), 60.

10. See also ibid., 60–61.

11. Ranjani Mazumdar, "From Subjectification to Schizophrenia: The 'Angry Man' and the 'Psychotic' Hero of Bombay Cinema," in *Making Meaning in Indian Cinema*, ed. Ravi S. Vasudevan (New Delhi: Oxford University Press, 2000), 238–264, esp. 240–241.

12. Ibid., 241–242.

13. André Bazin, "Theater and Cinema," in *Film Theory and Criticism: Introductory Readings*, 6th ed., ed. Leo Braudy and Marshall Cohen (New York: Oxford University Press, 2004), 418–428, esp. 419, 420.

14. Mazumdar, "From Subjectification to Schizophrenia," 243–244.

15. Ibid., 247.

16. Samir Dayal, "Professing Spirituality: Bollywood Fantasies and the Return of Religion," Special Issue, "FilmFocus," *Weber Studies* 24, no. 2 (Winter 2008): 74–97.

17. Thomas Waugh, "Queer Bollywood, or 'I'm the Player, You're the Naive One': Patterns of Sexual Subversion in Recent Indian Popular Cinema," in *Keyframes: Popular Cinema and Cultural Studies*, ed. Matthew Tinkcom and Amy Villarejo (New York: Routledge, 2001), 280–297.

18. Ashok Row Kavi, "The Changing Image of the Hero in Hindi Films," *Journal of Homosexuality* 39, nos. 3–4 (2000): 307–312.

19. M. Madhava Prasad, *Ideology of the Hindi Film: A Historical Construction* (Delhi: Oxford University Press, 2001), 83–84.

20. Fredric Jameson, *The Antinomies of Realism* (London: Verso, 2013), 28–29.

21. Partha Chatterjee, "The Nationalist Resolution of the Women's Question," in *Recasting Women: Essays in Indian Colonial History*, ed. Kumkum Sangari and Sudesh Vaid (New Brunswick: Rutgers University Press, 1990), 233–253. See also Ratna Kapur, "Postcolonial Erotic Disruptions: Legal Narratives of Culture, Sex, and Nation in India," *Columbia Journal of Gender and Law* 10, no. 2 (2001): 333–384.

22. K. Moti Gokulsing and Wimal Dissanayake, eds., *Popular Culture in a Globalised India* (London: Routledge, 2009), 79.

23. Gopalan, *Cinema of Interruptions*, 35, 40–41. Gopalan draws here on M. Rahman's report on the Indian film industry of the 1980s. See M. Rahman, "Women Strike Back," *India Today* (July 15, 1988): 80–82.

24. Sundar Kaali, "Narrating Seduction: Vicissitudes of the Sexed Subject in Tamil Nativity Film," in *Making Meaning in Indian Cinema*, ed. Ravi S. Vasudevan (New Delhi: Oxford University Press, 2000), 168–191, esp. 175.

25. See George Ritzer, *The Globalization of Nothing 2* (Thousand Oaks, CA: Pine Forge, 2007), 36. In the Introduction I invoked Ritzer's opposition of globalization and glocalization as a useful framing of the point. It is important not to see globalization, glocalization, or even autochthony as monotonically "good" or "bad." After all, even the assertion of autochthonous identity poses its own perils. Nira Yuval-Davis writes that while "the 'old racism' basically constructed 'the other' as essentially racially different, and the 'new racism' constructed her/him as essentially culturally different, autochthony is a racist discourse which uses origin, culture and religion as signifiers of immutable boundaries like other forms of racism, but its focus is spatial/territorial, a mode of what Manuel Castells called 'defensive identity communities,' except that these days it often applies to majoritarian as well as minoritarian community discourses." See Nira Yuval-Davis, "The Dark Side of Democracy: Autochthony and the Radical Right," *OpenDemocracy*, July 26, 2011, available at http://tinyurl.com/ms3z4eb (accessed June 20, 2013).

26. Sangeeta Ray, "Introduction," in *En-Gendering India: Woman and Nation in Colonial and Postcolonial Narratives* (Durham, NC: Duke University Press, 2000), 6–7.

27. Naila Kabeer, "Grief and Rage in India: Making Violence against Women History?" *OpenDemocracy*, January 5, 2013, available at http://www.opendemocracy.net/5050/naila-kabeer/grief-and-rage-in-india-making-violence-against-women-history.

28. Ashish Rajadhyaksha and Paul Willemen, *Encyclopaedia of Indian Cinema*, 2nd ed. (New Delhi: Oxford University Press, 1999 [1995]), 416.

29. Ruchira Gupta, "India: Examining the Motivation for Rape," *OpenDemocracy*, January 8, 2013, available at http://www.opendemocracy.net/5050/ruchira-gupta/india-examining-motivation-for-rape.

30. Kabeer, "Grief and Rage in India."

31. Gupta, "India: Examining the Motivation for Rape."

32. Ibid.

33. Madhu Kishwar and Ruth Vanita, "Male Fantasies of Female Revenge," *Manushi* 48 (September–October 1988): 43–44, esp. 44.

34. See http://www.vakilno1.com/bareacts/indianpenalcode/s376.htm (accessed November 12, 2012). There were some changes to the language in 2010, generally not

material to my argument here except that "rape" was replaced by "sexual assault" and the language on rape of a spouse was deleted, for which see http://www.prsindia.org/uploads/media/draft/Draft%20Criminal%20Law%20(Amendment)%20Bill%202010.pdf (accessed November 12, 2012).

35. Rajeswari Sunder Rajan, *The Scandal of the State: Women, Law, and Citizenship in Postcolonial India* (Durham, NC: Duke University Press, 2003), 215.

36. "Why BJP? Because MP Went beyond Women's Welfare Rhetoric," available at http://www.niticentral.com/?p=146053.

37. Praful Bidwai, "Gujarat under Barbarism's Spell: Modi Must Be Sent Packing," *Transnational Institute*, March 8, 2002, available at http://www.tni.org/archives/archives_bidwai_modi.

38. Gopalan, *Cinema of Interruptions*, 43–44.

39. Rajadhyaksha and Willemen, *Encyclopaedia of Indian Cinema*, 416.

40. Carol J. Clover, *Men, Women, and Chain Saws: Gender in the Modern Horror Film* (Princeton, NJ: Princeton University Press, 1992).

41. Nira Gupta-Casale, "Bearing Witness: Rape, Female Resistance, Male Authority and the Problems of Gender Representation in Popular Indian Cinema," *Indian Journal of Gender Studies* 7, no. 2 (2000): 231–248, esp. 240.

42. Ibid., 240.

43. Sharon Marcus, "Fighting Bodies, Fighting Words: A Theory and Politics of Rape Prevention," in *Feminists Theorize the Political,* ed. Judith Butler and Joan W. Scott (New York: Routledge, 1992), 385–403, esp. 399.

44. Ibid., 181.

45. Brenda Longfellow, "Rape and Translation in *Bandit Queen,*" in *Translating Desire: The Politics of Gender and Culture in India*, ed. Brinda Bose (New Delhi: Katha Press, 2002), 238–254, esp. 239.

46. Ibid.

47. Ibid., 239–240.

CHAPTER 4

1. International Monetary Fund, *World Economic Outlook Database,* October 2007, and World Bank, *World Development Indicators Database,* September 2007, available at http://siteresources.worldbank.org/DATASTATISTICS/Resources/GDP_PPP.pdf (accessed August 6, 2012).

2. A. Virmani, "World Economy: From Uni-Polar to Tri-Polar," *Hindu Business Line,* February 8, 2005, available at www.thehindubusinessline.com/2005/02/08/stories/2005020800030800.htm (accessed August 7, 2012).

3. Ctd. in Basharat Peer, "India's Broken Promise: How a Would-Be Great Power Hobbles Itself," *Foreign Affairs,* May–June 2012, 158–170, esp. 158.

4. Jean Drèze and Amartya Sen, "Putting Growth in Its Place," 1, available at http://aajeevika.gov.in/studies/important-analysis/Putting-growth-in-its-Place.pdf (accessed October 28, 2013).

5. Amartya Sen and Jean Drèze, *India: Development and Participation* (New Delhi: Oxford University Press, 2002 [1996]), 5, 24, 32–33.

6. Karl Polanyi, *The Great Transformation* (Boston: Beacon Press, 2002 [1944]), 4, 11–13.

7. Igor Primoratz, *Terrorism: A Philosophical Investigation* (Cambridge: Polity Press, 2013), 31.

8. Gayatri C. Spivak, "How to Read a 'Culturally Different' Book," in *Colonial Discourse/Postcolonial Theory*, ed. Francis Baker, Peter Hulme, and Margaret Iversen (Manchester, UK: Manchester University Press, 1994), 126–150, esp. 142.

9. Mark Seltzer, "Wound Culture: Trauma in the Pathological Public Sphere," *October* 80 (Spring 1997): 3–26, esp. 4–5.

10. V. D. Savarkar, *Hindutva: Who Is a Hindu?* (Bombay: S. S. Savarkar, 1969 [1923]), 33, 82, 5.

11. Ashutosh Varshney, "Contested Meanings: India's National Identity, Hindu Nationalism, and the Politics of Anxiety," *Daedalus* 122, no. 3 (Summer 1993): 227–261, esp. 249.

12. Christophe Jaffrelot, *Religion, Caste, and Politics in India* (New York: Columbia University Press, 2011), 170–171; emphasis added.

13. Gayatri C. Spivak, interview with Afsaneh Najmabadi, *Social Text*, no. 28 (1991): 122–134, esp. 133.

14. Saba Mahmood, "Secularism, Sexuality, and Sectarian Conflict," paper delivered at MIT, November 12, 2013, Cambridge, MA.

15. Srimati Basu, "Shading the Secular: Law at Work in the Indian Higher Courts," *Cultural Dynamics* 15, no. 2 (2003): 131–152, esp. 132.

16. Michel de Certeau, *The Writing of History*, trans. Tom Conley (New York: Columbia University Press, 1988), 4; emphasis original.

17. Ibid., 3.

18. Jean Laplanche, *Life and Death in Psychoanalysis*, trans. Jeffrey Mehlman (Baltimore: Johns Hopkins University Press, 1976), 88, 42.

19. Louis Dumont, "Le Problème de l'histoire," in *La Civilization indienne et nous*, Cahiers des Annales 23 (Paris: Colin, 1964), 31–54, ctd. in de Certeau, *Writing of History*, 4.

20. Jasbir K. Puar and Amit S. Rai, "Monster, Terrorist, Fag: The War on Terrorism and the Production of Docile Patriots," *Social Text* 72, no. 3 (Fall 2002): 117–148, esp. 140.

21. Mahmood Mamdani, *Good Muslim, Bad Muslim: America, the Cold War, and the Roots of Terror* (New York: Pantheon, 2004), 15.

22. Sumita Chakravarty, "Fragmenting the Nation: Images of Terrorism in Indian Popular Cinema," in *Cinema and Nation*, ed. Mette Hjort and Scott MacKenzie (London: Routledge, 2000), 222–238, esp. 228.

23. Amit Rai, "Patriotism and the Muslim Citizen in Hindi Films," *Harvard Asia Quarterly* 7, no. 3 (Summer 2003), available at http://www.asiaquarterly.com/content/view/136/5.

24. Susan Stewart, *Crimes of Writing* (New York: Oxford University Press, 1991), 280.

25. Bhaskar Sarkar, *Mourning the Nation: Indian Cinema in the Wake of Partition* (Durham, NC: Duke University Press, 2009).

26. Rai, "Patriotism."

27. Antonio Gramsci, "The Intellectuals," in *Selections from the Prison Notebooks*, ed. Quintin Hoare and Geoffrey Nowell Smith (New York: International Publishers, 1971), 12.

28. Jaffrelot, *Religion, Caste, and Politics*, 31–32, 35.

29. Nicholas Dirks, "The Home and the Nation: Consuming Culture and Politics in *Roja*," in *Pleasure and the Nation: The History, Politics and Consumption of Public Culture in India*, ed. Rachel Dwyer and Christopher Pinney (New Delhi: Oxford University Press, 2001), 161–185, esp. 162–163, 175.

30. Prasad, *Ideology of the Hindi Film*, 112–113.

31. Bruno Latour, "On Recalling ANT," in *Actor Network Theory and After*, ed. J. Law and J. Hassard (Oxford: Blackwell, 1999), 15–25, esp. 20.

32. Tejaswini Niranjana, "Integrating Whose Nation? Tourists and Terrorists in 'Roja,'" *Economic and Political Weekly,* January 15, 1994, 81.

33. See Ulf Hannerz, *Cultural Complexity: Studies in the Social Organization of Meaning* (New York: Columbia University Press, 1992), 23.

34. Chakravarty, "Fragmenting the Nation," 232–233.

35. Ibid., 234.

36. Ella Shohat and Robert Stam, "From the Imperial Family to the Transnational Imaginary: Media Spectatorship in the Age of Globalization," in *Global/Local: Cultural Production and the Transnational Imaginary,* ed. Rob Wilson and Wimal Dissanayake (Durham, NC: Duke University Press, 1996), 145–170, qtd. in Chakravarty, "Fragmenting the Nation," 233.

37. Geoffrey Galt Harpham, "Symbolic Terror," *Critical Inquiry* 28, no. 2 (Winter 2002): 573–579, esp. 578.

38. Mike Dillon, "'Patriotism and Valor Are in Your Blood': Necropolitical Subjectivities in The Terrorist (1999)," *Studies in South Asian Film and Media* 1, no. 2 (2009), doi: 10.1386/safm.1.2.209/1.

39. Nissim Mannathukkaren, "Subalterns, Cricket and the 'Nation': The Silences of 'Lagaan,'" *Economic and Political Weekly,* Special Article, December 8, 2001, available at http://www.epw.in/special-articles/subalterns-cricket-and-nation.html.

40. See Samir Dayal, "The Inadequately Violent State?" *In Media Res,* May 17, 2010, available at http://mediacommons.futureofthebook.org/imr/2010/05/17/inadequately-violent-state.

41. Lauren Berlant, "The Face of America and the State of Emergency," in *Disciplinarity and Dissent in Cultural Studies,* ed. Cary Nelson and Dilip Parameshwar Gaonkar (New York: Routledge, 1996), 397–439.

42. Slavoj Žižek, *Less Than Nothing: Hegel and the Shadow of Dialectical Materialism* (London: Verso, 2012), 679.

43. Giorgio Agamben, *What Is an Apparatus? And Other Essays,* trans. David Kishik and Stefan Pedatella (Stanford, CA: Stanford University Press, 2009), 23.

44. Jaffrelot, *Religion, Caste, and Politics,* 175, 171.

45. Slavoj Žižek, *For They Know Not What They Do: Enjoyment as a Political Factor* (London: Verso, 2002 [1991]), 70–71; emphasis original.

46. Chandan Reddy, *Freedom with Violence: Race, Sexuality, and the U.S. State* (Durham, NC: Duke University Press, 2011).

47. Agamben, *What Is an Apparatus?* 21, 14.

CHAPTER 5

1. George Ritzer, *The Globalization of Nothing 2* (Thousand Oaks, CA: Pine Forge, 2007), ix.

2. Eric Hobsbawm and Terence Ranger, *The Invention of Tradition* (Cambridge: Cambridge University Press, 1983), 10.

3. Jacqueline Rose, *States of Fantasy,* Clarendon Lectures in English Literature (Oxford: Oxford University Press, 1996), qtd. in Edward Said, "Fantasy's Role in the Making of Nations," in Said, *Reflections on Exile and Other Essays* (Cambridge, MA: Harvard University Press, 2000), 494.

4. See Uma Narayan, "Undoing the 'Package Picture' of Cultures," *Signs: Journal of Women in Culture and Society* 25, no. 4 (Spring 2000): 1084.

5. Judith Butler, *Bodies That Matter* (New York: Routledge, 1993), 112. See also Butler, *Gender Trouble: Feminism and the Subversion of Identity* (New York: Routledge, 1990).

6. Linda Bozniak reminds us, for instance, of denationalized subjects who appear in non-elite city-space. See Bozniak, "Citizenship Denationalized," *Indiana Journal of Global Law Studies* 7 (2000): 447–507.

7. Fredric Jameson, *The Antinomies of Realism* (London: Verso, 2013), 18.

8. C.L.R. James, *Beyond a Boundary* (Durham, NC: Duke University Press, 1983), 158. See also Gayatri C. Spivak, "Psychoanalysis in Left Field and Fieldworking: Examples to Fit the Title," in *Speculations after Freud: Psychoanalysis, Philosophy, and Culture*, ed. Sonu Shamdasani and Michael Münchow (New York: Routledge, 1994), 46.

9. James, *Beyond a Boundary*, 225.

10. Sandy Gordon, *India's Rise to Power: In the Twentieth Century and Beyond* (New York: St. Martin's, 1995), 157.

11. Sudipta Kaviraj, *The Imaginary Institution of India: Politics and Ideas* (New York: Columbia University Press, 2010), 6.

12. C. A. Bayly, "Patrons and Politics in Northern India," *Modern Asian Studies* 7, no. 3 (1973): 349–388, ctd. in Christophe Jaffrelot, *Religion, Caste, and Politics in India* (New York: Columbia University Press, 2011), 350.

13. C. A. Bayly, *The Local Roots of Indian Politics: Allahabad, 1880–1920* (Oxford: Clarendon Press, 1975), 273.

14. Kenneth Ballhatchet, *Race, Sex, and Class under the Raj: Imperial Attitudes and Policies and Their Critics, 1793–1905* (New York: St. Martin's Press, 1980), and Mrinalini Sinha, *Colonial Masculinity: The "Manly Englishman" and The "Effeminate Bengali" in the Late Nineteenth Century* (Manchester, UK: Manchester University Press, 1995).

15. See Eve Kosofsky Sedgwick, *Between Men: English Literature and Male Homosocial Desire* (Durham, NC: Duke University Press, 1985) It is not entirely ridiculous that some level of attraction or affection could emerge between Indian colonized and British colonizer. Ben Kingsley, the actor who played Gandhi, pointed out in a radio interview that Gandhi himself had affection for the British even as he was struggling against them (interview with Tom Ashbrook, "On Point Radio," January 13, 2012, available at http://onpoint.wbur.org/2012/01/13/actor-sir-ben-kingsley).

16. Pavitra Sundar, "Meri Awaaz Suno: Women, Vocality, and Nation in Hindi Cinema," *Meridians: Feminism, Race, Transnationalism* 8, no. 1 (2007): 144–179, esp. 169.

17. Ibid., 158.

18. Ibid., 170.

19. Ravi S. Vasudevan, "Addressing the Spectator of a 'Third World' National Cinema: The Bombay 'Social' Film of the 1940s and 1950s," *Screen* 36, no. 4 (Winter 1995): 316–317.

20. Arjun Appadurai, *Modernity at Large: Cultural Dimensions of Globalization* (Minneapolis: University of Minnesota Press, 1996), 44.

21. See Madhu Jain and Nandita Chowdhury, "Cinema: Coming Home," *India Today*, August 4, 1997, 28b–28c, qtd. in Purnima Mankekar, "Brides Who Travel: Gender, Transnationalism and Nationalism in Hindi Film," *Positions: East Asia Cultures Critique* 7, no. 3 (Winter 1999): 747.

22. See Naomi Schor, *Reading in Detail: Aesthetics and the Feminine* (New York: Methuen, 1987), xlv, 4, 10; Lalitha Gopalan, *Cinema of Interruptions: Action Genres in Contemporary Indian Cinema* (London: British Film Institute, 2002), 16–22. Gopalan discusses in those pages the aesthetics of the interruptive fantasy sequence.

23. See Homi Bhabha, "Of Mimicry and Man: The Ambivalence of Colonial Discourse," *October (Discipleship: A Special Issue on Psychoanalysis)* 28 (Spring 1984): 125–133.

24. Luce Irigaray, *This Sex Which Is Not One* (Ithaca, NY: Cornell University Press, 1985), 76, and Bhabha, "Of Mimicry and Man."

25. During the recent ethnic tensions between Muslims and Hindus in Gujarat, a neighborhood (Mohalla) committee organized a cricket match between teams that had equal numbers of Hindus and Muslims. Perhaps the central conceit of the game as an emollient to ethnic violence is not such a far-fetched idea after all?

26. Boria Majumdar reminds us that such inclusiveness was not unprecedented in the annals of Indian cricket: like Bhuvan, nineteenth-century figures such as Nagendra-prasad Sarbadhikary voiced a critique of caste-based discrimination in the arena of sports. Majumdar, "Politics of Leisure in Colonial India, 'Lagaan'—Invocation of a Lost History," *Economic and Political Weekly*, September 1, 2001, 3399–3404.

27. Ravi S. Vasudevan, "National Pasts and Futures: Indian Cinema," *Screen* 41, no. 1 (Spring 2000): 120.

28. Majumdar, "Politics of Leisure," 3400.

29. Ernest Renan, "What Is a Nation?" in *Nation and Narration*, ed. Homi K. Bhabha (London: Routledge, 1990), 8–22, esp. 11.

30. Arundhati Roy's *Power Politics* (Cambridge, MA: South End Press, 2001) is one example of a scathing rejection of the hype about globalization's promise (see esp. 35–36).

31. Fredric Jameson, "Third-World Literature in the Era of Multinational Capitalism," *Social Text* 15 (Fall 1986): 65–88. For Ahmad's critique, see Aijaz Ahmad, *In Theory: Classes, Nations, Literatures* (London: Verso, 1992).

32. See Johannes Fabian, *Time and the Other: How Anthropology Makes Its Object* (New York: Columbia University Press, 2002); Dipesh Chakrabarty, *Provincializing Europe: Postcolonial Thought and Historical Difference* (Princeton, NJ: Princeton University Press, 2000), 8–9.

33. Nissim Mannathukkaren adduces *Lagaan* as his primary example, but as I hope will be clear, my approach is very different from his. See "Subalterns, Cricket and the 'Nation': The Silences of 'Lagaan,'" *Economic and Political Weekly*, Special Article, December 8, 2001, available at http://www.epw.in/special-articles/subalterns-cricket-and-nation.html.

34. The category of the "not-yet" is developed in an interesting parallel by David N. Rodowick (*Gilles Deleuze's Time Machine* [Durham, NC: Duke University Press, 2003]), who extends Gilles Deleuze's work to postcolonial cinema studies, arguing that the simultaneous invocation of multiple pasts implies that, as Srinivas Aravamudan puts it, "a conceptual structure that is 'not yet' summons a people who are 'not yet'" (see Aravamudan, *Tropicopolitans: Colonialism and Agency, 1688–1804* [Durham, NC: Duke University Press, 1999], 17).

35. M. Madhava, Prasad, *Ideology of the Hindi Film: A Historical Construction* (Delhi: Oxford University Press, 1998), esp. 6, 9.

36. Étienne Balibar, "Borders of Europe," trans. J. Swenson, in *Cosmopolitics: Thinking and Feeling beyond the Nation*, ed. Pheng Cheah and Bruce Robbins (Minneapolis: University of Minnesota Press, 1998), esp. 216. See also Ulf Hannerz, "Scenarios for Peripheral Cultures," in *Culture, Globalization, and the World System: Contemporary Conditions for the Representation of Identity*, ed. Anthony D. King (London: Macmillan, 1991), 107–128, esp. 108.

37. Prasad, *Ideology of the Hindi Film*, 12.

38. Saskia Sassen, "Spatialities and Temporalities of the Global Elements for Theorization," *Public Culture* 12 (2000): 215.

39. See Richard Corliss, "The All-TIME 25 Best Sports Movies,"*Time*, September 22, 2012, available at http://entertainment.time.com/2011/09/22/the-all-time-25-best-sports-movies/slide/lagaan-2001/; *Empire*, August 2013, available at http://www.empireonline.com/features/100-greatest-world-cinema-films/default.asp?film=55.

40. Stuart Hall, "The Local and the Global: Globalization and Ethnicity," in *Culture, Globalization, and the World-System: Contemporary Conditions for the Representation of Identity*, ed. Anthony King (London: Macmillan, 1991), 21. See Benedict Anderson, *Imagined Communities: Reflections on the Origin and Spread of Nationalism* (London: Verso, 1991 [1983]), 315.

41. Arjun Appadurai, "Grassroots Globalization and the Research Imagination," *Public Culture* 12, no. 1 (Winter 2000): 3.

42. Ramachandra Guha, *A Corner of a Foreign Field: The Indian History of a British Sport* (Delhi: Picador, 2002).

43. David Washbrook, talk delivered at the Fletcher School of Law and Diplomacy, Tufts University, December 5, 2001.

44. Roland Robertson, "Social Theory, Cultural Relativity and the Problem of Globality," in *Culture, Globalization, and the World-System: Contemporary Conditions for the Representation of Identity*, ed. Anthony King (London: Macmillan, 1991), 87.

45. Vasudevan, "National Pasts," 123.

46. Orlando Patterson "The Ritual of Cricket," in *Liberation Cricket: West Indies Cricket Culture*, ed. Hilary McD. Beckles and Brian Stoddart (Manchester, UK: Manchester University Press, 1995), 141–147, esp. 141–142.

47. Appadurai, *Modernity*, 106.

48. Purnima Mankekar, *Screening Culture, Viewing Politics: An Ethnography of Television, Womanhood, and Nation in Postcolonial India* (Durham, NC: Duke University Press, 1999), 47; Dilip Gaonkar, ed., *Alternative Modernities* (Durham, NC: Duke University Press, 2001), 21.

49. Sumita Chakravarty, *National Identity in Indian Popular Cinema, 1947–1987* (Austin: University of Texas Press, 1993), 3; emphasis added.

50. See Sassen, "Spatialities," 219.

51. Vasudevan, "National Pasts," esp. 122–123.

52. See Immanuel Wallerstein, *Politics of the World Economy: The States, the Movements and the Civilizations* (Cambridge: Cambridge University Press, 1984), 166, and "The National and the Universal: Can There Be Such a Thing as World Culture?" in *Culture, Globalization, and the World System: Contemporary Conditions for the Representation of Identity*, ed. Anthony D. King (London: Macmillan, 1991), 92. Also see Arjun Appadurai, "Disjuncture and Difference in the Global Cultural Economy," in *Modernity at Large* (Minneapolis: University of Minnesota Press, 1996), 5.

53. Anderson, *Imagined Communities*, 319.

54. Walter Mignolo, keynote address, "Dewesternizing/Deorientalizing/Decolonizing Citizenship," Oecumene Project's Second Symposium, "Deorientalizing Citizenship," London, November 12–13, 2012, video, available at http://www.oecumene.eu/news/walter-mignolo-on-citizenship-knowledge-and-the-limits-of-humanity.

55. C.L.R. James, *Beyond a Boundary* (Durham, NC: Duke University Press, 1983), 348.

56. Sudipta Kaviraj, "The Imaginary Institution of India," in *Subaltern Studies VII*, ed.

Partha Chatterjee and Gyanendra Pandey, 1–39 (Delhi: Oxford University Press, 1996), ctd. in Sankaran Krishna, *Postcolonial Insecurities: India, Sri Lanka, and the Question of Nationhood* (Minneapolis: University of Minnesota Press, 1999), 72.

57. Qadri Ismail, "Batting against the Break: On Cricket, Nationalism, and the Swashbuckling Sri Lankans," *Social Text* 50, no. 1 (Spring 1997): 33–56, esp. 50.

58. Andreas Huyssen, *Present Pasts: Urban Palimpsests and the Politics of Memory* (Stanford, CA: Stanford University Press, 2003), 12, 26–27.

59. Sean Cubitt *The Cinema Effect* (Cambridge, MA: MIT Press, 2005), 301.

60. Appadurai, *Modernity*, 111.

61. See Kenneth Surin, "C.L.R. James' Material Aesthetic of Cricket," in *Liberation Cricket*, ed. Beckles and Stoddart, 326–327, 332–333.

62. Appadurai, *Modernity*, 93.

63. Ashis Nandy, *The Savage Freud and Other Essays on Possible and Retrievable Selves* (Delhi: Oxford University Press, 1995), 39.

64. Vijay Prashad, "From Multiculture to Polyculture in South Asian American Studies," *Diaspora: A Journal of Transnational Studies* 8, no. 2 (Fall 1999): 185–204, esp. 195; see also Samir Dayal, "The Emergence of the Fragile Subject: Amitav Ghosh's An Antique Land," in *India: Hybridity/Postcoloniality*, ed. Monika Fludernik (Tubingen, Germany: Stauffenburg, 1998), 103–133.

65. Qtd. in Krishna, *Postcolonial Insecurities*, 72.

66. "Countermodernity," as I conceptualize it, follows Dipesh Chakrabarty's theorization of a pluralizing and contestation of European modernity. See his *Provincializing Europe: Postcolonial Thought and Historical Difference* (Princeton, NJ: Princeton University Press, 2000), 46, 148.

67. Roland Barthes, *The Preparation of the Novel* (New York: Columbia University Press, 2011 [1980]), 107.

68. See Appadurai, *Modernity*, 90, 110.

69. Ashis Nandy, *The Tao of Cricket: On Games of Destiny and the Destiny of Games* (New Delhi: Penguin, 1989), 1–2.

70. Appadurai, *Modernity*, 90.

71. Majumdar, "Politics of Leisure," 3401.

72. Partha Chatterjee, *Nationalist Thought and the Colonial World: A Derivative Discourse?* (London: Zed Books for the United Nations University, 1986), 2.

73. Homi K. Bhabha, "Looking Global," paper delivered at a conference on globalization, Harvard University, April 3, 2001.

CHAPTER 6

1. Rosie Thomas, "Indian Cinema: Pleasures and Popularity," in *Asian Cinemas: A Reader and Guide*, ed. Dimitris Eleftheriotis and Gary Needham (Honolulu: University of Hawai'i Press, 2006), 280–294, esp. 290.

2. Gilles Deleuze, *The Time-Image*, trans. Hugh Tomlinson and Robert Galeta (Minneapolis: University of Minnesota Press, 1989), 130.

3. Gayatri Gopinath, *Impossible Desires: Queer Diasporas and South Asian Public Cultures* (Durham, NC: Duke University Press, 2005), 15–16, 1.

4. Gilles Deleuze and Félix Guattari, *Kafka: Toward a Minor Literature*, trans. Dana Polan (Minneapolis: University of Minnesota Press, 1986 [1975]), 16.

5. Jacques Lacan, *Écrits: A Selection*, trans. Alan Sheridan (London: Tavistock, 1977),

272, 760. See also Lacan, *The Seminar, Book XI: The Four Fundamental Concepts of Psychoanalysis,* 1964, trans. Alan Sheridan (London: Hogarth Press and Institute of Psycho-Analysis, 1977), 273.

6. See Kamala Visveswaran and Ali Mir, "On the Politics of Community in South Asian American Studies," *Amerasia Journal* 25, no. 3 (1999/2000): 97–108, esp. 100.

7. K. C. Kaleta, *Hanif Kureishi: Postcolonial Storyteller* (Austin: University of Texas Press, 1980), 40–41.

8. Stuart Hall, "New Ethnicities," in *Black Film, British Cinema*, ed. Kobena Mercer (London: ICA, 1988), 29–30.

9. Ambalavaner Sivanandan, *A Different Hunger: Writings on Black Resistance* (London: Pluto Press, 1982), 45.

10. Aimé Césaire, *Discourse on Colonialism,* excerpted in *Colonial Discourse and Post-colonial Theory: A Reader,* ed. Patrick Williams and Laura Chrisman (New York: Columbia University Press, 1994), 172–180, esp. 174.

11. Jasbir K. Puar, "To Be Gay and Racist Is No Anomaly," *The Guardian*, June 2, 2010, available at http://www.theguardian.com/commentisfree/2010/jun/02/gay-lesbian-islamophobia.

12. Jasbir K. Puar, *Terrorist Assemblages: Homonationalism in Queer Times* (Durham, NC: Duke University Press, 2007), xii–xiii.

13. Gopinath, *Impossible Desires*, 1, 3.

14. Eva Rueschmann, ed., *Moving Pictures, Migrating Identities* (Jackson: University Press of Mississippi, 2003), xix.

15. Ctd. in Sujata Moorti, "Inflamed Passions: *Fire,* the Woman Question, and the Policing of Cultural Borders," *Genders* 32 (2000), available at http://www.genders.org/g32/g32_moorti.html.

16. See ibid.

17. Qtd. in Gautaman Bhaskaran, "*Fire* Explores Women's Dilemma in Modern World," *Hindu*, December 20, 1998, 10.

18. Arif Dirlik and Rob Wilson, "Introduction," *boundary 2* 21, no. 1 (1994): 1–14, esp. 11.

19. Moorti, "Inflamed Passions."

20. For an account of some of the protests, including the attacks on movie theaters screening Mehta's film, see Moorti, "Inflamed Passions."

21. My reading is thus fundamentally at odds with Moorti's. In her view "Mehta opts to present a rosy, happy-ever-after ending that papers over the social conditions that render lesbians invisible in India." See Moorti, "Inflamed Passions."

22. Gayatri Chakravorty Spivak, "Can the Subaltern Speak?" in *Colonial Discourse and Post-colonial Theory: A Reader,* ed. Patrick Williams and Laura Chrisman (New York: Columbia University Press, 1994), 66–111.

23. G.W.F. Hegel, *Hegel's Phenomenology of Self-Consciousness: Text and Commentary,* ed. Leo Rauch and David Sherman (Albany: State University of New York Press, 1999), 20.

24. Spivak, "Can the Subaltern Speak?" 93.

25. Sikata Banerjee, "Women, Muscular Nationalism and Hinduism in India: Roop Kanwar and the *Fire* Protest," *Totalitarian Movements and Political Religions* 11, nos. 3–4 (September–December 2010): 271–287, esp. 281, 283. EBSCO.

26. Spivak, "Can the Subaltern Speak?" 91.

27. Moorti, "Inflamed Passions."

28. Terry Castle, *The Apparitional Lesbian: Female Homosexuality and Modern Culture* (New York: Columbia University Press, 1993), 2.

29. Slavoj Žižek, *Looking Awry: An Introduction to Jacques Lacan through Popular Culture* (Cambridge, MA: MIT Press, 1992), 6; emphasis original.

30. Bonnie Zimmerman, "What Has Never Been: An Overview of Lesbian Feminist Literary Criticism," in *Feminisms: An Anthology of Literary Theory and Criticism*, ed. Robyn R. Warhol and Diane Price Herndl (New Brunswick, NJ: Rutgers University Press, 1991), 128.

31. Bowers v. Hardwick, 478 U.S. 186 (1986), available at http://caselaw.lp.findlaw.com/scripts/getcase.pl?court=US&vol=478&invol=186.

32. Luce Irigaray, "Women on the Market," in *The Logic of the Gift: Toward an Ethic of Generosity*, ed. Alan D. Schrift (New York: Routledge, 1997), 174–189, esp. 174.

33. Rujuta Chincholkar-Mandelia, "Fire: A Subaltern Existence?" *Journal of Third World Studies* 22, no. 1 (2005): 197–209, esp. 205–206.

34. Zafaryab Jilani, Muslim leader and petitioner in the case, Lucknow; and Vivek Gunpal, student in Nagore, Rajasthan, from interviews conducted by Divya Arya and Geeta Pandey, "India Gay Sex Ruling: 'It Is a Huge Setback,'" *BBC News India* (December 11, 2013), available at http://www.bbc.com/news/world-asia-india-25329067.

35. Castle, *Apparitional Lesbian*, 15.

36. Monique Wittig, *The Straight Mind and Other Essays* (Boston: Beacon Press, 1992).

37. Judith Butler, "Imitation and Gender Insubordination," in *The Lesbian and Gay Studies Reader*, ed. Henry Abelove, Michèle Aina Barale, and David M. Halperin (New York: Routledge, 1993), 307–320, esp. 312.

38. Jasbir K. Puar and Amit S. Rai, "Perverse Projectiles under the Specter of (Counter)Terrorism," *Social Text 80* 22, no. 3 (2004), 75–194, esp. 75.

39. Ibid., 75–76.

CHAPTER 7

Acknowledgments: I thank members of audiences at the Universities of Bordeaux, Padua, Tampere, and Riga, before whom I delivered earlier versions of this chapter.

1. Stephen Toulmin, *Cosmopolis: The Hidden Agenda of Modernity* (New York: Free Press, 1990), 8.

2. Tejaswini Ganti, *Bollywood: A Guidebook to Popular Hindi Cinema* (New York: Routledge, 2004), 92.

3. The term "cosmopolitan" is, of course, interpreted in a wide variety of ways. My use of the term here falls somewhere between Bruce Robbins's conception as "the provocatively impure but irreducible combination of a certain privilege at home, as part of a real belonging in institutional places, with a no less real but much less common (and therefore highly desirable) extension of democratic, anti-imperial principles abroad" (*Secular Vocations: Intellectuals, Professionalism, Culture* [London: Verso, 1993], 188 ff.) and the more everyday understanding of cosmopolitanism: "having constituent elements from all over the world or from many different parts of the world" and "so sophisticated as to be at home in all parts of the world or conversant with many spheres of interest" (*American Heritage Dictionary*, 4th ed.)

4. Toulmin, *Cosmopolis*, 3.

5. Homi Bhabha, *The Location of Culture* (London: Routledge, 1994), 66.

6. Rajinder Kumar Dudrah, "Vilayati Bollywood: Popular Hindi Cinema-Going and Diasporic South Asian Identity in Birmingham (UK)," *Javnost* 9, no. 1 (2002): 19–36, esp. 29.

7. Asha Varadharajan, "Dissolution, Dissensus, and the Possibility of Community," *University of Toronto Quarterly* 66, no. 4 (Fall 1997): 621–633, esp. 631.

8. Edward W. Said, *Reflections on Exile and Other Essays* (Cambridge, MA: Harvard University Press, 2000), 26.

9. David Harvey, "Cosmopolitanism and the Banality of Geographical Evils," *Public Culture* 12, no. 2 (Spring 2000): 529–564, esp. 529.

10. Bruce Robbins, "Introduction Part I," in *Cosmopolitics: Thinking and Feeling beyond the Nation*, ed. Pheng Cheah and Bruce Robbins (Minneapolis: University of Minnesota Press, 1998), 4.

11. See Cheah and Robbins, *Cosmopolitics*, 1–2.

12. Jenny Sharpe, "Is the United States Postcolonial? Transnationalism, Immigration, and Race," *Diaspora: A Journal of Transnational Studies* 4, no. 2 (1995): 181–199, esp. 185.

13. Martha Nussbaum, "Patriotism and Cosmopolitanism," *Boston Review*, October–November 1994, available at http://bostonreview.net/martha-nussbaum-patriotism-and-cosmopolitanism.

14. Benjamin Barber, "Constitutional Faith," in *For Love of Country?* ed. Martha Nussbaum and Joshua Cohen (Boston: Beacon Press, 2002 [1996]), 30–37, esp. 36. See also Masao Miyoshi, "A Borderless World?" *Politics, Poetics: Documenta X, the Book*, ed. Documenta and Museum Fredercianum Veranstaltungs-GmbH (Kassel, Germany: Cantz, 1997), 202, and Arundhati Roy, *Power Politics* (Cambridge, MA: South End Press, 2001), 14, 18–19.

15. Roy, *Power Politics*, 14, 33.

16. George Ritzer, *The Globalization of Nothing 2* (Thousand Oaks, CA: Pine Forge, 2007), 36.

17. Aihwa Ong, *Flexible Citizenship: The Cultural Logics of Transnationality* (Durham, NC: Duke University Press, 1999), 4. With Ong, I take transnationalism to denote "both moving through space or across lines, as well as changing the nature of something. Besides suggesting new relations between nation states and capital, transnationality also alludes to the *trans*versal, the *trans*actional, the *trans*lational, and the *trans*gressive aspects of contemporary behavior and imagination that are incited, enabled, and regulated by the changing logics of states and capitalism" (ibid.; emphases original).

18. Cheah and Robbins, *Cosmopolitics*.

19. See also Jagdish Bhagwati, "Coping with Antiglobalization: A Trilogy of Discontents," *Foreign Affairs*, January–February 2002, 2–7, esp. 7.

20. See John L. Comaroff and Jean Comaroff, "Law and Disorder in the Postcolony," in *Law and Disorder in the Postcolony*, ed. Comaroff and Comaroff (Chicago: University of Chicago Press, 2006), 1–56, esp. 32.

21. Timothy Brennan, *At Home in the World: Cosmopolitanism Now* (Cambridge, MA: Harvard University Press, 1997), 2.

22. Michael Walzer, "Spheres of Affection," in Nussbaum and Cohen, *For Love of Country*, 125–130, esp. 125. Also see Gertrude Himmelfarb's essay, "The Illusions of Cosmopolitanism," which makes the astonishing claim that the ideas of justice, right, reason, and "love of humanity" are perhaps uniquely "Western values" (in Nussbaum and Cohen, *For Love of Country?* 72–77, esp. 75).

23. Anthony Appiah, "Cosmopolitan Patriots," in Nussbaum and Cohen, *For Love of Country?* 28–29.

24. Martha Nussbaum, "Reply," in Nussbaum and Cohen, *For Love of Country?* 133.

25. Saskia Sassen, "Spatialities and Temporalities of the Global Elements for Theorization," *Public Culture* 12 (2000): 215–216.

26. Nussbaum, "Patriotism and Cosmopolitanism."

27. Ibid.

28. Judith N. Shklar, "Putting Cruelty First," *Democratiya* 4 (Spring 2006): 81–94, esp. 91.

29. Amy Gutmann, "Democratic Citizenship," in Nussbaum and Cohen, *For Love of Country?* 69–71.

30. Arjun Appadurai, "Grassroots Globalization and the Research Imagination," *Public Culture* 12, no. 1 (Winter 2000): 1–19, esp. 6, 12, 13.

31. See Thomas McCarthy, "On Reconciling Cosmopolitan Unity and National Diversity," in *Alternative Modernities*, ed. Dilip P. Gaonkar (Durham, NC: Duke University Press, 2001), 197–235, esp. 202.

32. Walter Benjamin, "The Task of the Translator," in Benjamin, *Illuminations*, ed. Hannah Arendt, trans. Harry Zohn (New York: Schocken Books, 1969 [1955]), 69–82, esp. 81.

33. Graham Huggan, *The Post-colonial Exotic: Marketing the Margins* (London: Routledge Press, 2001), 19, 23.

34. Rey Chow, *Writing Diaspora: Tactics of Intervention in Contemporary Cultural Studies* (Bloomington: Indiana University Press, 1993), 53.

35. Richard Falk, "Revisioning Cosmopolitanism," in Nussbaum and Cohen, *For Love of Country?* 59.

36. James Clifford, "Traveling Cultures," in *Cultural Studies*, ed. Lawrence Grossberg, Cary Nelson, and Paula A. Treichler (New York: Routledge, 1992), 106–107.

37. Jacques Rancière, "Politics, Identification, and Subjectivization," *October* 61 (Summer 1992): 58–64, esp. 60.

38. Jenny Sharpe, "Gender, Nation, and Globalization in *Monsoon Wedding* and *Dilwale Dulhania Le Jayenge*," *Meridians: Feminism, Race, Transnationalism* 6, no. 1 (2005): 58–81, esp. 62.

39. Rancière, "Politics," 63.

40. Gayatri Chakravorty Spivak, "Subaltern Studies: Deconstructing Historiography," in *Selected Subaltern Studies*, ed. Ranajit Guha and Gayatri Chakravorty Spivak (Oxford: Oxford University Press, 1988), 3–32; and Jürgen Habermas, *The Philosophical Discourse of Modernity*, trans. Frederick Lawrence (Cambridge, MA: MIT Press, 1987). See also Habermas, *The Inclusion of the Other: Studies in Political Theory*, ed. Ciaran Cronin and Pablo De Greiff (Cambridge, MA: MIT Press, 1998).

41. Paul Willemen, "Introduction," in *Encyclopaedia of Indian Cinema*, 2nd ed., ed. Ashish Rajadhyaksha and Paul Willemen (New Delhi: Oxford University Press, 1999), 9.

42. See keynote address by Walter Mignolo, "Dewesternizing/ Deorientalizing/Decolonizing Citizenship," Oecumene Project's Second Symposium, "Deorientalizing Citizenship," London, November 12–13, 2012, video, available at http://www.oecumene.eu/news/walter-mignolo-on-citizenship-knowledge-and-the-limits-of-humanity.

43. Rancière, "Politics," 63.

44. Pnina Werbner, "Introduction: The Materiality of Diaspora—Between Aesthetic and 'Real' Politics," *Diaspora: A Journal of Transnational Studies* 9, no. 1 (Spring 2000): 5–20, esp. 11.

45. Sandhya Rajendra Shukla, *India Abroad: Diasporic Cultures of Postwar America and England* (Princeton, NJ: Princeton University Press, 2003), 2.

46. Shakuntala Rao, "The Globalization of Bollywood: An Ethnography of Non-elite Audiences in India," *Communication Review* 10, no. 1 (2007): 57–76, esp. 74.

47. See Patricia Uberoi, "The Diaspora Comes Home: Disciplining Desire in DDLJ," *Contributions to Indian Sociology* 32, no. 2 (1988): 305–336.

48. Purnima Mankekar, "Brides Who Travel: Gender, Transnationalism and Nationalism in Hindi Film," *Positions: East Asia Cultures Critique* 7, no. 3 (Winter 1999): 731–761, esp. 732.

49. P. Sainath, "17,368 Farm Suicides in 2009," *The Hindu*, December 27, 2010, available at http://tinyurl.com/krmb5lq.

50. Ayesha Jalal, *Democracy and Authoritarianism in South Asia: A Comparative and Historical Perspective* (Lahore, Pakistan: Sang-e-Meel Publications, 1995), 252, qtd. in Sankaran Krishna, *Postcolonial Insecurities: India, Sri Lanka and the Question of Nationhood* (Minneapolis: University of Minnesota Press, 1999), 240.

51. Few figures could so powerfully capture, even today, the virulence of antiforeigner sentiment as Enoch Powell did in his infamous "Rivers of Blood" speech. In that speech, delivered in the August of that annus mirabilis, 1968, he wrote, "As I look ahead, I am filled with foreboding; like the Roman, I seem to see 'the River Tiber foaming with much blood.'" Powell, qtd. in Kobena Mercer, "1968: Periodizing Politics and Identity," in *Cultural Studies*, ed. Lawrence Grossberg, Cary Nelson, and Paula A. Treichler (New York: Routledge, 1992), 424–449, esp. 435.

52. Ian Aspinall, promotional notes to DVD of *East Is East*.

53. Stuart Klawans, "On Tyson vs. Downey, Review of *East Is East*," *The Nation*, May 15, 2000, 34–36.

54. Mignolo's terms will find echo in Étienne Balibar (*Politics and the Other Scene* [London: Verso, 2002 (1998)], 24); Tariq Modood, "'Difference,' Cultural Racism and Anti-Racism," in *Debating Cultural Hybridity: Multicultural Identities and the Politics of Anti-racism*, ed. Pnina Werbner and Tariq Modood (London: Zed Books, 1997), 155. See also Molly Sackler, "Stereotypes and Social Critique Spar in This Culture-Clash Dramedy," *Bright Lights* 30 (October 2000), available at http://www.brightlightsfilm.com/30/eastiseast.html (accessed September 9, 2001).

55. Hall, "When Was the 'Post-colonial?' Thinking at the Limit," in *The Post-Colonial Question: Common Skies, Divided Horizons*, ed. Iain Chambers and Lidia Curti (London: Routledge, 1996).

56. Kim Knott and Sadja Khokher, "Religious and Ethnic Identity among Young Muslim Women in Bradford," *New Community* 19 (1993): 593–610, esp. 596.

57. Paul Gilroy, *The Black Atlantic: Modernity and Double Consciousness* (London: Verso, 1993), 80.

58. Patricia E. Roy, "The Fifth Force: Multiculturalism and the English Canadian Identity," *Annals of the American Academy of Political and Social Science (Being and Becoming Canada)* 538 (March 1995): 199–209, esp. 200.

59. Janet McLellan and Anthony H. Richmond, "Multiculturalism in Crisis: A Postmodern Perspective on Canada," *Ethnic and Racial Studies* 17, no. 4 (1994): 662–683, esp. 665.

60. Will Kymlicka and Wayne Norman, "Return of the Citizen: A Survey of Recent Work on Citizenship Theory," *Ethics* 104 (January 1994): 352–381, esp. 352.

61. Linda Basch, Nina Glick Schiller, and Cristina Szanton Blanc, *Nations Unbound: Transnational Projects, Postcolonial Predicaments, and Deterritorialized Nation-States* (Basel: Gordon and Breach, 1994), 12.

62. Karl Marx, Notebook III (November 29 to circa mid-December 1857), in *Grundrisse: Foundations of the Critique of Political Economy*, trans. Martin Nicolaus (New York: Vintage Books, 1973), 361.

63. Michael Hardt and Antonio Negri, "Preface: Dionysos," in *Labor of Dionysos: A Critique of the State Form* (Minneapolis: University of Minnesota Press, 1994), 15.

64. Oskar Negt and Alexander Kluge, *Public Sphere and Experience: Toward an Analysis of the Bourgeois and Proletarian Public Sphere*, trans. Peter Labanyi, Jamie Owen Daniel, and Assenka Oksiloff (Minneapolis: University of Minnesota Press, 1993), 36.

65. Keith Spicer, "So Great a Heritage as Ours," *Hamilton Spectator*, April 15, 1987, A7.

66. See Vijay Prashad, *Everybody Was Kung Fu Fighting: Afro-Asian Connections and the Myth of Cultural Purity* (Boston: Beacon Press, 2001). See also Prashad, *The Karma of Brown Folk* (Minneapolis: University of Minnesota Press, 2000).

67. Sheila L. Croucher, *Globalization and Belonging: The Politics of Identity in a Changing World* (Lanham, MD: Rowman and Littlefield, 2004), 333–335.

68. J. C. Naidoo and R. G. Edwards, "Combating Racism Involving Visible Minorities: A Review of Relevant Research and Policy Development," *Canadian Social Work* 8, no. 2 (1991): 211–236, esp. 217.

69. Kymlicka and Norman, "Return of the Citizen," 380.

70. bell hooks and Anuradha Dingwaney, "*Mississippi Masala*," *Z Magazine*, July–August 1992, 41–43.

71. Ibid., 43.

72. In her interview with Charlie Rose on May 1, 2002, Nair commented that she intended the film to "refuse to pander" to expectations about what an "Indian film" ought to portray; available at http://www.amazon.com/Charlie-Emanuel-Waxman-Jhumpa-Lahiri/dp/B000P29HH0.

73. Sunaina Maira, "Chaste Identities, Ethnic Yearnings: Second Generation Indian Americans in New York City" (Ph.D. diss., Harvard University, 1998), 283–287, ctd. in Prashad, *Karma of Black Folk*, 181.

74. Prashad, *Karma of Black Folk*, 190.

75. Jay Chandrasekhar, qtd. in Arthur J. Pais, "Comic's Coup," *India Today International*, January 22, 2001, 24d.

76. Rajadhyaksha and Willemen, *Encyclopaedia of Indian Cinema*, 10.

77. Samir Dayal, "Min(d)ing the Gap: South Asian Americans," in *A Part, yet Apart: South Asians in America*, ed. Lavina Shankar and Rajini Srikanth (Philadelphia: Temple University Press, 1998), 235–265. See also Amritjit Singh and Peter Schmidt, "On the Borders between U.S. Studies and Postcolonial Theory," in *Postcolonial Theory and the United States: Race, Ethnicity, and Literature*, ed. Amritjit Singh and Peter Schmidt (Jackson: University Press of Mississippi, 2000), 3–70, esp. 13.

78. Karen Shimakawa, *National Abjection: The Asian American Body Onstage* (Durham, NC: Duke University Press, 2002), 3; emphasis original.

79. Manish Khagram, Manish Desai, and Jason Varughese, "Seen, Rich, but Unheard? The Politics of Asian Indians in the United States," in *Asian Americans and Politics: Perspectives, Experiences, Prospects*, ed. Gordon H. Chang (Washington, DC: Woodrow Wilson Center Press, 2000), 258–284, esp. 260, 262.

80. Sumita S. Chakravarty, *National Identity in Indian Popular Cinema, 1947–1987* (Austin: University of Texas Press, 1993), 3.

81. Bhishnupriya Ghosh and Bhaskar Sarkar, "The Cinema of Displacement," *Film Criticism* 20, nos. 1–2 (Winter 1995–1996): 102–113, esp. 105, 109.

82. Keya Ganguly, *Cinema, Emergence, and the Films of Satyajit Ray* (Berkeley: University of California Press, 2010), 24.

83. Cheah and Robbins, *Cosmopolitics*, 11.

84. Bill Ashcroft, *Post-colonial Transformation* (New York: Routledge, 2001), 16.

85. Stuart Hall, "Cultural Identity and Diaspora," in *Identity: Community, Culture,*

Difference, ed. Jonathan Rutherford (London: Lawrence and Wishart, 1990), 222–237, esp. 224–225.

86. Said, *Reflections on Exile*, 184, 185, 186.

87. Ibid., 186; emphasis original.

88. Nussbaum, "Patriotism and Cosmopolitanism."

89. Dennis Altman, *Global Sex* (Chicago: University of Chicago Press, 2001).

90. Prashad, *Karma of Black Folk*, 43.

91. Appadurai, "Grassroots Globalization," esp. 6, 13.

92. Bok, "From Part to Whole," in Nussbaum and Cohen, *For Love of Country?* 42–43.

CHAPTER 8

1. Katherine Boo, "Opening Night: The Scene from the Airport Slums; Letter from Mumbai," *New Yorker*, February 23, 2009, 22–29, esp. 29.

2. Qtd. in Arthur J. Pais, "*Slumdog* Gets 4 Golden Globe Noms," Rediff.com, December 12, 2008, available at http://www.rediff.com/movies/2008/dec/12slumdog-gets-four-golden-globe-noms.htm.

3. Rebecca Tuhus-Dubrow, "Learning from Slums," Ideas section, *Boston Globe*, March 1, 2009, C1+.

4. Jyotika Virdi and Corey Creekmur, "India: Bollywood's Global Coming of Age," in *Contemporary Asian Cinema: Popular Culture in a Global Frame*, ed. Anne Tereska Ciecko (Oxford: Berg, 2006), 134–135.

5. Bhaskar Sarkar, *Mourning the Nation: Indian Cinema in the Wake of Partition* (Durham, NC: Duke University Press, 2009), 40.

6. Qtd. in ibid., 40.

7. Ibid., 39.

8. M. Madhava Prasad, "Surviving Bollywood," in *Global Bollywood*, ed. Anandam P. Kavoori and Aswin Punathambekar (New York: New York University Press, 2008), 41–51, esp. 45. At the same time, it is important to recognize as Prasad does that films made in regional variants of Hindi such as *Bhojpuri* and *khadi boli* are increasingly popular, especially in art or quasi-art films, ranging from *Ankur* (Shyam Benegal, 1974) to *Omkara* (Vishal Bharadwaj, 2006).

9. Rochona Mazumdar, ctd. in Mark Magnier, "'Slumdog Millionaire' and the Many Indian Realities," *Boston Globe*, January 25, 2009, A12.

10. Ashis Nandy, *Intimate Enemy: Loss and Recovery of Self under Colonialism* (Delhi: Oxford University Press, 1988 [1983]), 27.

11. Ravi Vasudevan, *Making Meaning in Indian Cinema* (New Delhi: Oxford University Press, 2000), 279, 302, 299.

12. Jigna Desai, "Bombay Boys and Girls: The Gender and Sexual Politics of Transnationality in the New Indian Cinema in English," in *Transnational Cinema: The Film Reader*, ed. Elizabeth Ezra and Terry Rowden (London: Routledge, 2006), 57–69, esp. 57. See also Vasudevan, *Making Meaning*, 29.

13. Shohini Chaudhuri, *Contemporary World Cinema: Europe, The Middle East, East Asia and South Asia* (Edinburgh: Edinburgh University Press, 2005), 156.

14. Smithu Radhakrishnan, "Slumdog Sincerity," UCLA Asia Initiative, available at http://www.asiaarts.ucla.edu/article.asp?parentid=101268 (accessed April 14, 2009; emphasis added).

15. Randeep Ramesh, "Bollywood Icon Amitabh Bachchan Rubbishes Slumdog Mil-

lionaire," *The Guardian*, January 14, 2009, available at http://www.theguardian.com/film/2009/jan/14/amitabh-bachchan-rubbishes-slumdog-millionaire.

16. Amitabh Bachchan, qtd. in Nirpal Dhaliwal, "Slumdog Millionaire Could Only Have Been Made by a Westerner," *The Guardian*, January 15, 2009, available at http://www.theguardian.com/film/filmblog/2009/jan/15/danny-boyle-shows.

17. Ctd. in Kashaan, "Shilpa Shetty Takes a Dig at Slumdog Millionaire," Bwoodz. Blogspot, available at http://bwoodz.blogspot.com/2009/02/shilpa-shetty-takes-dig-at-slumdog.html.

18. Boo, "Opening Night," 27.

19. Vasudevan, *Making Meaning*, 295.

20. Tuhus-Dubrow, "Learning from Slums," esp. C1.

21. Arundhati Roy, "Caught on Film: India Not-Shining," *Dawn*, March 2, 2009, available at http://dawn.com/news/921599/caught-on-film-india-not-shining (accessed March 11, 2009). See also Roy, *Power Politics* (Cambridge, MA: South End Press, 2001).

22. Qtd. in Magnier, "Slumdog Millionaire," A12.

23. Gayatri Chakravorty Spivak, *The Post-colonial Critic: Interviews, Strategies, Dialogues*, ed. Sarah Harasym (New York: Routledge, 1990), 108.

24. Anandam P. Kavoori and Aswin Punathambekar, eds., *Global Bollywood* (New York: New York University Press, 2008), 289, 295.

25. Sara Dickey, "Opposing Faces: Film Star Fan Clubs and the Construction of Class Identities in South India," in *Pleasure and the Nation: The History, Politics, and Consumption of Public Culture in India*, ed. Rachel Dwyer and Christopher Pinney (New Delhi: Oxford University Press, 2001), 212–246, esp. 213–214, 238.

26. Roy, "Caught on Film."

27. Nasreen Munni Kabir, 'Now, *Apna* Bollywood Has Become Cool,' *Daily News and Analysis*, September 24, 2005, 8.

28. Sara Dickey makes a similar point; see Dickey, "Opposing Faces," 214.

29. See Prasad, *Ideology of the Hindi Film*, 47.

30. Ien Ang, *Watching Dallas: Soap Opera and the Melodramatic Imagination*, trans. Della Couling (London: Methuen, 1985), 52.

31. Sigmund Freud, *Beyond the Pleasure Principle*, trans. and ed. James Strachey (New York: W. W. Norton, 1989 [1959]), 38.

32. Ibid., 14–15, 16–17.

33. Octave Mannoni, "I Know Well, but All the Same . . ." in *Perversion and the Social Relation*, ed. Molly Anne Rothenberg, Dennis A. Foster, and Slavoj Žižek (Durham, NC: Duke University Press, 2003), 68–92.

34. A. R. Rahman, Oscar Acceptance Speech, Academy Awards Acceptance Speech Database, February 22, 2009, available at http://aaspeechesdb.oscars.org/link/081-16/.

35. Lauren Berlant, *Cruel Optimism* (Durham, NC: Duke University Press, 2011), 14, 13.

36. Ibid., 14.

37. Peter Brooks, *The Melodramatic Imagination: Balzac, Henry James, Melodrama, and the Mode of Excess* (New Haven, CT: Yale University Press, 1976), 211–212.

38. Avital Ronell, *Stupidity* (Urbana: University of Illinois Press, 2002).

39. Boo, "Opening Night," 28.

40. Freud, *Beyond the Pleasure Principle*, 36.

41. Chetan Bhatt, *Hindu Nationalism: Origins, Ideologies and Modern Myths* (Oxford: Berg, 2001), 3.

CONCLUSION

1. Gayatri C. Spivak, *The Post-colonial Critic: Interviews, Strategies, Dialogues*, ed. Sarah Harasym (New York: Routledge, 1990), 39.

2. Fernand Braudel, *Afterthoughts on Material Civilization and Capitalism*, trans. Patricia M. Ranum (Baltimore: Johns Hopkins University Press, 1977).

3. Immanuel Kant, "Perpetual Peace: A Philosophical Sketch" in *Political Writings*, ed. Hans Reiss (Cambridge: Cambridge University Press, 1991), 108; emphasis original.

4. Immanuel Kant, "Idea for a Universal History with a Cosmopolitan Purpose," in *Political Writings*, 51; emphasis original.

5. Immanuel Kant, "On the Common Saying: 'This May Be True in Theory, but It Does Not Apply in Practice," in *Political Writings*, ed. Hans Reiss (Cambridge: Cambridge University Press, 1991), 92.

6. See Pheng Cheah, "Introduction Part II: The Cosmopolitical Today," in *Cosmopolitics: Thinking and Feeling beyond the Nation*, ed. Pheng Cheah and Bruce Robbins (Minneapolis: University of Minnesota Press, 1998).

7. For related discussion of the "powers of the false," see also Gayatri Gopinath, *Impossible Desires: Queer Diasporas and South Asian Public Cultures* (London: Duke University Press, 2005).

8. William Mazzarella, "Culture, Globalization, Mediation," *Annual Review of Anthropology* 33 (2004): 345–367; see esp. 345.

9. Rajini Vaidyanathan, BBC radio broadcast, December 6, 2011.

10. Benedict R. Anderson, *Imagined Communities: Reflections on the Origin and Spread of Nationalism* (London: Verso, 1991 [1983]), 7.

11. See also Gopinath, *Impossible Desires*; my deployment of the term, emphasizing an "aftereffect" or belatedness in the operation of the "powers of the false," is significantly different from Gopinath's approach.

12. W.J.T. Mitchell, *What Do Pictures Want? The Lives and Loves of Images* (Chicago: University of Chicago Press, 2004), 145, 2.

13. W.J.T. Mitchell, "Migration, Law, and the Image," in *The Migrant's Time: Rethinking Art History and Diaspora*, ed. Saloni Mathur (Williamstown, MA: Sterling and Francine Clark Art Institute, 2011), 59–77, esp. 60.

14. Aswin Punathambekar, "Bollywood in the Indian-American Diaspora: Mediating a Transitive Logic of Culture Citizenship," *International Journal of Cultural Studies* 8 (2005): 151–173, esp. 164.

15. Jesse Washington, "Some Asians' College Strategy: Don't Check 'Asian,'" December 3, 2011, available at http://news.yahoo.com/asians-college-strategy-dont-check-asian-174442977.html.

16. Douglas Kellner, "Popular Culture and the Construction of Postmodern Identities," in *Modernity and Identity*, ed. Scott Lash and Jonathan Friedman (Oxford: Blackwell, 1992), 141–177, esp. 153, 158.

17. Gayatri Spivak, "Subaltern Studies: Deconstructing Historiography," in *Selected Subaltern Studies*, ed. Ranajit Guha and Gayatri Chakravorty Spivak (Oxford: Oxford University Press, 1988), 3–32.

18. Ernst Bloch, *The Spirit of Utopia* (Stanford, CA: Stanford University Press, 2000 [1964]), 2.

19. See Raminder Kaur and Ajay Sinha, *Bollyworld: Popular Indian Cinema through a Transnational Lens* (New Delhi: Sage, 2005), 16.

20. Sean Cubitt, *The Cinema Effect* (Cambridge, MA: MIT Press, 2004), 310.

21. See Dipesh Chakrabarty, *Habitations of Modernity: Essays in the Wake of Subaltern Studies* (Chicago: University of Chicago Press, 2002), esp. 115–137.

22. Other Hinglish films include *Amritsar to LA* (Deepak Nayyar and Gurinder Chadha, 2004), *Monsoon Wedding* (Mira Nair, 2001), *Being Cyrus* (Homi Adjania, 2005), *Bollywood Hollywood* (Deepa Mehta, 2002), *Mitr, My Friend* (Revathy, 2002), *Hyderabad Blues* (Nagesh Kukunoor, 1998), *Mississippi Masala* (Mira Nair, 1991), *Bend It Like Beckham* (Gurinder Chadha, 2003), *Bombay Boys* (Kaizad Gustad, 1998), and *Slumdog Millionaire* (Danny Boyle, 2010).

23. Kingsley Bolton, "Constructing the Global Vernacular: American English and the Media," in *Media, Popular Culture, and the American Century*, ed. Kingsley Bolton and Jan Olsson (Stockholm: National Library of Sweden, 2010), 125–153, esp. 125.

24. Thomas Babington Macaulay, "Minute on Indian Education, February 2, 1835," rpt. in *Postcolonialisms: An Anthology of Cultural Theory and Criticism*, ed. Gaurav Desai and Supriya Nair (New Brunswick, NJ: Rutgers University Press, 2005), 121–131, esp. 130, 123–124.

25. See Sir Henry Yule and Arthur Coke Burnell, *Hobson-Jobson: A Glossary of Colloquial Anglo-Indian Words and Phrases, and of Kindred Terms* (London: John Murray, 1903).

26. This hybrid is based on the Khariboli of Delhi, Western Uttar Pradesh, the southern areas of Uttarakhand and Haryana in India. Standard Urdu is mutually intelligible with Standard Hindi. Together Hindi and Urdu speakers constitute the fourth-largest linguistic community in the world.

27. Bhaskar Sarkar, *Mourning the Nation: Indian Cinema in the Wake of Partition* (Durham, NC: Duke University Press, 2009).

28. Jacques Derrida, *Monolingualism of the Other*, trans. Patrick Mensah (Stanford, CA: Stanford University Press, 1998), 46.

29. Arjun Appadurai, *Modernity at Large: Cultural Dimensions of Globalization* (Minneapolis: University of Minnesota Press, 1996), 46. See also Judith M. Brown, *Global South Asians: Introducing the Modern Diaspora* (Cambridge: Cambridge University Press, 2006): 178.

30. Appadurai, *Modernity*, 199.

31. Peter Geschiere, *The Perils of Belonging: Autochthony, Citizenship, and Exclusion in Africa and Europe* (Chicago: University of Chicago Press, 2009).

32. Vidar Helgesen, "2012, the Age of the Citizen," *OpenDemocracy*, December 24, 2011, available at http://www.opendemocracy.net/vidar-helgesen/2012-age-of-citizen (accessed December 27, 2011).

33. Appadurai, *Modernity*, 199.

34. Ibid., 176.

35. Inderpal Grewal, *Transnational America: Feminisms, Diasporas, Neoliberalisms* (Durham, NC: Duke University Press, 2005), 2.

36. See Will Kymlicka, *Multicultural Citizenship: A Liberal Theory of Minority Rights* (Oxford: Oxford University Press, 1995); Marion Young, *Justice and the Politics of Difference* (Princeton, NJ: Princeton University Press, 1990); Carole Pateman, *The Sexual Contract* (Cambridge: Polity Press, 1988).

37. See Grewal, *Transnational America*, 17.

38. Jyotika Virdi and Corey Creekmur, "India: Bollywood's Global Coming of Age," in *Contemporary Asian Cinema: Popular Culture in a Global Frame*, ed. Anne Tereska Ciecko (Oxford: Berg, 2006), 137.

39. Freida Pinto, interview with Charlie Rose, August 5, 2011, available at http://www.charlierose.com/view/interview/11832 (accessed August 10, 2011). Unusual identity posi-

tions for Indian women have been depicted in films discussed in this book, such as *Mississippi Masala, Bandit Queen, Monsoon Wedding, Bend It Like Beckham,* and *Fire.*

40. Avtar Brah, *Cartographies of Desire: Contesting Identities* (London: Routledge, 1996), 15.

41. See "United States v. Bhagat Singh Thind," *American Journal of International Law* 17 (1923): 572–573.

42. Jasbir K. Puar and Amit S. Rai, "Perverse Projectiles under the Specter of (Counter)Terrorism," *Social Text* 22, no. 3 (Fall 2004): 75–104, esp. 75–76.

43. Virdi and Creekmur, "India," 138.

44. Sunaina Maira, *Desis in the House: Indian American Youth Culture in New York City* (Philadelphia: Temple University Press, 2002), 87–88.

45. Puar and Rai, "Perverse Projectiles," 77.

46. Engin Isin and Patricia Wood, *Citizenship and Identity* (London: Sage, 1999).

47. Sandhya Shukla, *India Abroad: Diasporic Cultures of Postwar America and England* (Princeton, NJ: Princeton University Press, 2003), 3.

48. Carl Schmitt, *The Concept of the Political,* expanded ed., trans. G. Schwab (Chicago: University of Chicago Press, 2007 [1932]), 12–13.

49. Akhil Gupta, "Blurred Boundaries: The Discourse of Corruption, the Culture of Politics, and the Imagined State," in *The Anthropology of the State: A Reader,* ed. Aradhana Sharma and Akhil Gupta (Malden, MA: Blackwell, 2006), 211–242, esp. 213.

50. Ctd. in Kamala Visveswaran and Ali Mir, "On the Politics of Community in South Asian American Studies," *Amerasia Journal* 25, no. 3 (1999/2000): 97–108, esp. 104.

51. Sudesh Mishra, "News from the Crypt: India, Modernity, and the West," *New Literary History* 40 (2009): 315–344, esp. 326–327.

52. Sheldon Wolin, *Politics and Vision: Continuity and Vision in Western Political Thought* (Princeton, NJ: Princeton University Press, 2004 [1960]), 404.

53. See Shani Mootoo, *Out on Main Street and Other Stories* (Vancouver, B.C.: Press Gang, 1993). In the work of other writers such as G. V. Desani, V. S. Naipaul, and more recently Amitav Ghosh, deracinated signifiers of Indianness become the currency of self-construction.

54. Zygmunt Bauman, *Liquid Modernity* (London: Polity Press, 2000), 7.

55. Sunaina Maira, "Desis Reprazent: Bhangra Remix and Hip Hop in New York City," *Postcolonial Studies* 1, no. 3 (1998): 357–370, esp. 362; emphasis mine.

56. Ulrich Beck, *Was ist Globalisierung? Irrtümer des Globalismus, Antworten auf Globalisierung* (Frankfurt: Suhrkamp, 1997), 16, qtd. in Hartmut Rosa, *Social Acceleration: A New Theory of Modernity,* trans. Jonathan Trejo-Mathys (New York: Columbia University Press, 2013), 211.

57. Anderson, *Imagined Communities,* 7.

58. See Aihwa Ong, *Flexible Citizenship: The Cultural Logics of Transnationality* (Durham, NC: Duke University Press, 1999).

59. See William Connolly, *Political Theory and Modernity* (Oxford: Blackwell, 1988).

60. Rosa, *Social Acceleration,* 213.

61. Samir Dayal, "Geography Isn't History: Agency in the Indian Call Center," in *Global Babel: Questions of Discourse and Communication in a Time of Globalization,* ed. Samir Dayal and Margueritte Murphy (Newcastle, UK: Cambridge Scholars, 2007).

62. Rosa, *Social Acceleration,* 221; emphasis original.

63. George Lipsitz, *Dangerous Cross-Roads: Popular Music, Postmodernism and the Poetics of Place* (London: Verso, 1994), esp. 4, 14–15, 18, ctd. in Peter Burke, *Cultural Hybridity* (Cambridge: Polity Press, 2009), 26.

64. Stuart Hall, "New Ethnicities," in *Black Film, British Cinema*, ed. Kobena Mercer (London: ICA, 1988), 27–31, esp. 29–30.

65. Gilles Deleuze and Félix Guattari, *Anti-Oedipus: Capitalism and Schizophrenia*, trans. Robert Hurley (New York: Viking Press, 1977), 42.

66. Gayatri C. Spivak, *Outside in the Teaching Machine* (New York: Routledge, 1993), 54.

67. Bruno Latour, "On Recalling ANT," in *Actor Network Theory and After*, ed. J. Law and J. Hassard (Oxford: Blackwell, 1999), 15–25, esp. 20.

68. Nabeel Zuberi, "Sampling South Asian Music," in *South Asian Technospaces*, ed. Radhika Gajjala and Venkataramana Gajjala (New York: Peter Lang, 2008), 49–69, esp. 50. Zuberi himself quotes the text by Latour I cited above, "On Recalling ANT," 20.

69. Available at http://www.questioncopyright.com/sstb-dvd-std01-ntsc.html.

70. Raminder Kaur, "Cruising on the *Vilayeti* Bandwagon: Diasporic Representations and Reception of Popular Indian Movies," in *Bollyworld: Popular Indian Cinema through a Transnational Lens*, ed. Raminder Kaur and Ajay J. Sinha (New Delhi: Sage, 2005), 309–329, esp. 323.

71. Available at http://www.youtube.com/watch?feature=player_embedded&v=F-osrK8Cl5o, accessed November 13, 2012 (no longer available).

72. Hamid Naficy, *The Making of Exile Culture: Iranian Television in Los Angeles* (Minneapolis: University of Minnesota Press, 1993), 150.

73. Susan Stewart, *On Longing: Narratives of the Miniature, the Gigantic, the Souvenir, the Collection* (Baltimore: Johns Hopkins University Press, 1984), 145.

74. See a video at http://www.youtube.com/watch?feature=player_embedded&v=6rbFyBedolM.

75. Qtd. in Rosa, *Social Acceleration*, 225–226.

76. Homi K. Bhabha, "Preface: Arrivals and Departures," in *Home, Exile, Homeland: Film, Media, and the Politics of Place*, ed. Hamid K. Naficy (New York: Routledge, 1998), vii–xii, esp. ix; emphasis original.

77. Ctd. in Sangita Gopal and Sujata Moorti, eds., *Global Bollywood: Travels of Hindi Song and Dance* (Minneapolis: University of Minnesota Press, 2008), 7–8. The Absolut vodka advertisement can be viewed at http://www.youtube.com/watch?v=YxSH64k0KfA.

78. David Morley and Kevin Robins, *Spaces of Identity: Global Media, Electronic Landscapes and Cultural Boundaries* (London: Routledge, 1997), 86 ff.

79. Daphne Berdahl, "'(N)Ostalgie' for the Present: Memory, Longing, and East German Things," *Ethnos* 64, no. 2 (1999): 192–211, esp. 202.

80. Julia Kristeva, *Intimate Revolt: The Powers and Limits of Psychoanalysis* (New York: Columbia University Press, 2002), 5–6.

81. See Maira, "Desis Reprazent," and Gayatri Gopinath, "'Bombay, UK, Yuba City': Bhangra Music and the Engendering of Diaspora," *Diaspora: A Journal of Transnational Studies* 4, no. 3 (Winter 1995): 303–321, esp. 312.

82. Cornelius Castoriadis, *The Imaginary Institution of Society*, trans. Kathleen Blamey (Cambridge, MA: MIT Press, 1987 [1975]), 292.

83. Sheldon Wolin, "Fugitive Democracy," in *Democracy and Difference: Contesting the Boundaries of the Political*, ed. Seyla Benhabib (Princeton, NJ: Princeton University Press, 1996), 31–45, esp. 36.

84. Gayatri Spivak, "Practical Politics of the Open End," in *Deconstruction: A Reader*, ed. Martin McQuillan (New York: Routledge, 2000), 397–404; Achille Mbembe, *On the Postcolony* (Berkeley: University of California Press, 2001), 16.

Bibliography

Abelove, Henry, Michèle Aina Barale, and David M. Halperin, eds. *The Lesbian and Gay Studies Reader.* New York: Routledge, 1993.

Abu-Lughod, Janet. "Going beyond Global Babble." In King, *Culture, Globalization, and the World-System*, 131–137.

Agamben, Giorgio. *What Is an Apparatus? And Other Essays.* Trans. David Kishik and Stefan Pedatella. Stanford, CA: Stanford University Press, 2009.

Ahmad, Aijaz. *In Theory: Classes, Nations, Literatures.* London: Verso, 1992.

——. "Jameson's Rhetoric of Otherness and the 'National Allegory.'" *Social Text* 17 (Autumn 1987): 3–25.

Ahmed, Akbar S. "Bombay Films: The Cinema as Metaphor for Indian Society and Politics." *Modern Asian Studies* 26, no. 2 (1992): 289–320.

Altman, Dennis. *Global Sex.* Chicago: University of Chicago Press, 2001.

Anderson, Benedict R. *Imagined Communities: Reflections on the Origin and Spread of Nationalism.* London: Verso, 1991 [1983].

Ang, Ien. *Watching Dallas: Soap Opera and the Melodramatic Imagination.* Trans. Della Couling. London: Methuen, 1985.

Appadurai, Arjun. "Disjuncture and Difference in the Global Cultural Economy." In Appadurai, *Modernity at Large*, 27–47. Minneapolis: University of Minnesota Press, 1996.

——. "Global Ethnoscapes: Notes and Queries for a Transnational Anthropology." In Appadurai, *Modernity at Large*, 48–65.

——. "Grassroots Globalization and the Research Imagination." *Public Culture* 12, no. 1 (Winter 2000): 1–19.

——. *Modernity at Large: Cultural Dimensions of Globalization.* Minneapolis: University of Minnesota Press, 1996.

——. "Playing with Modernity: The Decolonisation of Indian Cricket." In Breckenbridge, *Consuming Modernity*, 23–48.

Aravamudan, Srinivas. *Tropicopolitans: Colonialism and Agency, 1688–1804.* Durham, NC: Duke University Press, 1999.

Armes, Roy. *Third World Film Making and the West.* Berkeley: University of California Press, 1987.

Arya, Divya, and Geeta Pandey. "India Gay Sex Ruling: 'It Is a Huge Setback.'" *BBC News India,* December 11, 2013. Available at http://www.bbc.com/news/world-asia-india-25329067.

Ashcroft, Bill. *Post-colonial Transformation.* New York: Routledge, 2001.

Aspinall, Ian. *East Is East.* Promotional Notes to DVD.

Augé, Marc. *Non-places: Introduction to an Anthropology of Supermodernity.* London: Verso, 1995.

Bachchan, Amitabh. Public Service Announcement. Available at http://www.youtube.com/watch?v=wP-TwHwLc98.

Baker, Francis, Peter Hulme, and Margaret Iversen, eds. *Colonial Discourse/Postcolonial Theory.* Manchester, UK: Manchester University Press, 1994.

Balibar, Étienne. "Borders of Europe." Trans. J. Swenson. In Cheah and Robbins, *Cosmopolitics,* 216–229.

———. "Is There a 'Neo-Racism?" In Balibar and Wallerstein, *Race, Nation, Class,* 17–28.

———. *Politics and the Other Scene.* London: Verso, 2002 [1998].

Balibar, Etienne, and Immanuel Wallerstein. *Race, Nation, Class: Ambiguous Identities.* London: Verso, 1991.

Ballhatchet, Kenneth. *Race, Sex, and Class under the Raj: Imperial Attitudes and Policies and Their Critics, 1793–1905.* New York: St. Martin's Press, 1980.

Banaji, Shakuntala. *Reading "Bollywood": The Young Audience and Hindi Films.* Basingstoke, UK: Palgrave Macmillan, 2006.

Banerjee, Sikata. "Women, Muscular Nationalism and Hinduism in India: Roop Kanwar and the Fire Protest." *Totalitarian Movements and Political Religions* 11 (September–December 2010): 271–287. EBSCO.

Barber, Benjamin. "Constitutional Faith." In Nussbaum and Cohen, *For Love of Country?* 30–37.

Barnouw, Eric, and S. Krishnaswamy. *Indian Film.* New York: Oxford University Press, 1980.

Barthes, Roland. *The Preparation of the Novel.* New York: Columbia University Press, 2011 [1980].

Basch, Linda G., Nina Glick Schiller, and Cristina Szanton Blanc. *Nations Unbound: Transnational Projects, Postcolonial Predicaments, and Deterritorialized Nation-States.* Basel: Gordon and Breach, 1994.

Basu, Durga Das. *Introduction to the Constitution of India.* 18th ed. Nagpur: Wadhwa, 1999.

Basu, Srimati. "Shading the Secular: Law at Work in the Indian Higher Courts." *Cultural Dynamics* 15, no. 2 (2003): 131–152.

Bauman, Zygmunt. *Liquid Modernity.* London: Polity Press, 2000.

Bayly, C. A. *The Local Roots of Indian Politics: Allahabad, 1880–1920.* Oxford: Clarendon Press, 1975.

———. "Patrons and Politics in Northern India." *Modern Asia Studies* 7, no. 3 (1973): 349–388.

Bazin, André. "The Ontology of the Photographic Image." In Braudy and Cohen, *Film Theory and Criticism,* 195–199.

———. "Theater and Cinema." In Braudy and Cohen, *Film Theory and Criticism,* 418–428.

Beck, Ulrich. *Was Ist Globalisierung? Irrtümer des Globalismus, Antworten auf Globalisierung.* Frankfurt: Suhrkamp, 1997.

Beckles, Hilary McD. "The Political Ideology of West Indies Cricket Culture." In Beckles and Stoddart, *Liberation Cricket*, 148–164.

Beckles, Hilary McD., and Brian Stoddart, eds. *Liberation Cricket: West Indies Cricket Culture*. Manchester, UK: Manchester University Press, 1995.

Benegal, Shyam. "Secularism and Popular Indian Cinema." In Needham and Rajan, *Crisis of Secularism*, 225–238.

Benhabib, Seyla. *The Rights of Others: Aliens, Residents and Citizens*. Cambridge: Cambridge University Press, 2004.

———, ed. *Democracy and Difference: Contesting the Boundaries of the Political*. Princeton, NJ: Princeton University Press, 1996.

Benjamin, Walter. "The Task of the Translator." In *Illuminations*, ed. Hannah Arendt, trans. Harry Zohn, 69–82. New York: Schocken Books, 1969 [1955].

Berdahl, Daphne. "'(N)Ostalgie' for the Present: Memory, Longing, and East German Things." *Ethnos* 64, no. 2 (1999): 192–211.

Berlant, Lauren. *Cruel Optimism*. Durham, NC: Duke University Press, 2011.

———. "The Face of America and the State of Emergency." In Nelson and Gaonkar, *Disciplinarity and Dissent*, 397–439.

Berman, Marshall. *All That Is Solid Melts into Air: The Experience of Modernity*. London: Verso, 1983.

Bhabha, Homi K. "Foreword." In Fanon, *Black Skin, White Masks*.

———. *The Location of Culture*. London: Routledge, 1994.

———. "Looking Global." Paper delivered at a conference on globalization, Harvard University, April 3, 2001.

———. "Of Mimicry and Man: The Ambivalence of Colonial Discourse." *October* (Discipleship: A Special Issue on Psychoanalysis) 28 (Spring 1984): 125–133.

———. "Preface: Arrivals and Departures." In Naficy, *Home, Exile, Homeland*, xii–vii.

Bhagwati, Jagdish. "Coping with Antiglobalization: A Trilogy of Discontents." *Foreign Affairs*, January–February 2002, 2–7.

Bhaskaran, Gautaman. "*Fire* Explores Women's Dilemma in Modern World." *Hindu*, December 20, 1998, 10.

Bhatt, Chetan. *Hindu Nationalism: Origins, Ideologies and Modern Myths*. Oxford: Berg, 2001.

Bhugra, Dinesh, and Susham Gupta. "Psychoanalysis and the Hindi Cinema." *International Review of Psychiatry* 21, no. 3 (June 2009): 234–240.

Bidwai, Praful. "Bringing Down the Temple: Democracy at Risk in India." *The Nation*, January 25, 1993, 86.

Bloch, Ernst. *The Spirit of Utopia*. Stanford, CA: Stanford University Press, 2000.

Bok, Sissela. "From Part to Whole." In Nussbaum and Cohen, *For Love of Country?* 38–44.

Bolton Kingsley. "Constructing the Global Vernacular: American English and the Media." In Bolton and Olsson, 125–153.

Bolton, Kingsley, and Jan Olsson, eds. *Media, Popular Culture, and the American Century*. Stockholm: National Library of Sweden, 2010.

Boo, Katherine. "Opening Night: The Scene from the Airport Slums." Letter from Mumbai. *New Yorker*, February 23, 2009, 22–29.

Bordwell, David. "Space in the Classical Film." In Bordwell, Staiger, and Thompson, *Classical Hollywood Cinema*, 50–59.

Bordwell, David, Janet Staiger, and Kristin Thompson. *The Classical Hollywood Cinema: Film Style and Mode of Production to 1960*. London: Routledge, 1985.

Bose, Brinda, ed. *Translating Desire: The Politics of Gender and Culture in India*. New Delhi: Katha Press, 2002.

Bose, Sugata, and Ayesha Jalal. *Modern South Asia: History, Culture, Political Economy.* London: Routledge Press, 1997.
Bozniak, Linda. "Citizenship Denationalized." *Indiana Journal of Global Law Studies* 7 (2000): 447–507.
Brah, Avtar. *Cartographies of Desire: Contesting Identities.* London: Routledge, 1996.
Braudel, Fernand. *Afterthoughts on Material Civilization and Capitalism.* Trans. Patricia M. Ranum. Baltimore: Johns Hopkins University Press, 1977.
Braudy, Leo, and Marshall Cohen, eds. *Film Theory and Criticism: Introductory Readings.* 6th ed. New York: Oxford University Press, 2004.
Breckenbridge, Carol A., ed. *Consuming Modernity: Public Culture in a South Asian World.* Minneapolis: University of Minnesota Press, 1995.
Brennan, Timothy. *At Home in the World: Cosmopolitanism Now.* Cambridge, MA: Harvard University Press, 1997.
Brooks, Peter. *The Melodramatic Imagination: Balzac, Henry James, Melodrama, and the Mode of Excess.* New Haven, CT: Yale University Press, 1976.
Brown, Judith M. *Global South Asians: Introducing the Modern Diaspora.* Cambridge: Cambridge University Press, 2006.
Brubaker, Rogers, and Frederick Cooper. "Beyond 'Identity.'" *Theory and Society* 29 (2000): 1–47.
Buckland, Warren. *Teach Yourself Film Studies.* London: Hodder and Stoughton, 2003.
Burgin, Victor, James Donald, and Cora Kaplan, eds. *Formations of Fantasy.* London: Routledge, 1986.
Burke, Peter. *Cultural Hybridity.* Cambridge: Polity Press, 2009.
Butler, Judith. *Bodies That Matter: On the Discursive Limits of "Sex."* New York: Routledge, 1993.
———. *Gender Trouble: Feminism and the Subversion of Identity.* New York: Routledge, 1990.
———. "Imitation and Gender Insubordination." In Abelove, Barale, and Halperin, *Lesbian and Gay Studies Reader,* 307–320.
Butler, Judith, and Joan W. Scott, eds. *Feminists Theorize the Political.* New York: Routledge, 1992.
Castle, Terry. *The Apparitional Lesbian: Female Homosexuality and Modern Culture.* New York: Columbia University Press, 1993.
Castoriadis, Cornelius. *The Imaginary Institution of Society.* Trans. Kathleen Blamey. Cambridge, MA: MIT Press, 1987 [1975].
Cavell, Stanley. *The World Viewed: Reflections on the Ontology of Film.* Cambridge, MA: Harvard University Press, 1979.
Césaire, Aimé. "Discourse on Colonialism." In Williams and Chrisman, *Colonial Discourse and Post-colonial Theory,* 172–180.
Chakrabarty, Dipesh. *Habitations of Modernity: Essays in the Wake of Subaltern Studies.* Chicago: University of Chicago Press, 2002.
———. *Provincializing Europe: Postcolonial Thought and Historical Difference.* Princeton, NJ: Princeton University Press, 2000.
Chakravarty, Sumita S. "Fragmenting the Nation: Images of Terrorism in Indian Popular Cinema." In Hjort and MacKenzie, *Cinema and Nation,* 222–237.
———. *National Identity in Indian Popular Cinema, 1947–1987.* Austin: University of Texas Press, 1993.
Chambers, Iain. *Migrancy, Culture, Identity.* London: Routledge, 1994.

Chang, Gordon H., ed. *Asian Americans and Politics: Perspectives, Experiences, Prospects.* Washington, DC: Woodrow Wilson Center Press, 2000.

Chatterjee, Gayatri. *Awara.* New Delhi: Wiley Eastern, 1992.

———. *Mother India.* London: British Film Institute, 2002.

Chatterjee, Partha. "The Nationalist Resolution of the Women's Question." In Sangari and Vaid, *Recasting Women*, 233–253.

———. *Nationalist Thought and the Colonial World: A Derivative Discourse?* London: Zed Books for the United Nations University, 1986.

———. *The Nation and Its Fragments: Colonial and Postcolonial Histories.* Princeton, NJ: Princeton University Press, 1993.

———. "When Melody Ruled the Day." In Vasudev, *Frames of Mind*, 51–65.

Chaudhry, Lakshmi. "Slumdog President." *The Nation,* February 2, 2009, 19–20.

Chaudhuri, Shohini. *Contemporary World Cinema: Europe, The Middle East, East Asia and South Asia.* Edinburgh: Edinburgh University Press, 2005.

Cheah, Pheng, and Bruce Robbins, eds. *Cosmopolitics: Thinking and Feeling beyond the Nation.* Minneapolis: University of Minnesota Press, 1998.

Chen, Kuan-Hsing. *Asia as Method: Toward Deimperialization.* Durham, NC: Duke University Press, 2010.

Chincholkar-Mandelia, Rujuta. "Fire: A Subaltern Existence?" *Journal of Third World Studies* 22, no. 1 (2005): 197–209.

Chopra, Anupama. *Dilwale Dulhania Le Jayenge.* London: British Film Institute, 2002.

Chow, Rey. *Writing Diaspora: Tactics of Intervention in Contemporary Cultural Studies.* Bloomington: Indiana University Press, 1993.

Ciecko, Anne Tereska, ed. *Contemporary Asian Cinema: Popular Culture in a Global Frame.* English ed. Oxford: Berg, 2006.

Clifford, James. "Traveling Cultures." In Grossberg, Nelson, and Treichler, *Cultural Studies*, 96–116.

Clover, Carol J. *Men, Women and Chain Saws: Gender in the Modern Horror Film.* Princeton, NJ: Princeton University Press, 1992.

Comaroff, John L., and Jean Comaroff. "Law and Disorder in the Postcolony: An Introduction." In Comaroff and Comaroff, *Law and Disorder*, 1–56.

———, eds. *Law and Disorder in the Postcolony.* Chicago: University of Chicago Press, 2006.

Conley, Tom. *Cartographic Cinema.* Minneapolis: University of Minnesota Press, 2007.

Connolly, William. *Political Theory and Modernity.* Oxford: Blackwell, 1988.

Corliss, Richard. "The All-TIME 25 Best Sports Movies." *Time*, September 22, 2012. Available at http://entertainment.time.com/2011/09/22/the-all-time-25-best-sports-movies/slide/lagaan-2001/.

Corrigan, Timothy, and Patricia White. *The Film Experience.* 2nd ed. New York: St. Martin's Press, 2008.

Creekmur, Corey. "Review of Jigna Desai, *Beyond Bollywood: The Cultural Politics of South Asian Diasporic Film.*" *Film Quarterly* 59, no. 1 (Fall 2005): 49–51.

Cronin, Ciaran, and Pablo De Greiff, eds. *The Inclusion of the Other: Studies in Political Theory.* Cambridge, MA: MIT Press, 1998.

Croucher, Sheila L. *Globalization and Belonging: The Politics of Identity in a Changing World.* Lanham, MD: Rowman and Littlefield, 2004.

Cubitt, Sean. *The Cinema Effect.* Cambridge, MA: MIT Press, 2004.

Daiya, Kavita. *Violent Belongings: Partition, Gender, and National Culture in Postcolonial India.* Philadelphia: Temple University Press, 2008.

Dayal, Samir. "Blackness as Symptom: Josephine Baker and European Identity." In Raphael-Hernandez, *Blackening Europe*, 35–53.

———. "Constructing Nation as Family: Gandhi, Ambedkar, and Postnationality." *Socialist Review* 99, nos. 1+2 (1999): 97–142.

———. "The Emergence of the Fragile Subject: Amitav Ghosh's An Antique Land." In Fludernik, *India*, 103–133.

———. "Ethical Antihumanism in Frantz Fanon." In Karavanta and Morgan, *Edward Said and Jacques Derrida*, 220–249.

———. "Geography Isn't History: Agency in the Indian Call Center." In *Global Babel: Questions of Discourse and Communication in a Time of Globalization*, ed. Samir Dayal and Margueritte S. Murphy, 64–105. Newcastle, UK: Cambridge Scholars, 2007.

———. "The Inadequately Violent State?" *In Media Res*, May 17, 2010. Available at http://mediacommons.futureofthebook.org/imr/2010/05/17/inadequately-violent-state.

———. "Managing Ecstasy: A Subaltern Performative of Resistance." Special Issue, "Subaltern Affect," *Angelaki: Theoretical Journal of the Humanities* 6, no. 3 (2001): 75–90.

———. "Min(d)ing the Gap: South Asian Americans." In Shankar and Srikanth, *A Part, Yet Apart*, 235–265.

———. "The Modern Reader's Dilemma: Something Old, Something New . . ."; Review Essay on Simona Sawhney's *The Modernity of Sanskrit* (Minneapolis: University of Minnesota Press, 2010)." *Twentieth-Century Literature* 56, no. 2 (Summer 2010): 245–253.

———. "Professing Spirituality: Bollywood Fantasies and the Return of Religion." Special Issue, "FilmFocus," *Weber Studies* 24, no. 2 (Winter 2008): 74–97.

Debord, Guy. *The Society of the Spectacle*. Trans. Donald Nicholson-Smith. New York: Zone Books, 1994 [1967].

De Certeau, Michel. *The Writing of History*. Trans. Tom Conley. New York: Columbia University Press, 1988.

Deleuze, Gilles. *The Time-Image*. Trans. Hugh Tomlinson and Robert Galeta. Minneapolis: University of Minnesota Press, 1989.

Deleuze, Gilles, and Félix Guattari. *Anti-Oedipus: Capitalism and Schizophrenia*. Trans. Robert Hurley. London: Viking, 1977.

———. *Kafka: Toward a Minor Literature*. Trans. Dana Polan. Minneapolis: University of Minnesota Press, 1986.

Derrida, Jacques. *The Animal That Therefore I Am*. Ed. Marie-Louise Mallet. Trans. David Wills. New York: Fordham University Press, 2008.

———. *Monolingualism of the Other*. Trans. Patrick Mensah. Stanford, CA: Stanford University Press, 1998.

Desai, Jigna. "Bombay Boys and Girls: The Gender and Sexual Politics of Transnationality in the New Indian Cinema in English." In Ezra and Rowden, *Transnational Cinema*, 57–69.

Devonish, Hubert. "African and Indian Consciousness at Play: A Study in West Indies Cricket and Nationalism." In Beckles and Stoddart, *Liberation Cricket*, 179–191.

Dickey, Sara. "Opposing Faces: Film Star Fan Clubs and the Construction of Class Identities in South India" In *Pleasure and the Nation: The History, Politics, and Consumption of Public Culture in India*, ed. Rachel Dwyer and Christopher Pinney, 212–246. New Delhi: Oxford University Press, 2001.

Dillon, Mike. "'Patriotism and Valor Are in Your Blood': Necropolitical Subjectivities in The Terrorist (1999)." *Studies in South Asian Film and Media* 1, no. 2 (2009). doi: 10.1386/safm.1.2.209/1. Available at http://www.intellectbooks.co.uk/journals/view-Article,id=9117/.

Dirks, Nicholas. "The Home and the Nation: Consuming Culture and Politics in *Roja*." In *Pleasure and the Nation: The History, Politics and Consumption of Public Culture in India*, ed. Rachel Dwyer and Christopher Pinney, 161–185. New Delhi: Oxford University Press, 2001.

Dirlik, Arif, and Rob Wilson. "Introduction." *boundary 2* 21, no. 1 (1994): 1–14.

Dissanayake, Wimal. "Critical Approaches to World Cinema." In *The Oxford Guide to Film Studies*, ed. John Hill and Pamela Church Gibson, 527–534. New York: Oxford University Press, 1998.

———. "Rethinking Indian Popular Cinema: Towards Newer Frames of Understanding." In Guneratne and Dissanayake, *Rethinking Third Cinema*, 202–225.

Doane, Mary Ann. "The Indexical and the Concept of Medium Specificity." *Differences: A Journal of Feminist Cultural Studies* 18, no. 1 (2007): 129–152.

Dollar, David, and Aart Kraay. "Spreading the Wealth." *Foreign Affairs*, January–February 2002, 120–133.

Donald, J. *Fantasy and the Cinema*. London: British Film Institute, 1989.

Drèze, Jean, and Amartya Sen. "Putting Growth in Its Place." Available at http://aajeevika.gov.in/studies/important-analysis/Putting-growth-in-its-Place.pdf. Accessed October 28, 2013.

Dudrah, Rajinder Kumar. *Bollywood: Sociology Goes to the Movies*. New Delhi: Sage, 2006.

———. "Vilayati Bollywood: Popular Hindi Cinema-Going and Diasporic South Asian Identity in Birmingham (UK)." *Javnost* 9, no. 1 (2002): 19–36.

Dumont, Louis. "Le Problème de l'histoire." In *La Civilization indienne et nous*, 31–54. Cahiers des Annales 23. Paris: Colin, 1964.

Dunne, T., and N. J. Wheeler, eds. *Human Rights in Global Politics*. Cambridge: Cambridge University Press, 1999.

Dwyer, Rachel. *All You Want Is Money, All You Need Is Love: Sex and Romance in Modern India*. London: Cassell, 2000.

———. *Filming the Gods*. London: Routledge, 2006.

Eleftheriotis, Dimitris, and Gary Needham, eds. *Asian Cinemas: A Reader and Guide*. Honolulu: University of Hawai'i Press, 2006.

Empire, August 2013. Available at http://www.empireonline.com/features/100-greatest-world-cinema-films/default.asp?film=55.

Ezra, Elizabeth, and Terry Rowden, eds. *Transnational Cinema: The Film Reader*. London: Routledge, 2006.

Fabian, Johannes. *Time and the Other: How Anthropology Makes Its Object*. New York: Columbia University Press, 2002.

Falk, Richard. "Revisioning Cosmopolitanism." In Nussbaum and Cohen, *For Love of Country?* 53–60.

Fanon, Frantz. *Black Skin, White Masks*. London: Pluto Press, 1986.

Farred, Grant. "Wankerdom: Trainspotting as a Rejection of the Postcolonial." *South Atlantic Quarterly* 103, no. 1 (2004): 215–226.

Fludernik, Monika, ed. *India: Hybridity/Postcoloniality*. Tubingen, Germany: Stauffenburg, 1998.

Foucault, Michel. "Nietzsche, Genealogy, History." In *Language, Counter-Memory, Practice: Selected Essays and Interviews by Michel Foucault*, ed. D. Bouchard. Ithaca, NY: Cornell University Press, 1977.

Freud, Sigmund. *Beyond the Pleasure Principle*. Trans. and ed. James Strachey. New York: W. W. Norton 1989 [1959].

Friedman, Jonathan. "Global Crises, the Struggle for Cultural Identity and Intellectual Porkbarrelling: Cosmopolitans versus Locals, Ethnics and Nationals in an Era of Dehegemonization." In Werbner and Modood, *Debating Cultural Hybridity*, 70–89.

Fullinwider, Robert K., ed. *Public Education in a Multicultural Society: Policy, Theory, Critique*. Cambridge: Cambridge University Press, 1996.

Fuss, Diana. *Identification Papers: Readings in Psychoanalysis*. New York: Routledge, 1995.

Gajjala, Radhika, and Venkataramana Gajjala, eds. *South Asian Technospaces*. New York: Peter Lang, 2008.

Gandhy, Behroze, and Rosie Thomas. "Three Indian Film Stars." In Gledhill, *Stardom*, 107–131.

Ganguly, Keya. *Cinema, Emergence, and the Films of Satyajit Ray*. Berkeley: University of California Press, 2010.

Ganti, Tejaswini. *Bollywood: A Guidebook to Popular Hindi Cinema*. London: Routledge, 2004.

Gaonkar, Dilip P., ed. *Alternative Modernities*. Durham, NC: Duke University Press, 2001.

Garga, B. D. "The Turbulent Thirties." In Vasudev, *Frames of Mind*, 17–28.

Gellner, Ernest. *Nations and Nationalism*. Oxford: Blackwell, 1983.

Geschiere, Peter. *The Perils of Belonging: Autochthony, Citizenship, and Exclusion in Africa and Europe*. Chicago: University of Chicago Press, 2009.

Ghosh, Amitav. "The Diaspora in Indian Culture." *Public Culture* 2 (1989): 73–78.

Ghosh, Bhishnupriya, and Bhaskar Sarkar. "The Cinema of Displacement." *Film Criticism* 20, nos. 1-2 (Winter 1995–1996): 102–113.

Gilroy, Paul. *The Black Atlantic: Modernity and Double Consciousness*. London: Verso, 1993.

———. "One Nation under a Groove: The Cultural Politics of 'Race.'" In Goldberg, *Anatomy of Racism*, 263–282.

———. *There Ain't No Black in the Union Jack*. London: Routledge, 1987.

Gledhill, Christine, ed. *Stardom: Industry of Desire*. New York: Routledge, 1991.

Gokulsing, K. Moti, and Wimal Dissanayake. *Indian Popular Cinema: A Narrative of Cultural Change*. Stoke-on-Trent, UK: Trentham Books, 2004.

———, eds. *Popular Culture in a Globalised India*. London: Routledge, 2009.

Goldberg, Jonathan, ed. *Anatomy of Racism*. Minneapolis: University of Minnesota Press, 1990.

Gopal, Sangita. "Between State and Capital: Women Make Movies." Talk at the "Imperfect Futures" conference, Brandeis University, May 7–8, 2014.

Gopal, Sangita, and Sujata Moorti, eds. *Global Bollywood: Travels of Hindi Song and Dance*. Minneapolis: University of Minnesota Press, 2008.

Gopalan, Lalitha. "Avenging Women in Indian Cinema." *Screen* 38, no. 1 (Spring 1997): 42–59.

———. *Cinema of Interruptions: Action Genres in Contemporary Indian Cinema*. London: British Film Institute, 2002.

Gopinath, Gayatri. "'Bombay, UK, Yuba City': Bhangra Music and the Engendering of Diaspora." *Diaspora: A Journal of Transnational Studies* 4, no. 3 (Winter 1995): 303–321.

———. *Impossible Desires: Queer Diasporas and South Asian Public Cultures*. Durham, NC: Duke University Press, 2005.

Gordon, Sandy. *India's Rise to Power: In the Twentieth Century and Beyond*. New York: St. Martin's Press, 1995.

Gramsci, Antonio. "The Intellectuals." In *Selections from the Prison Notebooks*, ed. Quintin Hoare and Geoffrey Nowell Smith, 131-161. New York: International Publishers, 1971.

Grewal, Inderpal. *Transnational America: Feminisms, Diasporas, Neoliberalisms*. Durham, NC: Duke University Press, 2005.

Grossberg, Lawrence, Cary Nelson, and Paula A. Treichler, eds. *Cultural Studies*. New York: Routledge, 1992.

Guha, Ramachandra. *A Corner of a Foreign Field: The Indian History of a British Sport*. Delhi: Picador, 2002.

Guha, Ranajit, and Gayatri Chakravorty Spivak, eds. *Selected Subaltern Studies*. Oxford: Oxford University Press, 1988.

Guneratne, Anthony R., and Wimal Dissanayake, eds. *Rethinking Third Cinema*. New York: Routledge, 2003.

Gupta, Akhil. "Blurred Boundaries: The Discourse of Corruption, the Culture of Politics, and the Imagined State." In *The Anthropology of the State: A Reader*, ed. Akhil Gupta and Aradhana Sharma, 211-242. Malden, MA: Blackwell, 2006.

Gutmann, Amy. "Democratic Citizenship." In Nussbaum and Cohen, *For Love of Country?* 69–71.

Habermas, Jürgen. *The Inclusion of the Other: Studies in Political Theory*. Ed. Ciaran Cronin and Pablo De Greiff. Cambridge, MA: MIT Press, 1998.

———. *The Philosophical Discourse of Modernity*. Trans. Frederick Lawrence. Cambridge, MA: MIT Press, 1987.

———. *The Structural Transformations of the Public Sphere: An Inquiry into a Category of Bourgeois Society*. Trans. Thomas Burger and Frederick Lawrence. Cambridge, MA: MIT Press, 1991.

Hall, Stuart. "Cultural Identity and Diaspora." In *Identity: Community, Culture, Difference*, ed. Jonathan Rutherford. London: Lawrence and Wishart, 1990.

———. "The Local and the Global: Globalization and Ethnicity." In King, *Culture, Globalization, and the World-System*, 19–40.

———. "New Ethnicities." In *Black Film, British Cinema*, ed. Kobena Mercer, 27–31. London: ICA, 1988.

———. "When Was the 'Post-Colonial?' Thinking at the Limit." In *The Post-colonial Question: Common Skies, Divided Horizons*, ed. Iain Chambers and Lidia Curti, 242–259. London: Routledge, 1996.

Hannerz, Ulf. *Cultural Complexity: Studies in the Social Organization of Meaning*. New York: Columbia University Press, 1992.

———. "Scenarios for Peripheral Cultures." In King, *Culture, Globalization, and the World System*, 107–128.

Hardt, Michael, and Antonio Negri. *Empire*. Cambridge, MA: Harvard University Press, 2000.

———. "Preface: Dionysos." In *Labor of Dionysos: A Critique of the State Form*, ed. Michael Hardt and Antonio Negri, xiii–xiv. Minneapolis: University of Minnesota Press, 1994.

Harpham, Geoffrey Galt. "Symbolic Terror." *Critical Inquiry* 28, no. 2 (Winter 2002): 573–579.

Harvey, David. "Cosmopolitanism and the Banality of Geographical Evils." *Public Culture* 12, no. 2 (Spring 2000): 529–564.

Hayward, Susan. *Cinema Studies: The Key Concepts*. 3rd ed. London: Routledge, 2006 [1996].

Hegel, G.W.F. *Hegel's Phenomenology of Self-Consciousness: Text and Commentary*. Ed. Leo Rauch and David Sherman. New York: State University of New York, 1999.

———. *The Phenomenology of Mind*. Trans. J. B. Baillie. New York: Harper Torchbooks, 1967 [1910].

Helgesen, Vidar. "2012, the Age of the Citizen." *OpenDemocracy*, 2011. Available at http://www.opendemocracy.net/vidar-helgesen/2012-age-of-citizen. Accessed December 24, 2011.

Himmelfarb, Gertrude. "The Illusions of Cosmopolitanism." In Nussbaum and Cohen, *For Love of Country?* 72–77.

Hjort, Mette, and Scott MacKenzie, eds. *Cinema and Nation*. London: Routledge, 2000.

Hobsbawm, Eric. "Introduction." In Hobsbawm and Ranger, *Invention of Tradition*, 1–14.

Hobsbawm, Eric, and Terence O. Ranger. *The Invention of Tradition*. Cambridge: Cambridge University Press, 1983.

hooks, bell, and Anuradha Dingwaney. "*Mississippi Masala*." *Z Magazine*, July–August 1992, 41–43.

Huggan, Graham. *The Post-colonial Exotic: Marketing the Margins*. London: Routledge, 2001.

Hutnyk, John. "Adorno at Womad: South Asian Crossovers and the Limits of Hybridity-Talk." In Werbner and Modood, *Debating Cultural Hybridity*, 119–120.

Huyssen, Andreas. *Present Pasts: Urban Palimpsests and the Politics of Memory*. Stanford, CA: Stanford University Press, 2003.

International Monetary Fund, *World Economic Outlook Database*, October 2007; World Bank, *World Development Indicators Database*, September 2007. Available at http://siteresources.worldbank.org/DATASTATISTICS/Resources/GDP_PPP.pdf. Accessed August 6, 2012.

Irigaray, Luce. *This Sex Which Is Not One*. Ithaca, NY: Cornell University Press, 1985.

———. "Women on the Market." In Schrift, *Logic of the Gift*, 174–189.

Isin, Engin F., and Patricia K. Wood. *Citizenship and Identity*. London: Sage, 1999.

Ismael, Qadri. "Batting against the Break: On Cricket, Nationalism, and the Swashbuckling Sri Lankans." *Social Text* 50, no. 1 (Spring 1997): 33–56.

Israel, Milton, and N. K. Wagle, eds. *Ethnicity, Identity, Migration: The South Asian Context*. Toronto: University of Toronto Press, 1993.

Jaffrelot, Christophe. *Religion, Caste, and Politics in India*. New York: Columbia University Press, 2011.

Jalal, Ayesha. *Democracy and Authoritarianism in South Asia: A Comparative and Historical Perspective*. Lahore, Pakistan: Sang-e-Meel, 1995.

James, C.L.R. *Beyond a Boundary*. Durham, NC: Duke University Press, 1983.

Jameson, Fredric. *The Antinomies of Realism*. London: Verso, 2013.

———. *Postmodernism, or The Cultural Logic of Late Capitalism*. Durham, NC: Duke University Press, 1991.

———. "Reification and Utopia in Mass Culture." In Jameson, *Signatures of the Visible*, 9–34. New York: Routledge, 1992.

———. "Third World Literature in the Era of Multinational Capitalism." *Social Text* 15 (Fall 1986): 65–88.

Jha, Priya. "Lyrical Nationalism: Gender Friendship, and Excess in 1970s Hindi Cinema." *Velvet Light Trap* 51 (Spring 2003): 43–53.

Kaali, Sundar. "Narrating Seduction: Vicissitudes of the Sexed Subject in Tamil Nativity Film." In Vasudevan, *Making Meaning in Indian Cinema*, 168–191.

Kabir, Nasreen Munni. *Bollywood: The Indian Cinema Story*. London: Channel 4 Books, 2001.

———. "Now, *Apna* Bollywood Has Become Cool." *Daily News and Analysis*, September 24, 2005, 8.

Kakar, Sudhir. "East Meets West: The Psychohistory of Sudhir Kakar." Interview with Paul H. Elovitz. *Clio's Psyche: Psychological and Historical Insights without Jargon* 5, no. 3

(December 1998): 100–104. Available at http://www.cliospsyche.org/PDFs/Clios%20Psyche%205-3%20Dec%201998.pdf.

———. *Intimate Relations: Exploring Indian Sexuality.* Chicago: University of Chicago Press, 1989.

Kaleta, K. C. *Hanif Kureishi: Postcolonial Storyteller.* Austin: University of Texas Press, 1980.

Kant, Immanuel. "An Answer to the Question, 'What Is Enlightenment?'" In *Kant: Political Writings*, 54–63.

———. *Critique of Practical Reason.* Trans. L. W. Beck. Indianapolis: Bobbs-Merrill, 1956.

———. *Kant: Political Writings.* 2nd ed. Ed. Hans Reiss. Trans. H. B. Nisbet. Cambridge: Cambridge University Press, 1992 [1970].

———. "Perpetual Peace: A Philosophical Sketch." In *Kant: Political Writings*, 93–130.

Kapur, Ratna. "Postcolonial Erotic Disruptions: Legal Narratives of Culture, Sex, and Nation in India." *Columbia Journal of Gender and Law* 10, no. 2 (2001): 333–384.

Karavanta, Mina, and Nina Morgan, eds. *Edward Said and Jacques Derrida: Reconstellating Humanism and the Global Hybrid.* Newcastle, UK: Cambridge Scholars, 2009.

Kaur, Raminder. "Cruising on the Vilayeti Bandwagon: Diasporic Representations and Reception of Popular Indian Movies." In Kaur and Sinha, *Bollyworld*, 309–328.

Kaur, Raminder, and Ajay J. Sinha, eds. *Bollyworld: Popular Indian Cinema through a Transnational Lens.* New Delhi: Sage, 2005.

Kavi, Ashok Row. "The Changing Image of the Hero in Hindi Films." *Journal of Homosexuality* 39, nos. 3–4 (2000): 307–312.

Kaviraj, Sudipta. *The Imaginary Institution of India: Politics and Ideas.* New York: Columbia University Press, 2010.

———. "Indira Gandhi and Indian Politics." *Economic and Political Weekly* 21 (1986): 1697–1708.

———. "On State, Society and Discourse in India." In Manor, *Rethinking Third World Politics*, 72–99.

Kavoori, Anandam P., and Aswin Punathambekar, eds. *Global Bollywood.* New York: New York University Press, 2008.

Kazmi, Farid. "How Angry Is the Angry Man?" in Nandy, *Secret Politics of Our Desires*, 134–155.

Kellner, Douglas. "Popular Culture and the Construction of Postmodern Identities." In Lash and Friedman, *Modernity and Identity*, 141–177.

Khagram, Sanjeev, Manish Desai, and Jason Varughese. "Seen, Rich, but Unheard? The Politics of Asian Indians in the United States." In Chang, *Asian Americans and Politics*, 258–284.

Khan-Din, Ayub. "A Quick Chat with Ayub Khan-Din." Interview by Mark Olden. *Kamera.co.uk*, October 6, 1999. Available at http://www.kamera.co.uk/interviews/ayubkhandin.html.

King, Anthony, ed. *Culture, Globalization, and the World-System: Contemporary Conditions for the Representation of Identity.* Current Debates in Art History 3. Binghamton, NY: Department of Art and Art History, 1991.

Kingsley, Ben. Interview with Tom Ashbrook. *On Point Radio.* Available at http://onpoint.wbur.org/2012/01/13/actor-sir-ben-kingsley.

Kishwar, Madhu, and Ruth Vanita. "Male Fantasies of Female Revenge." *Manushi* 48 (September–October 1988): 43–44.

Klawans, Stuart. "On Tyson vs. Downey." Review of *East Is East. The Nation*, May 15, 2000, 34–36.

Knott, Kim, and Sadja Khokher. "Religious and Ethnic Identity among Young Muslim Women in Bradford." *New Community* 19 (1993): 593–610.

Kolanad, Gitanjali. *Culture Shock! India: A Guide to Customs and Etiquette.* Singapore: Times Editions, 2004 [1994].

Krishna, Sankaran. *Postcolonial Insecurities: India, Sri Lanka, and the Question of Nationhood.* Minneapolis: University of Minnesota Press, 1999.

Kristeva, Julia. *Intimate Revolt: The Powers and Limits of Psychoanalysis.* New York: Columbia, 2002.

———. *This Incredible Need to Believe.* Trans. Beverly Bie Brahic. New York: Columbia, 2009 [2006].

Kumar, Shanti. *Gandhi Meets Primetime: Globalization and Nationalism in Indian Television.* Urbana: University of Illinois Press, 2006.

Kymlicka, Will. *Multicultural Citizenship: A Liberal Theory of Minority Rights.* Oxford: Oxford University Press, 1995.

Kymlicka, Will, and Wayne Norman. "Return of the Citizen: A Survey of Recent Work on Citizenship Theory." *Ethics* 104, no. 2 (January 1994): 352–381.

Lacan, Jacques. Écrits: A Selection. Trans. Alan Sheridan. London: Tavistock, 1977.

———. *The Seminar, Book XI: The Four Fundamental Concepts of Psychoanalysis.* 1964. Trans. Alan Sheridan. London: Hogarth Press and Institute of Psycho-Analysis, 1977.

Laplanche, Jean. *Life and Death in Psychoanalysis.* Trans. Jeffrey Mehlman. Baltimore: Johns Hopkins University Press, 1976.

Laplanche, Jean, and Jean-Bertrand Pontalis. "Fantasy and the Origins of Sexuality." In Burgin, Donald, and Kaplan, *Formations of Fantasy,* 5–34.

Lash, Scott, and Jonathan Friedman, eds. *Modernity and Identity.* Oxford: Blackwell, 1992.

Latour, Bruno. "On Recalling ANT." In Law and Hassard, *Actor Network Theory and After,* 15–25.

Law, J., and J. Hassard, eds. *Actor Network Theory and After.* Oxford: Blackwell, 1999.

Lazarus, Neil. "Cricket and National Culture in the Writings of C.L.R. James." In Beckles and Stoddart, *Liberation Cricket,* 342–355.

Leitch, Vincent B., ed. *The Norton Anthology of Theory and Criticism.* 2nd ed. New York: W. W. Norton, 2010 [2001].

Leonard, Karen. "Ethnic Identity and Gender: South Asians in the United States." In Israel and Wagle, *Ethnicity, Identity, Migration,* 165–180.

———. *Making Ethnic Choices: California's Punjabi Mexican Americans.* Philadelphia: Temple University Press, 1992.

Lipsitz, George. *Dangerous Cross-Roads: Popular Music, Postmodernism and the Poetics of Place.* London: Verso, 1997.

Longfellow, Brenda. "Rape and Translation in *Bandit Queen.*" In Bose, *Translating Desire,* 238–254.

Loomba, Ania. *Colonialism/Post-colonialism.* London: Routledge, 1998.

Lukács, György. "The Classical Form of the Historical Novel." From *The Historical Novel.* In Leitch, *Norton Anthology of Theory and Criticism,* 909–921.

Macaulay, Thomas Babington. "Minute on Indian Education, February 2, 1835." In *Postcolonialisms: An Anthology of Cultural Theory and Criticism,* ed. Gaurav Gajanan Desai and Supriya Nair, 121–131. New Brunswick, NJ: Rutgers University Press, 2005.

Macgregor, J. "Bollywood Seduces the West." Netribution, March 19, 2006. Available at http://www.netribution.co.uk/finance/bollywood-seduces-the-west.

MacIntyre, Alasdair. *After Virtue: A Study in Moral Theory.* Notre Dame, IN: Notre Dame Press, 1981.

Magnier, Mark. "'Slumdog Millionaire' and the Many Indian Realities." *Boston Globe*, January 25, 2009, A12.

Mahmood, Saba. "Secularism, Sexuality, and Sectarian Conflict." Paper delivered at MIT, Cambridge, MA, November 12, 2013.

Maira, Sunaina. "Chaste Identities, Ethnic Yearnings: Second Generation Indian Americans in New York City." Ph.D. diss., Harvard University, 1998.

———. *Desis in the House: Indian American Youth Culture in New York City*. Philadelphia: Temple University Press, 2002.

———. "Desis Reprazent: Bhangra Remix and Hip Hop in New York City." *Postcolonial Studies* 1, no. 3 (1998): 357–370.

Majumdar, Boria. "Politics of Leisure in Colonial India, 'Lagaan'—Invocation of a Lost History." *Economic and Political Weekly*, September 1, 2001, 3399–3404.

Majumdar, Neepa. "The Embodied Voice: Song Sequences and Stardom in Popular Hindi Cinema." In Wojcik and Knight, *Soundtrack Available*, 161–181.

Mamdani, Mahmood. *Good Muslim, Bad Muslim: America, the Cold War, and the Roots of Terror*. New York: Pantheon, 2004.

Mankekar, Purnima. "Brides Who Travel: Gender, Transnationalism and Nationalism in Hindi Film." *Positions: East Asia Cultures Critique* 7, no. 3 (Winter 1999): 731–761.

———. "Reflections on Diasporic Identities: A Prolegomena to an Analysis of Political Bifocality." *Diaspora: A Journal of Transnational Studies* 3, no. 3 (1994): 349–371.

———. *Screening Culture, Viewing Politics: An Ethnography of Television, Womanhood, and Nation in Postcolonial India*. Durham, NC: Duke University Press, 1999.

Mannathukkaren, Nissim. "Subalterns, Cricket and the 'Nation': The Silences of 'Lagaan.'" *Economic and Political Weekly*, Special Article, December 8, 2001. Available at http://www.epw.in/special-articles/subalterns-cricket-and-nation.html.

Mannoni, Octave. "I Know Well, but All the Same . . ." In Rothenberg, Foster, and Žižek, *Perversion and the Social Relation*, 68–92.

Manor, James ed. *Rethinking Third World Politics*. New York: Longman, 1991.

Marcus, Sharon. "Fighting Bodies, Fighting Words: A Theory and Politics of Rape Prevention." In Butler and Scott, *Feminists Theorize the Political*, 385–403.

Marx, Karl. *Grundrisse: Foundations of the Critique of Political Economy*. Trans. Martin Nicolaus. New York: Vintage Books, 1973.

Masud, Iqbal. "The Great Four of the Golden Fifties." In Vasudev, *Frames of Mind*, 29–41.

Mazumdar, Ranjani. "From Subjectification to Schizophrenia: The 'Angry Man' and the 'Psychotic' Hero of Bombay Cinema." In Vasudevan, *Making Meaning in Indian Cinema*, 238–264.

Mazzarella, William. "Culture, Globalization, Mediation." *Annual Review of Anthropology* 33, no. 1 (2004): 345–367.

Mbembe, Achille. *On the Postcolony*. Berkeley: University of California Press, 2001.

McCarthy, Thomas. "On Reconciling Cosmopolitan Unity and National Diversity." In Gaonkar, *Alternative Modernities*, 197–235.

McLellan, Janet, and Anthony H. Richmond. "Multiculturalism in Crisis: A Postmodern Perspective on Canada." *Ethnic and Racial Studies* 17, no. 4 (1994): 662–683.

McQuillan, Martin, ed. *Deconstruction: A Reader*. New York: Routledge, 2000.

Mercer, Kobena. "1968: Periodizing Politics and Identity." In Grossberg, Nelson, and Treichler, *Cultural Studies*, 424–449.

———, ed. *Black Film, British Cinema*. London: ICA, 1988.

Mignolo, Walter. "Dewesternizing/Deorientalizing/Decolonizing Citizenship." Oecumene Project's Second Symposium, "Deorientalizing Citizenship." London, November 12–13,

2012. Video. Available at http://www.oecumene.eu/news/walter-mignolo-on-citizenship-knowledge-and-the-limits-of-humanity.
Mishra, Sudesh. "News from the Crypt: India, Modernity, and the West." *New Literary History* 40, no. 2 (2009): 315–344.
Mishra, Vijay. *Bollywood Cinema: Temples of Desire*. New York: Routledge, 2002.
———. "Towards a Theoretical Critique of Bombay Cinema." *Screen* 6, nos. 3–4 (1985): 133–146.
Mitchell, W.J.T. "Migration, Law, and the Image." In *The Migrant's Time: Rethinking Art History and Diaspora*, ed. Saloni Mathur, 59–77. Williamstown, MA: Sterling and Francine Clark Art Institute, 2011.
———. *What Do Pictures Want? The Lives and Loves of Images*. Chicago: University of Chicago Press, 2004.
Miyoshi, Masao. "A Borderless World?" In *Politics, Poetics: Documenta X, the Book*, ed. Documenta and Museum Fredercianum Veranstaltungs-GmbH. Kassel, Germany: Cantz, 1997.
Modood, Tariq. "'Difference,' Cultural Racism and Anti-racism." In Werbner and Modood, *Debating Cultural Hybridity*, 154–172.
Moorti, Sujata. "Inflamed Passions: *Fire*, the Woman Question, and the Policing of Cultural Borders." *Genders* 32 (2000). Available at http://www.genders.org/g32/g32_moorti.html.
Mootoo, Shani. *Out on Main Street and Other Stories*. Vancouver, BC: Press Gang, 1993.
Morley, David, and Kuan-Hsing Chen, eds. *Stuart Hall: Critical Dialogues in Cultural Studies*. London: Routledge, 1996.
Morley, David, and Kevin Robins. *Spaces of Identity: Global Media, Electronic Landscapes and Cultural Boundaries*. London: Routledge, 1997.
Mufti, Aamir. *Enlightenment in the Colony: The Jewish Question and the Crisis of Postcolonial Culture*. Princeton, NJ: Princeton University Press, 2007.
Naficy, Hamid. *Home, Exile, Homeland: Film, Media, and the Politics of Place*. New York: Routledge, 1998.
———. *The Making of Exile Cultures: Iranian Television in Los Angeles*. Minneapolis: University of Minnesota Press, 1993.
Naidoo, J. C., and R. G. Edwards. "Combating Racism Involving Visible Minorities: A Review of Relevant Research and Policy Development." *Canadian Social Work* 8, no. 2 (1991): 211–236.
Nair, Mira. Interview with Charlie Rose. Broadcast May 1, 2002. Available at http://www.amazon.com/Charlie-Emanuel-Waxman-Jhumpa-Lahiri/dp/B000P29HH0.
Nandy, Ashis. "The Discreet Charms of Indian Terrorism." *Journal of Commonwealth and Comparative Politics* 12 (1990): 25–43.
———. *The Intimate Enemy: Loss and Recovery of Self under Colonialism*. Delhi: Oxford, 1988 [1983].
———. *The Savage Freud and Other Essays on Possible and Retrievable Selves*. Delhi: Oxford University Press, 1995.
———. *The Secret Politics of Our Desires: Innocence, Culpability and Indian Popular Cinema*. London: Zed Books, 1999.
———. *The Tao of Cricket: On Games of Destiny and the Destiny of Games*. New Delhi: Penguin, 1989.
Narayan, Uma. "Undoing the 'Package Picture' of Cultures." *Signs: Journal of Women in Culture and Society* 25, no. 4 (Spring 2000): 1083–1086.
Nayar, Pramod K. *Seeing Stars: Spectacle, Society and Celebrity Culture*. New Delhi: Sage, 2009.

Nayar, Sheila J. "The Values of Fantasy: Indian Popular Cinema through Western Scripts." *Journal of Popular Culture* 31, no. 1 (Summer 1997): 73–90.

Needham, Anuradha Dingwaney, and Rajeswari Sunder Rajan, eds. *The Crisis of Secularism in India.* Durham, NC: Duke University Press, 2007.

Negri, Antonio, and Michael Hardt. *Empire.* Cambridge, MA: Harvard University Press, 2000.

Negt, Oskar, and Alexander Kluge. *Public Sphere and Experience: Toward an Analysis of the Bourgeois and Proletarian Public Sphere.* Trans. Peter Labanyi, Jamie Owen Daniel, and Assenka Oksiloff. Minneapolis: University of Minnesota Press, 1993.

Nelson, Cary, and Dilip Parameshwar Gaonkar, eds. *Disciplinarity and Dissent in Cultural Studies.* New York: Routledge, 1996.

Niranjana, Tejaswini. "Integrating Whose Nation? Tourists and Terrorists in 'Roja.'" *Economic and Political Weekly,* January 15, 1994, 79–81.

Nowell-Smith, Geoffrey, ed. *The Oxford History of World Cinema.* Oxford: Oxford University Press, 1996.

Nussbaum, Martha, and Joshua Cohen. "Patriotism and Cosmopolitanism." *Boston Review,* October–November 1994, 3–6. Available at http://bostonreview.net/martha-nussbaum-patriotism-and-cosmopolitanism.

———. "Reply." In Nussbaum and Cohen, *For Love of Country?* 131–144.

———, eds. *For Love of Country?* Boston: Beacon Press, 2002 [1996]. "100 Greatest World Cinema Films." *Empire,* August 2013. Available at http://www.empireonline.com/features/100-greatest-world-cinema-films/default.asp?film=55.

Ong, Aihwa. *Flexible Citizenship: The Cultural Logics of Transnationality.* Durham, NC: Duke University Press, 1999.

Pais, Arthur J. "Comic's Coup." *India Today International,* January 22, 2001, 22c–24d.

———. "*Slumdog* Gets 4 Golden Globe Noms." Rediff.com, December 12, 2008. Available at http://www.rediff.com/movies/2008/dec/12slumdog-gets-four-golden-globe-noms.htm.

Pandey, Gyan. "In Defense of the Fragment: Writing about Hindu-Muslim Riots in India Today." *Economic and Political Weekly* 26, nos. 11–12 (March 1991): 559–572.

Pateman, Carole. *The Sexual Contract.* Cambridge: Polity Press, 1988.

Patterson, Orlando. "The Ritual of Cricket." In Beckles and Stoddart, *Liberation Cricket,* 141–147.

Peer, Basharat. "India's Broken Promise: How a Would-Be Great Power Hobbles Itself." *Foreign Affairs,* May–June 2012, 158–170.

Pinto, Freida. "Freida Pinto: Interview with Charlie Rose." August 5, 2011. Available at http://www.charlierose.com/view/interview/11832.

Planning Commission, India. *First Five Year Plan, Chapter 8. 1951.* Available at http://planningcommission.nic.in/plans/planrel/fiveyr/1st/1planch8.html.

Polan, Dana. "Review of *Cinema 1: L'Image-Mouvement by Gilles Deleuze.*" *Film Quarterly* 38, no. 1 (Autumn 1984): 50–52.

Polanyi, Karl. *The Great Transformation.* Boston: Beacon Press, 2002 [1944].

Prasad, M. Madhava. *Ideology of the Hindi Film: A Historical Construction.* Delhi: Oxford University Press, 1998.

———. "Surviving Bollywood." In Kavoori and Punathambekar, *Global Bollywood,* 41–51.

———. "This Thing Called Bollywood." Available at http://www.india-seminar.com/2003/525/525%20madhava%20prasad.htm.

Prashad, Vijay. *The Darker Nations: A People's History of the Third World.* New York: New Press, 2007.

———. *Everybody Was Kung Fu Fighting: Afro-Asian Connections and the Myth of Cultural Purity.* Boston: Beacon Press, 2001.
———. "From Multiculture to Polyculture in South Asian American Studies." *Diaspora: A Journal of Transnational Studies* 8, no. 2 (Fall 1999): 185–204.
———. *The Karma of Brown Folk.* Minneapolis: University of Minnesota Press, 2000.
Pratt, Mary Louise. *Imperial Eyes: Travel Writing and Transculturation.* New York: Routledge, 1992.
Primoratz, Igor. *Terrorism: A Philosophical Investigation.* Cambridge: Polity Press, 2013.
Puar, Jasbir K. *Terrorist Assemblages: Homonationalism in Queer Times.* Durham, NC: Duke University Press, 2007.
———. "To Be Gay and Racist Is No Anomaly." *The Guardian,* June 2, 2010. Available at http://www.theguardian.com/commentisfree/2010/jun/02/gay-lesbian-islamophobia.
Puar, Jasbir K., and Amit S. Rai. "Monster, Terrorist, Fag: The War on Terrorism and the Production of Docile Patriots." *Social Text* 72, no. 3 (Fall 2002): 117–148.
———."Perverse Projectiles under the Specter of (Counter)Terrorism." *Social Text* 22, no. 3 (2004): 75–104.
Punathambekar, Aswin. "Bollywood in the Indian-American Diaspora: Mediating a Transitive Logic of Culture Citizenship." *International Journal of Cultural Studies* 8 (2005): 151–173.
———. "We're Online, Not on the Streets." In Kavoori and Punathambekar, *Global Bollywood,* 282–299.
Putnam, Hilary. "Must We Choose?" In Nussbaum and Cohen, *For Love of Country?* 91–97.
Radhakrishnan, Smithu. "Slumdog Sincerity." UCLA Asia Initiative. April 14, 2009. Available at http://www.asiaarts.ucla.edu/article.asp?parentid=101268. Accessed December 12, 2009.
Raghavendra, M. K. "Local Resistance to Global Bangalore: Reading Minority Indian Cinema." In Gokulsing and Dissanayake, *Popular Culture in a Globalised India,* 15–27.
Raha, Kironmoy. "Bengal in the Forefront." In Vasudev, *Frames of Mind,* 69–78.
Rahman, M. "Women Strike Back." *India Today* (July 15, 1988): 80–82.
Rai, Amit. "Patriotism and the Muslim Citizen in Hindi Films." *Harvard Asia Quarterly* 7, no. 3 (Summer 2003). Available at http://www.asiaquarterly.com/content/view/136/5. Last accessed June 2, 2007; site now unavailable.
———. *Untimely Bollywood: Globalization and India's New Media Assemblage.* Durham, NC: Duke University Press, 2009.
Rajadhyaksha, Ashish. "The 'Bollywoodization' of the Indian Cinema: Cultural Nationalism in a Global Arena." *Inter-Asia Cultural Studies* 4, no. 1 (2003): 25–39.
———. "India: Filming the Nation." In Nowell-Smith, *Oxford History of World Cinema,* 678–689.
———. *Indian Cinema in the Time of Celluloid: From Bollywood to the Emergency.* Bloomington: Indiana University Press, 2009.
Rajadhyaksha, Ashish, and Paul Willemen, eds. *Encyclopaedia of Indian Cinema.* 2nd ed. Published in arrangement with British Film Institute. New Delhi: Oxford University Press, 1999.
Rajagopal, Arvind. "The Rise of National Programming: The Case of Indian Television." *Media, Culture, and Society* 15 (1993): 91–131.
Raju, A. Raghurama. "Problematising Nationalism." *Economic and Political Weekly,* July 3–10, 1993, 1433–1438.

Ramaswamy, Sumathi. *The Goddess and the Nation*. Durham, NC: Duke University Press, 2010.

Rancière, Jacques. "Politics, Identification, and Subjectivization." *October* 61 (Summer 1992): 58–64.

Rao, Shakuntala. "The Globalization of Bollywood: An Ethnography of Non-elite Audiences in India." *Communication Review* 10, no. 1 (2007): 57–76.

Raphael-Hernandez, Heike. *Blackening Europe*. Ed. Paul Gilroy. New York: Routledge Press, 2004.

Ray, Sangeeta. *En-Gendering India: Woman and Nation in Colonial and Postcolonial Narratives*. Durham, NC: Duke University Press, 2000.

Reddy, Chandan. *Freedom with Violence: Race, Sexuality, and the U.S. State*. Durham, NC: Duke University Press, 2011.

Renan, Ernest. "What Is a Nation?" In *Nation and Narration*, ed. Homi K. Bhabha, 8–22. London: Routledge Press, 1990.

Reports of the Planning Commission. Available at http://planningcommission.nic.in/plans/planrel/fiveyr/welcome.html. Accessed January 4, 2011.

Ritzer, George. *The Globalization of Nothing 2*. Thousand Oaks, CA: Pine Forge, 2007.

Robbins, Bruce. *Secular Vocations: Intellectuals, Professionalism, Culture*. London: Verso, 1993.

Robertson, Roland. *Globalization: Social Theory and Global Culture*. London: Sage, 1992.

———. "Social Theory, Cultural Relativity and the Problem of Globality." In King, *Culture, Globalization, and the World-System*, 69–90.

Rodowick, David N. *Gilles Deleuze's Time Machine*. Durham, NC: Duke University Press, 2003 [1997].

Ronell, Avital. *Stupidity*. Urbana: University of Illinois Press, 2002.

Rosa, Hartmut. *Social Acceleration: A New Theory of Modernity*. Trans. Jonathan Trejo-Mathys. New York: Columbia University Press, 2013.

Rothenberg, Molly Anne, Dennis A. Foster, and Slavoj Žižek, eds. *Perversion and the Social Relation*. Durham, NC: Duke University Press, 2003.

Roy, Arundhati. "Caught on Film: India Not-Shining." *Dawn*, March 2, 2009. Available at http://dawn.com/news/921599/caught-on-film-india-not-shining.

———. *Power Politics*. Cambridge, MA: South End Press, 2001.

Roy, Patricia E. "The Fifth Force: Multiculturalism and the English Canadian Identity." *Annals of the American Academy of Political and Social Science (Being and Becoming Canada)* 538 (March 1995): 199–209.

Rudrappa, Sharmila. *Ethnic Routes to Becoming American: Indian Immigrants and the Cultures of Citizenship*. New Brunswick, NJ: Rutgers University Press, 2004.

Rueschmann, Eva, ed. *Moving Pictures, Migrating Identities*. Jackson: University Press of Mississippi, 2003.

Rushdie, Salman. "Imaginary Homelands." In *Imaginary Homelands: Essays and Criticism, 1981–1991*. New York: Penguin, 1991.

———. *The Moor's Last Sigh*. London: Jonathan Cape, 1995.

———. *The Satanic Verses*. New York: Picador, 1988.

Sackler, Molly. "Stereotypes and Social Critique Spar in This Culture-Clash Dramedy." *Bright Lights* 30 (October 2000). Available at http://www.brightlightsfilm.com/30/eastiseast.html. Accessed September 9, 2001.

Said, Edward W. "Bitter Dispatches from the Third World." In Said, *Reflections on Exile and Other Essays*, 98–104.

———. *Culture and Imperialism*. London: Chatto and Windus, 1993.

———. "Fantasy's Role in the Making of Nations." In Said, *Reflections on Exile and Other Essays*, 493–499.
———. *Reflections on Exile and Other Essays*. Cambridge, MA: Harvard University Press, 2000.
Sainath, P. "17,368 Farm Suicides in 2009." *The Hindu*, December 27, 2010. Available at http://tinyurl.com/krmb5lq.
Sangari, Kumkum, and Sudesh Vaid, eds. *Recasting Women: Essays in Indian Colonial History*. New Brunswick: Rutgers University Press, 1990 [1989].
Sarkar, Bhaskar. "The Melodramas of Globalization." *Cultural Dynamics* 20, no. 1 (March 2008): 31–51.
———. *Mourning the Nation: Indian Cinema in the Wake of Partition*. Durham, NC: Duke University Press, 2009.
Sassen, Saskia. "Spatialities and Temporalities of the Global Elements for Theorization." *Public Culture* 12 (2000): 215–232.
Savarkar, V. D. *Hindutva: Who Is a Hindu?* Bombay: S. S. Savarkar, 1969 [1923].
Schmitt, Carl. *The Concept of the Political*. Expanded ed. Trans. G. Schwab. Chicago: University of Chicago Press, 2007 [1932].
Schor, Naomi. *Reading in Detail: Aesthetics and the Feminine*. New York: Methuen, 1987.
Schrift, Alan D., ed. *The Logic of the Gift: Toward an Ethic of Generosity*. New York: Routledge, 1997.
Sconce, Jeffrey. "Bollywood Bad: Toward an Aesthetics of the Failed Future." *In Media Res*, March 17, 2009. Available at http://tinyurl.com/6aodt2t.
Scott, Joan W. "Fantasy Echo: History and the Construction of Identity." *Critical Inquiry* 27, no. 2 (Winter 2001): 284–304.
Sedgwick, Eve Kosofsky. *Between Men: English Literature and Male Homosocial Desire*. Durham, NC: Duke University Press, 1985.
Seltzer, Mark. "Wound Culture: Trauma in the Pathological Public Sphere." *October* 80 (Spring 1997): 3–26.
Sen, Amartya. *Reason before Identity: The Romanes Lecture for 1998*. Oxford: Oxford University Press, 1999.
Sen, Amartya, and Jean Drèze. *India: Development and Participation*. New Delhi: Oxford University Press, 2002 [1996].
Shamdasani, Sonu, and Michael Münchow, eds. *Speculations after Freud: Psychoanalysis, Philosophy, and Culture*. New York: Routledge, 1994.
Shankar, Lavina Dhingra, and Rajini Srikanth, eds. *A Part, Yet Apart: South Asians in Asian America*. Philadelphia: Temple University Press, 1998.
Sharma, Arvind. "On Hindu, Hindustan, Hinduism and Hindutva." *Numen* 49, no. 1 (2002): 1–36.
Sharpe, Jenny. "Gender, Nation, and Globalization in *Monsoon Wedding* and *Dilwale Dulhania Le Jayenge*." *Meridians: Feminism, Race, Transnationalism* 6, no. 1 (2005): 58–81.
———. "Is the United States Postcolonial? Transnationalism, Immigration, and Race." *Diaspora: A Journal of Transnational Studies* 4, no. 2 (1995): 181–199.
Shimakawa, Karen. *National Abjection: The Asian American Body Onstage*. Durham, NC: Duke University Press, 2002.
Shklar, Judith N. "Putting Cruelty First." *Democratiya* 4 (2006): 81–94.
Shohat, Ella, and Robert Stam. "From the Imperial Family to the Transnational Imaginary: Media Spectatorship in the Age of Globalization." In *Global/Local: Cultural Production and the Transnational Imaginary*, ed. Rob Wilson and Wimal Dissanayake, 145–170. Durham, NC: Duke University Press, 1996.

Shukla, Sandhya Rajendra. *India Abroad: Diasporic Cultures of Postwar America and England.* Princeton, NJ: Princeton University Press, 2003.

Singh, Amritjit, and Peter Schmidt. "On the Borders between U.S. Studies and Postcolonial Theory." In Singh and Schmidt, *Postcolonial Theory and the United States*, 3–70.

———, eds. *Postcolonial Theory and the United States: Race, Ethnicity, and Literature.* Jackson: University Press of Mississippi, 2000.

Sinha, Mrinalini. *Colonial Masculinity: The "Manly Englishman" and the "Effeminate Bengali" in the Late Nineteenth Century.* Manchester, UK: Manchester University Press, 1995.

Sircar, Ajanta. "Of 'Metaphorical' Politics: Bombay Films and Indian Society." *Modern Asian Studies* 29, no. 2 (1995): 325–335.

Sivanandan, Ambalavaner. *A Different Hunger: Writings on Black Resistance.* London: Pluto, 1982.

"South Asian Psychoanalytic Forum Screens 'My Son the Fanatic.'" Available at http://www.indiainnewyork.com/iny2k1110/Arts/SAPsychoanaly.html. Accessed September 9, 2001.

Spicer, Keith. "So Great a Heritage as Ours." *Hamilton Spectator*, April 15, 1987.

Spivak, Gayatri Chakravorty. "Can the Subaltern Speak?' In Williams and Chrisman, *Colonial Discourse and Post-colonial Theory*, 66–111.

———. "How to Read a 'Culturally Different' Book." In Baker, Hulme, and Iversen, *Colonial Discourse/Postcolonial Theory*, 126–150.

———. Interview with Afsaneh Najmabadi. *Social Text* 28 (1991): 122–134.

———. *Other Asias.* Malden, MA: Blackwell, 2008.

———. *Outside in the Teaching Machine.* New York: Routledge, 1993.

———. "The Politics of Translation." In Spivak, *Outside in the Teaching Machine*, 179–200.

———. *The Post-colonial Critic: Interviews, Strategies, Dialogues.* Ed. Sarah Harasym. New York: Routledge, 1990.

———. "Practical Politics of the Open End." In McQuillan, *Deconstruction*, 397–404.

———. "Psychoanalysis in Left Field and Fieldworking: Examples to Fit the Title." In Shamdasani and Münchow, *Speculations after Freud*, 41–75.

———. "Subaltern Studies: Deconstructing Historiography." In Guha and Spivak, *Selected Subaltern Studies*, 3–32.

Srivastava, Sanjay. "Voice, Gender and Space in Time of Five-Year Plans: The Idea of Lata Mangeshkar." *Economic and Political Weekly*, May 15, 2004. Available at http://www.epw.org.in/showArticles.php?root=2004&leaf=05&filename=7189&filetype=html. Accessed November 10, 2012.

Stewart, Susan. *Crimes of Writing.* New York: Oxford University Press, 1991.

———. *On Longing: Narratives of the Miniature, the Gigantic, the Souvenir, the Collection.* Baltimore: Johns Hopkins University Press, 1984.

Stiegler, Bernard. *Technics and Time, 3: Cinematic Time and the Question of Malaise.* Stanford, CA: Stanford University Press, 2011.

Stoddart, Brian. "Cricket and Colonialism in the English-Speaking Caribbean to 1914: Towards a Cultural Analysis." In Beckles and Stoddart, *Liberation Cricket*, 9–32.

Stratton, Jon, and Ien Ang. "On the Impossibility of a Global Cultural Studies: British Cultural Studies in an International Frame." In Morley and Chen, *Stuart Hall*, 360–392.

Sundar, Pavitra. "Meri Awaaz Suno: Women, Vocality, and Nation in Hindi Cinema." *Meridians: Feminism, Race, Transnationalism* 8, no. 1 (2007): 144–179.

Sunder Rajan, Rajeswari. *Real and Imagined Women: Gender, Culture and Postcolonialism.* London: Routledge, 1993.

———. *The Scandal of the State: Women, Law, and Citizenship in Postcolonial India.* Durham, NC: Duke University Press, 2003.

Surin, Kenneth. "C.L.R. James' Material Aesthetic of Cricket." In Beckles and Stoddart, *Liberation Cricket*, 313–341.

———. *Freedom Not Yet: Liberation and the Next World Order.* Durham, NC: Duke University Press, 2009.

Thomas, Rosie. "Indian Cinema: Pleasures and Popularity." In Eleftheriotis and Needham, *Asian Cinemas*, 280–294.

———. "Sanctity and Scandal: The Mythologization of Mother India." *Quarterly Review of Film and Video* 11 (1989): 11–30.

Thompson, L. O'Brien. "How Cricket Is West Indian Cricket? Class, Racial, and Color Conflict." In Beckles and Stoddart, *Liberation Cricket*, 165–178.

Tinkcom, Matthew, and Amy Villarejo, eds. *Keyframes: Popular Cinema and Cultural Studies.* New York: Routledge, 2001.

Tololyan, Khachig. "The Nation-State and Its Others: In Lieu of a Preface." *Diaspora: A Journal of Transnational Studies* 1, no. 1 (Spring 1991): 3–7.

Toulmin, Stephen. *Cosmopolis: The Hidden Agenda of Modernity.* New York: Free Press, 1990.

Tuhus-Dubrow, Rebecca. "Learning from Slums." *Boston Globe*, March 1, 2009, Ideas section.

Uberoi, Patricia. "The Diaspora Comes Home: Disciplining Desire in DDLJ." *Contributions to Indian Sociology* 32, no. 2 (1988): 305–336.

"United States v. Bhagat Singh Thind." *American Journal of International Law* 17 (1923): 572–573.

Vaidyanathan, Rajini. "Indian Music." BBC. December 6, 2011. Radio. Available at http://www.bbc.co.uk/programmes/p00mc4s4.

Van der Veer, Peter. "'The Enigma of Arrival': Hybridity and Authenticity in the Global Space." In Werbner and Modood, *Debating Cultural Hybridity*, 90–105.

Varadharajan, Asha. "Dissolution, Dissensus, and the Possibility of Community." *University of Toronto Quarterly* 66, no. 4 (Fall 1997): 621–633.

Varshney, Ashutosh. "Contested Meanings: India's National Identity, Hindu Nationalism, and the Politics of Anxiety," *Daedalus* 122, no. 3 (Summer 1993): 227–261.

Vasudev, Aruna, ed. *Frames of Mind: Reflections on Indian Cinema.* New Delhi: UBS, 1995.

Vasudevan, Ravi S. "Addressing the Spectator of a 'Third World' National Cinema: The Bombay 'Social' Film of the 1940s and 1950s." *Screen* 36, no. 4 (Winter 1995): 305–325.

———. "Cinema in Urban Space." Seminar 525, *Unsettling Cinema: A Symposium on the Place of Cinema in India.* July 29, 2011. Available at http://www.india-seminar.com/2003/525/525%20ravi%20vasudevan.htm.

———. "Film Studies: New Cultural History and Experience of Modernity." *Economic and Political Weekly* 30, no. 44 (November 4, 1995): 2809–2814.

———. "The Melodramatic Mode and Commercial Hindi Cinema." *Screen* 30, no. 3 (1989): 29–50.

———. "National Pasts and Futures: Indian Cinema." *Screen* 41, no. 1 (Spring 2000): 119–125.

———. "Shifting Codes, Dissolving Identities: The Hindi Social Film of the 1950s as Popular Culture." In Vasudevan, *Making Meaning in Indian Cinema*, 99–121.

——, ed. *Making Meaning in Indian Cinema*. New Delhi: Oxford, 2000.

Virdi, Jyotika. *The Cinematic ImagiNation: Indian Popular Films as Social History*. New Brunswick, NJ: Rutgers University Press, 2003.

——. "Reverence, Rape—and Then Revenge: Popular Hindi Cinema's 'Woman's Film.'" *Screen* 40, no. 1 (Spring 1999): 17–37.

Virdi, Jyotika, and Corey Creekmur. "India: Bollywood's Global Coming of Age." In Ciecko, *Contemporary Asian Cinema*, 134–135.

Virmani, A. "World Economy: From Uni-Polar to Tri-Polar." In *Hindu Business Line*, February 8, 2005. Available at www.thehindubusinessline.com/2005/02/08/stories/2005020800030800.htm.

Visveswaran, Kamala, and Ali Mir, "On the Politics of Community in South Asian American Studies." *Amerasia Journal* 25, no. 3 (1999–2000): 97–108.

Vitali, Valentina, and Paul Willemen, eds. *Theorising National Cinema*. London: British Film Institute, 2008.

Waldron, Jeremy. "Minority Cultures and the Cosmopolitan Alternative." In *The Rights of Minority Cultures*, ed. Will Kymlicka, 93–119. Oxford: Oxford University Press, 1995.

——. "Multiculturalism and Mélange." In Fullinwider, *Public Education in a Multicultural Society*, 90–118.

Wallerstein, Immanuel. "The National and the Universal: Can There Be Such a Thing as World Culture?" In King, *Culture, Globalization, and the World-System*, 91–105.

——. *The Politics of the World-Economy: The States, the Movements and the Civilizations*. Cambridge: Cambridge University Press, 1984.

Walzer, Michael. "Spheres of Affection." In Nussbaum and Cohen, *For Love of Country?* 125–130.

Warhol, Robyn R., and Diane Price Herndl. *Feminisms: An Anthology of Literary Theory and Criticism*. New Brunswick, NJ: Rutgers University Press, 1991.

Washbrook, David. Talk presented at the Fletcher School of Law and Diplomacy, Tufts University, December 5, 2001.

Washington, Jesse. "Some Asians' College Strategy: Don't Check 'Asian.'" *Yahoo News*, December 3, 2011. Available at http://news.yahoo.com/asians-college-strategy-dont-check-asian-174442977.html.

Waugh, Thomas. "Queer Bollywood, or 'I'm the Player, You're the Naive One': Patterns of Sexual Subversion in Recent Indian Popular Cinema." In Tinkcom and Villarejo, *Keyframes*, 280–297.

Werbner, Pnina. "Introduction: The Materiality of Diaspora—Between Aesthetic and 'Real' Politics." *Diaspora: A Journal of Transnational Studies* 9, no. 1 (Spring 2000): 5–20.

Werbner, Pnina, and Tariq Modood, eds. *Debating Cultural Hybridity: Multicultural Identities and the Politics of Anti-racism*. London: Zed Books, 1997.

Willemen, Paul. "Introduction." In Rajadhyaksha and Willemen, *Encyclopaedia of Indian Cinema*, 10–11.

Williams, Patrick, and Laura Chrisman, eds. *Colonial Discourse and Post-colonial Theory: A Reader*. New York: Columbia University Press, 1994.

Wittig, Monique. *The Straight Mind and Other Essays*. Boston: Beacon Press, 1992.

Wojcik, Pamela Robertson, and Arthur Knight, eds. *Soundtrack Available: Essays on Film and Popular Music*. Durham, NC: Duke University Press, 2001.

Wolin, Sheldon. "Fugitive Democracy." In Benhabib, *Democracy and Difference*, 31–45.

——. *Politics and Vision: Continuity and Innovation in Western Political Thought*. Princeton, NJ: Princeton University Press, 2004 [1960].

Wüst, Sarah. "Young German Heimatfilm: Negotiations of a Powerful Myth." *Austausch* 1, no. 1 (April 2011): 76–94.

Yelvington, Kevin A. "Ethnicity 'Not Out': The Indian Cricket Tour of the West Indies and the 1976 Elections in Trinidad and Tobago." In Beckles and Stoddart, *Liberation Cricket*, 205–221.

Yoshimoto, Mitsuhiro. "A Search for a National Community." In *Film Analysis: A Norton Reader*, ed. Jeffrey Geiger and R. L. Rutsky, 495–508. New York: W. W. Norton, 2005.

Young, Marion. *Justice and the Politics of Difference*. Princeton, NJ: Princeton University Press, 1990.

Yule, Sir Henry, and Arthur Coke Burnell. *Hobson-Jobson: A Glossary of Colloquial Anglo-Indian Words and Phrases, and of Kindred Terms*. London: John Murray, 1903.

Yuval-Davis, Nira. "The Dark Side of Democracy: Autochthony and the Radical Right." *OpenDemocracy*, June 20, 2011. Available at http://tinyurl.com/ms3z4eb.

Zimmerman, Bonnie. "What Has Never Been: An Overview of Lesbian Feminist Literary Criticism." In Warhol and Herndl, *Feminisms*, 117–137.

Žižek, Slavoj. *Demanding the Impossible*. Ed. Yong-june Park. Cambridge: Polity Press, 2013.

———. *For They Know Not What They Do: Enjoyment as a Political Factor*. London: Verso, 2002 [1991].

———. *Less Than Nothing: Hegel and the Shadow of Dialectical Materialism*. London: Verso, 2012.

———. *Living in the End Times*. London: Verso, 2010.

———. *Looking Awry: An Introduction to Jacques Lacan through Popular Culture*. Cambridge, MA: MIT Press, 1992.

———. *The Sublime Object of Ideology*. London: Verso, 1989.

———. *Tarrying with the Negative: Kant, Hegel, and the Critique of Ideology*. Durham, NC: Duke University Press, 1993.

Zuberi, Nabeel. "Sampling South Asian Music." In Gajjala and Gajjala, *South Asian Technospaces*, 49–69.

Index

Samir Dayal is a Professor of English and Media Studies at Bentley University in Massachusetts. He is the author of *Resisting Modernity: Counternarratives of Nation and Masculinity in Pre-Independence India*; a co-editor, with Margueritte Murphy, of *Global Babel: Questions of Discourse and Communication in a Time of Globalization*; and the editor of the Cultural Studies Series, which includes Julia Kristeva's *Crisis of the European Subject.*

www.ingramcontent.com/pod-product-compliance
Lightning Source LLC
LaVergne TN
LVHW090554110826
845146LV00001B/118

* 9 7 8 1 4 3 9 9 1 0 6 4 1 *